THE
BATHROOM
DEVOTIONAL

By the
Backdraft Media

THE BATHROOM DEVOTIONAL

Cover Design by Rich Praytor, Colorado Springs, CO.
(richdp@comcast.net)

OUR SINCEREST THANKS!

Backdraft Media would like to thank the following organizations and people for providing life changing information to the book.

EternalProductions.Org

GodAndScience.Org

ChangingLives.AU.com

GodQuestions.Org

Carm.Org

Skip Pennington

TABLE OF CONTENTS

INTRODUCTION

Welcome to the first edition of the Bathroom Devotional!
The Bathroom Devotional has been a labor of love in
research, developing and creating information specifically
for people wanting to learn about the Christian faith.

And when we say Christian faith, we mean, well, the belief
in one God. So that includes First Baptists, Second
Baptists, Third Baptists (and so on) Presbyterians,
Catholics, Mormons, Jehovah Witnesses, Methodists,
Lutherans, Episcopalians, Republicans, Democrats,
vegetarians well, you get the picture.

We're not here to promote any particular religion or
denomination. We just want to provide thought provoking
articles, fun facts and interesting information so our readers
will be more fulfilled after reading our book.

TOILET FACTS

- Some other terms for the toilet include: washroom, outhouse, powder room, ladies, lavatory, potty, women's room, bog, necessary, dunny, bathroom, gents, men's room, khazi, convenience, garderobe, restroom, place of easement, privy, john, potty, water closet, the smallest room, can, little girls' or boys' room, facilities, and throne room.

- Only seven percent of Afghanistan homes have flush toilets. Nineteen percent, however, have television sets.

- Every year, there are more than 40,000 toilet-related injuries in the US. The odds are 1 out of 10000 that you will get a toilet-related injury this year.

- You're probably wondering how astronauts relieve themselves in outer space. Space shuttles do not have bathrooms the way airplanes do. Air pressure is key in determining where toilet wastes go. Waste is usually disposed of outside of the shuttle and out into space. Astronauts do not shower. They cleanse themselves using washcloths.

- November 19 is world Toilet Day. Bet you can learn a lot of fun toilet facts on Toilet Day.

- In 1890, Scott Paper Company produced toilet paper in rolls –the one you are accustomed to using today- for the first time.

- The most luxurious toilet in the world was made of pure gold. This 24 carat gold toilet existed in the Hall of Gold in Honk Kong. It was owned by the Hang Fung jewelers who had the toilet built as a marketing strategy to attract tourists from around the world. Unfortunately,

the toilet might not be around for long due to changes in the Hang Fung jewelers' operations. They have decided to melt the golden toilet in order to finance their expansion to Mainland China.

- The average life expectancy of a toilet is 50 years.

- The film "Psycho" was the first movie to show a toilet flushing – the scene caused an in pouring of complaints about indecency.

- Hermann Goering refused to use regulation toilet paper instead he bought soft white handkerchiefs in bulk and used them.

- Over $100,000 US dollars was spent on a study to determine whether most people put their toilet paper on the holder with the flap in front or behind; the answer: three out of four people have the flap in the front.

- King George II of Great Britain died falling off a toilet on the 25th of October 1760.

- The average person spends three whole years of their life sitting on the toilet.

- The first toilet cubicle in a row is the least used (and consequently cleanest).

- An estimated 2.6 billion people worldwide do not have access to proper toilet facilities, particularly in rural areas of China and India.

- The Roman army didn't have toilet paper so they used a water soaked sponge on the end of a stick instead!

- The toilet is flushed more times during the super bowl halftime than at any time during the year.

- Lack of suitable toilets and sanitation kills approximately 1.8 million people a year, many of them children.

- The toilet handle in a public restroom can have up to 40,000 germs per square inch.

- While he didn't invent the toilet, Thomas Crapper perfected the siphon flush system we use today. He was born in the village of Thorne – which is an anagram of throne.

- In a 1992 survey, British public toilets were voted the worst in the world. Following quickly behind were Thailand, Greece, and France.

- An average person visits the toilet 2,500 times per year. (6-8 times per day).

- People spend at least 3 years of their lives on the toilet.

- Seven million cell phones are dropped in the toilet per year.

- Americans use a lot more toilet paper than any other country. (7 sheets on average).

- People have flushed down the toilet: goldfish, false teeth, socks, underwear, bras, shirts, shoes, mice, hamsters, toy cars, action figures, Barbies, toothbrushes, and whole rolls of toilet paper.

- Most toilets flush on an E-flat note.

- 10,000 times you have to change a baby's diaper until it learns how to go to the bathroom itself.

- Men spend 140 days of his life shaving.

- Brushing your teeth with the water on wastes 5 gallons of water.

- Shaving with the water on wastes 15 to 20 gallons.

- Females take 3 times longer than males in the bathroom.

- 433 million miles of toilet paper is how much Americans use annually and this could stretch to the sun and back.

- 43 percent of homes in the U.S. have two or more bathrooms, and 18 percent of those homeowners scrub and clean their shower in the nude.

- The sink has 100,000 germs per square inch, where the toilet seat only has 100 germs per square inch.

- Paper towels decrease hand bacteria by 29 percent, a hand dryer increases it by 162 percent

- Pomegranates studded with cloves were used as the first attempt at making toilet air-freshener.

- King George II of Great Britain died falling off a toilet on the 25th of October 1760.

- The first toilet cubicle in a row is the least used (and consequently cleanest).

- The toilet is flushed more times during the super bowl halftime than at any time during the year.

- The toilet handle in a public restroom can have up to 40,000 germs per square inch.

- 55.2% will let someone else come in the bathroom while they're using the toilet.

- There are 45.2% of people that pee in the shower.

- When a person pees, a small deposit of urine enters the mouth through the saliva glands.

- Ninety percent of pharmaceuticals taken by people are excreted through urination. As a result our sewer systems contain large doses of the excreted drugs.

- A toilet consumes more water than any other appliance in the home.

- A normal person flushes close to twenty gallons of fresh potable water everyday.

- A lady in Kansas was stuck on the toilet for nearly 2 years. The Kansas' woman skin had actually formed around the toilet seat.

- The first time male and female toilets were separated was in Paris during a high-class party in 1739.

- Hermann Goering, a senior Nazi, refused to use regulation toilet paper so he bought large supplies of soft white handkerchiefs instead.

- The most expensive toilet in the galaxy is found in space. Each toilet in space costs about 19 million dollars.

- A rat can survive after being flushed down in a toilet. It can return through the same route.

- John Mayer is known to have tweeted from a nightclub toilet. Mayer made an update on his twitter account using his cell phone in the restroom.

- The first toilet paper was produced in England in 1880

but was not sold in rolls. Instead, it came in boxes with individual sheets.

- People use about 57 sheets of toilet paper everyday.

- The first World Summit on Toilets was conducted in Singapore in 2001.

- The White House has thirty bathrooms. The Pentagon uses about 636 toilet paper rolls per day.

- The toilet is the home appliance that uses up the most amount of water.

IS OUR COPY OF THE BIBLE A RELIABLE COPY OF THE ORIGINAL?

Many skeptics believe that the Bible has been drastically changed over the centuries. In reality, the Bible has been *translated* into a number of different languages. However, the ancient manuscripts (written in Hebrew, Aramaic, and Greek) have been reliably copied over the centuries - with very few alterations.

Old Testament.
How do we know the Bible has been kept in tact for over 2,000 years of copying? Before the discovery of the Dead Sea Scrolls, our earliest Hebrew copy of the Old Testament was the Masoretic text, dating around 800 A.D. The Dead Sea Scrolls date to the time of Jesus and were copied by the Qumran community, a Jewish sect living around the Dead Sea. We also have the Septuagint, which is a Greek translation of the Old Testament dating in the second century B.C. When we compare these texts which have an 800-1000 years gap between them we are amazed that 95% of the texts are identical with only minor variations and a few discrepancies.

New Testament.
There are tens of thousands of manuscripts from the New Testament, in part or in whole, dating from the second century A.D. to the late fifteenth century, when the printing press was invented. These manuscripts have been found in Egypt, Palestine, Syria, Turkey, Greece, and Italy, making collusion unlikely. The oldest manuscript, the John Ryland's manuscript, has been dated to 125 A.D. and was

found in Egypt, some distance from where the New Testament was originally composed in Asia Minor. Many early Christian papyri, discovered in 1935, have been dated to 150 A.D., and include the four gospels. The Papyrus Bodmer II, discovered in 1956, has been dated to 200 A.D., and contains 14 chapters and portions of the last seven chapters of the gospel of John. The Chester Beatty biblical papyri, discovered in 1931, has been dated to 200-250 A.D. and contains the Gospels, Acts, Paul's Epistles, and Revelation. The number of manuscripts is extensive compared to other ancient historical writings, such as Caesar's "Gallic Wars" (10 Greek manuscripts, the earliest 950 years after the original), the "Annals" of Tacitus (2 manuscripts, the earliest 950 years after the original), Livy (20 manuscripts, the earliest 350 years after the original), and Plato (7 manuscripts).

Manuscript Evidence for Ancient Writings

Author	Written	Earliest Copy	Time Span	# Mss.
Caesar	100-44 B.C.	900 A.D.	1,000 yrs	10
Plato	427-347 B.C.	900 A.D.	1,200 yrs	7
Thucydides	460-400 B.C.	900 A.D.	1,300 yrs	8
Tacitus	100 A.D.	1100 A.D.	1,000 yrs	20
Suetonius	75-160 A.D.	950 A.D.	800 yrs	8
Homer (Iliad)	900 B.C.	400 B.C.	500 yrs	643
New Testament	40-100 A.D.	125 A.D.	25-50 yrs	24,000

Thousands of early Christian writings and lexionaries (first and second century) cite verses from the New Testament. In fact, it is nearly possible to put together the entire New Testament just from early Christian writings. For example, the Epistle of Clement to the Corinthians (dated 95 A.D.) cites verses from the Gospels, Acts, Romans, 1 Corinthians, Ephesians, Titus, Hebrews, and 1 Peter. A the letter of Ignatius (dated 115 A.D.) were written to several churches in Asia Minor and cites verses from Matthew, John, Romans, 1 & 2 Corinthians, Galatians, Ephesians, Philippians, 1 & 2 Timothy and Titus.

These letters indicate that the entire New Testament was written in the first century A.D. In addition, there is internal evidence for a first century date for the writing of the New Testament. The book of Acts ends abruptly with Paul in prison, awaiting trial (Acts 28:30-31 (1)). It is likely that Luke wrote Acts during this time, before Paul finally appeared before Nero.

This would be about 62-63 A.D., meaning that Acts and Luke were written within thirty years of ministry and death of Jesus. Another internal evidence is that there is no mention of the destruction of Jerusalem in 70 A.D. Although Matthew, Mark and Luke record Jesus' prophecy that the temple and city would be destroyed within that generation (Matthew 24:1-2 (2),Mark 13:1-2 (3), Luke 21:5-9,20-24,32(4)), no New Testament book refers to this event as having happened.

If they had been written after 70 A.D., it is likely that letters written after 70 A.D. would have mentioned the fulfillment of Jesus' prophecy. As stated by Nelson Glueck, former president of the Jewish Theological Seminary in the Hebrew Union College in Cincinnati, and renowned Jewish archaeologist, "In my opinion, every book of the New

Testament was written between the forties and eighties of the first century A.D."

Conclusion
With all of the massive manuscript evidence you would think there would be massive discrepancies - just the opposite is true. New Testament manuscripts agree in 99.5% (5) of the text (compared to only 95% for the Iliad).

Most of the discrepancies are in spelling and word order. A few words have been changed or added. There are two passages that are disputed but no discrepancy is of any doctrinal significance (i.e., none would alter basic Christian doctrine).

Most Bibles include the options as footnotes when there are discrepancies. How could there be such accuracy over a period of 1,400 years of copying? Two reasons: The scribes that did the copying had meticulous methods for checking their copies for errors. 2) The Holy Spirit made sure we would have an accurate copy of God's word so we would not be deceived. The Mormons, theological liberals as well as other cults and false religions such as Islam that claim the Bible has been tampered with are completely proven false by the extensive, historical manuscript evidence.

GodandScience.Org

FUN FACTS

Bible Basics

- The word "Bible" is derived from the Greek work "bibla," which translates to "books." The term is accurate. Although the Bible is presented as a single text, it is actually a collection of 66 different books.

- Are you interested in reading the Bible aloud? Hope you have some time on your hands! It would take you approximately 70 hours to get through the 773, 692 words in the book.

- The Bible took a long time to finish. According to What Saith The Scripture, the Bible was compiled over a course of 1600 years. Scripture was compiled beginning in 1500 B.C with the final pieces being added by approximately 100 A.D.

- The Bible has been published in over 6,000 languages. The original language of the Old Testament was Hebrew. The New Testament was originally written in Greek.

- Obadiah is the shortest book in the Old Testament, with 21 verses. John 2 is the shortest book in the New Testament. It has 13 verses.

- Acts is the longest book in the New Testament. It has 28 chapters.

- There are 1189 chapters in the Bible.

Bible Fun Facts - People of The Bible

The Bible is chockfull of fascinating people. How well do you know them? Check out these Bible fun facts for a look into their lives.

- King Solomon was definitely a busy man. According to Bible accounts, he played host to 700 wives and over 300 concubines.

- Large and powerful people and corporations are often referred to as Goliath, and for good reason. In the Bible, Goliath stands at nine and a half feet tall.

- There are some remarkable stories of life and death in the Bible. Methuselah lived to be 969. He is said to have died seven days before the great flood. It is further said that God delayed the flood to allow for seven days of mourning. Enoch, Methuselah's father, and Elijah are said to have never died at all. They are believed to have ascended to heaven while alive.

- Gideon fought off 135,000 Midianites invaders with only an army of 300 men and 300 trumpets.

- In his book, Isaiah offered the most accurate predications about Jesus. He made 20 predictions, and they all turned out to be true.

- Samson is the strongest man in the Bible, while King Solomon is said to the wisest.

The Bible and Numbers

Many number patterns in the Bible are significant. Check out the following facts:

- Be Not Afraid is a well-known Christian hymn inspired by an often repeated phrase in the Bible. "Do not be afraid" is repeated 365 times in the Bible – the same number of days in a year.

- The number seven has particular significance in the Bible and is usually used a symbol of completion. This is the source of the idea that seven is a "lucky" number.

- The number 40 is also symbolic in the Bible. Forty is normally associated with the dawn of a new era. Jesus fasted for 40 days in the desert, it rained for 40 days in the great flood, spies were in Canaan for 40 days and Nineveh was warned by Jonah for 40 days.

- The Bible mentions 12 tribes of Israel. There were also 12 apostles.

- Can you believe it that the Bible is the number one most shoplifted book in America? Don't you wonder if the shoplifter knows the Ten Commandments?

- Of all the books in the Bible, the book of Esther never once mentioned the name of God.

- According to Genesis 1:20-22, the chicken came before the egg. So, now we can stop pondering which comes first, the chicken or the egg.

- Throughout the world, 47 bibles are being sold or distributed every minute. That is a lot of bibles around the world.

- Shakespeare was believed to be 46 when the King James Version of the Bible was written. That is nothing to be awed about. However, the following fact might really make you wonder if it's just a coincidence or a

design on the part of the writers of the King James Version. In Psalms 46, the 46th word from the first word is "shake" and the 46th word from the last word is "spear". And put them together, you'll get

- The Bible has been translated to Klingon. Klingon is a fictional tribe invented by the creators of Star Trek. Maybe they converted some Klingons to Christianity.

- The ten most mentioned animals in the Bible are sheep, lamb, lion, ox, ram, horse, bullock, ass, goat and camel.

- The shortest verse in the Bible? Jesus wept (John 11:35).

- Almonds and pistachios are the only nuts mentioned in the Bible.

- Only 2 books are named after women and they are the book of Esther and the book of Ruth.

- The first book in the Old Testament is the Genesis and the last book is Malachi.

- The first book in the Old Testament is the Gospel according to St Matthew and the last book is Revelation.

- There are 66 books and 929 chapters in the Bible and 27 books and 260 chapters in the New Testament.

- The oldest person mentioned in the Bible is Methuselah. He was 969 years old.

- The only miracle Jesus Christ performed that was mentioned in all the four Gospels is the feeding of the 5000.

Other Random Facts

- Almonds and pistachios are the only nuts mentioned in the Bible.

- As specified by the Christian church, the canonical hours are matins, lauds, prime, terce, sext, none, vespers, and compline.

- Gabriel, Michael, and Lucifer are the three angels mentioned by name in the Bible.

- In Christian theology there are nine choirs of angels. From highest to lowest, they are: seraphim, cherubim, thrones, dominions, virtues, powers, principalities, archangels, and angels.

- One of the holiest Christian holidays is named after a pagan goddess. The name "Easter" derives from the Anglo-Saxon goddess Eostre, who governed the vernal equinox.

- Salt is mentioned more than 30 times in the Bible.

- Scholars estimate that the 66 books of the King James Version of the Bible were written by some 50 different authors.

- Seven suicides are recorded in the Bible.

- Some biblical scholars believe that Aramaic (the language of the ancient Bible) did not contain an easy way to say 'many things' and used a term which has come down to us as 40. This means that when the bible -- in many places -- refers to '40 days,' they meant many days.

- Strict Puritan laws had their origins from practical

reasons. Smoking was banned - farmers would raise
badly needed food crops instead of tobacco. Cooking
was banned on Sundays - to prevent house fires during
the long hours the family was at church. Young men
were banned from hunting - to prevent weapons from
falling into Indian hands.

- The 1st US Mormon temple was dedicated in Kirtland,
  Ohio in 1836.

- The 3 Magi:(or Wise Men) and their gifts: Melchoir,
  "king of light," offered Gold, Gaspar," or the white
  one," offered frankincense, and Balthazar, "lord of
  treasures," offered myrrh.

- The Bible devotes some 500 verses on prayer, less than
  500 verses on faith, but over 2000 verses on money and
  possessions.

- The Bible was written by about 40 men over a period of
  about 1600 years dating from 1500 BC to about 100
  years after Christ.

- The Church of Scientology was founded in 1953, at
  Washington DC, by US science fiction writer L. Ron
  Hubbard.

- The first translation of the English Bible was initiated
  by John Wycliffe and completed by John Purvey in
  1388.

- The Four Horsemen of the Apocalypse, named in the
  Bible's Book of Revelation, are Conquest, Slaughter,
  Famine, and Death.

- The Hindu holy day begins at sunrise, the Jewish holy
  day begins at sunset, and the Christian holy day begins
  at midnight.

- The longest name in the Bible Mahershalalhashbaz (Isaiah 8:1).

- The patron saint of dentists is St. Apollonia. She reportedly had her teeth pulled out in 249 AD by an anti-Christian mob.

- The seven archangels are Michael, Gabriel, Raphael, Uriel, Chamuel, Jophiel, and Zadkiel.

- The Seven Deadly Sins are lust, pride, anger, envy, sloth, avarice and gluttony.

- The seven virtues are prudence, courage, temperance, justice, faith, hope and charity.

- The shortest verse in the Bible consists of two words: "Jesus wept" (John 11:35).

- The Three Wise Men of the East brought gold, frankincense and myrrh to the infant Jesus. Frankincense is a gum resin used as a base for incense. Myrrh, also a gum resin, was valued as a perfume and unguent used in embalming.

- The two robbers crucified next to Jesus were named Dismas and Gestas.

- There are 1189 chapters in the Bible: 929 chapters in the Old Testament and 260 chapters in the New Testament.

- There are 49 different foods mentioned in the Bible.

- Zipporah was the wife of Moses.

"THE LOST TOMB OF JESUS": HAVE THE BONES OF JESUS CHRIST BEEN FOUND IN JERUSALEM?

James Cameron is producing a 90-minute film for the Discovery Channel entitled, "The Lost Tomb of Jesus," claiming that the actual bones of Jesus of Nazareth were buried in a tomb near Jerusalem. A companion book, *The Jesus Tomb* written by Simcha Jacobovici and Charles Pellegrino, is also being offered. In addition, in the tradition of the discredited Dan Brown, the film claims that these bones of "Jesus" were once married to Mary Magdalene, with whom he had a son name Judah.

The timing of the release
The timing of Discovery's special right before Christianity's Holy Week was not by accident. Last year it was *National Geographic's* "Gospel of Judas" special on the high Christian holiday of Palm Sunday. One can be certain that the next big "special" will be aired at the same time next year to attempt to discredit Christianity's founder at a time of the year when popular interest focuses on His death and resurrection.

Dating of the bones
It was Jewish custom in the first century A.D. that the bones of the deceased were transferred from burial caves to limestone boxes called ossuaries one year after their death. This practice was abandoned after the destruction of the Jewish Temple in 70 A.D. Frank Moore Cross, a professor emeritus in the Department of Near Eastern Languages and Civilizations at Harvard University, indicated, "The

inscriptions are from the Herodian Period (which occurred from around 1 B.C. to 1 A.D.). The use of limestone ossuaries and the varied script styles are characteristic of that time." Since Jesus did not die until 30 A.D., the date is problematic for those claiming they represent the bones of Jesus.

What was found?
The tomb containing the bones was first found by a construction crew in 1980 in the Jerusalem suburb of Talpiyot. According to Jerusalem-based biblical expert Joe Zias the tomb would have held more than 200 ossuaries. Ten ossuaries were taken to the Rockefeller Archaeological Museum near Jerusalem, where one disappeared. Six of the ossuaries were inscribed with names that would be translated as Jeshua (Joshua or Jesus), Mara (Mary), Matthew, Josa (Joseph), Mariamene (Mary Magdalene?) and Judah, son of Jeshua.

Are the names those of the Holy Family?
Stephen Pfann, a biblical scholar at the University of the Holy Land in Jerusalem, is unsure that the name "Jesus" on the ossuary was read correctly, since ancient Semitic script is difficult to read. He thinks it's more likely that the name is "Hanun." Bar-Ilan University Prof. Amos Kloner indicated that "Jesus son of Joseph" inscriptions had been found on several other ossuaries over the years. In addition, Kloner indicated, "There is no likelihood that Jesus and his relatives had a family tomb. They were a Galilee family with no ties in Jerusalem. The Talpiot tomb belonged to a middle-class family from the 1st century CE."

What does the DNA testing tell us?
According to the film's website, DNA testing was attempted on only two samples - those of "Jesus" and those of Mariamene. The DNA was so degraded that no

sequencing could be determined from the nuclear DNA (the main chromosomes). Only mitochondrial DNA (mtDNA) was available for sequencing. Since mtDNA is much smaller than nuclear DNA, the average person's mtDNA differs from another's by only 8 base pairs. In closely-related communities, differences would be much less. The film's website did not give any details about the testing other than the claim that the individuals "were not related." Since "Jesus" and Mariamene were "unrelated," the filmmakers assumed they were married and had a son named Judah (from the ossuary "Judah, son of Jeshua"). However, the conclusion that "Jesus" and Mariamene were married cannot be ascertained from the DNA evidence. Since mtDNA is only transferred from mother to daughter (or son), "Jesus" could very well be the father of Mariamene (or any other relative on the paternal side), and the mtDNA testing would indicate that they were "not related." Only nuclear DNA analysis could determine if "Jesus" and Mariamene were truly related or not. So, the mtDNA testing tells us only that "Jesus" and Mariamene were not siblings or related maternally. No other relationship can be determined from the mtDNA testing.

Is Mariamene Mary Magdalene?
The assumption that Mariamene is really Mary Magdalene is quite overstated, since the name of "Mariamne" from the Acts of Philip is not the same as Mariamene. In addition, the Acts of Philip is the work of a heretical community that lived in the fourth century - at least two hundred fifty years after the events of the New Testament. For more information, see The Acts of Philip, Mariamne and the Jesus Tomb.

Conclusion
Jerusalem-based biblical expert Joe Zias has called the documentary nonsense, saying those involved in the

project have "no credibility whatsoever... It's an old story that's been recycled. The story first broke in 1996 by the BBC. It burst in a couple of days." The fact that the inscriptions on the ossuaries date to the beginning of the first century and Jesus and the others died much later, makes it extremely unlikely that "Jeshua" from the "Jesus Tomb" is really Jesus Christ. According to Stephen Pfann, "How possible is it? On a scale of one through 10 - 10 being completely possible - it's probably a one, maybe a one and a half."

GodandScience.Org

FAMOUS SCIENTISTS THAT
BELIEVED IN GOD

Nicholas Copernicus (1473-1543): Copernicus was the Polish astronomer who put forward the first mathematically based system of planets going around the sun. He attended various European universities, and became a Canon in the Catholic Church in 1497. His new system was actually first presented in the Vatican gardens in 1533 before Pope Clement VII who approved, and urged Copernicus to publish it around this time. Copernicus was never under any threat of religious persecution - and was urged to publish both by Catholic Bishop Guise, Cardinal Schonberg, and the Protestant Professor George Rheticus. Copernicus referred sometimes to God in his works, and did not see his system as in conflict with the Bible.

Sir Francis Bacon (1561-1627): Bacon was a philosopher who is known for establishing the scientific method of inquiry based on experimentation and inductive reasoning. In *De Interpretatione Naturae Prooemium*, Bacon established his goals as being the discovery of truth, service to his country, and service to the church. Although his work was based upon experimentation and reasoning, he rejected atheism as being the result of insufficient depth of philosophy, stating, "It is true, that a little philosophy inclineth man's mind to atheism, but depth in philosophy bringeth men's minds about to religion; for while the mind of man looketh upon second causes scattered, it may sometimes rest in them, and go no further; but when it beholdeth the chain of them confederate, and linked together, it must needs fly to Providence and Deity."

Johannes Kepler (1571-1630): Kepler was a brilliant mathematician and astronomer. He did early work on light,

and established the laws of planetary motion about the sun. He also came close to reaching the Newtonian concept of universal gravity - well before Newton was born! His introduction of the idea of force in astronomy changed it radically in a modern direction. Kepler was an extremely sincere and pious Lutheran, whose works on astronomy contain writings about how space and the heavenly bodies represent the Trinity. Kepler suffered no persecution for his open avowal of the sun-centered system, and, indeed, was allowed as a Protestant to stay in Catholic Graz as a Professor (1595-1600) when other Protestants had been expelled!

Galileo Galilei (1564-1642): Galileo is often remembered for his conflict with the Roman Catholic Church. His controversial work on the solar system was published in 1633. It had no proofs of a sun-centered system (Galileo's telescope discoveries did not indicate a moving earth) and his one "proof" based upon the tides was invalid. It ignored the correct elliptical orbits of planets published twenty-five years earlier by Kepler. Since his work finished by putting the Pope's favorite argument in the mouth of the simpleton in the dialogue, the Pope (an old friend of Galileo's) was very offended. After the "trial" and being forbidden to teach the sun-centered system, Galileo did his most useful theoretical work, which was on dynamics. Galileo expressly said that the Bible cannot err, and saw his system as an alternate interpretation of the biblical texts.

Rene Descartes (1596-1650): Descartes was a French mathematician, scientist and philosopher who has been called the father of modern philosophy. His school studies made him dissatisfied with previous philosophy: He had a deep religious faith as a Roman Catholic, which he retained to his dying day, along with a resolute, passionate desire to discover the truth. At the age of 24 he had a dream, and felt

the vocational call to seek to bring knowledge together in one system of thought. His system began by asking what could be known if all else were doubted - suggesting the famous "I think therefore I am". Actually, it is often forgotten that the next step for Descartes was to establish the near certainty of the existence of God - for only if God both exists and would not want us to be deceived by our experiences - can we trust our senses and logical thought processes. God is, therefore, central to his whole philosophy. What he really wanted to see was that his philosophy be adopted as standard Roman Catholic teaching. Rene Descartes and Francis Bacon (1561-1626) are generally regarded as the key figures in the development of scientific methodology. Both had systems in which God was important, and both seem more devout than the average for their era.

Blaise Pascal (1623-1662): Pascal was a French mathematician, physicist, inventor, writer and theologian. In mathematics, he published a treatise on the subject of projective geometry and established the foundation for probability theory. Pascal invented a mechanical calculator, and established the principles of vacuums and the pressure of air. He was raised a Roman Catholic, but in 1654 had a religious vision of God, which turned the direction of his study from science to theology. Pascal began publishing a theological work, *Lettres provinciales*, in 1656. His most influential theological work, the *Pensées* ("Thoughts"), was a defense of Christianity, which was published after his death. The most famous concept from *Pensées* was Pascal's Wager. Pascal's last words were, "May God never abandon me."

Isaac Newton (1642-1727): In optics, mechanics, and mathematics, Newton was a figure of undisputed genius and innovation. In all his science (including chemistry) he

saw mathematics and numbers as central. What is less well known is that he was devoutly religious and saw numbers as involved in understanding God's plan for history from the Bible. He did a considerable work on biblical numerology, and, though aspects of his beliefs were not orthodox, he thought theology was very important. In his system of physics, God was essential to the nature and absoluteness of space. In *Principia* he stated, "The most beautiful system of the sun, planets, and comets, could only proceed from the counsel and dominion of an intelligent and powerful Being."

Robert Boyle (1791-1867): One of the founders and key early members of the Royal Society, Boyle gave his name to "Boyle's Law" for gases, and also wrote an important work on chemistry. *Encyclopedia Britannica* says of him: "By his will he endowed a series of Boyle lectures, or sermons, which still continue, 'for proving the Christian religion against notorious infidels...' As a devout Protestant, Boyle took a special interest in promoting the Christian religion abroad, giving money to translate and publish the New Testament into Irish and Turkish. In 1690 he developed his theological views in *The Christian Virtuoso*, which he wrote to show that the study of nature was a central religious duty." Boyle wrote against atheists in his day (the notion that atheism is a modern invention is a myth), and was clearly much more devoutly Christian than the average in his era.

Michael Faraday (1791-1867): Michael Faraday was the son of a blacksmith who became one of the greatest scientists of the 19th century. His work on electricity and magnetism not only revolutionized physics, but led to much of our lifestyles today, which depends on them (including computers and telephone lines and, so, web sites). Faraday was a devoutly Christian member of the

Sandemanians, which significantly influenced him and strongly affected the way in which he approached and interpreted nature. Originating from Presbyterians, the Sandemanians rejected the idea of state churches, and tried to go back to a New Testament type of Christianity.

Gregor Mendel (1822-1884): Mendel was the first to lay the mathematical foundations of genetics, in what came to be called "Mendelianism". He began his research in 1856 (three years before Darwin published his *Origin of Species*) in the garden of the Monastery in which he was a monk. Mendel was elected Abbot of his Monastery in 1868. His work remained comparatively unknown until the turn of the century, when a new generation of botanists began finding similar results and "rediscovered" him (though their ideas were not identical to his). An interesting point is that the 1860's were notable for formation of the X-Club, which was dedicated to lessening religious influences and propagating an image of "conflict" between science and religion. One sympathizer was Darwin's cousin Francis Galton, whose scientific interest was in genetics (a proponent of eugenics - selective breeding among humans to "improve" the stock). He was writing how the "priestly mind" was not conducive to science while, at around the same time, an Austrian monk was making the breakthrough in genetics. The rediscovery of the work of Mendel came too late to affect Galton's contribution.

William Thomson Kelvin (1824-1907): Kelvin was foremost among the small group of British scientists who helped to lay the foundations of modern physics. His work covered many areas of physics, and he was said to have more letters after his name than anyone else in the Commonwealth, since he received numerous honorary degrees from European Universities, which recognized the value of his work. He was a very committed Christian, who

was certainly more religious than the average for his era. Interestingly, his fellow physicists George Gabriel Stokes (1819-1903) and James Clerk Maxwell (1831-1879) were also men of deep Christian commitment, in an era when many were nominal, apathetic, or anti-Christian. The *Encyclopedia Britannica* says "Maxwell is regarded by most modern physicists as the scientist of the 19th century who had the greatest influence on 20th century physics; he is ranked with Sir Isaac Newton and Albert Einstein for the fundamental nature of his contributions." Lord Kelvin was an Old Earth creationist, who estimated the Earth's age to be somewhere between 20 million and 100 million years, with an upper limit at 500 million years based on cooling rates (a low estimate due to his lack of knowledge about radiogenic heating).

Max Planck (1858-1947): Planck made many contributions to physics, but is best known for quantum theory, which revolutionized our understanding of the atomic and sub-atomic worlds. In his 1937 lecture "Religion and Naturwissenschaft," Planck expressed the view that God is everywhere present, and held that "the holiness of the unintelligible Godhead is conveyed by the holiness of symbols." Atheists, he thought, attach too much importance to what are merely symbols. Planck was a churchwarden from 1920 until his death, and believed in an almighty, all-knowing, beneficent God (though not necessarily a personal one). Both science and religion wage a "tireless battle against skepticism and dogmatism, against unbelief and superstition" with the goal "toward God!"

Albert Einstein (1879-1955): Einstein is probably the best known and most highly revered scientist of the twentieth century, and is associated with major revolutions in our thinking about time, gravity, and the conversion of matter to energy ($E=mc^2$). Although never coming to belief in a

personal God, he recognized the impossibility of a non-created universe. The *Encyclopedia Britannica* says of him: "Firmly denying atheism, Einstein expressed a belief in "Spinoza's God who reveals himself in the harmony of what exists." This actually motivated his interest in science, as he once remarked to a young physicist: "I want to know how God created this world, I am not interested in this or that phenomenon, in the spectrum of this or that element. I want to know His thoughts, the rest are details." Einstein's famous epithet on the "uncertainty principle" was "God does not play dice" - and to him this was a real statement about a God in whom he believed. A famous saying of his was "Science without religion is lame, religion without science is blind."

GodandScience.Org

WHERE IS HELL?

Skeptics claim that the Bible says that Hell is a place located under the Earth. Since the earth is solid or semi-molten all the way to the core, it would seem unlikely that humans (even the souls of the damned) would be able to live there. Atheists love to use the King James Version (KJV), since it uses the English word "hell" in lots of different places in the Bible—even where it doesn't really belong. So, let's see what the Bible really says hell and where it is.

Hell is under the Earth

Here are some of the verses skeptics cite to "prove" their point that the Bible says hell refers to a place under the earth:

- It is as high as heaven; what canst thou do? Deeper than hell; what canst thou know? (Job 11:8 KJV)

- For great is thy mercy toward me: and thou hast delivered my soul from the lowest hell. (Psalm 86:13 KJV)

- But he knoweth not that the dead are there; and that her guests are in the depths of hell. (Proverbs 9:18 KJV)

- The way of life is above to the wise, that he may depart from hell beneath. (Proverbs 15:24 KJV)

- Yet thou shalt be brought down to hell, to the sides of the pit. (Isaiah 14:15 KJV)

- I made the nations to shake at the sound of his fall, when I cast him down to hell with them that descend into the pit: and all the trees of Eden, the choice and best

of Lebanon, all that drink water, shall be comforted in the nether parts of the earth. (Ezekiel 31:16 KJV)

- Though they dig into hell, thence shall mine hand take them; though they climb up to heaven, thence will I bring them down: (Amos 9:2 KJV)

- If I ascend up into heaven, thou art there: if I make my bed in hell, behold, thou art there. (Psalm 139:8 KJV)

Sheol refers to the grave
Even though the verses above seem to imply that "hell" is under the earth, some of the verses are difficult to reconcile, given the context. First, one would have to ask why God would be in both heaven *and* hell (Psalm 139:8)? Isn't God supposed to be in heaven? And why is hell described as a "pit?" Unless it were a really *big* pit, it would be difficult to fit all the damned into such a "pit." The mystery is solved when one looks at the Hebrew word translated in the KJV Bible as "hell." The Hebrew word common to all these verses is *sheol*, which actually refers to the grave. However, atheists will not cite the following verses, which also contain the word *sheol*.

- And all his sons and all his daughters rose up to comfort him; but he refused to be comforted; and he said, For I will go down into the grave [*sheol*] unto my son mourning. Thus his father wept for him. (*Genesis 37:35 KJV*)

- The LORD killeth, and maketh alive: he bringeth down to the grave [*sheol*], and bringeth up. (*1 Samuel 2:6 KJV*)

- O that thou wouldest hide me in the grave [*sheol*], that thou wouldest keep me secret, until thy wrath be past, that thou wouldest appoint me a set time, and remember

2me! (*Job 14:13 KJV*)

- They spend their days in wealth, and in a moment go down to the grave [*sheol*]. (*Job 21:13 KJV*)

- Let us swallow them up alive as the grave [*sheol*]; and whole, as those that go down into the pit: (*Proverbs 1:12 KJV*)

- Thy pomp is brought down to the grave [*sheol*], and the noise of thy viols: the worm is spread under thee, and the worms cover thee. (*Isaiah 14:11 KJV*)

The reason why atheists don't cite the verses above is because they make it clear that *sheol* refers to the grave and not hell, the real the place of exile and judgment. Yes, the grave is *under the earth*!

Where is hell?
The Greek word for hell, *genna*, occurs only 11 times in the Bible, none of which refer to a place under the Earth. In fact, all the references to under the Earth refer to either *sheol* (Hebrew) or its Greek equivalent (Hades). Here is a list of all verses that refer to Hell:

- "But I say to you that everyone who is angry with his brother shall be guilty before the court; and whoever shall say to his brother, 'Raca,' shall be guilty before the supreme court; and whoever shall say, 'You fool,' shall be guilty *enough to go* into the fiery hell." (*Matthew 5:22*)

- "And if your right eye makes you stumble, tear it out, and throw it from you; for it is better for you that one of the parts of your body perish, than for your whole body to be thrown into hell." (*Matthew 5:29*)

- "And if your right hand makes you stumble, cut it off, and throw it from you; for it is better for you that one of the parts of your body perish, than for your whole body to go into hell." (*Matthew 5:30*)

- "And do not fear those who kill the body, but are unable to kill the soul; but rather fear Him who is able to destroy both soul and body in hell." (*Matthew 10:28*)

- "And if your eye causes you to stumble, pluck it out, and throw it from you. It is better for you to enter life with one eye, than having two eyes, to be cast into the fiery hell." (*Matthew 18:9*)

- "Woe to you, scribes and Pharisees, hypocrites, because you travel about on sea and land to make one proselyte; and when he becomes one, you make him twice as much a son of hell as yourselves." (*Matthew 23:15*)

- "You serpents, you brood of vipers, how shall you escape the sentence of hell?" (*Matthew 23:33*)

- "And if your hand causes you to stumble, cut it off; it is better for you to enter life crippled, than having your two hands, to go into hell, into the unquenchable fire," (*Mark 9:43*)

- "And if your foot causes you to stumble, cut it off; it is better for you to enter life lame, than having your two feet, to be cast into hell," (*Mark 9:45*)

- "And if your eye causes you to stumble, cast it out; it is better for you to enter the kingdom of God with one eye, than having two eyes, to be cast into hell," (*Mark 9:47*)

- "But I will warn you whom to fear: fear the One who after He has killed has authority to cast into hell; yes, I

tell you, fear Him!" (*Luke 12:5*)

- And the tongue is a fire, the *very* world of iniquity; the tongue is set among our members as that which defiles the entire body, and sets on fire the course of *our* life, and is set on fire by hell. (*James 3:6*)

As noted before, none of these verses says that Hell is under the Earth. In fact, the Bible says that the Earth will be destroyed[1] and that Hades (or the grave) will be thrown into Hell (Lake of Fire). It would be rather difficult for Hell to be thrown into itself, or for Hades to be thrown into the Earth, especially when the Earth was already destroyed. So, it is pretty clear that the Bible does *not* say that Hell is under the earth, but is a place separate from earth (and probably separate from the universe, since the entire universe will be destroyed and replaced with the new creation).

Conclusion

Verses cited by skeptics reportedly referring to hell being under the earth really refer to the grave, the common destination of all human beings. In fact, the Bible says that the grave will be thrown into hell after the judgment, ending death altogether. Although the Bible does not describe where hell is, it is apparent that it is outside the universe, since it will still exist, at least temporarily, after the present universe is destroyed by God. After this creation is destroyed, God will create again—a new heavens and new earth, where righteousness dwells (2 Peter 3:13).

GodandScience.Org

RANDOM FACTS

- The longest one-syllable word in the English language is "screeched."

- "Dreamt" is the only English word that ends in the letters "mt".

- Almonds are members of the peach family.

- The symbol on the "pound" key (#) is called an octothorpe.

- The dot over the letter 'i' is called a tittle.

- The word "set" has more definitions than any other word in the English language.

- "Underground" is the only word in the English language that begins and ends with the letters "und."

- There are only four words in the English language which end in "-dous": tremendous, horrendous, stupendous, and hazardous.

- The longest word in the English language, according to the Oxford English Dictionary, is *pneumonoultramicroscopicsilicovolcanoconiosis. The only other word with the same amount of letters is pneumonoultramicroscopicsilicovolcanoconioses, its plural.

- The longest place-name still in use is Taumatawhakatangihangakoauauotamateaturipukakapi kimaungahoronukupokaiw en uaitnatahu, a New Zealand hill.

- Los Angeles's full name is "El Pueblo de Nuestra Senora la Reina de los Angeles de Porciuncula" and can be abbreviated to 3.63% of its size, "L.A."

- An ostrich's eye is bigger than its brain.

- Tigers have striped skin, not just striped fur.

- Donald Duck's middle name is Fauntleroy.

- The muzzle of a lion is like a fingerprint - no two lions have the same pattern of whiskers.

- A pregnant goldfish is called a twit.

- The Ramses brand condom is named after the great pharaoh Ramses II who fathered over 160 children.

- There is a seven letter word in the English language that contains ten words without rearranging any of its letters, "therein": the, there, he, in, rein, her, here, ere, therein, herein.

- Dueling is legal in Paraguay as long as both parties are registered blood donors.

- It's impossible to sneeze with your eyes open.

- Cranberries are sorted for ripeness by bouncing them; a fully ripened cranberry can be dribbled like a basketball.

- The male gypsy moth can "smell" the virgin female gypsy moth from 1.8 miles away.

- The letters KGB stand for Komitet Gosudarstvennoy Bezopasnosti.

- "Stewardesses" is the longest word that can be typed

with only the left hand.

- To "testify" was based on men in the Roman court swearing to a statement made by swearing on their testicles.

- The combination "ough" can be pronounced in nine different ways. The following sentence contains them all: "A rough-coated, dough-faced, thoughtful ploughman strode through the streets of Scarborough; after falling into a slough, he coughed and hiccoughed."

- Emus and kangaroos cannot walk backwards, and are on the Australian coat of arms for that reason.

- Cats have over one hundred vocal sounds, while dogs only have about ten.

- The word "Checkmate" in chess comes from the Persian phrase "Shah Mat," which means "the king is dead."

- The reason firehouses have circular stairways is from the days of yore when the engines were pulled by horses. The horses were stabled on the ground floor and figured out how to walk up straight staircases.

- The first episode of "Joanie Loves Chachi" was the highest rated American program in the history of Korean television.

- "Chachi" is Korean for "penis."

- A snail can sleep for three years.

- Babies are born without kneecaps. They don't appear until the child reaches 2 to 6 years of age.

- Cats have over one hundred vocal sounds. Dogs only have about 10.

- February 1865 is the only month in recorded history not to have a full moon.

- If the population of China walked past you in single file, the line would never end because of the rate of reproduction.

- Leonardo DiVinci invented the scissors.

- Our eyes are always the same size from birth, but our nose and ears never stop growing.

- Shakespeare invented the word 'assassination' and 'bump'.

- The cruise liner, QE2, moves only six inches for each gallon of diesel that it burns.

- TYPEWRITER is the longest word that can be made using the letters only on one row of the keyboard.

- Women blink nearly twice as much as men.

- Your stomach has to produce a new layer of mucus every two week otherwise it will digest itself.

- There are two words in the English language that have all five vowels in order: "abstemious" and "facetious."

- There is a word in the English language with only one vowel, which occurs five times: "indivisibility."

- The Bible does not say there were three wise men; it only says there were three gifts.

- Did you know that crocodiles never outgrow the pool in

which they live? That means that if you put a baby croc in an aquarium, it would be little for the rest of its life.

- Thirty-five percent of the people who use personal ads for dating are already married.

- The only 15-letter word that can be spelled without repeating a letter is "uncopyrightable"

- It is impossible to lick your elbow.

- A crocodile can't stick its tongue out.

- A shrimp's heart is in their head.

- People say, "Bless you" when you sneeze because when you sneeze, your heart stops for a milli-second.

- In a study of 200,000 ostriches over a period of 80 years, no one reported a single case where an ostrich buried its head in the sand, or attempted to do so (apart from bones).

- It is physically impossible for pigs to look up into the sky.

- A pregnant goldfish is called a twit.

- Between 1937 and 1945 Heinz produced a version of Alphabetti Spaghetti especially for the German market that consisted solely of little pasta swastikas.

- On average, a human being will have sex more than 3,000 times and spend two weeks kissing in their lifetime.

- More than 50% of the people in the world have never made or received a telephone call.

- Rats and horses can't vomit.

- The "sixth sick sheik's sixth sheep's sick" is said to be the toughest tongue twister in the English language.

- If you sneeze too hard, you can fracture a rib.

- If you try to suppress a sneeze, you can rupture a blood vessel in your head or neck and die.

- If you keep your eyes open by force, they can pop out.

- Rats multiply so quickly that in 18 months, two rats could have over a million descendants.

- Wearing headphones for just an hour will increase the bacteria in your ear by 700 times.

- If the U.S. government has no knowledge of aliens, then why does Title 14, Section 1211 of the Code of Federal Regulations, implemented on July 16, 1969, make it illegal for U.S. citizens to have any contact with extraterrestrials or their vehicles?

- In every episode of Seinfeld there is a Superman somewhere.

- The cigarette lighter was invented before the match.

- Thirty-five percent of the people who use personal ads for dating are already married.

- A duck's quack doesn't echo, and no one knows why.

- 23% of all photocopier faults worldwide are caused by people sitting on them and photocopying their buttocks.

- In the course of an average lifetime you will, while sleeping, eat 70 assorted insects and 10 spiders.

- Most lipstick contains fish scales.

- Cat's urine glows under a black light.

- Like fingerprints, everyone's tongue print is different.

- Over 75% of people who read this will try to lick their elbow.

- The king of hearts is the only king without a mustache.

- A Boeing 747s wingspan is longer than the Wright brother's first flight.

- American Airlines saved $40,000 in 1987 by eliminating 1 olive from each salad served in first-class.

- Venus is the only planet that rotates clockwise.

- Apples, not caffeine, are more efficient at waking you up in the morning.

- The plastic things on the end of shoelaces are called aglets.

- Most dust particles in your house are made from dead skin.

- The first owner of the Marlboro Company died of lung cancer.

- Michael Jordan makes more money from Nike annually than all of the Nike factory workers in Malaysia combined.

- All US Presidents have worn glasses. Some just didn't like being seen wearing them in public.

- Walt Disney was afraid of mice.

- Pearls melt in vinegar.

- The three most valuable brand names on earth Marlboro, Coca Cola, and Budweiser, in that order.

- It is possible to lead a cow upstairs...but not downstairs.

- Richard Millhouse Nixon was the first US president whose name contains all the letters from the word "criminal." William Jefferson Clinton is the second.

- Turtles can breathe through their butts.

DEBUNKING DAWKINS: THE GOD DELUSION CHAPTER 1: A DEEPLY RELIGIOUS NON BELIEVER

In his first chapter, Dawkins introduces us to the target of his book- theistic belief in a personal God. He does this is a round about way, primarily using the "beliefs" of Albert Einstein as an example. Einstein was at most a deist (one who believes God created the universe, but does not interact with it) or a pantheist (one who ascribes to "God" everything that exists in the universe). The title of the chapter, "A deeply religious non believer" is a partial quote from Albert Einstein, who described his "religion" as an awe of nature and its "magnificent structure." The main thrust of the chapter is that science deserves respect (which is doesn't get) whereas religion deserves little or no respect (which it receives).

Deserved Respect

The god of religions is a "little god"
In attempting to prove his point that religions are stupid, Dawkins quotes Carl Sagan in *Pale Blue Dot*:

"How is it that hardly any major religion has looked at science and concluded, 'This is much better than we thought! The Universe is much bigger than our prophets said, grander more subtle, more elegant? Instead they say, 'No, no, no! My god is a little god, and I want him to stay that way.' A religion, old or new, that stressed the magnificence of the Universe as revealed by modern

science might be able to draw forth reserves of reverence and awe hardly tapped by the conventional faiths."

What Sagan failed to understand (and Dawkins, by quoting him) is that there *is* such a religion that directly ascribes the magnificence of the universe to the glory of the God who created it. The Christian scriptures say that God created time and the entire universe from what is not visible, and, as immense as it is, it cannot contain Him. This is certainly no "little god." These same scriptures tell us that the awesome nature of the created universe reveals God's glory and power:

- The heavens are telling of the glory of God; And their expanse is declaring the work of His hands. (Psalm 19:1)

- The heavens declare His righteousness, And all the peoples have seen His glory. (Psalm 97:6)

- Lift up your eyes on high And see who has created these stars, The One who leads forth their host by number, He calls them all by name; Because of the greatness of His might and the strength of His power, Not one of them is missing. (*Isaiah 40:26*)

- Let heaven and earth praise Him, The seas and everything that moves in them. (*Psalm 69:34*)

- Praise the LORD from the earth, Sea monsters and all deeps; Fire and hail, snow and clouds; Stormy wind, fulfilling His word; Mountains and all hills; Fruit trees and all cedars; Beasts and all cattle; Creeping things and winged fowl; Kings of the earth and all peoples; Princes and all judges of the earth; Both young men and virgins; Old men and children. Let them praise the name of the LORD, For His name alone is exalted; His glory is

above earth and heaven. (*Psalm 148:7-13*)

- For the wrath of God is revealed from heaven against all ungodliness and unrighteousness of men who suppress the truth in unrighteousness, because that which is known about God is evident within them; for God made it evident to them. For since the creation of the world His invisible attributes, His eternal power and divine nature, have been clearly seen, being understood through what has been made, so that they are without excuse. (*Romans 1:18-20*)

The God of Christianity is only a "little god" to those who have not read and understood what the Bible says about Him.

Let's quote some obscure off-the-wall Christians
After many words about the differences between "supernatural religion" (i.e. theism) and an awe of nature (i.e., deism or pantheism) Dawkins goes on to quote some obscure (and unnamed) Christians who attacked Einstein's view of God. Who are these people? Dawkins doesn't even tell us their names. Does Dawkins really expect us to believe that they represent mainstream Christianity? One particularly glaring example is a quote from a letter from some "president of a historical society in New Jersey," who says, "As everyone knows, religion is based on Faith, not knowledge." I am sure Dawkins must have searched long and hard to find such an off-the-wall quote. Does this idea really exist within the pages of Christianity's scriptures?

The Bible actually tells believers to test everything.4 In His revelation to Isaiah, God Himself stated, "Come now, and let us reason together..." God, the Creator of humans and human reasoning ability wants us to use that ability. Psalm 19 tells us that the universe "declares the glory of God" and that this "voice goes out into all the earth."

In fact, the Bible says that the evidence for God's design of the universe is so strong that people are "without excuse" in rejecting God and His plan of salvation. The Bible says that God created humans and endowed them with a mind so that they would use it. The Bible says that God and Jesus Christ will test the minds (as well as the hearts) of people. One of the most important prophecies for Christianity, the coming of the New Covenant fulfilled in the coming of the Messiah, Jesus of Nazareth, describes the changes God does in both the heart *and* the mind of those who are transformed.

The Bible says that those who do not believe do so, in part, because of deception in their minds. This deception leads to hostility to God and defiling of their minds and consciences. The Christian is encouraged to direct our "mind to know, to investigate, and to seek wisdom and an explanation."

Christians should use their minds in all aspects of life and "always be prepared to give an answer to everyone who asks you to give the reason for the hope that you have." Many verses from Proverbs discuss the importance of acquiring knowledge and wisdom, even to the degree of choosing knowledge over riches.

Faith is of utmost importance to the Christian, but the Bible doesn't say to limit your belief to faith alone. In fact, it commands us to add first moral excellence then second knowledge. The Bible encourages believers to have a knowledge-based faith, built upon sound biblical doctrine.

When Paul preached the gospel, he did it through reasoning from the scriptures and not an appeal to blind faith. In fact, he commended the Berea's, because they examined the

prophecies to determine if what he was saying was the truth. Paul, in his letters to the churches told believers to do away with childish thinking and reasoning.

Christians are advised to set an example for others in teaching by modeling "integrity, seriousness, and soundness of speech." Jesus, in one of His most famous quotes said, "Love the Lord your God with all your heart and with all your soul and with all your *mind*." (Matthew 22:37) Blind faith is never taught in the Bible.

Dawkins' response to the letter from some "president of a historical society in New Jersey" is, "What a devastatingly revealing letter! Every sentence drips with intellectual and moral cowardice." However, only really naïve atheists are going to believe that some unnamed "president of a historical society in New Jersey" really represents what Christianity teaches about faith and reason. How does Dawkins really think he is going to get away with such deception?

Undeserved respect
The section entitled "undeserved respect" claims that religious ideas receive too much respect and tend to be "hands off" as far as being criticized or even discussed. On this account, I agree with Dawkins. Religious ideas should be up to debate and scrutiny. That is why on this website we discuss and refute all manner of religious claims that are not consistent with the facts.

More "atheistic pride"
Richard Dawkins likes to pat himself on the back throughout the book. He quotes the late Douglas Adams, "...We are used to not challenging religious ideas but it's very interesting how much furor Richard [Dawkins] creates when he does it!..." Such shameless self-promotion does

nothing to dispel his image as a "bad boy" who is only interested in bashing religion to create controversy, instead engaging in intelligent debate.

Confusing group dynamics with religion

Dawkins goes on to explain how "religious conflicts" are mislabeled under group or ethnic strife. He cites the conflict in Northern Ireland, where the parties are labeled "Nationalists" and "Loyalists" instead of Catholics and Protestants. Likewise, Dawkins complains that the conflict in Iraq between the Sunni and Shia Muslims has been called "ethnic cleansing" instead of a "religious conflict."

However, Dawkins fails to point out what part of these conflicts is truly religious in nature. Are these disputes over religious doctrines or principles or disagreements about the nature of God? If so, he should have pointed out exactly which parts of the conflicts were religious in nature. Of course these are not conflicts about religion. They are conflicts involving different religious groups, but as with virtually all conflicts, the disagreements are about power.

Dawkins seems to have forgotten his studies in psychology of human group dynamics. Groups of humans in power will oppress other groups, just based upon membership within each group. The membership could involve religion, language, or just geography.

In fact, the demarcation could be as simple as labeling each group. Psychological studies of group behavior have shown that groups of people will become adversaries with others outside of their own group. Just watch your son's next soccer game. However, Richard Dawkins has only one daughter, so maybe he was never involved in sports.

Even so, Philip Zimbardo's famous Stanford prison experiment showed that students assigned to the category of "guards" physically abused their fellow students just because they were labeled as "prisoners." In fact, the study went so much out-of-control that it had to be ended early.

Dawkins conveniently leaves out of the discussion the fact that atheists (who are not religious) have killed far more people than all "religious" conflicts combined. Joseph Stalin killed 20 million Soviet citizens between 1929 and 1939. Mao Tse-tung killed 34 to 62 million Chinese during the Chinese civil war of the 1930s and 1940s. Pol Pot, the leader of the Marxist regime in Cambodia, Kampuchea, in the 1970's killed 1.7 million of his own people.
In fact, the Pol Pot regime specifically preached atheism and sought to exterminate all religious expression in Cambodia. And, since atheist-led states were largely unheard of before the 20th century, atheists have just begun to get in on the killing rampage.

Let's find the most extreme court rulings regarding religious liberty
Dawkins cites as examples of the "privilege" of religion citing some rather surprising court decisions. The first involved the case where a small church, Centro Espirita Beneficiente Uniao do Vegetal sued to prevent the government from interfering with their religious practices (which involved ingesting hallucinogenic tea during religious ceremonies).

Now, I agree with Dawkins that one is not going to find God by getting stoned. However, the Supreme Court decision involved application of the Religious Freedom Restoration Act of 1993, which required the government to prove a compelling government interest in preventing the

use of the controlled substance during a religious ceremony.

The problem the government experienced was that the religious participants only used the tea during religious ceremonies and did not distribute it to those outside the group. So, the government failed to prove that they had a compelling interest in preventing the use of this controlled substance during a religious practice. The decision was 8-0, with both court liberals and conservatives agreeing that the government failed to prove its case. Similar court cases have found in favor of Native American religious practices, which involved the use of peyote, another controlled substance.

Dawkins cites a recent Los Angeles Time article that reportedly shows how Christian groups are suing to stop "universities from enforcing anti-discrimination rules, including prohibitions against harassing or abusing homosexuals."

What Dawkins doesn't explain is that these "anti-discrimination rules" are really anti-free speech rules that were instituted to prevent discussion of non-politically-correct topics. A number of these rules have been overturned through court decisions (based upon free speech, not freedom of religion), and most other universities have modified or eliminated their speech codes. Harassment and abuse has always been illegal, whether it is directed against homosexuals or heterosexuals. Maybe something was lost in Dawkins translation from British English?

The second court case involved a student who wore a T-shirt stating, "Homosexuality is a sin! Islam is a lie! Abortion is murder! Some issues are just black and white."

Obviously, wearing such a T-short to school is in very poor taste, even if the student was a Christian (presumably). Dawkins goes on to claim that the reason why the student won was because he sued for his *religious* freedom and not free speech rights:

"The parents might have had a conscionable case if they had based it on the First Amendment's guarantee of freedom of speech. But they didn't: indeed, they couldn't, because free speech is deemed not to include 'hate speech'... So, instead of freedom of speech, the Nixons' lawyers appealed to the constitutional right to freedom of religion."

Dawkins statement is a lie. In fact, the student won on the basis of his *free speech* rights. The district court ruled that the school would be in the right if the T-shirt contained "symbols and words that promote values that are so patently contrary to the school's educational mission."

However, they said that "Speech that contains a potentially offensive political viewpoint is not included in this category of regulated expression." (note the word "political", not "religious"). The court also found that the message was not hate speech, saying "there is no evidence that James' silent, passive expression of opinion interfered with the work of Sheridan Middle School or collided with the rights of other students to be let alone. Therefore, the Court rejects defendants' assertion that James' T-shirt invaded on the rights of others."

So, Dawkins just lied that the case revolved around religious rights instead of free speech rights. He also lied that the T-shirt would have been classified as hate speech. He must have known that somebody would check up on his bogus claims.

Danish newspaper cartoons depicting the prophet Muhammad

Dawkins ends chapter one with a description of a recent incident in which Moslem reaction to certain Danish cartoons ended in murder and riots. As it turned out, certain imams added some more offensive cartoons and falsified the treatment of Muslims in Denmark to generate outrage throughout the Muslim world. Most of the targets of the murders were Christians, since we are obviously responsible for all the evil in the world. Of course the entire incident is cited as an example of typical religious reaction to insults. Obviously, we Christians need to step things up to keep up with other religious groups. Dawkins seems strangely unperturbed by insults leveled against religious people, since this is a clear case of free speech, whereas a few pages before, he was highly incensed that anyone would criticize homosexuality, since this is clearly hate speech. It almost seems hypocritical. No, Richard Dawkins would never be prejudiced!

Conclusion

Chapter 1 of Richard Dawkins' book, *The God Delusion* uses all the classic disreputable techniques that Dawkins has complained about in his dealings with certain creationists. He misrepresents Christian understanding of God and the role of evidence and faith. In addition, he quotes from unnamed sources, representing them as standard examples of religious believers, when they are obviously not mainline.

Dawkins mistakenly categorizes conflicts as being religious in nature, when, in reality, none of the disputes involve any theological issues at all. In fact, the examples all involve political power struggles of groups that just happen to be

from different religious affiliations. He fails to point out the atheists who have committed even greater atrocities.

Finally, Dawkins lies outright about how the U.S. courts are protecting "hate speech" on the basis of "religious freedom," when the cases were judged not to be hate speech, nor even religious speech. Despite its popularity, *The God Delusion* has to be Richard Dawkins' most poorly written book to date.

__GodandScience.Org__

SCIENTIFIC STUDIES THAT SHOW A POSITIVE EFFECT OF RELIGION ON HEALTH

Scientific studies over the last four decades have examined the role of both public and private religious expression on health and longevity. The studies have shown that the practice of religious activity improves health and increases longevity.

The effect is seen even when other social/psychological differences are taken into account. For example, one 16-year study examined mortality rates in 11 religious vs. 11 secular kibbutzim in Israel. Although both communities were demographically-matched and provided similar levels of social support, three time more people died in the secular kibbutzim compared to the religious kibbutazim.

The following is a short list of some recent studies that have shown the positive influence of religion on health and longevity.

Tully J, Viner RM, Coen PG, Stuart JM, Zambon M, Peckham C, Booth C, Klein N, Kaczmarski E, Booy R. 2006. Risk and Protective Factors for Meningococcal Disease in Adolescents: Matched Cohort Study. BMJ 332: 445-450.

A study of meningococcal disease in adolescents in the UK showed that religious observance was as effective as meningococcal vaccination for preventing meningococcal disease.

O'Connor P.J., N.P. Pronk, A. Tan, and R.P. Whitebird.

- 54 -

2005. Characteristics of adults who use prayer as an alternative therapy. Am. J. Health Promot. 19:369-375.

A study of prayer use by patients showed that 47% of study subjects prayed for their health, and 90% of these believed prayer improved their health. Those who prayed had significantly less smoking and alcohol use and more preventive care visits, influenza immunizations, vegetable intake, satisfaction with care, and social support, and were more likely to have a regular primary care provider. The study concluded that those who pray had more favorable health-related behaviors, preventive service use, and satisfaction with care.

Krucoff, M. W., et al. 2005. Music, imagery, touch, and prayer as adjuncts to interventional cardiac care: the Monitoring and Actualisation of Noetic Trainings (MANTRA) II randomised study. Lancet 366:211-217.

This double blind study used prayer in combination with music, imagery, and touch in four randomly assigned groups of cardiac patients. Intercessory prayer groups included Christian, Muslim, Jewish, and Buddhist religious traditions. Overall, the study found no significant effect of prayer. However, major adverse cardiac events were reduced in the prayer group (23% to 27%), as were death and readmission rates (33% to 35%). The inclusion of intercessors of multiple religious traditions may have reduced the effectiveness of prayer, especially since Buddhists (who do not believe in God) were included in the study.

D'Souza, R.F. and A. Rodrigo. 2004. Spiritually augmented cognitive behavioural therapy. Australas Psychiatry 12: 148-152.

This study used spiritually augmented cognitive behavior therapy in a mental health study. The study demonstrated that spiritually augmented cognitive behavior therapy helped reduce hopelessness and despair, improved treatment collaboration, reduced relapse, and enhanced functional recovery.

Palmer, R. F., D. Katerndahl, and J. Morgan-Kidd. 2004. A Randomized Trial of the Effects of Remote Intercessory Prayer: Interactions with Personal Beliefs on Problem-Specific Outcomes and Functional Status. J. Alt. Compl. Med. 10: 438-448.

A randomized clinical trial found a significant reduction in the amount of pain in the intercessory prayer group compared to controls. In addition, the amount of concern for baseline problems at follow-up was significantly lower in the prayer group when the subject initially believed that the problem could be resolved. Those who did not believe that their problem could be resolved did not differ from controls. Better physical functioning was observed in the prayer group for those with a higher belief in prayer. However, better mental health scores were observed in the control group with lower belief in prayer scores.

Krucoff, M. W., S. W. Crater, C. L. Green, A. C. Maas, J. E. Seskevich, J. D. Lane, K. A. Loeffler, K. Morris, T. M. Bashore, and H. G. Koenig. 2001. Integrative noetic therapies as adjuncts to percutaneous intervention during unstable coronary syndromes: Monitoring and Actualization of Noetic Training (MANTRA) feasibility pilot. Am. Heart J. 142: 760-767.

A pilot study[8] (limited to 150 patients) examining the efficacy of noetic (non-pharmacological) therapies (stress relaxation, imagery, touch therapy, and prayer) found that

"Of all noetic therapies, off-site intercessory prayer had the lowest short- and long-term absolute complication rates." The results did not reach statistical significance due to the small sample size, but a full study is planned.

Pargament, K. I., H. G. Koenig, N. Tarakeshwar, J. Hahn. 2001. Religious Struggle as a Predictor of Mortality Among Medically Ill Elderly Patients A 2-Year Longitudinal Study. Arch. Intern Med. 161: 1881-1883.

A study examined the effect of "religious struggle" (defined by such things as being angry at God or feeling punished by God) was predictive of poorer physical recovery and higher mortality. According to the authors, "Our findings suggest that patients who indicate religious struggle during a spiritual history may be at particularly high risk for poor medical outcomes. Referral of these patients to clergy to help them work through these issues may ultimately improve clinical outcomes; further research is needed to determine whether interventions that reduce religious struggles might also improve medical prognosis."

Hughes M. Helma, Judith C. Haysb, Elizabeth P. Flintb, Harold G. Koeniga and Dan G. Blazera. 2000. Does Private Religious Activity Prolong Survival? A Six-Year Follow-up Study of 3,851 Older Adults. The Journals of Gerontology Series A: Biological Sciences and Medical Sciences 55: M400-M405.

A six-year study of 3,851 elderly persons revealed that those who reported having rarely to never participating in private religious activity had an increased relative hazard of dying over those who participated more frequently in religious activity. Whereas most previous studies showed a positive effect for organized religious activities, this study showed that personal religious activity was also effective at

reducing mortality.

Koenig HG, Hays JC, Larson DB, et al. 1999. Does religious attendance prolong survival? A six-year follow-up study of 3,968 older adults. J Gerontol Med Sci. 54A: M370-M377.

Hummer R, Rogers R, Nam C, Ellison CG, 1999. Religious involvement and U.S. adult mortality. Demography 36: 273-285.

This study examined the effect of religious attendance on mortality. People who never attended religious activities exhibited 1.87 times the risk of death compared with people who attend more than once a week, which results in a seven-year difference in life expectancy at age 20 between those who never attend and those who attend more than once a week. People who did not attend church or religious services were more likely to be unhealthy and, consequently, to die. However, religious attendance also increased social ties and behavioral factors to decrease the risks of death.

Koenig, H.G. 1998. Religious attitudes and practices of hospitalized medically ill older adults. International Journal of Geriatric Psychiatry 13: 213-224.

When a random sample of 338 hospitalized patients were asked an open-ended question about what the most important factor was that enabled them to cope, 42.3% mentioned their religious faith.

Koenig H.G, et al. 1998. The relationship between religious activities and blood pressure in older adults. International Journal of Psychiatry in Medicine 28: 189-213.

The relationship between religious activities and blood pressure was examined in 6-year prospective study of 4,000 older adults. Among subjects who attended religious services once a week or more *and* prayed or studied the Bible once a day or more, the likelihood of diastolic hypertension was 40 percent lower than among those who attended services and prayed less often ($p<.0001$, after controlling for age, sex, race, smoking, chronic illness and body mass index).

Koenig, H.G., Pargament, K.I., and Nielsen, J. 1998. Religious coping and health status in medically ill hospitalized older adults. Journal of Nervous and Mental Disease 186: 513-521.

The authors concluded that religious coping behaviors related to better mental health were at least as strong, if not stronger, than were non-religious coping behaviors. A survey of 577 hospitalized medically ill patients age 55 or over examined the relationship between 21 different types of religious coping and mental and physical health. Religious coping behaviors that were associated with better mental health were re-appraisal of God as benevolent, collaboration with God, and giving religious help to others. Re-appraisals of God as punishing, re-appraisals involving demonic forces, pleading for direct intersection, and spiritual discontent were associated with worse mental and physical health. Of the 21 religious coping behaviors, 16 were significantly related to greater psychological growth, 15 were related to greater cooperativeness, and 16 were related to greater spiritual growth.

Koenig, H.G., George, L.K., Peterson, B.L. 1998. Use of health services by hospitalized medically ill depressed elderly patients. American Journal of Psychiatry 155: 536-542.

Found that depressed patients who had a strong intrinsic religious faith recovered over 70% faster from depression than those with less strong faith; among a subgroup of patients whose physical illness was not improving, intrinsically religious patients recovered 100% faster.

Koenig, H.G., and Larson, D.B. 1998. Use of hospital services, religious attendance, and religious affiliation. Southern Medical Journal 91: 925-932.

Found an inverse relationship between frequency of religious service attendance and likelihood of hospital admission in a sample of 455 older patients. Those who attended church weekly or more often were significantly less likely in the previous year to have been admitted to the hospital, had fewer hospital admissions, and spent fewer days in the hospital than those attending less often; these associations retained their significance after controlling for covariates. Patients unaffiliated with a religious community had significantly longer index hospital stays than those affiliated. Unaffiliated patients spent an average of 25 days in the hospital, compared with 11 days for affiliated patients (p<.0001); this association strengthened when physical health and other covariates were controlled.

Koenig, H.G., et al. 1998. The relationship between religious activities and cigarette smoking in older adults. Journal of Gerontology A Biol Sci Med Sci 53: 6.

Substantially lower rates of smoking among persons more religiously involved is likely to translate into lower rates of lung cancer, hypertension, coronary artery disease and chronic obstructive pulmonary disease. Cigarette smoking and religious activities were examined in a 6-year prospective study of 3,968 persons age 65 or older in North Carolina. Both likelihood of current smoking and total

number of pact years smoked were inversely related to attendance at religious services and private religious activities. Higher participation in religious activities at one wave predicted lower rates of smoking at future waves. If persons both attended religious services at least weekly and read the Bible or prayed at least daily, they were 990% less likely to smoke than persons involved in these religious activities less frequently (p<.0001, after multiple covariates were taken into account).

Oman, D., and Reed, D. 1998. Religion and mortality among the community-dwelling elderly. American Journal of Public Health 88: 1469-1475.

In a 5-yer prospective cohort study of 1,931 older residents of Marin County, California, persons who attended religious services were 36% less likely to die during the follow up period. When the variables (including age, sex, marital status, number of chronic diseases, lower body disability, balance problems, exercise, smoking status, alcohol use, weight, two measures of social functioning and social support, and depression) were controlled, persons who attended religious services were still 24% less likely to die during the 5-yer follow up. During the 5-year follow up, there were 454 deaths. Subjects were divided into 2 categories: "attenders" (weekly or occasional attenders) and "non-attenders" (never attend).

Idler, E.L., & Kasl, S.V. 1997. Religion among disabled and nondisabled persons II: attendance at religious services as a predictor of the course of disability. Journal of Gerontology 52: S306-S316.

A longitudinal study of 2,812 older adults in New Haven, CT, found that frequent religious attenders in 1982 were significantly less likely than infrequent attenders to be

physically disabled 12 years later, a finding that persisted after controlling for health practices, social ties, and indicators of well being.

Koenig HG, et al. 1997. Attendance at religious services, interleukin-6, and other biological parameters of immune function in older adults. International Journal of Psychiatry in Medicine 27: 233-250.

Findings suggest that persons who attend church frequently have stronger immune systems than less frequent attenders, and may help explain why both better mental and better physical health are characteristic of frequent church attenders. Reported that frequent religious attendance in 1986, 1989, and 1992 predicted lower plasma interleukin-6 (IL-6) levels in a sample of 1,718 older adults followed over six years. IL-6 levels are elevated in patients with AIDS, osteoporosis, Alzheimer's disease, diabetes, and other serious medical conditions, and is an indicator of immune system function.

Strawbridge, W.J., et al. 1997. Frequent attendance at religious services and mortality over 28 years. American Journal of Public Health 87: 957-961.

Frequent church attendees were more likely to stop smoking, increase exercising, increase social contacts, and stay married; even after these factors were controlled for, however, the mortality difference persisted.

Study reports the results of a 28-year follow-up study of 5,000 adults involved in the Berkeley Human Population Laboratory. Mortality for persons attending religious services once/week or more often was almost 25% lower than for persons attending religious services less

frequently; for women, the mortality rate was reduced by 35%.

Kark, JD., G Shemi, Y Friedlander, O Martin, O Manor and SH Blondheim. 1996. Does religious observance promote health? mortality in secular vs religious kibbutzim in Israel. American Journal of Public Health 86: 341-346.

Even after eliminating social support and conventional health behaviors as possible confounders, members of religious kibbutzim still lived longer than those in secular kibbutzim. A 16-year mortality study, where 11 religious kibbutzim were matched with 11 secular kibbutzim (n=3,900); careful matching was performed to ensure that secular and religious kibbutzim were as similar as possible in characteristics that might affect mortality (social support, selection and retaining of members, etc.), and controlled for conventional risk factors (drinking, smoking, plasma cholesterol levels. Of the 268 deaths that occurred, 69 were in religious and 199 in secular kibbutzim; hazard ratio was 1.93 (95% CI 1.44-2.59, p<.0001).

Oxman, T.E., Freeman, D.H., and Manheimer, E.D. 1995. Lack of social participation or religious strength and comfort as risk factors for death after cardiac surgery in the elderly. Psychosomatic Medicine 57: 5-15.

The mortality rate in persons with low social support who did not depend on their religious faith for strength, was 12 times that of persons with a strong support network who relied heavily on religion; even when social factors were accounted for, persons who depended on religion were only about one-third as likely to die as those who did not. Followed 232 adults for six months after open-heart surgery, examining predictors of mortality.

Bliss, J.R., McSherry, E., and Fassett, J. 1995. NIH Conference on Spirituality and Health Care Outcomes

Chaplain Intervention Reduces Costs in Major DRGs. Patients in the intervention group had an average 2 day shorter post-op hospitalization, resulting in an overall cost savings of $4,200 per patient. Randomized 331 open-heart surgery patients to either a chaplain intervention ("Modern Chaplain Care") or usual care.

Propst, L.R., et al. 1992. Comparative efficacy of religious and nonreligious cognitive-behavioral therapy for the treatment of clinical depression in religious individuals. Journal of Consulting and Clinical Psychology 60: 94-103.

Religious therapy resulted in significantly faster recovery from depression when compared with standard secular cognitive-behavioral therapy. Study examined the effectiveness of using religion-based psychotherapy in the treatment of 59 depressed religious patients. The religious therapy used Christian religious rationales, religious arguments to counter irrational thoughts, and religious imagery. What was surprising was that benefits from religious-based therapy were most evident among patients who received religious therapy from non-religious therapists.

Pressman, P., Lyons, J.S., Larson, D.B., and Strain, J.J. 1990. Religious belief, depression, and ambulation status in elderly women with broken hips. American Journal of Psychiatry 147: 758-759.

Reported that among 33 elderly women hospitalized with hip fracture, greater religiousness was associated with less depression and longer walking distances at the time of hospital discharge.

McSherry, E., Ciulla, M., Salisbury, S., and Tsuang, D. 1987. Social Compass 35: 515-537.

Heart surgery patients with higher than average personal religiousness scores on admission and post-op had lengths of stay 20% less than those with lower than average scores.

Chu, C.C., & Klein, H.E. 1985. Psychosocial and environmental variables in outcome of black schizophrenics. Journal of the National Medical Association. 77:793-796.

Studying 128 Black schizophrenics and their families, investigators reported that Black urban patients were less likely to be re-hospitalized if their families encouraged them to continue religious worship while they were in the hospital (p<.001).

Zuckerman DM, Kasl SV, Ostfeld AM, 1984. Psychosocial predictors of mortality among the elderly poor. Am J Epidemiol. 119:410-423.

This study examine mortality among 400 elderly poor residents of New Haven, Hartford, and West Haven, Connecticut, in 1972-1974. Results, controlled for demographic variables, showed that religiousness reduced mortality.

Florell, J.L. 1973. Bulletin of the American Protestant Hospital Association 37(2):29-36.

Crisis-intervention in orthopedic surgery: Empirical evidence of the effectiveness of a chaplain working with surgery patients. Randomized patients either to a chaplain intervention, which involved chaplain visits for 15 minutes/day per patient, or to a control group ("business as

usual"). The chaplain intervention reduced length of stay by 29% (p<.001), patient-initiated call on RN time to one-third, and use of PRN pain medications to one-third.

GodandScience.Org

FUNNY ONE LINERS

- I'm a humble person, really. I'm actually much greater than I think I am.

- Do not argue with an idiot. He will drag you down to his level and beat you with experience.

- The last thing I want to do is hurt you. But it's still on the list.

- Love is a temporary insanity curable by marriage.

- We live in a society where pizza gets to your house before the police.

- I asked God for a bike, but I know God doesn't work that way. So I stole a bike and asked for forgiveness.

- We never really grow up, we only learn how to act in public.

- Light travels faster than sound. This is why some people appear bright until you hear them speak.

- War does not determine who is right – only who is left.

- If I agreed with you we'd both be wrong.

- The early bird might get the worm, but the second mouse gets the cheese.

- Politicians and diapers have one thing in common. They should both be changed regularly, and for the same reason.

- Children: You spend the first 2 years of their life teaching them to walk and talk. Then you spend the

next 16 years telling them to sit down and shut-up.

- I want to die peacefully in my sleep, like my grandfather. Not screaming and yelling like the passengers in his car.

- Knowledge is knowing a tomato is a fruit; Wisdom is not putting it in a fruit salad.

- Evening news is where they begin with 'Good evening', and then proceed to tell you why it isn't.

- The future will soon be a thing of the past.

- I didn't fight my way to the top of the food chain to be a vegetarian.

- If you think nobody cares if you're alive, try missing a couple of payments.

- I thought I wanted a career, turns out I just wanted paychecks.

- If God is watching us, the least we can do is be entertaining.

- Better to remain silent and be thought a fool, than to speak and remove all doubt.

- Accept that some days you're the pigeon, and some days you're the statue.

- Some people are like Slinkies ... not really good for anything, but you can't help smiling when you see one tumble down the stairs.

- How is it one careless match can start a forest fire, but it takes a whole box to start a campfire?

- Did you know that dolphins are so smart that within a few

- Weeks of captivity, they can train people to stand on the very edge of the pool and throw them fish?

- A bank is a place that will lend you money, if you can prove that you don't need it.

- Why do they lock gas station bathrooms? Are they afraid someone will clean them?

- Never, under any circumstances, take a sleeping pill and a laxative on the same night.

- To steal ideas from one person is plagiarism. To steal from many is research.

- A computer once beat me at chess, but it was no match for me at kickboxing.

- I saw a woman who had pants that said "Guess" so I said "$2.50"

- Why does someone believe you when you say there are four billion stars, but check when you say the paint is wet?

- A clear conscience is usually the sign of a bad memory.

- The voices in my head may not be real, but they have some good ideas!

- Women will never be equal to men until they can walk down the street with a bald head and a beer gut, and still think they are sexy.

- Laugh at your problems, everybody else does.

- The shinbone is a device for finding furniture in a dark room.

- Whenever I fill out an application, in the part that says "If an emergency, notify:" I put "DOCTOR". What's my mother going to do?

- He who smiles in a crisis has found someone to blame.

- I didn't say it was your fault, I said I was blaming you.

- Artificial intelligence is no match for natural stupidity.

- God must love stupid people. He made SO many.

- Behind every successful man is his woman. Behind the fall of a successful man is usually another woman.

- The sole purpose of a child's middle name, is so he can tell when he's really in trouble.

- Never get into fights with ugly people, they have nothing to lose.

- Always borrow money from a pessimist. He won't expect it back.

- My opinions may have changed, but not the fact that I am right.

- Some people say, "If you can't beat them, join them". I say, "If you can't beat them, beat them", because they will be expecting you to join them, so you will have the element of surprise.

- Some cause happiness wherever they go. Others whenever they go.

- It's not the fall that kills you; it's the sudden stop at the

end.

- Crowded elevators smell different to midgets.

- Hospitality: making your guests feel like they're at home, even if you wish they were.

- You do not need a parachute to skydive. You only need a parachute to skydive twice.

- Nostalgia isn't what it used to be.

- I discovered I scream the same way whether I'm about to be devoured by a great white shark or if a piece of seaweed touches my foot.

- A bargain is something you don't need at a price you can't resist.

- My psychiatrist told me I was crazy and I said I want a second opinion. He said okay, you're ugly too.

- I intend to live forever. So far, so good.

- Money can't buy happiness, but it sure makes misery easier to live with.

- A diplomat is someone who can tell you to go to hell in such a way that you will look forward to the trip.

- We have enough gun control. What we need is idiot control.

- You're never too old to learn something stupid.

- A little boy asked his father, "Daddy, how much does it cost to get married?" Father replied, "I don't know son, I'm still paying."

- With sufficient thrust, pigs fly just fine.

- Women may not hit harder, but they hit lower.

- Knowledge is power, and power corrupts. So study hard and be evil.

- There's a fine line between cuddling and holding someone down so they can't get away.

- Worrying works! 90% of the things I worry about never happen.

- Why do Americans choose from just two people to run for president and 50 for Miss America?

- I always take life with a grain of salt, …plus a slice of lemon, …and a shot of tequila. (Joke not intended for Baptist)

- If at first you don't succeed, skydiving is not for you!

- I used to be indecisive. Now I'm not sure.

- When in doubt, mumble.

- I like work. It fascinates me. I sit and look at it for hours.

- To be sure of hitting the target, shoot first and call whatever you hit the target.

- A bus is a vehicle that runs twice as fast when you are after it as when you are in it.

- A TV can insult your intelligence, but nothing rubs it in like a computer.

- Circular Definition: see Definition, Circular.

- I got in a fight one time with a really big guy, and he said, "I'm going to mop the floor with your face." I said, "You'll be sorry."

- He said, "Oh, yeah? Why?" I said, "Well, you won't be able to get into the corners very well."

- Some people hear voices. Some see invisible people. Others have no imagination whatsoever.

- You are such a good friend that if we were on a sinking ship together and there was only one life jacket... I'd miss you heaps and think of you often.

- When tempted to fight fire with fire, remember that the Fire Department usually uses water.

- Hallmark Card: "I'm so miserable without you, it's almost like you're still here."

- Change is inevitable, except from a vending machine.

- If winning isn't everything why do they keep score?

- If you keep your feet firmly on the ground, you'll have trouble putting on your pants.

- If you are supposed to learn from your mistakes, why do some people have more than one child?

- Eagles may soar, but weasels don't get sucked into jet engines.

WHAT ABOUT DINASOURS?

Why would God have left out a description of the dinosaurs from the creation account found in the Bible? Skeptics claim that this omission proves that the Bible wasn't written by God's inspiration, but is just a compilation of the words of fallible men. First, we should understand the origin of the Genesis creation account and its purpose in the Bible. The first five books of the Bible, including Genesis, were written by Moses. Since nobody except God was present at the creation, the Genesis creation account was given to Moses by God. If one is attempting to second guess the Author of Genesis, one must take these facts into account.

Purpose of the creation account
God was not interested in giving Moses a scientific treatise on the creation of the world. The Bible indicates that God's communication to Moses was centered on the relationship between God and man and the rules by which God wanted man to live. Therefore, the creation account mirrors the content of the rest of the Bible, which centers on mankind and his relationship to God. The question, "Why would God leave out a description of the dinosaurs?" is a bad one to begin with. A more appropriate question should be "What would God want to relate to man about *His* description of the creation?"

Dinosaurs in the Bible?
Many who have studied the Bible believe that it does mention dinosaurs in the text. Specifically, Genesis 1:21 says that God created "great sea monsters" on the fifth day.[1] The Hebrew word *tannîyn*, can have several meanings, including "dragon," "serpent," "sea monster," or "venomous snake."[2] An analysis of other Old Testament

verses indicates that this word usually refers to contemporary aquatic animals or snakes:

So, although *tannîyn* could refer to a dinosaur in Genesis 1, in most other usage throughout the Old Testament, the word refers to species that existed at the time the Old Testament books were written.

The second instance where the Bible might refer to dinosaurs occurs first in the book of Job. The Leviathan4 is described as being an armored aquatic creature in the book of Job, the Psalms, and Isaiah.5 The descriptions claim that the creature was contemporary with the writers of the Bible, and are not inconsistent with large alligators or crocodiles. Although dinosaurs are not specifically mentioned in the Bible, the fossil deposits they produced are described as being used by early humans in the opening chapters of Genesis.6

Problems with including dinosaurs
There are some technical problems that God would have faced in including dinosaurs in the creation account. There is no word for "dinosaur" in the Hebrew language. Now, God could have invented a Hebrew word for dinosaur and explained what those animals were like and how they had died out. However, this is a *one page* description of the creation of the world and life in it. Trying to explain about an extinct group of creatures would have taken a lot of space and distracted from the rest of the creation account.

Obviously, there were a lot more creatures than just dinosaurs that were left out of the creation account. If God were to have included every creature in the creation account (well over one billion), such inclusion would have completely lost the spiritual significance of the passage (and would be much longer than the Bible itself). The

purpose of the Genesis creation account is to give an account of how God created mankind and provided for him. The account, like the entire Bible, centers on God and His miraculous workings *for mankind*. Therefore, in the creation account, we find the supernatural creation of the universe by God, indicating that the universe wasn't always here, but created by God *for man*. Next, it talks about the creation of plants, which are important to humans, since we eat them, and also important to the animals that we rely upon, which also eat them. Then, it talks about the sea creatures and birds, which we also eat. It next talks about the beasts of the field, which we eat and use for labor. Then it talks about the creation of mankind and how he is to have dominion and manage the earth and its creatures.

The second chapter of Genesis gives a spiritual account of the creation of mankind and man's relationship to God. The entire account is centered on God and man. Therefore, one would expect the creation account to describe events that are important to mankind.

Dinosaurs - a modern mindset
Those who claim that the lack of dinosaurs in the creation account is a mistake are looking at the topic on the basis of our modern perspective, which values sensationalism over practicality. Dinosaurs are fascinating! The idea that these creatures walked the same earth that we live on intrigues us. However, the fact that they lived has virtually no effect upon our practical lives.

Some might say that dinosaurs were important in providing fossil fuels (which products were important even in biblical events[1]). Even the fossil fuel argument is not a strong one, since the overwhelming majority of oil came from the bodies of plants and trees - not dinosaurs. Most of those who complain about the lack of dinosaurs in the Bible are

looking at the natural world from an evolutionary perspective, in which mankind is just an evolutionary fluke - a recent upstart who doesn't figure prominently in the overall evolutionary history of the earth. Even from a naturalistic perspective, dinosaurs are a failed evolutionary experiment that couldn't compete with their mammalian descendents.

Conclusion

The fact is that dinosaurs are as unimportant to us as they were to the Hebrews to whom the creation account was given. The purpose of the creation account is to provide an explanation of how God provided for mankind and created him as the one spiritual animal on earth. The account is purposely brief and centered upon mankind - the only creature God created on earth to enter into a personal relationship with Him. The Genesis creation account contains all the information necessary to fulfill the purpose given for the recording of the pages of the Bible. As an exercise to illustrate the point, you might want to write your own one page creation account. In doing this, you should center the account on mankind and the creation miracles God used to prepare the earth for him. What you will find is that there is not room to discuss dinosaurs or any other extinct species of life.

Dinosaurs FAQ
Did dinosaurs and humans coexist?
No. All the dinosaurs were wiped out 65 million years ago by a huge asteroid that impacted near the Yucatan Peninsula. The impact was so devastating that if wiped out 30%-80% of other land-dwelling species, as well as over 50% of plant species.[7] This is *Scientific American's* (August, 1995, page 86) description of the result of a collision of the large asteroid with the earth:

"Sixty-five million years ago an object somewhat larger than Haley's comet slammed into what is now the coast of Mexico's Yucatan peninsula. The impact gouged a crater 170 kilometers across and launched debris worldwide. As the multitude of tiny ballistic missiles fell beck to earth, meteors filled the sky, and the atmosphere became red-hot. Fires erupted over the earth's surface, but the global inferno was soon followed by persistent darkness."

What about dinosaur along side human footprints?
Carl Baugh made famous the idea that there exist human footprints along side dinosaur ones at the Paluxy Riverbed near Glen Rose, Texas. However, the "human" prints are huge at about 2 feet long. In addition, they are highly filled in so that the prints are not clear at all. However, some of the prints show three separate areas, suggestive that they come from a three-toed dinosaur. We don't see any biblical evidence of three-toed people, so we are guessing that the "human" prints are really just the prints of smaller dinosaurs. In fact, ICR president John Morris admitted in 1986 that the Paluxy footprints are probably not human but are eroded dinosaur footprints (ICR Impact #151).

What about cave drawings showing dinosaurs?
We haven't seen any caveman drawings that suggest they saw dinosaurs. Some of the better drawings allow us to identify now extinct large mammals. However, when one is trying to interpret caveman scribbles, they could be just about anything, including aliens, rockets or Twinkies.

Did Noah take dinosaurs on the ark?
No. There weren't any dinosaurs to take along at that point in time, since they had died 65 million years ago. In fact, since the flood was likely local in extent, Noah probably did not take Polar Bears, penguins, or giraffes.
GodandScience.Org

DOESN'T SCIENCE CONTRADICT THE BIBLE?

Numerous genetic studies over the last few decades have shown that human genetic diversity is greatest within African populations, leading scientists to proclaim that modern human populations originated in Africa. However, the Bible says that humans were created in Eden, which is described as being in or near Mesopotamia. Can we stretch the biblical creation narrative to place Eden in Africa or is it possible that the science is wrong? Alternatively, is the Bible just wrong about where humans originated?

Eden in Africa?
Some Christians have suggested that the Bible is not specific enough to conclude that Eden is in Mesopotamia. Let's look at the biblical description of Eden to see if it could be stretched to include eastern Africa.

The LORD God planted a garden toward the east, in Eden; and there He placed the man whom He had formed. Out of the ground the LORD God caused to grow every tree that is pleasing to the sight and good for food; the tree of life also in the midst of the garden, and the tree of the knowledge of good and evil. Now a river flowed out of Eden to water the garden; and from there it divided and became four rivers. The name of the first is Pishon; it flows around the whole land of Havilah, where there is gold. The gold of that land is good; the bdellium and the onyx stone are there. The name of the second river is Gihon; it flows around the whole land of Cush. The name of the third river is Tigris; it flows east of Assyria. And the fourth river is the Euphrates. (*Genesis 2:8-14*)

Garden of Eden?

The location of Eden has always been somewhat uncertain. However, the Bible describes four rivers, two of which (the Tigris and Euphrates) are in Mesopotamia. The other two rivers are unknown. However, the Bible describes the river Gihon as being associated with Cush, which is described as being near Egypt, probably being on the Arabian peninsula. The other river (Pishon) is said to be in the land of Havila, which is described as being east of Egypt, toward Assyria,1 . A tentative map of the area is shown to the right. If modern humans originated during the last ice age then the Persian Gulf would have been dry (due to sea levels at least 400 feet lower than present). So, it is entirely possible that the location of the Eden is currently under water.

Persian Gulf Oasis

A new review of the archeological literature reveals evidence that the Persian Gulf region was once a lush oasis, during the last glacial maximum. At that time, sea levels were much lower, meaning that virtually all of the Persian Gulf was a large floodplain above sea level. More than 60 archeological sites, some of which are currently submerged, show that the area was extensively inhabited. The study describes four rivers, the Tigris and Euphrates Rivers from Mesopotamia, the Karun River (biblical Pishon?) draining the Iranian Plateau, and the Wadi Batin River (biblical Gihon?) flowing across northern Arabia. The convergence of the four rivers, along with subterranean aquifers, resulted in what the author described as the "Persian Gulf Oasis." According to the study, "This evidence is used to construct a model of human occupation around the basin over the course of the last 100,000 years."

Although it is possible that the garden of Eden was in Africa, it would have to be at the very boundary of potential locations. In addition, such a location would

contradict the Genesis 2 narrative that says that God planted the garden "toward the east" (presumably east of Israel). Ethiopia is to the southwest. Therefore, the Persian Gulf region matches the description of the biblical narrative the best.

Out of Africa?

Numerous scientific studies have proposed to have shown that a small group of individuals migrated out of eastern Africa and eventually expanded into most of today's populations. In reality, what the studies have shown is that African populations exhibit the most genetic diversity among all people groups. The theory is that once a population has been founded, the amount of genetic diversity increases over time. The theory is generally good, but does make some assumptions. One of the assumptions is that the populations have undergone little or no interbreeding with other populations. For Africa, the assumption is generally good, since Africa is geographically isolated from the rest of the world. The only route to get into Africa is through Suez. Likewise, for Native Americans, there was only one route - over the Aleutians near the end of an ice age, when sea levels were low and temperatures were beginning to moderate. However, for people groups in Mesopotamia and the Middle East, there was no geographic isolation. Being at the intersection of three continents, the Middle East has seen numerous people groups migrate through and back. So, it would be *very unlikely* that peoples of the Middle East would have the greatest genetic diversity of modern humans, *even if humans originated there*.

Middle Easterners have second highest genetic diversity

Two new studies, the result of the human genome project, examined the genetic diversity of over 1,000 individuals from 51 population groups all over the world.6' 7 As in previous studies, peoples of Africa were the most genetically diverse. However, these studies also determined that those from the Middle East were the second most genetically diverse. The authors of one study admitted that Middle Eastern population genetics was not just simple gene flow, saying, "The Middle Eastern populations may have experienced both continuous gene flow and shared ancestry with the rest of Eurasia."7 The authors of either study did not consider the possibility that humans originated in Mesopotamia, as the Bible says, since the out of Africa hypothesis is the current reigning paradigm. However, given the evidence of admixture in Middle Eastern populations and the fact that those populations are still the second most genetically diverse, it is entirely possible that modern humans originated in the Middle East, but lost much of their genetic diversity through subsequent migrations and replacement.

Conclusion

Out of Eden
New genetic analysis of human population groups shows that peoples of the Middle East represent the second most genetically diverse group among world-wide populations. A hypothesis is proposed that modern humans originated in the garden of Eden, in or near Mesopotamia, through the direct creation of God, and subsequently migrated world-wide, first into Africa, then Asia and Europe, and eventually the Americas and Polynesia. Subsequent back migrations diluted the genetic diversity of this founder population, making them appear to be less ancient than the Africans. The hypothesis can potentially be tested by carefully examining more Middle Eastern populations in

more detail to attempt to reconstruct the original founder population.

GodandScience.Org

IS CHRISTIANITY A MADE-UP MYTH WRITTEN BY THE DISCIPLES?

Skeptics say that the writings of the Bible have the character of mythology. In addition, stories of numerous miracles make it unlikely that the Bible is true. However, if God is powerful enough to have created the entire universe, He would certainly be able to perform miracles. Although there are miracles in the Bible, greater than 99% of the text describes non-miraculous events. So, who wrote the Bible? If the disciples made up the events in the Bible, would they write it in the way it is written?

Virgin birth
The virgin birth of Jesus Christ is one of the most unbelievable aspects of Christianity. It would have been very risky to document and claim that Jesus was born of a virgin. In the Middle East there were "honor killings" for women who conceived out of wedlock, so to speak of a virgin birth was extremely dishonorable. In fact, the Bible alludes to some disparaging remarks made by the religious opponents of Jesus.[1] In addition, if you look at the anti-Christian literature at the time, much of it focused on this aspect of Christianity. This makes one wonder why, if Christians were just making up a religion, they say something that would offend virtually everybody in the Middle East. It makes no sense to make up something offensive - unless it were true.

GodandScience.Org

THE DISCIPLES

If I had been Jesus, I certainly wouldn't have chosen the band of misfits that He picked. There was Peter, the loudmouth, John, his main competitor (and Jesus' favorite, according to his own words) Matthew, the corrupt taxman, and Thomas, the ultimate skeptic. As a group, they were slow learners who constantly demonstrated a lack of faith in Jesus[4] despite all the miracles He performed in their presence.

Peter was an interesting choice as the disciple to lead the early church. As an uneducated fisherman, he would often act first and think about it later. Peter himself admitted to Jesus that he was "a sinful man." In one instance, Jesus blessed Peter and not five verses later called him "Satan." Peter made the pronouncement that he would never leave Jesus, being even willing to die before denying Him. However, Peter denied knowing Jesus three times after He was arrested and fled to go into hiding with the rest of the disciples.

John is thought of being a quiet disciple who was deeply devoted to Jesus. However, John had definite jealousy issues with Peter. After being told of Jesus' resurrection by the women who followed Him, John describes in his gospel racing Peter to the empty tomb - and winning! Peter was actively involved in this rivalry, being jealous of John at the last supper, asking Jesus, "Lord, and what about this man?" Jesus solidly rebuked Peter, basically telling him to mind his own business. The rivalry among the disciples was not limited to just Peter and John. At one point, they all started to argue about which of the disciples was the greatest. Jesus suggested that those who would be greatest would serve others.[17]

THE SCANDALOUS WOMEN

Jesus helped a number of women, many of whom followed Him, along with the disciples. After Jesus was arrested and crucified, the disciples all fled and hid, being afraid that they would suffer the same fate. However, the women wanted to finish the burial, which had been left unfinished because of the approaching Sabbath. So Mary Magdalene, Mary, the mother of James, and Salome, wife of Zebedee, walked to the tomb early in the morning of the third day. However, they found the stone rolled away, the body of Jesus gone, and angels sitting in His place. The fact that the discovery of the empty tomb was made by women is not something that would have been fabricated, since, at the time, women were not considered to be reliable witnesses.

The Church is female!

This is going to come to a shock to most non-Christians (and maybe even some Christians), but God's people are referred to as female, *not* male. In the Old Testament, God's people are the "daughters of Zion." The Church or body of Christ (including us men) is referred to as the "bride" of Christ and God is said to be our "husband." Paul even describes the members of the church as being presented to her husband, Jesus, "as a pure virgin." Whenever referred to by sex, the Church is described as "she" or "her." In addition, the Greek word for "church" is a feminine noun. Obviously, if men had made up the Bible, they would have made the church a male!

No marriage or sex in heaven

Jesus was asked a complicated question about heaven by the Sadducees (a religious sect that did not believe in the resurrection of the dead) that directly leads us to the conclusion that there will be no marriage or sex in heaven.

The Sadducees gave a scenario of a woman who married 7 men (sequentially, since they all died prematurely) in her lifetime. They asked whose wife she would be in heaven. Jesus answered:

"You are mistaken, not understanding the Scriptures, or the power of God. "For in the resurrection they neither marry, nor are given in marriage, but are like angels in heaven. (*Matthew 22:29-30*)

In other words, there will be no marriage or sexual differences among those in heaven, since reproduction is unnecessary. This concept is supported by other biblical verses that indicate that males and females are spiritually equal.[28] Obviously, if the disciples (who were men) had created a fictitious story about heaven, it would most certainly have included sex (probably with multiple virgin sexual partners), as is found in several other religions.

However, in heaven, we will be "married" to Jesus, who will be our spiritual "husband."[29] A marriage is described in heaven. The "bride" is composed of all believers in Jesus Christ. The "groom" is none other than Jesus Himself. This kind of idea seems okay for women, but tends to make us men a little nervous. I find it difficult to consider myself as a bride. The disciples would have never come up with the idea of being the bride of Jesus. There is no way that that was made up!

Other not quite perfect Bible leaders

Paul (or Saul)
Paul, the apostle who first took the gospel to the gentiles, began life as a super-religious Pharisee. However, when Christians were preaching their gospel in Damascus, Paul sought to get letters from the high priest in order to bring

the Christians to Jerusalem to stand trial as heretics. Paul was present at the stoning of Stephen, and "was in hearty agreement with putting him to death." Paul readily admitted his former unrighteous acts of persecution against the early Christians. However, Paul personally met Jesus on the road to Damascus in a rather spectacular way, at which point he became the primary spokesman for Christianity. As with the disciples and other Christian and Jewish leaders, Paul is presented as a real person - complete with his faults, including being an accessory to murder.

Other leaders in the Bible
- Noah - drunkenness

- Abraham - lack of trust in God

- Lot - drunkenness

- Moses - avoiding God's call, killing the Egyptian

- Isaac and Rebekah - favoritism

- Jacob - stealing the birthright

- Joseph - deceiving his brothers

- David - adultery and murder

- Job - justified himself

- Jonah - ran from God

- John Mark - left Paul on a missionary journey

- Paul - unable to free himself from a "thorn in the flesh"

Conclusion

Skeptics often claim that the New Testament was fabricated by the disciples. Although the Bible contains many stories of miracles, it also includes doctrines that the average male would not have included, if they were making up a religion. For example, in other religions, heaven consists of males engaging in eternal sex with multiple virgins. However, in the Bible there are no sexual relationships in heaven, but believers are "married" to Jesus. Realistically, no males I know of (including myself) would ever make up the Christian concept of heaven. To make the picture complete, the members of the Church are described as being female. How insulting that would be to the average male ego? Another doctrine that would be considered offensive in first century Jewish culture is the virgin birth of Jesus. In addition, first century Jewish culture considered women to be unreliable witnesses, making the discovery of the empty tomb by women unlikely to have been fabricated. The leaders in the Bible are presented realistically, with all their faults and shortcomings. When presenting themselves, most people tend to tell about their positive traits, eliminating negative traits, such as drunkenness, adultery, and murder. The inclusion of the good and the bad of God's leaders indicate that the biblical accounts are not just fabricated stories.

GodandScience.Org

IS CHRISTIANITY SEXIST?

The claim is often made that the Bible is sexist and that Christianity demeans women and makes them into second class citizens. While I do agree that sexism exists in Christian churches and that portions of scripture have been used to perpetuate sexism, the Bible does not condone discrimination in any manner. Men have cited verses about submission of women to keep believing women "in their place." Get out your Bibles and let's see what the Bible really says about women, submission, and equality.

Created in the image of God
Most people know that the Bible says God created man in His own image. However, many do not know that "man" includes both males and females. Both males and females are created in the image of God:
And God created man in His own image, in the image of God He created him; **male and female He created them**. (*Genesis 1:27*)

This verse implies that the "image of God" encompasses traits found in both males and females and that the physical sexual differences between the sexes are not important characteristics in terms of how mankind was created in God's image.

Women as just helpers?
The story of women in the Bible begins in Genesis 2, where God says that it is not good that man should be alone. So God made a woman as a "helper suitable for him." Some would say that making woman as a "helper" is sexist. The Hebrew word translated "helper" is *ezer*, which occurs 21 times in the Old Testament. In 2 instances in Genesis, *ezer* refers to the woman Eve. In 16 of the other

19 instances the word is used to describe God Himself!
Obviously, the term cannot be said to represent some sort
of subservient role. An interesting sidelight to the phrase
"helper suitable for him" is that the translation "suitable" is
not the most common translation for the Hebrew word. In
fact, the most common translation is "opposite." Anyone
who is married knows that their spouse is often completely
opposite from themselves.

Women in the Bible - not just mommies
The women described in the Bible are not always
homemakers and mothers. Obviously, the biological
function of women is to produce and care for children.
However, Deborah was both a judge and leader of Israel.
Other women were involved in ridding Israel of her
enemies. Quite a number of women are described as being
prophetesses. Other women in the Bible were involved in
teaching the Word of God or serving as deaconesses in the
early Christian church.

There are a number of other very strong women of faith
described in the Bible. In fact, two books of the Bible are
specifically about women, as indicated by their titles,
"Ruth" and "Esther." Ruth is the story of the compassion
and redemption of the gentile woman, Ruth. Naomi, Ruth's
mother-in-law, fell into the unfortunate circumstances of
losing both her husband and her two sons, one of whom
was Ruth's husband. With nobody to provide for her and
Naomi being "too old" to be remarried, she chose to go to
Israel, where the laws and traditions required the Israelites
to take care of widows, even if they were strangers. One of
Naomi's daughter-in-laws chose to stay in the land in order
to find another husband. But Ruth chose to go with her
mother-in-law, even though this meant that she would
probably never be married. However, Ruth was
"redeemed" by Boaz, who married her despite the fact that

she was a gentile. The line of Ruth and Boaz led directly to King David, and, of course, eventually to the Messiah, Jesus of Nazareth.

The book of Esther is the story of the rise of a young Jewish woman who found favor in the eyes of the Persian king, Ahasuerus (Xerxes), and became the queen of Persia. The former queen, Vashti, had refused to appear before the court when called by the king, and had been removed from the royal position. The king's prime minister, Haman hated the Jews and sought to destroy all of them through a plot of getting the king to unsuspectingly sign a decree calling for their execution. However, through the actions of the righteous Jew Mordecai, and the bravery of Esther in confronting the king, the decree was revoked and the conspirator, Haman, hanged. The Bible says that Esther had "come to royal position for such a time as this" - destined by God to save the Jews.

Other strong women of the Bible included Sarah, the wife of Abraham, who was preserved by the Lord despite the cowardly actions of Abraham in saying that she was his sister, and thus allowing her to enter into the courts of two kings (as a potential wife). Hannah is another example of a woman who had a strong spiritual walk. She was a woman of prayer and faith. Although she was childless for years, she had faith in God and her prayers were answered in giving birth to her son Samuel. She promised to give him back to the Lord, which she did by taking him to the priest as soon as he was weaned. Probably the strongest woman in the New Testament was Mary, the mother of Jesus. When the angel Gabriel told her she was to give birth to a son although a virgin, her response was, "May it be to me as you have said." A famous prayer of praise from Mary is recorded in the book of Luke.

The ideal biblical wife

The book of Proverbs (which records the wisdom of Solomon) describes the ideal wife in its last chapter. She is, by no means, a weak woman who grovels at the feet of her husband. Instead, she takes charge over the care and needs of her family, and, in addition, the needs of the poor. She also manages her servants. In addition, she maintains her own business and from her own earnings buys land and plants vineyards. She is described as being wise, strong, and dignified, yet able to laugh. She is praised by her husband and children, who appreciate her hard work and commitment.

How Jesus treated women

When we look at how Jesus treated women, we discover the difference between the way God wants men to treat women and the way they were (and still are) treated by men in societies. The woman at the well is a prime example. When Jesus asked her for a drink, her first reaction was disbelief that he would even talk to her. When Jesus' disciples came back, they were surprised that He was talking to a woman. Jewish customs had become so legalistic that men (and especially rabbis) did not associate with women who were not their wives. Even now, orthodox Jewish men and women are prohibited from touching members of the opposite sex.

In contrast, Jesus touched many women and allowed them to touch Him as He healed them. Although this was in direct opposition to the customs of the time, it reveals the nature of the personal God who directly touches people's lives. Jesus was compassionate to sinners and ministered to prostitutes and adulteresses. In a well-known example, some of the religious leaders brought a woman to Jesus who was "caught in the act of adultery." Obviously, the man involved in the adultery would have been there also,

but they didn't bring him. As Jesus alluded to their own sins, the woman's accusers left. Jesus did not condemn the woman, but admonished her to leave her life of sin.

Although all of Jesus' twelve disciples were men (there is good reason for this, there were a number of women who were loyal followers and who ministered to Him and His disciples. The gospels record that the women were the first to hear the news of Jesus' resurrection from the angels and the first to see Him (since the men had gone into hiding or back to their original jobs after Jesus was crucified). In contrast to the gentleness and kindness with which Jesus treated women, He reserved His more scathing comments for the arrogant male religious leaders of His time. These He labeled as "serpents," "brood of vipers," and "whitewashed tombs."

That "S" word - biblical submission
Many women don't like what the Bible says because it calls wives to "submit to their husbands." However, submission is not limited to wives submitting to their husbands. We are told to submit to God, governmental authorities, our boss, and leaders in the church. We are also told to submit to one another, which includes men submitting women and vice versa. God is a God of order. In a sinful world, submission to those in authority is the only way to maintain order. What form does this submission to authority take? In every instance where submission is called for wives, it is conditioned with the phrase "as to the Lord" or some other reference to Jesus Christ. The submission takes on the form of being in the will of God. If the husband asks the wife to do something outside the will of Christ, she is under no obligation to follow him. Accompanying each command for wives to submit to their husbands is the command for the husband to love his wife. In the book of Ephesians, this love is to be "just as Christ loved the church and gave

himself up for her." Such a love is not one that dominates and subjugates another person, but a self-sacrificing love that will give up its own life for another's.

The Christian Church is female!
This is going to come to a shock to most non-Christians (and maybe even some Christians), but God's people are referred to as female, *not* male. In the Old Testament, God's people are the "daughters of Zion. "The Church or body of Christ (including us men) is referred to as the "bride" of Christ and God is said to be our "husband." Whenever referred to by sex, the Church is described as "she" or "her." In addition, the Greek word for church is a feminine noun.

Conclusion
The essence of biblical equality can be summed up in Paul's letter to the Galatians:

There is neither Jew nor Greek, there is neither slave nor free man, there is neither male nor female; for you are all one in Christ Jesus. (*Galatians 3:28*)

Even though the world does not treat humans as equals, as members of the body of Christ, all are equal spiritually in the eyes of Jesus. In fact, those who exalt themselves (which includes many men) will be humbled and those who serve others (which characterize many women I know) will be exalted to a higher status in the kingdom of heaven. It seems likely that heaven will be a place that will be run by caring mothers and women who will have served others while living on earth.

Objections

On "headship" - This was probably more of a concession to culture than anything else. In first century Israel, women didn't have many rights or much opportunity for independence, so the husband was a sort of "covering" for her. Since he was legally and morally responsible for pretty much everything his wife did (Numbers 30:6-16), it made sense that she would defer to him in domestic matters. Besides, submission doesn't mean becoming a doormat - it means voluntarily laying aside one's own rights for the sake of the other, and husbands are instructed to love their wives sacrificially as well: "just as Christ loved the church and gave himself up for her." (Ephesians 5:25)

On "keeping silent in church" - Women are more verbal than men, and when they get together, they tend to move from subject to subject. In the synagogues, the women were segregated from the men. If they had any questions on the worship or the teachings, they would have had to shout them over to the men, or discuss them among themselves, which would have resulted in an inability to maintain order. In addition, Paul emphasizes that his rules for church are given so that everything would be "done in a fitting and orderly way." (1 Corinthians 14:40) Disorderly communication, such as uninterrupted speaking in tongues, was also prohibited.

On "not being permitted to teach" - Some interpret this passage to mean that women should never teach in the assembled church. However, commentators point out that Paul did not forbid women from ever teaching. Paul's commended co-worker, Priscilla, taught Apollos, the great preacher (Acts 18:24-26). In addition, Paul frequently mentioned other women who held positions of authority in the church. Phoebe worked in the church (Romans 16:1). Mary, Tryphena, and Tryphosa were the Lord's workers (Romans 16:6, 12). Paul was very likely prohibiting the

Ephesian women, not all women, from teaching. To understand these verses (Ephesians 2:9-15), we must understand the situation in which Paul and Timothy worked. In first-century Jewish culture, women were not allowed to study. When Paul said that women should learn in quietness and full submission, he was offering them an amazing new opportunity. Paul did not want the Ephesian women to teach because they didn't yet have enough knowledge or experience. The Ephesian church had a particular problem with false teachers. Evidently, the women were especially susceptible to the false teachings (2 Timothy 3:1-9), because they did not yet have enough Biblical knowledge to discern the truth. In addition, some women were apparently flaunting their new-found Christian freedom by wearing inappropriate clothing (1 Timothy 2:9). Paul was telling Timothy not to put anyone (in this case, women) into a position of leadership who was not yet mature in the faith (1 Timothy 3:6). The same principle applies to churches today.

GodandScience.Org

FUNNY AND UNUSUAL
BIBLE VERSES

Genesis 25:30 (Holman Christian Standard Bible)
He said to Jacob, "Let me eat some of that red stuff, because I'm exhausted."

Proverbs 21:19 (New Living Translation)
It is better to live alone in the desert than with a crabby, complaining wife.

Proverbs 27:15-16 (New Living Translation)
A quarrelsome wife is as annoying as constant dripping on a rainy day. Stopping her complaints is like trying to stop the wind or trying to hold something with greased hands.

Did you know there is a talking donkey in the Bible?

Numbers 22:21-29 (New King James Version)
Balaam got up in the morning, saddled his donkey and went with the princes of Moab. But God was very angry when he went, and the angel of the LORD stood in the road to oppose him. Balaam was riding on his donkey, and his two servants were with him. When the donkey saw the angel of the LORD standing in the road with a drawn sword in his hand, she turned off the road into a field. Balaam beat her to get her back on the road.

Then the angel of the LORD stood in a narrow path between two vineyards, with walls on both sides. When the donkey saw the angel of the LORD, she pressed close to the wall, crushing Balaam's foot against it. So he beat her again.

Then the angel of the LORD moved on ahead and stood in a narrow place where there was no room to turn, either to the right or to the left. When the donkey saw the angel of the LORD, she lay down under Balaam, and he was angry and beat her with his staff. Then the LORD opened the donkey's mouth, and she said to Balaam, "What have I done to you to make you beat me these three times?" Balaam answered the donkey, "You have made a fool of me! If I had a sword in my hand, I would kill you right now."

Here's how God deals with whiners—

Numbers 11:18- (New Living Translation)

"And tell the people to purify themselves, for tomorrow they will have meat to eat. Tell them, 'The LORD has heard your whining and complaints: "If only we had meat to eat! Surely we were better off in Egypt!" Now the LORD will give you meat, and you will have to eat it. And it won't be for just a day or two, or for five or ten or even twenty. You will eat it for a whole month until you gag and are sick of it. For you have rejected the LORD, who is here among you, and you have complained to him, "Why did we ever leave Egypt?"

One time, Jesus was asked to leave town-- for killing all the pigs!

Matthew 8:28-34 (New International Version)

When he arrived at the other side in the region of the Gadarenes, two demon-possessed men coming from the tombs met him. They were so violent that no one could pass that way. "What do you want with us, Son of God?" they shouted. "Have you come here to torture us before the appointed time?"

Some distance from them a large herd of pigs was feeding. The demons begged Jesus, "If you drive us out, send us into the herd of pigs." He said to them, "Go!" So they came out and went into the pigs, and the whole herd rushed down the steep bank into the lake and died in the water.

Those tending the pigs ran off, went into the town and reported all this, including what had happened to the demon-possessed men. Then the whole town went out to meet Jesus. And when they saw him, they pleaded with him to leave their region.

Did you know Alabama is mentioned in the book of Ezekiel?

Ezekiel 20:29 (New International Version)
Then I said to them: What is this high place you go to? It is called Bamah to this day.

Do you know the disciples had to share a car?

Philippians 2:2 (American Standard Version)
Make full my joy, that ye be of the same mind, having the same love, being of one accord...

They all met at a famous hotel in Washington, D.C....
Neimeiah 8:1 (New International Version)
...all the people assembled as one man in the square before the Water Gate.

And there are bad drivers...

2 Kings 9:20 (New International Version)
The lookout reported, "He has reached them, but he isn't coming back either. The driving is like that of Jehu son of Nimshi--he drives like a madman."

There's the story of Isaac's son, who smelled like a farm.
Genesis 27:27 (New International Version)
So he went to him and kissed him. When Isaac caught the smell of his clothes, he blessed him and said, "Ah, the smell of my son is like the smell of a field that the LORD has blessed.

Job 13:5 (New International Version)
If only you would be altogether silent! For you, that would be wisdom.

2 Kings 2:23-24 (New International Version)
From there Elisha went up to Bethel. As he was walking along the road some youths came out of the town and jeered at him. "Go on up, you baldhead!" they said. "Go on up, you baldhead!"

He turned around, and looked at them and called down a curse on them in the name of the Lord.

Then two bears came out of the woods and mauled forty-two of the youths.

The book of Proverbs is full of funny verses...

Proverbs 29:20 (New Living Translation)
There is more hope for a fool than for someone who speaks without thinking.

Proverbs 31:6 (New International Version)
As a dog returns to its vomit, so a fool repeats his folly.

Proverbs 26:11 (New International Version)
Gray is a crown of splendor: it is attained by a righteous life.

Proverbs 27:14 (New International Version)
If a man loudly blesses his neighbor early in the morning, it will be taken as a curse.

Proverbs 31:6 (New International Version)
Give beer to those who are perishing, wine to those who are in anguish.

Then there are the weird stories and verses...

Job 19:17 (New International Version)
My breath is offensive to my wife; I am loathsome to my own brothers.

Acts 20:9 (New Living Translation)
As Paul spoke on and on, a young man named Eutychus, sitting on the windowsill, became very drowsy. Finally, he fell sound asleep and dropped three stories to his death below.

Zechariah 6:7 (New International Version)
When the powerful horses went out, they were straining to go throughout the earth. And he said, "Go throughout the earth!" So they went throughout the earth.

Deuteronomy 14:21 (New International Version)
Do not eat anything you find already dead. You may give it to an alien living in any of your towns and he may eat it, or you may sell it to a foreigner...

When Gideon was building an army, God helped him choose soldiers...

Judges 7:4-8 (New International Version)

But the LORD said to Gideon, "There are still too many men. Take them down to the water, and I will sift them for you there. If I say, 'This one shall go with you,' he shall go; but if I say, 'This one shall not go with you,' he shall not go."

So Gideon took the men down to the water. There the LORD told him, "Separate those who lap the water with their tongues like a dog from those who kneel down to drink." Three hundred men lapped with their hands to their mouths. All the rest got down on their knees to drink.

The LORD said to Gideon, "With the three hundred men that lapped I will save you and give the Midianites into your hands. Let all the other men go, each to his own place." So Gideon sent the rest of the Israelites to their tents but kept the three hundred, who took over the provisions and trumpets of the others.

And when you go to the store this Sunday afternoon, think about this one...

Exodus 35:1-3 (New International Version)
Moses assembled the whole Israelite community and said to them, "These are the things the LORD has commanded you to do: For six days, work is to be done, but the seventh day shall be your holy day, a Sabbath of rest to the LORD. Whoever does any work on it must be put to death. Do not light a fire in any of your dwellings on the Sabbath day."

Here's a "duh" moment...

Judges 16:17 (New International Version)
So he told her everything. "No razor has ever been used on my head," he said, "because I have been a Nazirite set apart to God since birth. If my head were shaved, my strength

would leave me, and I would become as weak as any other man."

Here's a story that is pretty amazing…

By the way, an ephod is like an apron. With no backside.

2 Samuel 6:1-14 (New International Version)
David again brought together out of Israel chosen men, thirty thousand in all. He and all his men set out from Baalah of Judah to bring up from there the ark of God, which is called by the Name, the name of the LORD Almighty, who is enthroned between the cherubim that are on the ark.

They set the ark of God on a new cart and brought it from the house of Abinadab, which was on the hill. Uzzah and Ahio, sons of Abinadab, were guiding the new cart with the ark of God on it, and Ahio was walking in front of it. David and the whole house of Israel were celebrating with all their might before the LORD, with songs and with harps, lyres, tambourines, sistrums and cymbals.

When they came to the threshing floor of Nacon, Uzzah reached out and took hold of the ark of God, because the oxen stumbled. The LORD's anger burned against Uzzah because of his irreverent act; therefore God struck him down and he died there beside the ark of God.

Then David was angry because the LORD's wrath had broken out against Uzzah, and to this day that place is called Perez Uzzah.

David was afraid of the LORD that day and said, "How can the ark of the LORD ever come to me?" He was not willing to take the ark of the LORD to be with him in the City of

David. Instead, he took it aside to the house of Obed-Edom the Gittite. The ark of the LORD remained in the house of Obed-Edom the Gittite for three months, and the LORD blessed him and his entire household.

Now King David was told, "The LORD has blessed the household of Obed-Edom and everything he has, because of the ark of God." So David went down and brought up the ark of God from the house of Obed-Edom to the City of David with rejoicing.

When those who were carrying the ark of the LORD had taken six steps, he sacrificed a bull and a fattened calf. David, wearing a linen ephod, danced before the LORD with all his might, while he and the entire house of Israel brought up the ark of the LORD with shouts and the sound of trumpets.

As the ark of the LORD was entering the City of David, Michal daughter of Saul watched from a window. And when she saw King David leaping and dancing before the LORD, she despised him in her heart. They brought the ark of the LORD and set it in its place inside the tent that David had pitched for it, and David sacrificed burnt offerings and fellowship offerings before the LORD. After he had finished sacrificing the burnt offerings and fellowship offerings, he blessed the people in the name of the LORD Almighty.

Then he gave a loaf of bread, a cake of dates and a cake of raisins to each person in the whole crowd of Israelites, both men and women. And all the people went to their homes.

When David returned home to bless his household, Michal daughter of Saul came out to meet him and said, "How the king of Israel has distinguished himself today, disrobing in

the sight of the slave girls of his servants as any vulgar fellow would!"

David said to Michal, "It was before the LORD, who chose me rather than your father or anyone from his house when he appointed me ruler over the LORD's people Israel-I will celebrate before the LORD. I will become even more undignified than this, and I will be humiliated in my own eyes. But by these slave girls you spoke of, I will be held in honor." And Michal daughter of Saul had no children to the day of her death.

There are some pretty funny names in the Bible too-- Zippor, Balaam, Ham, Nimrod, Uz, Mash, Diklah, Jobab (like Joe Bob), Dorcas, There is also the town of Shur.

There's proof that there will be no women in heaven: Revelations 8:1 (New International Version)
When he opened the seventh seal, there was silence in heaven for about half an hour.

There is the very interesting Psalms 118...

- Psalm 118 is the middle chapter of the entire Bible.

- Psalm 117, before Psalm 118 is the shortest chapter in the Bible.

- Psalm 119, after Psalm 118 is the longest chapter in the Bible.

- The Bible has 594 chapters before Psalm 118 and 594 chapters after Psalm 118.

- If you add up all the chapters except Psalm 118, you get a total of 1188 chapters.

- 1188 or Psalm 118 verse 8 is the middle verse of the

entire Bible.

And what is the message found in verse 118? "It is better to take refuge in the Lord than to trust in man." - Psalm 118:8

FUN FACTS

The longest one-syllable word in the English language is "screeched."

"Dreamt" is the only English word that ends in the letters "mt".

Almonds are members of the peach family.

The symbol on the "pound" key (#) is called an octothorpe.

The dot over the letter 'i' is called a tittle.

The word "set" has more definitions than any other word in the English language.

"Underground" is the only word in the English language that begins and ends with the letters "und."

There are only four words in the English language which end in "-dous": tremendous, horrendous, stupendous, and hazardous.

The longest word in the English language, according to the Oxford English Dictionary, is *pneumonoultramicroscopicsilicovolcanoconiosis. The only other word with the same amount of letters is pneumonoultramicroscopicsilicovolcanoconioses, its plural.

The longest place-name still in use is Taumatawhakatangihangakoauauotamateaturipukakapikim aungahoronukupokaiw en uaitnatahu, a New Zealand hill.

Los Angeles's full name is "El Pueblo de Nuestra Senora la Reina de los Angeles de Porciuncula" and can be abbreviated to 3.63% of its size, "L.A."

An ostrich's eye is bigger than its brain.

Tigers have striped skin, not just striped fur.

Donald Duck's middle name is Fauntleroy.

The muzzle of a lion is like a fingerprint - no two lions have the same pattern of whiskers.

A pregnant goldfish is called a twit.

The Ramses brand condom is named after the great pharaoh Ramses II who fathered over 160 children.

There is a seven letter word in the English language that contains ten words without rearranging any of its letters, "therein": the, there, he, in, rein, her, here, ere, therein, herein.

Dueling is legal in Paraguay as long as both parties are registered blood donors.

It's impossible to sneeze with your eyes open.

Cranberries are sorted for ripeness by bouncing them; a fully ripened cranberry can be dribbled like a basketball.

The male gypsy moth can "smell" the virgin female gypsy moth from 1.8 miles away.

The letters KGB stand for Komitet Gosudarstvennoy Bezopasnosti.

"Stewardesses" is the longest word that can be typed with only the left hand.

To "testify" was based on men in the Roman court swearing to a statement made by swearing on their testicles.

The combination "ough" can be pronounced in nine different ways. The following sentence contains them all: "A rough-coated, dough-faced, thoughtful ploughman strode through the streets of Scarborough; after falling into a slough, he coughed and hiccoughed."

The only 15 letter word that can be spelled without repeating a letter is uncopyrightable.

Emus and kangaroos cannot walk backwards, and are on the Australian coat of arms for that reason.

Cats have over one hundred vocal sounds, while dogs only have about ten.

The word "Checkmate" in chess comes from the Persian phrase "Shah Mat," which means, "The king is dead."

The reason firehouses have circular stairways is from the days of yore when the engines were pulled by horses. The horses were stabled on the ground floor and figured out how to walk up straight staircases.

The first episode of "Joanie Loves Chachi" was the highest rated American program in the history of Korean television. "Chachi" is Korean for "penis."

*pneumonoultramicroscopicsilicovolcanoconiosis

Let me define this for you;
pneumono = lungs
ultramicroscopic = just what it says
silico=silicon
volcano=just what it says
coni = dust
osis = inflammation

So, this big word indicates ultramicroscopic silicon volcano dust has caused inflammation of the lungs. Stick that in your hat :).

A snail can sleep for three years.

Babies are born without kneecaps. They don't appear until the child reaches 2 to 6 years of age.

Cats have over one hundred vocal sounds. Dogs only have about 10.

February 1865 is the only month in recorded history not to have a full moon.

If the population of China walked past you in single file, the line would never end because of the rate of reproduction.

Leonardo DiVinci invented the scissors.

Our eyes are always the same size from birth, but our nose and ears never stop growing.

Shakespeare invented the word 'assassination' and 'bump'.

The cruise liner, QE2, moves only six inches for each gallon of diesel that it burns.

TYPEWRITER is the longest word that can be made using the letters only on one row of the keyboard.

Women blink nearly twice as much as men.

Your stomach has to produce a new layer of mucus every two week otherwise it will digest itself.

There are two words in the English language that have all five vowels in order: "abstemious" and "facetious."

There is a word in the English language with only one vowel, which occurs five times: "indivisibility."

The Bible does not say there were three wise men; it only says there were three gifts.

Did you know that crocodiles never outgrow the pool in which they live?
That means that if you put a baby croc in an aquarium, it would be little for the rest of its life.

The only 15-letter word that can be spelled without repeating a letter is "uncopyrightable"

Thirty-five percent of the people who use personal ads for dating are already married.

<u>DID YOU KNOW.........</u>

It is impossible to lick your elbow.

A crocodile can't stick its tongue out.

A shrimp's heart is in their head.

People say "Bless you" when you sneeze because when you sneeze, your heart stops for a milli-second.

In a study of 200,000 ostriches over a period of 80 years, no one reported a single case where an ostrich buried its head in the sand, or attempted to do so (apart from bones).

It is physically impossible for pigs to look up into the sky.

A pregnant goldfish is called a twit

Between 1937 and 1945 Heinz produced a version of Alphabetti Spaghetti especially for the German market that consisted solely of little pasta swastikas.

On average, a human being will have sex more than 3,000 times and spend two weeks kissing in their lifetime.

More than 50% of the people in the world have never made or received a telephone call.

Rats and horses can't vomit.

The "sixth sick sheik's sixth sheep's sick" is said to be the toughest tongue twister in the English language.

If you sneeze too hard, you can fracture a rib.

If you try to suppress a sneeze, you can rupture a blood vessel in your head or neck and die.

If you keep your eyes open by force, they can pop out.

Rats multiply so quickly that in 18 months, two rats could have over a million descendants.

Wearing headphones for just an hour will increase the bacteria in your ear by 700 times.

If the U.S. government has no knowledge of aliens, then why does Title 14, Section 1211 of the Code of Federal Regulations, implemented on July 16, 1969, make it illegal for U.S. citizens to have any contact with extraterrestrials or their vehicles?

In every episode of Seinfeld there is a Superman somewhere.

The cigarette lighter was invented before the match.

Thirty-five percent of the people who use personal ads for dating are already married.

A duck's quack doesn't echo, and no one knows why.

23% of all photocopier faults worldwide are caused by people sitting on them and photocopying their buttocks.

In the course of an average lifetime you will, while sleeping, eat 70 assorted insects and 10 spiders.

Most lipstick contains fish scales.

Cat's urine glows under a black light. Like fingerprints,

Everyone's tongue print is different.

Over 75% of people who read this will try to lick their elbow.

The king of hearts is the only king without a mustache

A Boeing 747s wingspan is longer than the Wright brother's first flight.

American Airlines saved $40,000 in 1987 by eliminating 1 olive from each salad served in first-class.

Venus is the only planet that rotates clockwise.

Apples, not caffeine, are more efficient at waking you up in the morning.

The plastic things on the end of shoelaces are called aglets.

Most dust particles in your house are made from dead skin.

The first owner of the Marlboro Company died of lung cancer.

Michael Jordan makes more money from Nike annually than all of the Nike factory workers in Malaysia combined.

All US Presidents have worn glasses. Some just didn't like being seen wearing them in public.

Walt Disney was afraid of mice.

Pearls melt in vinegar.

The three most valuable brand names on earth Marlboro, Coca Cola, and Budweiser, in that order.

It is possible to lead a cow upstairs...but not downstairs.

Richard Millhouse Nixon was the first US president whose name contains all the letters from the word "criminal." William Jefferson Clinton is the second.

And, the best for last...Turtles can breathe through their butts.

COULD NOAH'S ARK HOLD ALL THE ANIMALS?

One issue that is often raised against Christianity is Noah's Ark and the Flood. Did it really happen? Did the flood really cover the whole world? Is there enough water on earth to cover all the land? Could the ark really hold two of every kind of animal in the world? Though these might be intimidating questions, the answer to each is a resounding, "Yes."

God said to Noah in Genesis 6:14-16, "So make yourself an ark of cypress wood; make rooms in it and coat it with pitch inside and out. This is how you are to build it: The ark is to be 450 feet long, 75 feet wide and 45 feet high. Make a roof for it and finish the ark to within 18 inches of the top. Put a door in the side of the ark and make lower, middle and upper decks" (NIV). According to God's Word, Noah built the ark. Eight people entered it and all humanity died in the ensuing flood.

Did the flood really happen? Yes. Jesus said in Matt. 24:37-39 that the flood happened. If you can't trust Jesus, you can't trust anyone. As far as physical evidence goes there are numerous sedimentary deposits worldwide which suggest a universal flood. There are countless fossil deposits world-wide (fossilization occurs when organisms are buried rapidly within sediment.). Every major culture has a flood legend. Of over 200 flood legends, 95% say the flood was universal; 70% say survival depended upon a boat; 66% say the wickedness of man was the cause; 88% say there was a favored family; 66% say the remnant was warned; 67% say animals were also saved; 57% say the survivors ended up on a mountain; 35% say birds were sent

out; 9% say eight people were saved; and 7% mention a rainbow.

Is there enough water to flood the entire earth? Absolutely! If the earth were perfectly spherical the oceans would cover all the land by more than a mile in depth. The biblical account is that it rained for 40 days and nights in which the floodgates of the heavens were opened up as well as the fountains from the earth (Gen. 7:11;8:2). There is a theory known as the canopy theory that states it had never rained on the earth up to the time of Noah and that a mist watered the plants (Gen. 2:6). The theory goes on to state that there may have been a heavy cloud or water vapor layer over the entire earth and that it was this canopy of water that became torrential rains during the flood period.

Did the flood cover all the earth? Yes it did. The depth of the floodwaters is described in Gen. 7:19 as covering "all the high mountains under the entire heavens." Also, there are many references in the Bible to it being global: Gen. 6:1,4-5,12,13,17,19;7:4,6,10,19;8:3;9:15. There were 40 days of rain (Gen. 7:12), 110 days of flooding (Gen. 7:24) and 221 more days of draining (Gen. 8:1-5,13-14). That is a total of 371 days of flooding. That could not be a local flood.

Could the ark really contain all the animals of the world? Again the answer is "Yes." But let's look at the last question in more detail. The ark took about 120 years to build. Noah was 480 years old when he began the work and he had the help of his wife, three sons, and his son's wives. He probably hired local people to help in the construction.

The dimensions of the ark have a ratio of six to one. The Ark was six times longer than it was wide. This is the best ratio for modern shipbuilding. Model stability tests have

shown that the design is stable for waves up to 200 feet high and that the ark could have rotated 90 degrees and still righted itself.

The volume of the ark would be 450 feet long by 75 feet wide by 45 feet high. This equals 1,518,750 cubic feet and is comparable to 569 modern railroad boxcars. Therefore each boxcar, by comparison, would be 1,518,750 divided by 569, or 2,669 cubic feet of space. The average size of an animal on the earth is smaller than a cat. But, just to keep it safe let's consider the average size of an animal to be a sheep. The average double deck stock car holds 240 sheep. The Ark capacity would be about 569 x 240 equaling 136,560 animals of that size. However, that still is not accurate for our needs. Since most birds, reptiles, and amphibians are much smaller, let's double the boxcar capacity for them. Therefore, the boxcars could each hold 480 different kinds of birds, reptiles, and amphibians.

Noah had to take two or seven of every kind of animal on the earth. Though it is not really known exactly what is meant by a biblical kind, it is generally considered to be animals that are fertile within their own groups. Any dog can breed with any dog, therefore, dogs are one kind. It would only be necessary to bring representatives of each kind since the parents could produce offspring that would carry the genetic information for all variations within their kind.

Classification	# of Species	# of Kinds on the Ark
Mammals	3,700	3,700
Birds	8,600	60,200
Reptiles	6,	6,300
Amphibians	2,500	2,500
Fishes	20,600	zero
Other marine life	192,605	zero

Insects	850,000	(Since insects are very small, and a great many could be stored in a small area, calculation would be difficult.)
Total	**1,072,305**	**72,700**

The total number of mammals would be 3,700 times two pair which equals 7,400 animals. 7,400 divided by 240 = 31 boxcars used.

Since Gen. 7:3 says to take seven pairs of every bird then the total for birds would be 8,600 times two pair times 7 or 120,400 animals. 120,400 x 480 = 250 boxcars. The reptiles and amphibians would be 6,300 plus 2,500 or 8,800. 8,800 times two pair equals 17,600 animals. 17,600 divided by 480 = 37 boxcars.

The total number of boxcars used would be 318 with a total number of animals at 145,400. There would be 251 boxcars left over. That means that only 56% of the ark would be used for storing the animals. Obviously, then, the rest of the space would be used for food for the people and animals and sleeping quarters. In addition, considering that insects are extremely small, it is easily conceivable that they could be housed in part of the remaining space.

It should also be considered that many animals can hibernate. Additionally, predators and prey have been known to live peacefully together during situations of stress like fire, flood, or earthquake. In the Ark, animal behavior probably would have been different from normal daily life. Specialists in animal behavior have noted that animals can sense danger and have often migrated to escape it. Perhaps God used their migratory instincts to get them to the Ark.

Though this is only a brief analysis, it should present enough evidence that the Ark account is certainly within the realm of possibility.

Carm.org.

WHAT DOES THE BIBLE SAY ABOUT DINOSAURS?

The topic of dinosaurs in the Bible is part of a larger ongoing debate within the Christian community over the age of the earth, the proper interpretation of Genesis, and how to interpret the physical evidences we find all around us. Those who believe in an older age for the earth tend to agree that the Bible does not mention dinosaurs, because, according to their paradigm, dinosaurs died out millions of years before the first man ever walked the earth. The men who wrote the Bible could not have seen living dinosaurs.

Those who believe in a younger age for the earth tend to agree that the Bible does mention dinosaurs, though it never actually uses the word "dinosaur." Instead, it uses the Hebrew word *tanniyn*, which is translated a few different ways in our English Bibles. Sometimes it's "sea monster," and sometimes it's "serpent." It is most commonly translated "dragon." The *tanniyn* appear to have been some sort of giant reptile. These creatures are mentioned nearly thirty times in the Old Testament and were found both on land and in the water.

In addition to mentioning these giant reptiles, the Bible describes a couple of creatures in such a way that some scholars believe the writers may have been describing dinosaurs. The behemoth is said to be the mightiest of all God's creatures, a giant whose tail is likened to a cedar tree (Job 40:15). Some scholars have tried to identify the behemoth as either an elephant or a hippopotamus. Others point out that elephants and hippopotamuses have very thin tails, nothing comparable to a cedar tree. Dinosaurs like the

brachiosaurus and the diplodocus, on the other hand, had huge tails, which could easily be compared to a cedar tree.

Nearly every ancient civilization has some sort of art depicting giant reptilian creatures. Petroglyphs, artifacts, and even little clay figurines found in North America resemble modern depictions of dinosaurs. Rock carvings in South America depict men riding diplodocus-like creatures and, amazingly, bear the familiar images of triceratops-like, pterodactyl-like, and tyrannosaurus rex-like creatures. Roman mosaics, Mayan pottery, and Babylonian city walls all testify to man's trans-cultural, geographically unbounded fascination with these creatures.

Sober accounts like those of Marco Polo's Il Milione mingle with fantastic tales of treasure-hoarding beasts. In addition to the substantial amount of anthropic and historical evidences for the coexistence of dinosaurs and man, there are physical evidences, like the fossilized footprints of humans and dinosaurs found together at places in North America and West-Central Asia.

So, are there dinosaurs in the Bible? The matter is far from settled. It depends on how you interpret the available evidences and how you view the world around you. If the Bible is interpreted literally, a young earth interpretation will result, and the idea that dinosaurs and man coexisted can be accepted. If dinosaurs and human beings coexisted, what happened to the dinosaurs? While the Bible does not discuss the issue, dinosaurs likely died out sometime after the flood due to a combination of dramatic environmental shifts and the fact that they were relentlessly hunted to extinction by man.

Carm.org.

- 123 -

WHERE DID CAIN GET HIS WIFE?

In Genesis 4:16-17 it says,

"Then Cain went out from the presence of the Lord, and settled in the land of Nod, east of Eden. [17]And Cain had relations with his wife and she conceived, and gave birth to Enoch; and he built a city, and called the name of the city Enoch, after the name of his son."

Genesis tells us that Adam and Eve had two sons: Cain and Abel. Cain killed Abel, was exiled by God, and then in Genesis 4:17 we read that Cain had relations with his wife. Where did Cain get his wife? The answer is simple: Cain married either his sister or a niece.

In Genesis 5:4 we see that Adam had other sons and daughters.

"This is the book of the generations of Adam. In the day when God created man, He made him in the likeness of God. [2]He created them male and female, and He blessed them and named them Man in the day when they were created. [3]When Adam had lived one hundred and thirty years, he became the father of a son in his own likeness, according to his image, and named him Seth. [4]Then the days of Adam after he became the father of Seth were eight hundred years, and he had other sons and daughters. [5]So all the days that Adam lived were nine hundred and thirty years, and he died," (Gen. 5:1-5).

Since Adam lived several hundred years, having lots of children was not a problem. The Genesis account does not tell us about the order of the births nor does it tell us how

old they were. It was the ancient custom to often extract relevant information (sometimes out of order) to emphasis a point. By having many children it is certainly possible that there were many women around. This would mean that Cain married either a sister or a niece or some other relation and their children had children, etc. Of course at this point, the question of inbreeding is raised. But it is not a problem early on in the human race because the genetic line was so pure. Therefore, the prohibition against incest was not proclaimed until much later (Lev. 18:6-18) when inbreeding started to become a problem.

Carm.org.

WHAT DOES THE BIBLE SAY ABOUT DIVORCE AND REMARRIAGE?

First of all, no matter what view one takes on the issue of divorce, it is important to remember Malachi 2:16: "I hate divorce, says the LORD God of Israel." According to the Bible, marriage is a lifetime commitment. "So they are no longer two, but one. Therefore what God has joined together, let man not separate" (Matthew 19:6). God realizes, though, that since marriages involve two sinful human beings, divorces are going to occur.

In the Old Testament, He laid down some laws in order to protect the rights of divorcees, especially women (Deuteronomy 24:1-4). Jesus pointed out that these laws were given because of the hardness of people's hearts, not because they were God's desire (Matthew 19:8). The controversy over whether divorce and remarriage is allowed according to the Bible revolves primarily around Jesus' words in Matthew 5:32 and 19:9. The phrase "except for marital unfaithfulness" is the only thing in Scripture that possibly gives God's permission for divorce and remarriage.

Many interpreters understand this "exception clause" as referring to "marital unfaithfulness" during the "betrothal" period. In Jewish custom, a man and a woman were considered married even while they were still engaged or "betrothed." According to this view, immorality during this "betrothal" period would then be the only valid reason for a divorce.

However, the Greek word translated "marital unfaithfulness" is a word, which can mean any form of sexual immorality. It can mean fornication, prostitution, adultery, etc. Jesus is possibly saying that divorce is permissible if sexual immorality is committed. Sexual relations are an integral part of the marital bond: "the two will become one flesh" (Genesis 2:24; Matthew 19:5; Ephesians 5:31). Therefore, any breaking of that bond by sexual relations outside of marriage might be a permissible reason for divorce. If so, Jesus also has remarriage in mind in this passage. The phrase "and marries another" (Matthew 19:9) indicates that divorce and remarriage are allowed in an instance of the exception clause, whatever it is interpreted to be. It is important to note that only the innocent party is allowed to remarry. Although it is not stated in the text, the allowance for remarriage after a divorce is God's mercy for the one who was sinned against, not for the one who committed the sexual immorality. There may be instances where the "guilty party" is allowed to remarry, but it is not taught in this text.

Some understand 1 Corinthians 7:15 as another "exception," allowing remarriage if an unbelieving spouse divorces a believer. However, the context does not mention remarriage, but only says a believer is not bound to continue a marriage if an unbelieving spouse wants to leave. Others claim that abuse (spousal or child) is a valid reason for divorce even though it is not listed as such in the Bible. While this may very well be the case, it is never wise to presume upon the Word of God.

Sometimes lost in the debate over the exception clause is the fact that whatever "marital unfaithfulness" means, it is an allowance for divorce, not a requirement for it. Even when adultery is committed, a couple can, through God's grace, learn to forgive and begin rebuilding their marriage.

God has forgiven us of so much more. Surely we can follow His example and even forgive the sin of adultery (Ephesians 4:32).

However, in many instances, a spouse is unrepentant and continues in sexual immorality. That is where Matthew 19:9 can possibly be applied. Many also look to quickly remarry after a divorce when God might desire them to remain single. God sometimes calls people to be single so that their attention is not divided (1 Corinthians 7:32-35). Remarriage after a divorce may be an option in some circumstances, but that does not mean it is the only option.

It is distressing that the divorce rate among professing Christians is nearly as high as that of the unbelieving world. The Bible makes it abundantly clear that God hates divorce (Malachi 2:16) and that reconciliation and forgiveness should be the marks of a believer's life (Luke 11:4; Ephesians 4:32). However, God recognizes that divorce will occur, even among His children. A divorced and/or remarried believer should not feel any less loved by God, even if the divorce and/or remarriage is not covered under the possible exception clause of Matthew 19:9. God often uses even the sinful disobedience of Christians to accomplish great good.

GotQuestions.org

IS ETERNAL SECURITY BIBLICAL?

When people come to know Christ as their Savior, they are brought into a relationship with God that guarantees their eternal security. Jude 24 declares, "To Him who is able to keep you from falling and to present you before His glorious presence without fault and with great joy." God's power is able to keep the believer from falling. It is up to Him, not us, to present us before His glorious presence.

Our eternal security is a result of God keeping us, not us maintaining our own salvation. The Lord Jesus Christ proclaimed, "I give them eternal life, and they shall never perish; no one can snatch them out of my hand. My Father, who has given them to me, is greater than all, no one can snatch them out of my Father's hand" (John 10:28-29b). Both Jesus and the Father have us firmly grasped in their hand. Who could possibly separate us from the grip of both the Father and the Son?

Ephesians 4:30 tells us that believers are "sealed for the day of redemption." If believers did not have eternal security, the sealing could not truly be unto the day of redemption, but only to the day of sinning, apostasy, or disbelief. John 3:15-16 tells us that whoever believes in Jesus Christ will "have eternal life." If a person were to be promised eternal life, but then have it taken away, it was never "eternal" to begin with. If eternal security is not true, the promises of eternal life in the Bible would be in error.

The most powerful argument for eternal security is Romans 8:38-39; "For I am convinced that neither death nor life, neither angels nor demons, neither the present nor the

future, nor any powers, neither height nor depth, nor anything else in all creation, will be able to separate us from the love of God that is in Christ Jesus our Lord." Our eternal security is based on God's love for those whom He has redeemed. Our eternal security is purchased by Christ, promised by the Father, and sealed by the Holy Spirit.

GotQuestions.org

"IS GAMBLING A SIN? WHAT DOES THE BIBLE SAY ABOUT GAMBLING?

The Bible does not specifically condemn gambling, betting, or the lottery. The Bible does warn us, however, to stay away from the love of money (1 Timothy 6:10; Hebrews 13:5). Scripture also encourages us to stay away from attempts to "get rich quick" (Proverbs 13:11; 23:5; Ecclesiastes 5:10). Gambling most definitely is focused on the love of money and undeniably tempts people with the promise of quick and easy riches.

What is wrong with gambling? Gambling is a difficult issue because if it is done in moderation and only on occasion, it is a waste of money, but it is not necessarily evil. People waste money on all sorts of activities. Gambling is no more or less of a waste of money than seeing a movie (in many cases), eating an unnecessarily expensive meal, or purchasing a worthless item. At the same time, the fact that money is wasted on other things does not justify gambling. Money should not be wasted. Excess money should be saved for future needs or given to the Lord's work, not gambled away.

While the Bible does not explicitly mention gambling, it does mention events of "luck" or "chance." As an example, casting lots is used in Leviticus to choose between the sacrificial goat and the scapegoat. Joshua cast lots to determine the allotment of land to the various tribes. Nehemiah cast lots to determine who would live inside the walls of Jerusalem. The apostles cast lots to determine the replacement for Judas. Proverbs 16:33 says, "The lot is cast in the lap, but its every decision is from the Lord."

What would the Bible say about casinos and lotteries? Casinos use all sorts of marketing schemes to entice gamblers to risk as much money as possible. They often offer inexpensive or even free alcohol, which encourages drunkenness, and thereby a decreased ability to make wise decisions. Everything in a casino is perfectly rigged for taking money in large sums and giving nothing in return, except for fleeting and empty pleasures. Lotteries attempt to portray themselves as a way to fund education and/or social programs.

However, studies show that lottery participants are usually those who can least afford to be spending money on lottery tickets. The allure of "getting rich quick" is too great a temptation to resist for those who are desperate. The chances of winning are infinitesimal, which results in many peoples' lives being ruined.

Can lotto/lottery proceeds please God? Many people claim to be playing the lottery or gambling so that they can give the money to the church or to some other good cause. While this may be a good motive, reality is that few use gambling winnings for godly purposes. Studies show that the vast majority of lottery winners are in an even worse financial situation a few years after winning a jackpot than they were before. Few, if any, truly give the money to a good cause.

Further, God does not need our money to fund His mission in the world. Proverbs 13:11 says, "Dishonest money dwindles away, but he who gathers money little by little makes it grow." God is sovereign and will provide for the needs of the church through honest means. Would God be honored by receiving donated drug money or money stolen in a bank robbery? Of course not. Neither does God need or

want money that was "stolen" from the poor in the temptation for riches.

First Timothy 6:10 tells us, "For the love of money is a root of all kinds of evil. Some people, eager for money, have wandered from the faith and pierced themselves with many griefs." Hebrews 13:5 declares, "Keep your lives free from the love of money and be content with what you have, because God has said, 'Never will I leave you; never will I forsake you.'" Matthew 6:24 proclaims, "No one can serve two masters. Either he will hate the one and love the other, or he will be devoted to the one and despise the other. You cannot serve both God and Money."

GotQuestions.org

EVIDENCES OF CREATION

1. Information

The instructions for how to build, operate, and repair living cells represent a vast amount of information (estimated at 12 billion bits). Information is a mental, non-material concept. It can <u>never</u> arise from a natural process and is <u>always</u> the result of intelligence. Just as a newspaper story transcends the ink on the paper, life's DNA itself (like the ink) is <u>not</u> the information, it is simply a <u>physical representation</u> or housing of the information (the story). Modifying the DNA via mutation can <u>never</u> produce new genetic information to drive upward evolution, just as spilling coffee on the newspaper, thereby modifying the distribution of the ink, will never improve the story.

2. Formation of Life

Dead chemicals cannot become alive on their own. The cell is a miniature factory with many active processes, not a simple blob of "protoplasm" as believed in Darwin's day. Lightening striking a mud puddle or some "warm little pond" will never produce life. This is another view of the core issue of information, as the simplest living cell requires a vast amount of information to be present. The "Law of Biogenesis" states that life comes only from prior life. Spontaneous generation has long been shown to be impossible (by Louis Pasteur in 1859). Numerous efforts to bring life from non-life (including the famous Miller-Urey experiment) have not succeeded. The probability of life forming from non-life has been likened to the probability of a tornado going through a junkyard and spontaneously assembling a working 747 airplane. The idea that life on earth may have been seeded from outer space just moves the problem elsewhere.

3. Design Of Living Things

Design is apparent in the living world. Even Richard Dawkins in his anti-creation book *The Blind Watchmaker* admits, "Biology is the study of complicated things that give the appearance of having been designed for a purpose." The amazing defense mechanism of the Bombardier Beetle is a classic example of design in nature, seemingly impossible to explain as the result of accumulating small beneficial changes over time, because if the mechanism doesn't work perfectly, "boom" - no more beetle! This is also another view of the core issue of information, as the design of living things is the result of processing the information in the DNA (following the blueprint) to produce a working organism.

4. Irreducible Complexity

The idea that "nothing works until everything works." The classic example is a mousetrap, which is irreducibly complex in that if one of its several pieces is missing or not in the right place, it will not function as a mousetrap and no mice will be caught. The systems, features, and processes of life are irreducibly complex. What good is a circulatory system without a heart? An eye without a brain to interpret the signals? What good is a half-formed wing? Doesn't matching male and female reproductive machinery need to exist at the same time, fully-functioning if any reproduction is to take place? Remember, natural selection has no foresight, and works to eliminate anything not providing an immediate benefit.

5. Second Law of Thermodynamics

The Second Law of Thermodynamics refers to the universal tendency for things, on their own, to "mix" with their surrounding environment over time, becoming less ordered and eventually reaching a steady state. A glass of hot water becomes room temperature, buildings decay into

rubble, and the stars will eventually burn out leading to the "heat death" of the universe. However, the evolutionary scenario proposes that over time things, on their own, became more ordered and structured. Somehow the energy of a "Big Bang" structured itself into stars, galaxies, planets, and living things, contrary to the Second Law. It is sometimes said that the energy of the Sun was enough to overcome this tendency and allow for the formation of life on earth. However, application of energy alone is not enough to overcome this tendency; the energy must be channeled by a machine. A human must repair a building to keep it from decaying. Likewise, it is the machinery of photosynthesis which harnesses the energy of the Sun, allowing life to exist, and photosynthesis is itself a complex chemical process. The maturing of an acorn into a tree, or a zygote (the first cell resulting from fertilization) into a mature human being does not violate the Second Law as these processes are guided by the information already present in the acorn or zygote.

6. Existence of the Universe

By definition, something must be eternal (as we have "something" today and something cannot come from "nothing", so there was never a time when there was "nothing"). Either the universe itself is eternal, or something/someone outside of and greater than the universe is eternal. We know that the universe is not eternal, it had a beginning (as evidenced by its expansion). Therefore, God (the something/someone outside of the universe) must exist and must have created the universe. Einstein showed that space and time are related. If there is no space there is no time. Before the universe was created there was no space and therefore no concept of time. This is hard for us to understand as we are space-time creatures, but it allows for God to be an eternal being, completely consistent with scientific laws. The question "who created

God" is therefore an improper/invalid question, as it is a time-based question (concerning the point in time at which God came into existence) but God exists outside of time as the un-caused first cause.

7. Fine-tuning of Earth for Life

Dozens of parameters are "just right" for life to exist on this planet. For example, if the Earth were just a little closer to the Sun it would be too hot and the ocean's water would boil away, much further and it would be covered continually in ice. Earth's circular orbit (to maintain a roughly constant temperature year-round), its rotation speed (to provide days and nights not too long or short), its tilt (to provide seasons), and the presence of the moon (to provide tides to cleanse the oceans) are just some of many other examples.

The presence of large amounts of water, with its amazing special properties, is also required. Water is a rare compound in that it is lighter in a solid state than in a liquid state. This allows ponds to freeze with the ice on the surface allowing the life beneath to survive. Otherwise bodies of water would freeze from the bottom up and become solid ice. Water is also the most universal "solvent" known, allowing for dissolving/mixing with the many different chemicals of life. In fact, our bodies are 75-85% comprised of water.

8. Fine-tuning of Physics

The **fine-tuning of the physical constants** that control the physics of the universe - the settings of the basic forces (strong nuclear force constant, weak nuclear force constant, gravitational force constant, and electromagnetic force constant) are on a knife's edge. A minor change in these or any of dozens of other universal parameters would make life impossible.

The "multiverse" idea that there may be many universes and ours "just happened" to have these proper values is outside of science and could never be proven. Even then we would have to ask, "what was the <u>cause</u> of all these universes?"

9. Abrupt Appearance in the Fossil Record

The oldest fossils for any creature are already fully formed and don't change much over time ("stasis"). The "Cambrian Explosion" in the "primordial strata" documents the geologically rapid appearance of most major groups of complex animals. There is no evidence of evolution from simpler forms. Birds are said to have evolved from reptiles but no fossil has ever been found having a "half-scale/half-wing". A reptile breathes using an "in and out" lung (like humans have), but a bird has a "flow-through" lung suitable for moving through the air. Can you even imagine how such a transition of the lung could have taken place? Abrupt appearance and stasis are consistent with the biblical concept of creation "according to its kind", and a world-wide flood that scoured the earth down to its basement rocks, depositing the "geologic column" and giving the appearance of a "Cambrian Explosion". Smarter, more mobile creatures would escape the flood waters longer, becoming buried in higher-level strata, leading to a burial order progressing from "simpler" forms to more complex/higher-level forms, which people now wrongly interpret as an evolutionary progression.

10. Human Consciousness

A person is a unity of body + mind/soul, the mind/soul being the immaterial part of you that is the real inner you. Chemicals alone cannot explain self-awareness, creativity, reasoning, emotions of love and hate, sensations of pleasure and pain, possessing and remembering

experiences, and free will. Reason itself cannot be relied upon if it is based only on blind neurological events.

11. Human Language
Language is one of the main things that separates man from the animals. No animal is capable of achieving anything like human speech, and all attempts to teach chimpanzees to talk have failed. Evolutionists have no explanation for the origin of human language. However, the Bible does. It says that the first man, Adam, was created able to speak. The Bible also explains why we have different human languages, as God had to "confuse" the common language being used in Babel after the flood, in order to force people to spread out around the world as He wanted. This was only a "surface" confusion though, as all languages express the same underlying basic ideas and concepts, enabling other languages to be learned and understood.

12. Sexual Reproduction
Many creatures reproduce asexually. Why would animals abandon simpler asexual reproduction in favor of more costly and inefficient sexual reproduction? Sexual reproduction is a very complex process that is only useful if fully in place. For sexual reproduction to have evolved complimentary male and female sex organs, sperm and eggs, and all the associated machinery in tandem defies the imagination.

13. The Bible's Witness
The Bible is true. The history of the Bible is true. The words of the Bible concerning our origins were given to men to write down, by God, who was the only living being present. We were not there! God said He created the universe. God said He created all living things. We know that life is much more than chemicals. God put His life into

Adam and that life has been transferred from generation to generation all the way down to us!

BestBibleScience.Org

"WHAT DOES THE BIBLE SAY ABOUT HOMOSEXUALITY?

The Bible consistently tells us that homosexual activity is a sin (Genesis 19:1-13; Leviticus 18:22; 20:13; Romans 1:26-27; 1 Corinthians 6:9). Romans 1:26-27 teaches specifically that homosexuality is a result of denying and disobeying God. When people continue in sin and unbelief, God "gives them over" to even more wicked and depraved sin in order to show them the futility and hopelessness of life apart from God. 1 Corinthians 6:9 proclaims that homosexual "offenders" will not inherit the kingdom of God. God does not create a person with homosexual desires.

The Bible tells us that people become homosexuals because of sin (Romans 1:24-27) and ultimately because of their own choice. A person may be born with a greater susceptibility to homosexuality, just as some people are born with a tendency to violence and other sins. That does not excuse the person's choosing to sin by giving in to sinful desires. If a person is born with a greater susceptibility to anger/rage, does that make it right for him to give into those desires? Of course not! The same is true with homosexuality.

However, the Bible does not describe homosexuality as a "greater" sin than any other. All sin is offensive to God. Homosexuality is just one of the many things listed in 1 Corinthians 6:9-10 that will keep a person from the kingdom of God. According to the Bible, God's forgiveness is just as available to a homosexual as it is to an adulterer, idol worshipper, murderer, thief, etc. God also

promises the strength for victory over sin, including homosexuality, to all those who will believe in Jesus Christ for their salvation (1 Corinthians 6:11; 2 Corinthians 5:17; Philippians 4:13).

Carm.org.

THE PURSUIT OF GOD, CHAPTER 1 BY A.W.TOZER

My soul followeth hard after thee: thy right hand upholdeth me Psa. 63:8

Christian theology teaches the doctrine of prevenient grace, which briefly stated means this, that before a man can seek God, God must first have sought the man.

Before a sinful man can think a right thought of God, there must have been a work of enlightenment done within him; imperfect it may be, but a true work nonetheless, and the secret cause of all desiring and seeking and praying which may follow.

We pursue God because, and only because, He has first put an urge within us that spurs us to the pursuit. "No man can come to me," said our Lord, "except the Father which hath sent me draw him," and it is by this very prevenient drawing that God takes from us every vestige of credit for the act of coming. The impulse to pursue God originates with God, but the out working of that impulse is our following hard after Him; and all the time we are pursuing Him we are already in His hand: "Thy right hand upholdeth me."

In this divine "upholding" and human "following" there is no contradiction. All is of God, for as von Hugel teaches, God is always previous. In practice, however, (that is, where God's previous working meets man's present response) man must pursue God. Or, our part there must be positive reciprocation if this secret drawing of God is to eventuate in identifiable experience of the Divine. In

the warm language of personal feeling this is stated in the Forty-second Psalm: "As the hart panteth after the water brooks, so panteth my soul after thee, O God. My soul thirsteth for God, for the living God: when shall I come. And appear before God?" This is deep calling unto deep, and the longing heart will understand it.

The doctrine of justification by faith-a Biblical truth, and a blessed relief from sterile legalism and unavailing self-effort has in our time fallen into evil company and been interpreted by many in such manner as actually to bar men from the knowledge of God. The whole transaction of religious conversion has been made mechanical and spiritless. Faith may now be exercised without a jar to the moral life and without embarrassment to the Adamic ego. Christ may be "received" without creating any special love for Him in the soul of the receiver. The man is "saved," but he not hungry nor thirsty after God. In fact he is specifically taught to be satisfied and encouraged to be content with little.

The modern scientist has lost God amid the wonders of His world; we Christians are in real danger of losing God amid the wonders of His Word. We have almost forgotten that God is a Person and, as such, can be cultivated as any person can. It is inherent in personality to be able to know other personalities, but full knowledge of one personality by another cannot be achieved in one encounter. It is only after long and loving mental intercourse that the full possibilities of both can be explored.

All social intercourse between human beings is a response of personality to personality, grading upward from the most casual brush between man and man to the fullest, most intimate communion of which the human soul is capable.

Religion, so far as it is genuine, is in essence the response of created personalities to the Creating Personality, God. "This is life eternal, that they might know thee the only true God, and Jesus Christ, whom thou hast sent."

God is a Person, and in the deep of His mighty nature He thinks, wills, enjoys, feels, loves, desires and suffers as any other person may. In making Himself known to us He stays by the familiar pattern of personality. He communicates with us through the avenues of our minds, our wills and our emotions. The continuous and unembarrassed interchange of love and thought between God and the soul of the redeemer man is the throbbing heart of New Testament religion. This intercourse between God and the soul is known to us in conscious personal awareness. It is personal: that is, it does not come through the body of believers, as such, but is known to the individual, and, to the body through the individuals which compose it. And it is conscious: that is, it does not stay below the threshold of consciousness and work there unknown to the soul (as, for instance, infant baptism is though by some to do), but comes within the field of awareness where the man can "know" it as he knows any other fact of experience.

You and I are in little (our sins excepted) what, God is in large. Being made in His image we have: I within us the capacity to know Him. In our sins we lack only the power. The moment the Spirit has quickened us to life in regeneration our whole being senses its kinship to God and leaps up in joyous recognition That is the heavenly birth without which we cannon: see the Kingdom of God. It is, however, not an end but an inception, for now begins the glorious pursuit the heart's happy exploration of the infinite

riches of the Godhead. That is where we begin, I say, but where: we stop no man has yet discovered, for there is in the awful and mysterious deaths of the Triune God neither limit nor end.

Shoreless Ocean, who can sound Thee? Thine own eternity is round Thee Majesty divine!

To have found God and still to pursue Him is the soul's paradox of love, scorned indeed by the too-easily-satisfied religionist, but justified in happy experience by the children of the burning heart. St. Bernard stated this holy paradox in a musical quatrain that will be instantly understood by every worshipping soul:

We taste Thee? O Thou Living Bread, And long teast upon Thee still: We drink of Thee, the Fountainhead And thirst our souls from Thee to fill.

Come near to the holy men and women of the past and you will soon feel the heat of their desire after God. They mourned for Him, they prayed and wrestled and sought for Him day and night, in season and out, and when they had found Him the finding was all the sweeter for the long seeking. Moses used the fact that he knew God as an argument for knowing Him better. "Now, therefore, I pray thee, if I have found grace in thy sight, show me now thy way, that I may know thee, that I may find grace in thy sight"; and from there he rose to make the daring request, "I beseech thee, show me thy glory." God was frankly pleased by this display of ardor, and the next day called Moses into the mount, and there in solemn procession made all His glory pass before him.

David's life was a torrent of spiritual desire, and his psalms ring with the cry of the seeker and the glad shout of the finder. Paul

confessed the mainspring of his life to be his burning desire after Christ. "That I may know Him," was the goal of his heart, and to this he sacrificed everything. "Yea doubtless, and I count all things but loss for the excellency of the knowledge of Christ Jesus my Lord: for whom I have suffered the loss of all things, and do count them but refuse, that I may win Christ."

Hymnody is sweet with the longing after God, the God whom, while the singer seeks, he knows he has already found. "His track I see and I'll pursue," sang our fathers only a short generation ago, but that song is heard no more in the great congregation. How tragic that we in this dark day have had our seeking done for us by our teachers. Everything is made to center upon the initial act of "accepting" Christ (a term, incidentally, which is not found in the Bible and we are not expected thereafter to crave any further

revelation of God to our souls. We have been snared in the coils of a spurious logic which insists that if we have found Him we need no more seek Him. This is set before us as the last word in orthodoxy, and it is taken for granted that no Bible-taught Christian ever believed otherwise. Thus the whole testimony of the worshipping, seeking, singing Church on that subject is crisply set aside. The experiential heart-theology of a grand army of fragrant saints is rejected in favor of a smug interpretation of Scripture which would certainly have sounded strange to an Augustine, a Rutherford or a Brainerd.

In the midst of this great chill there are some, I rejoice to acknowledge, who will not be content with shallow logic. They will admit the force of the argument, and then turn away with tears to hunt some lonely place and pray, "O God, show me thy glory." They want to taste,

to touch with their hearts, to see with their inner eyes the wonder that is God.

I want deliberately to encourage this mighty longing after God. The lack of it has brought us to our present low estate. The stiff and wooden quality about our religious lives is a result of our lack of holy desire. Complacency is a deadly foe of all spiritual growth. Acute desire must be present or there will be no manifestation of Christ to His people. He waits to be wanted. Too bad that with many of us He waits so long, so very long, in vain.

Every age has its own characteristics. Right now we are in an age of religious complexity. The simplicity which is in Christ is rarely found among us. In its stead are programs, methods, organizations and a world of nervous activities which occupy time and attention but can never satisfy the longing of the heart. The shallowness of our inner experience, the hollowness of our worship, and that servile imitation of the world which marks our promotional methods all testify that we, in this day, know God only imperfectly, and the peace of God scarcely at all.

If we would find God amid all the religious externals we must first determine to find Him, and then proceed in the way of simplicity. Now as always God discovers Himself to "babes" and hides Himself in thick darkness from the wise and the prudent. We must simplify our approach to Him. We must strip down to essentials (and they will be found to be blessedly few). We must put away all effort to impress, and come with the guileless candor of childhood. If we do this, without doubt God will quickly respond.

When religion has said its last word, there is little that we need other than God Himself. The evil habit of seeking God-and effectively prevents us from finding God in full revelation. In

the "and" lies our great woe. If we omit the "and" we shall soon find God, and in Him we shall find that for which we have all our lives been secretly longing.

We need not fear that in seeking God only we may narrow our lives or restrict the motions of our expanding hearts. The opposite is true. We can well afford to make God our All, to concentrate, to sacrifice the many for the One.

The author of the quaint old English classic, The Cloud of Unknowing, teaches us how to do this. "Lift up thine heart unto Gel with a meek stirring of love; and mean Himself, and none of His goods. And thereto, look thee loath to think on aught but God Himself. So that nought work in thy wit, nor in thy will, but only God Himself. This is the work of the soul that most pleaseth God."

Again, he recommends that in prayer we practice a further stripping down of everything, even of our theology. "For it sufficeth enough, a naked intent direct unto God without any other cause than Himself." Yet underneath all his thinking lay the broad foundation of New Testament truth, for he explains that by "Himself" he means "God that made thee, and bought thee, and that graciously called thee to thy degree." And he is all for simplicity: If we would have religion "lapped and folden in one word, for that thou shouldst have better hold thereupon, take thee but a little word of one syllable: for so it is better than of two, for even the shorter it is the better it accordeth with the work of the Spirit. And such a word is this word GOD or this word LOVE."

When the Lord divided Canaan among the tribes of Israel Levi received no share of the land. God said to him simply, "I am thy part and thine inheritance," and by those words made him richer than all his

brethren, richer than all the kings and rajas who have ever lived in the world. And there is a spiritual principle here, a principle still valid for every priest of the Most High God.

The man who has God for his treasure has all things in One. Many ordinary treasures may be denied him, or if he is allowed to have them, the enjoyment of them will be so tempered that they will never be necessary to his happiness. Or if he must see them go, one after one, he will scarcely feel a sense of loss, for having the Source of all things he has in One all satisfaction, all pleasure, all delight. Whatever he may lose he has actually lost nothing, for he now has it all in One, and he has it purely, legitimately and forever.

O God, I have tasted Thy goodness, and it has both satisfied me and made me thirsty for more. I am painfully conscious of my need of further grace. I am ashamed of my lack of desire. O God, the Triune God, I want to want Thee; I long to be filled with longing; I thirst to be made more thirsty still. Show me Thy glory, I pray Thee, that so I may know Thee indeed. Begin in mercy a new work of love within me. Say to my soul, "Rise up, any love, my fair one, and come away." Then give me grace to rise and follow T Thee up from this misty lowland where I have wandered so long. In Jesus' Name, Amen.

WHAT DOES THE BIBLE SAY ABOUT INTERRACIAL MARRIAGE?

The Old Testament Law commanded the Israelites not to engage in interracial marriage (Deuteronomy 7:3-4). However, the reason for this was not primarily racial in nature. Rather, it was religious. The reason God commanded against interracial marriage was that people of other races were idolaters and worshippers of false gods. The Israelites would be led astray from God if they intermarried with idol worshippers, pagans, or heathens.

A similar principle is laid out in the New Testament, but at a much different level: "Do not be yoked together with unbelievers. For what do righteousness and wickedness have in common? Or what fellowship can light have with darkness?" (2 Corinthians 6:14). Just as the Israelites (believers in the one true God) were commanded not to marry idolaters, so Christians (believers in the one true God) are commanded not to marry unbelievers. To answer this question specifically, no, the Bible does not say that interracial marriage is wrong.

As Martin Luther King noted, a person should be judged by his or her character, not by skin color. There is no place in the life of the Christian for favoritism based on race (James 2:1-10). When selecting a mate, a Christian should always first find out if the potential spouse is born again by faith in Jesus Christ (John 3:3-5). Faith in Christ, not skin color, is the biblical standard for choosing a spouse. Interracial marriage is not a matter of right or wrong, but of wisdom, discernment, and prayer.

The only reason interracial marriage should be considered carefully is the difficulties a mixed-race couple may experience because of others who have a hard time accepting them. Many interracial couples experience discrimination and ridicule, sometimes even from their own families. Some interracial couples experience difficulties when their children have skin tones of different shades from the parents and/or siblings. An interracial couple needs to take these things into consideration and be prepared for them, should they decide to marry. Again, though, the only biblical restriction placed on whom a Christian may marry is whether the other person is a member of the body of Christ.

BestBibleScience.Org

IS IT RIGHT TO LIE?

The Bible nowhere presents an instance where lying is considered to be the right thing to do. The ninth commandment prohibits bearing false witness (Exodus 20:16). Proverbs 6:16-19 lists "a lying tongue" and "a false witness who pours out lies" as two of the seven abominations to the Lord. Love "rejoices with the truth" (1 Corinthians 13:6). For other Scriptures that speak negatively of lying, see Psalm 19:29, 163; 120:2; Proverbs 12:22; 13:5; Ephesians 4:25; Colossians 3:9; and Revelation 21:8. There are many examples of liars in Scripture, from Jacob's deceit in Genesis 27 to the pretense of Ananias and Sapphira in Acts 5. Time after time, we see that falsehood leads to misery, loss, and judgment.

There are at least two instances in the Bible where lying produced a favorable result. For example, the lie the Hebrew mid- wives tell Pharaoh seems to result in the Lord's blessing on them (Exodus 1:15-21), and it probably saved the lives of many Hebrew babies. Another example is Rahab's lie to protect the Israelite spies in Joshua 2:5. It is important to note, however, that God never condones these lies. Despite the "positive" out- come of these lies, the Bible nowhere praises the lies them- selves. The Bible nowhere states that there are instances where lying is the right thing to do.

At the same time, the Bible does not declare that there is no possible instance in which lying is an acceptable option. The question then remains: is there ever a time when lying is the right thing to do? The most common illustration of this dilemma comes from the life of Corrie ten Boom in Nazi-occupied Holland. Essentially, the story is this: Corrie ten Boom is hiding Jews in her home to protect them from

the Nazis. Nazi soldiers come to her home and ask her if she knows where any Jews are hiding. What is she to do? Should she tell the truth and allow the Nazis to capture the Jews she was trying to protect? Or, should she lie and deny that she knows anything about them?

In an instance such as this, where lying may be the only possible way to prevent a horrible evil, perhaps lying would be an acceptable thing to do. Such an instance would be somewhat similar to the lies of the Hebrew midwives and Rahab. In an evil world, and in a desperate situation, it may be the right thing to commit a lesser evil, lying, in order to prevent a much greater evil. However, it must be noted that such instances are extremely rare. It is highly likely that the vast majority of people in human history have never faced a situation in which lying was the right thing to do.

CAN A CHRISTIAN LOSE SALVATION?

Before this question is answered, the term "Christian" must be defined. A "Christian" is not a person who has said a prayer, or walked down an aisle, or been raised in a Christian family. While each of these things can be a part of the Christian experience, they are not what "makes" a Christian. A Christian is a person who has, by faith, received and fully trusted in Jesus Christ as the only Savior (John 3:16; Acts 16:31; Ephesians 2:8-9).

So, with this definition in mind, can a Christian lose salvation? Perhaps the best way to answer this crucially important question is to examine what the Bible says occurs at salvation, and to study what losing salvation would therefore entail. Here are a few examples: A Christian is a new creation. "Therefore, if anyone is in Christ, he is a new creation; the old has gone, the new has come!" (2 Corinthians 5:17).

This verse speaks of a person becoming an entirely new creature as a result of being "in Christ." For a Christian to lose salvation, the new creation would have to be canceled and reversed. A Christian is redeemed. "For you know that it was not with perishable things such as silver or gold that you were redeemed from the empty way of life handed down to you from your forefathers, but with the precious blood of Christ, a lamb without blemish or defect" (1 Peter 1:18-19).

The word "redeemed" refers to a purchase being made, a price being paid. For a Christian to lose salvation, God Himself would have to revoke His purchase that He paid for with the precious blood of Christ. A Christian is

justified. "Therefore, since we have been justified through faith, we have peace with God through our Lord Jesus Christ" (Romans 5:1). To "justify" means to "declare righteous." All those who receive Jesus as Savior are "declared righteous" by God.

For a Christian to lose salvation, God would have to go back on His Word and "un-declare" what He had previously declared. A Christian is promised eternal life. "For God so loved the world that he gave his one and only Son, that whoever believes in him shall not perish but have eternal life" (John 3:16). Eternal life is a promise of eternity (forever) in heaven with God. God promises, "Believe and you will have eternal life." For a Christian to lose salvation, eternal life would have to be taken away.

If a Christian is promised to live forever, how then can God break this promise by taking away eternal life? A Christian is guaranteed glorification. "And those he predestined, he also called; those he called, he also justified; those he justified, he also glorified" (Romans 8:30). As we learned in Romans 5:1, justification is declared at the moment of faith. According to Romans 8:30, glorification is guaranteed for all those whom God justifies. Glorification refers to a Christian receiving a perfect resurrection body in heaven.

If a Christian can lose salvation, then Romans 8:30 is in error, because God could not guarantee glorification for all those whom He predestines, calls, and justifies. Many more illustrations of what occurs at salvation could be shared. Even these few make it abundantly clear that a Christian cannot lose salvation. Most, if not all, of what the Bible says happens to us when we receive Jesus Christ as Savior would be invalidated if salvation could be lost. Salvation cannot be reversed. A Christian cannot be un-newly

created. Redemption cannot be undone. Eternal life cannot be lost and still be considered eternal.

If a Christian can lose salvation, God would have to go back on His Word and change His mind—two things that Scripture tells us God never does. The most frequent objections to the belief that a Christian cannot lose salvation are 1) What about those who are Christians and continually live an immoral lifestyle? 2) What about those who are Christians but later reject the faith and deny Christ? The problem with these two objections is the phrase "who are Christians." The Bible declares that a true Christian will not live a continually immoral lifestyle (1 John 3:6). The Bible declares that anyone who departs the faith is demonstrating that he never truly was a Christian (1 John 2:19).

Therefore, neither objection is valid. Christians do not continually live immoral lifestyles, nor do they reject the faith and deny Christ. Such actions are proof that they were never redeemed. No, a Christian cannot lose salvation. Nothing can separate a Christian from God's love (Romans 8:38-39). Nothing can remove a Christian from God's hand (John 10:28-29).

God is both willing and able to guarantee and maintain the salvation He has given us. Jude 24-25, "To Him who is able to keep you from falling and to present you before his glorious presence without fault and with great joy—to the only God our Savior be glory, majesty, power and authority, through Jesus Christ our Lord, before all ages, now and forevermore! Amen."

BestBibleScience.Org

MASTURBATION - IS IT A SIN ACCORDING TO THE BIBLE?

The Bible never explicitly mentions masturbation or states whether or not masturbation is a sin. The Scripture most frequently pointed to in regards to masturbation is the story of Onan in Genesis 38:9-10. Some interpret this passage as saying that "spilling your seed" on the ground is a sin. However, that is not precisely what the passage is saying. God condemned Onan not for "spilling his seed" but because Onan refused to fulfill his duty to provide an heir for his brother. The passage is not about masturbation, but rather about fulfilling a family duty. A second passage sometimes used as evidence for masturbation's being a sin is Matthew 5:27-30. Jesus speaks against having lustful thoughts and then says, "If your right hand causes you to sin, cut it off and throw it away." While there are parallels between this passage and masturbation, it is unlikely that masturbation was what Jesus was alluding to.

While the Bible nowhere explicitly states that masturbation is a sin, there is no question as to whether the actions that lead to masturbation are sinful. Masturbation is nearly always the result of lustful thoughts, sexual stimulation, and/or pornographic images. It is these problems that need to be dealt with. If the sins of lust, immoral thoughts, and pornography are forsaken and overcome, masturbation will become a non-issue. Many people struggle with guilty feelings concerning masturbation, when in reality, the things that led to the act are far more worthy of repentance.

There are some biblical principles that can be applied to the issue of masturbation. Ephesians 5:3 declares, "Among you there must not be even a hint of sexual immorality, or of any kind of impurity." It is hard to see how masturbating can pass that particular test. The Bible teaches us, "So whether you eat or drink or whatever you do, do it all for the glory of God" (1 Corinthians 10:31).

If you cannot give God glory for something, you should not do it. If a person is not fully convinced that an activity is pleasing to God, then it is a sin: "Everything that does not come from faith is sin" (Romans 14:23). Further, we need to remember that our bodies have been redeemed and belong to God. "Do you not know that your body is a temple of the Holy Spirit, who is in you, whom you have received from God? You are not your own; you were bought at a price. Therefore honor God with your body" (1 Corinthians 6:19-20).

This great truth should have a real bearing on what we do with our bodies. In light of these principles, the conclusion that masturbation is a sin is biblical. Clearly, masturbation is not glorifying to God; it does not avoid the appearance of immorality, nor does it pass the test of God's having ownership over our bodies.

BestBibleScience.Org

ONCE SAVED ALWAYS SAVED?

O nce a person is saved are they always saved? When people come to know Christ as their Savior, they are brought into a relationship with God that guarantees their salvation as eternally secure. Numerous passages of Scripture declare this fact. (a) Romans 8:30 declares, "And those He predestined, He also called; those He called, He also justified; those He justified, He also glorified." This verse tells us that from the moment God chooses us, it is as if we are glorified in His presence in heaven.

There is nothing that can prevent a believer from one day being glorified because God has already purposed it in heaven. Once a person is justified, his salvation is guaranteed - he is as secure as if he is already glorified in heaven. (b) Paul asks two crucial questions in Romans 8:33-34 "Who will bring any charge against those whom God has chosen? It is God who justifies. Who is he that condemns? Christ Jesus, who died more than that, who was raised to life - is at the right hand of God and is also interceding for us."

Who will bring a charge against God's elect? No one will, because Christ is our advocate. Who will condemn us? No one will, because Christ, the One who died for us, is the one who condemns. We have both the advocate and judge as our Savior.   (c) Believers are born again (regenerated) when they believe (John 3:3; Titus 3:5). For a Christian to lose his salvation, he would have to be un-regenerated. The Bible gives no evidence that the new birth can be taken away. (d) The Holy Spirit indwells all believers (John 14:17; Romans 8:9) and baptizes all believers into the

Body of Christ (1 Corinthians 12:13). For a believer to become unsaved, he would have to be "un-indwelt" and detached from the Body of Christ. (e) John 3:15 states that whoever believes in Jesus Christ will "have eternal life."

If you believe in Christ today and have eternal life, but lose it tomorrow, then it was never "eternal" at all. Hence if you lose your salvation, the promises of eternal life in the Bible would be in error. (f) For the most conclusive argument, I think Scripture says it best itself, "For I am convinced that neither death nor life, neither angels nor demons, neither the present nor the future, nor any powers, neither height nor depth, nor anything else in all creation, will be able to separate us from the love of God that is in Christ Jesus our Lord" (Romans 8:38-39). Remember the same God who saved you is the same God who will keep you. Once we are saved we are always saved. Our salvation is most definitely eternally secure!

BestBibleScience.Org

WHY DID GOD ALLOW POLYGAMY IN THE BIBLE?

The question of polygamy is an interesting one in that most people today view polygamy as immoral while the Bible nowhere explicitly condemns it. The first instance of polygamy/bigamy in the Bible was that of Lamech in Genesis 4:19: "Lamech married two women."

Several prominent men in the Old Testament were polygamists. Abraham, Jacob, David, Solomon, and others all had multiple wives. In 2 Samuel 12:8, God, speaking through the prophet Nathan, said that if David's wives and concubines were not enough, He would have given David even more. Solomon had 700 wives and 300 concubines (essentially wives of a lower status), according to 1 Kings 11:3.

What are we to do with these instances of polygamy in the Old Testament? There are three questions that need to be answered:

1) Why did God allow polygamy in the Old Testament?
2) How does God view polygamy today?
3) Why did it change?
4) Why did God allow polygamy in the Old Testament?

The Bible does not specifically say why God allowed polygamy. As we speculate about God's silence, there are a few key factors to consider. First, while there are slightly more male babies than female babies, due to women having longer lifespans, there have always been more women in the world than men. Current statistics show that approximately 50.5 percent of the world population are women.

Assuming the same percentages in ancient times, and multiplied by millions of people, there would be tens of thousands more women than men. Second, warfare in ancient times was especially brutal, with an incredibly high rate of fatality. This would have resulted in an even greater percentage of women to men.

Third, due to patriarchal societies, it was nearly impossible for an unmarried woman to provide for herself. Women were often uneducated and untrained. Women relied on their fathers, brothers, and husbands for provision and protection. Unmarried women were often subjected to prostitution and slavery. The significant difference between the number of women and men would have left many, many women in an undesirable situation.

So, it seems that God may have allowed polygamy to protect and provide for the women who could not find a husband otherwise. A man would take multiple wives and serve as the provider and protector of all of them. While definitely not ideal, living in a polygamist household was far better than the alternatives: prostitution, slavery, or starvation.

In addition to the protection/provision factor, polygamy enabled a much faster expansion of humanity, fulfilling God's command to "be fruitful and increase in number; multiply on the earth" (Genesis 9:7). Men are capable of impregnating multiple women in the same time period, causing humanity to grow much faster than if each man was only producing one child each year.2)

How does God view polygamy today? Even while allowing polygamy, the Bible presents monogamy as the plan which conforms most closely to God's ideal for marriage. The

Bible says that God's original intention was for one man to be married to only one woman: "For this reason a man will leave his father and mother and be united to his wife [not wives], and they will become one flesh [not fleshes]" (Genesis 2:24). While Genesis 2:24 is describing what marriage is, rather than how many people are involved, the consistent use of the singular should be noted. In Deuteronomy 17:14-20; God says that the kings were not supposed to multiply wives (or horses or gold). While this cannot be interpreted as a command that the kings must be monogamous, it can be understood as declaring that having multiple wives causes problems. This can be clearly seen in the life of Solomon (1 Kings 11:3-4).

In the New Testament, 1 Timothy 3:2, 12 and Titus 1:6 give "the husband of one wife" in a list of qualifications for spiritual leadership. There is some debate as to what specifically this qualification means. The phrase could literally be translated "a one-woman man." Whether or not this phrase is referring exclusively to polygamy, in no sense can a polygamist be considered a "one-woman man."

While these qualifications are specifically for positions of spiritual leadership, they should apply equally to all Christians. Should not all Christians be "above reproach...temperate, self-controlled, respectable, hospitable, able to teach, not given to drunkenness, not violent but gentle, not quarrelsome, not a lover of money" (1 Timothy 3:2-4)? If we are called to be holy (1 Peter 1:16), and if these standards are holy for elders and deacons, then they are holy for all.

Ephesians 5:22-33 speaks of the relationship between husbands and wives. When referring to a husband (singular), it always also refers to a wife (singular). "For the husband is the head of the wife [singular] He who loves

his wife [singular] loves himself. For this reason a man will leave his father and mother and be united to his wife [singular], and the two will become one flesh....

Each one of you also must love his wife [singular] as he loves himself, and the wife [singular] must respect her husband [singular]." While a somewhat parallel passage, Colossians 3:18-19; refers to husbands and wives in the plural, it is clear that Paul is addressing all the husbands and wives among the Colossian believers, not stating that a husband might have multiple wives. In contrast, Ephesians 5:22-33 is specifically describing the marital relationship. If polygamy were allowable, the entire illustration of Christ's relationship with His body (the church) and the husband-wife relationship falls apart. 3) Why did it change? It is not so much God's disallowing something He previously allowed as it is God's restoring marriage to His original plan.

Even going back to Adam and Eve, polygamy was not God's original intent. God seems to have allowed polygamy to solve a problem, but it is not the ideal. In most modern societies, there is absolutely no need for polygamy. In most cultures today, women are able to provide for and protect themselves—removing the only "positive" aspect of polygamy. Further, most modern nations outlaw polygamy. According to Romans 13:1-7; we are to obey the laws the government establishes. The only instance in which disobeying the law is permitted by Scripture is if the law contradicts God's commands (Acts 5:29). Since God only allows for polygamy, and does not command it, a law prohibiting polygamy should be upheld.

Are there some instances in which the allowance for polygamy would still apply today? Perhaps, but it is unfathomable that there would be no other possible

solution. Due to the "one flesh" aspect of marriage, the need for oneness and harmony in marriage, and the lack of any real need for polygamy, it is our firm belief that polygamy does not honor God and is not His design for marriage.

BestBibleScience.Org

WHAT DOES THE BIBLE SAY ABOUT SEX BEFORE MARRIAGE?

There is no Hebrew or Greek word used in the Bible that precisely refers to sex before marriage. The Bible undeniably condemns adultery and sexual immorality, but is sex before marriage considered sexually immoral? According to 1 Corinthians 7:2, "yes" is the clear answer: "But since there is so much immorality, each man should have his own wife, and each woman her own husband." In this verse, Paul states that marriage is the "cure" for sexual immorality. First Corinthians 7:2 is essentially saying that, because people cannot control themselves and so many are having immoral sex outside of marriage, people should get married. Then they can fulfill their passions in a moral way.

Since 1 Corinthians 7:2 clearly includes sex before marriage in the definition of sexual immorality, all of the Bible verses that condemn sexual immorality as being sinful also condemn sex before marriage as sinful. Sex before marriage is included in the biblical definition of sexual immorality. There are numerous Scriptures that declare sex before marriage to be a sin (Acts 15:20; 1 Corinthians 5:1; 6:13, 18; 10:8; 2 Corinthians 12:21; Galatians 5:19; Ephesians 5:3; Colossians 3:5; 1 Thessalonians 4:3; Jude 7).

The Bible promotes complete abstinence before marriage. Sex between a husband and his wife is the only form of sexual relations of which God approves (Hebrews 13:4). Far too often we focus on the "recreation" aspect of sex without recognizing that there is another aspect—

procreation. Sex within marriage is pleasurable, and God designed it that way. God wants men and women to enjoy sexual activity within the confines of marriage. Song of Solomon and several other Bible passages (such as Proverbs 5:19) clearly describe the pleasure of sex. However, the couple must understand that God's intent for sex includes producing children.

Thus, for a couple to engage in sex before marriage is doubly wrong—they are enjoying pleasures not intended for them, and they are taking a chance of creating a human life outside of the family structure God intended for every child.

While practicality does not determine right from wrong, if the Bible's message on sex before marriage were obeyed, there would be far fewer sexually transmitted diseases, far fewer abortions, far fewer unwed mothers and unwanted pregnancies, and far fewer children growing up without both parents in their lives. Abstinence is God's only policy when it comes to sex before marriage. Abstinence saves lives, protects babies, gives sexual relations the proper value, and, most importantly, honors God.

BestBibleScience.Org

"WHAT SPEAKING IN TONGUES?

The first occurrence of speaking in tongues occurred on the day of Pentecost in Acts 2:1-4. The apostles went out and shared the gospel with the crowds, speaking to them in their own languages: "We hear them declaring the wonders of God in our own tongues!" (Acts 2:11). The Greek word translated tongues literally means "languages." Therefore, the gift of tongues is speaking in a language a person does not know in order to minister to someone who does speak that language.

In 1 Corinthians chapters 12–14, Paul discusses miraculous gifts, saying, "Now, brothers, if I come to you and speak in tongues, what good will I be to you, unless I bring you some revelation or knowledge or prophecy or word of instruction?" (1 Corinthians 14:6). According to the apostle Paul, and in agreement with the tongues described in Acts, speaking in tongues is valuable to the one hearing God's message in his or her own language, but it is useless to everyone else unless it is interpreted/translated.

A person with the gift of interpreting tongues (1 Corinthians 12:30) could understand what a tongues-speaker was saying even though he did not know the language that was being spoken. The tongues interpreter would then communicate the message of the tongues speaker to everyone else, so all could understand. "For this reason anyone who speaks in a tongue should pray that he may interpret what he says" (1 Corinthians 14:13). Paul's conclusion regarding tongues that were not interpreted is powerful: "But in the church I would rather speak five intelligible words to instruct others than ten thousand words in a tongue" (1 Corinthians 14:19).

Is the gift of tongues for today? First Corinthians 13:8 mentions the gift of tongues ceasing, although it connects the ceasing with the arrival of the "perfect" in 1 Corinthians 13:10. Some point to a difference in the tense of the Greek verbs referring to prophecy and knowledge "ceasing" and that of tongues "being ceased" as evidence for tongues ceasing before the arrival of the "perfect." While possible, this is not explicitly clear from the text. Some also point to passages such as Isaiah 28:11 and Joel 2:28-29 as evidence that speaking in tongues was a sign of God's oncoming judgment.

First Corinthians 14:22 describes tongues as a "sign to unbelievers." According to this argument, the gift of tongues was a warning to the Jews that God was going to judge Israel for rejecting Jesus Christ as Messiah. Therefore, when God did in fact judge Israel (with the destruction of Jerusalem by the Romans in A.D. 70), the gift of tongues would no longer serve its intended purpose. While this view is possible, the primary purpose of tongues being fulfilled does not necessarily demand its cessation. Scripture does not conclusively assert that the gift of speaking in tongues has ceased.

At the same time, if the gift of speaking in tongues were active in the church today, it would be performed in agreement with Scripture. It would be a real and intelligible language (1 Corinthians 14:10). It would be for the purpose of communicating God's Word with a person of another language (Acts 2:6-12). It would be in agreement with the command God gave through the apostle Paul, "If anyone speaks in a tongue, two—or at the most three—should speak, one at a time, and someone must interpret. If there is no interpreter, the speaker should keep quiet in the church and speak to himself and God" (1 Corinthians 14:27-28). It

would also be in accordance with 1 Corinthians 14:33, "For God is not the author of confusion, but of peace, as in all churches of the saints."

God most definitely can give a person the gift of speaking in tongues to enable him or her to communicate with a person who speaks another language. The Holy Spirit is sovereign in the dispersion of the spiritual gifts (1 Corinthians 12:11). Just imagine how much more productive missionaries could be if they did not have to go to language school, and were instantly able to speak to people in their own language.

However, God does not seem to be doing this. Tongues does not seem to occur today in the manner it did in the New Testament, despite the fact that it would be immensely useful. The vast majority of believers who claim to practice the gift of speaking in tongues do not do so in agreement with the Scriptures mentioned above. These facts lead to the conclusion that the gift of tongues has ceased or is at least a rarity in God's plan for the church today.

BestBibleScience.Org

WHAT DOES THE BIBLE SAY ABOUT SUICIDE?

The Bible mentions six specific people who committed suicide: Abimelech (Judges 9:54), Saul (1 Samuel 31:4), Saul's armor-bearer (1 Samuel 31:4-6), Ahithophel (2 Samuel 17:23), Zimri (1 Kings 16:18), and Judas (Matthew 27:5). Five of them were wicked, sinful men (not enough is said regarding Saul's armor-bearer to make a judgment as to his character).

Some consider Samson an instance of suicide (Judges 16:26-31), but Samson's goal was to kill the Philistines, not himself. The Bible views suicide as equal to murder, which is what it is—self-murder. God is the only one who is to decide when and how a person should die.

According to the Bible, suicide is not what determines whether a person gains entrance into heaven. If an unsaved person commits suicide, he has done nothing but "expedite" his journey to hell. However, that person who committed suicide will ultimately be in hell for rejecting salvation through Christ, not because he committed suicide.

What does the Bible say about a Christian who commits suicide? The Bible teaches that from the moment we truly believe in Christ, we are guaranteed eternal life (John 3:16). According to the Bible, Christians can know beyond any doubt that they possess eternal life (1 John 5:13). Nothing can separate a Christian from God's love (Romans 8:38-39).

If no "created thing" can separate a Christian from God's love, and even a Christian who commits suicide is a "created thing," then not even suicide can separate a

Christian from God's love. Jesus died for all of our sins, and if a true Christian, in a time of spiritual attack and weakness, commits suicide, that would still be a sin covered by the blood of Christ.

Suicide is still a serious sin against God. According to the Bible, suicide is murder; it is always wrong. Serious doubts should be raised about the genuineness of faith of anyone who claimed to be a Christian yet committed suicide. There is no circumstance that can justify someone, especially a Christian, taking his/her own life.

Christians are called to live their lives for God, and the decision on when to die is God's and God's alone. Although it is not describing suicide, 1 Corinthians 3:15 is probably a good description of what happens to a Christian who commits suicide: "He himself will be saved, but only as one escaping through the flames."

BestBibleScience.Org

WHAT DOES THE BIBLE SAY ABOUT TATTOOS AND BODY PIERCINGS?

The Old Testament law commanded the Israelites, "Do not cut your bodies for the dead or put tattoo marks on yourselves. I am the LORD" (Leviticus 19:28). So, even though believers today are not under the Old Testament law (Romans 10:4; Galatians 3:23-25; Ephesians 2:15), the fact that there was a command against tattoos should raise some questions. The New Testament does not say anything about whether or not a believer should get a tattoo.

In relation to tattoos and body piercings, a good test is to determine whether we can honestly, in good conscience, ask God to bless and use that particular activity for His own good purposes. "So whether you eat or drink or whatever you do, do it all for the glory of God" (1 Corinthians 10:31). The New Testament does not command against tattoos or body piercings, but it also does not give us any reason to believe God would have us get tattoos or body piercings.

An important scriptural principle on issues the Bible does not specifically address is if there is room for doubt whether it pleases God, then it is best not to engage in that activity. Romans 14:23 reminds us that anything that does not come from faith is sin. We need to remember that our bodies, as well as our souls, have been redeemed and belong to God. Although 1 Corinthians 6:19-20 does not directly apply to tattoos or body piercings, it does give us a principle: "Do you not know that your body is a temple of the Holy Spirit, who is in you, whom you have received from God?

You are not your own; you were bought at a price. Therefore honor God with your body." This great truth should have a real bearing on what we do and where we go with our bodies. If our bodies belong to God, we should make sure we have His clear "permission" before we "mark them up" with tattoos or body piercings.

BestBibleScience.Org

WHAT DOES THE BIBLE SAY ABOUT TITHING?

Many Christians struggle with the issue of tithing. In some churches tithing is over-emphasized. At the same time, many Christians refuse to submit to the biblical exhortations about making offerings to the Lord. Tithing/giving is intended to be a joy and a blessing. Sadly, that is sometimes not the case in the church today.

Tithing is an Old Testament concept. The tithe was a requirement of the law in which all Israelites were to give 10 percent of everything they earned and grew to the Tabernacle/Temple (Leviticus 27:30; Numbers 18:26; Deuteronomy 14:24; 2 Chronicles 31:5). In fact, the Old Testament Law required multiple tithes which would have pushed the total to around 23.3 percent, not the 10 percent which is generally considered the tithe amount today.

Some understand the Old Testament tithe as a method of taxation to provide for the needs of the priests and Levites in the sacrificial system. The New Testament nowhere commands, or even recommends, that Christians submit to a legalistic tithe system. Paul states that believers should set aside a portion of their income in order to support the church (1 Corinthians 16:1-2).   The New Testament nowhere designates a percentage of income a person should set aside, but only says it is to be "in keeping with income" (1 Corinthians 16:2).

Some in the Christian church have taken the 10 percent figure from the Old Testament tithe and applied it as a "recommended minimum" for Christians in their giving. The New Testament talks about the importance and

benefits of giving. We are to give as we are able. Sometimes that means giving more than 10 percent; sometimes that may mean giving less. It all depends on the ability of the Christian and the needs of the church. Every Christian should diligently pray and seek God's wisdom in the matter of participating in tithing and/or how much to give (James 1:5).

Above all, all tithes and offerings should be given with pure motives and an attitude of worship to God and service to the body of Christ. "Each man should give what he has decided in his heart to give, not reluctantly or under compulsion, for God loves a cheerful giver" (2 Corinthians 9:7).

BestBibleScience.Org

WHAT DOES THE BIBLE TEACH ABOUT THE TRINITY?

The most difficult thing about the Christian concept of the Trinity is that there is no way to perfectly and completely understand it. The Trinity is a concept that is impossible for any human being to fully understand, let alone explain. God is infinitely greater than we are; therefore, we should not expect to be able to fully understand Him. The Bible teaches that the Father is God, that Jesus is God, and that the Holy Spirit is God.

The Bible also teaches that there is only one God. Though we can understand some facts about the relationship of the different Persons of the Trinity to one another, ultimately, it is incomprehensible to the human mind. However, this does not mean the Trinity is not true or that it is not based on the teachings of the Bible.

The Trinity is one God existing in three Persons. Understand that this is not in any way suggesting three Gods. Keep in mind when studying this subject that the word "Trinity" is not found in Scripture. This is a term that is used to attempt to describe the triune God—three coexistent, co-eternal Persons who make up God. Of real importance is that the concept represented by the word "Trinity" does exist in Scripture.

The following is what God's Word says about the Trinity:
1) There is one God (Deuteronomy 6:4; 1 Corinthians 8:4; Galatians 3:20; 1 Timothy 2:5).   2) The Trinity consists of three Persons (Genesis 1:126, 3:22; 11:7; Isaiah 6:8; 48:16; 61:1; Matthew 3:16-17; 28:19; 2 Corinthians

13:14). In Genesis 1:1, the Hebrew plural noun "Elohim" is used. In Genesis 1:26; 3:22 11:7and Isaiah 6:8, the plural pronoun for "us" is used. The word "Elohim" and the pronoun "us" are plural forms, definitely referring in the Hebrew language to more than two.

While this is not an explicit argument for the Trinity, it does denote the aspect of plurality in God. The Hebrew word for "God," "Elohim," definitely allows for the Trinity.

In Isaiah 48:16 and 61:1, the Son is speaking while making reference to the Father and the Holy Spirit. Compare Isaiah 61:1 to Luke 4:14-19 to see that it is the Son speaking. Matthew 3:16-17 describes the event of Jesus' baptism. Seen in this passage is God the Holy Spirit descending on God the Son while God the Father proclaims His pleasure in the Son. Matthew 28:19 and 2 Corinthians 13:14 are examples of three distinct Persons in the Trinity. 3) The members of the Trinity are distinguished one from another in various passages.

In the Old Testament, "LORD" is distinguished from "Lord" (Genesis 19:24; Hosea 1:4). The LORD has a Son (Psalm 2:7, 12; Proverbs 30:2-4). The Spirit is distinguished from the "LORD" (Numbers 27:18) and from "God" (Psalm 51:10-12). God the Son is distinguished from God the Father (Psalm 45:6-7; Hebrews 1:8-9). In the New Testament, Jesus speaks to the Father about sending a Helper, the Holy Spirit (John 14:16-17). This shows that Jesus did not consider Himself to be the Father or the Holy Spirit. Consider also all the other times in the Gospels where Jesus speaks to the Father. Was He speaking to Himself? No. He spoke to another Person in the Trinity— the Father. 4) Each member of the Trinity is God. The Father is God (John 6:27; Romans 1:7; 1 Peter 1:2). The Son is God (John 1:1, 14; Romans 9:5; Colossians 2:9; Hebrews 1:8; 1 John 5:20). The Holy Spirit is God (Acts

5:3-4; 1 Corinthians 3:16). 5) There is subordination within the Trinity.

Scripture shows that the Holy Spirit is subordinate to the Father and the Son, and the Son is subordinate to the Father. This is an internal relationship and does not deny the deity of any Person of the Trinity. This is simply an area which our finite minds cannot understand concerning the infinite God. Concerning the Son see Luke 22:42, John 5:36, John 20:21, and 1 John 4:14. Concerning the Holy Spirit see John 14:16; 14:26; 15:26; 16:7; and especially John 16:13-14.   6) The individual members of the Trinity have different tasks. The Father is the ultimate source or cause of the universe (1 Corinthians 8:6; Revelation 4:11); divine revelation (Revelation 1:1); salvation (John 3:16-17); and Jesus' human works (John 5:17; 14:10). The Father initiates all of these things.

The Son is the agent through whom the Father does the following works: the creation and maintenance of the universe (1 Corinthians 8:6; John 1:3; Colossians 1:16-17); divine revelation (John 1:1; 16:12-15; Matthew 11:27; Revelation 1:1); and salvation (2 Corinthians 5:19; Matthew 1:21; John 4:42). The Father does all these things through the Son, who functions as His agent.

The Holy Spirit is the means by whom the Father does the following works: creation and maintenance of the universe (Genesis 1:2; Job 26:13; Psalm 104:30); divine revelation (John 16:12-15; Ephesians 3:5; 2 Peter 1:21); salvation (John 3:6; Titus 3:5; 1 Peter 1:2); and Jesus' works (Isaiah 61:1; Acts 10:38). Thus, the Father does all these things by the power of the Holy Spirit.

There have been many attempts to develop illustrations of the Trinity. However, none of the popular illustrations are

completely accurate. The egg (or apple) fails in that the shell, white, and yolk are parts of the egg, not the egg in themselves, just as the skin, flesh, and seeds of the apple are parts of it, not the apple itself. The Father, Son, and Holy Spirit are not parts of God; each of them is God. The water illustration is somewhat better, but it still fails to adequately describe the Trinity. Liquid, vapor, and ice are forms of water. The Father, Son, and Holy Spirit are not forms of God, each of them is God.

So, while these illustrations may give us a picture of the Trinity, the picture is not entirely accurate. An infinite God cannot be fully described by a finite illustration. The doctrine of the Trinity has been a divisive issue throughout the entire history of the Christian church. While the core aspects of the Trinity are clearly presented in God's Word, some of the side issues are not as explicitly clear. The Father is God, the Son is God, and the Holy Spirit is God—but there is only one God. That is the biblical doctrine of the Trinity. Beyond that, the issues are, to a certain extent, debatable and non-essential.

Rather than attempting to fully define the Trinity with our finite human minds, we would be better served by focusing on the fact of God's greatness and His infinitely higher nature. "Oh, the depth of the riches of the wisdom and knowledge of God! How unsearchable his judgments, and his paths beyond tracing out! Who has known the mind of the Lord? Or who has been his counselor?" (Romans 11:33-34).

BestBibleScience.Org

WHAT HAPPENS AFTER DEATH?

Within the Christian faith, there is a significant amount of confusion regarding what happens after death. Some hold that after death, everyone "sleeps" until the final judgment, after which everyone will be sent to heaven or hell. Others believe that at the moment of death, people are instantly judged and sent to their eternal destinations. Still others claim that when people die, their souls/spirits are sent to a "temporary" heaven or hell, to await the final resurrection, the final judgment, and then the finality of their eternal destination. So, what exactly does the Bible say happens after death?

First, for the believer in Jesus Christ, the Bible tells us that after death believers' souls/spirits are taken to heaven, because their sins are forgiven by having received Christ as Savior (John 3:16, 18, 36). For believers, death is to be "away from the body and at home with the Lord" (2 Corinthians 5:6-8; Philippians 1:23). However, passages such as 1 Corinthians 15:50-54 and 1 Thessalonians 4:13-17 describe believers being resurrected and given glorified bodies. If believers go to be with Christ immediately after death, what is the purpose of this resurrection?

It seems that while the souls/spirits of believers go to be with Christ immediately after death, the physical body remains in the grave "sleeping." At the resurrection of believers, the physical body is resurrected, glorified, and then reunited with the soul/spirit. This reunited and glorified body-soul-spirit will be the possession of believers for eternity in the new heavens and new earth (Revelation 21-22). Second, for those who do not receive

Jesus Christ as Savior, death means everlasting punishment.

However, similar to the destiny of believers, unbelievers also seem to be sent immediately to a temporary holding place, to await their final resurrection, judgment, and eternal destiny. Luke 16:22-23 describes a rich man being tormented immediately after death. Revelation 20:11-15 describes all the unbelieving dead being resurrected, judged at the great white throne, and then being cast into the lake of fire. Unbelievers, then, are not sent to hell (the lake of fire) immediately after death, but rather are in a temporary realm of judgment and condemnation. However, even though unbelievers are not instantly sent to the lake of fire, their immediate fate after death is not a pleasant one. The rich man cried out, "I am in agony in this fire" (Luke 16:24).

Therefore, after death, a person resides in a "temporary" heaven or hell. After this temporary realm, at the final resurrection, a person's eternal destiny will not change. The precise "location" of that eternal destiny is what changes. Believers will ultimately be granted entrance into the new heavens and new earth (Revelation 21:1). Unbelievers will ultimately be sent to the lake of fire (Revelation 20:11-15). These are the final, eternal destinations of all people— based entirely on whether or not they had trusted Jesus Christ alone for salvation (Matthew 25:46; John 3:36).

BestBibleScience.Org

WHERE WAS JESUS FOR THE THREE DAYS BETWEEN HIS DEATH AND RESURRECTION?

1 Peter 3:18-19 states, "For Christ died for sins once for all, the righteous for the unrighteous, to bring you to God. He was put to death in the body but made alive by the Spirit, through whom also he went and preached to the spirits in prison." The phrase, "by the Spirit," in verse 18 is exactly the same construction as the phrase, "in the flesh." So it seems best to relate the word "spirit" to the same realm as the word "flesh." The flesh and spirit are Christ's flesh and spirit. The words "made alive by (in) the spirit" point to the fact that Christ's sin-bearing and death brought about the separation of His human spirit from the Father (Matthew 27:46). The contrast is between flesh and spirit, as in Matthew 27:46 and Romans 1:3-4; and not between Christ's flesh and the Holy Spirit. When Christ's atonement for sin was completed, His spirit restored the fellowship which had been broken.

First Peter 3:18-22 describes a necessary link between Christ's suffering (verse 18) and His glorification (verse 22). Only Peter gives specific information about what happened between these two events. The word "preached" in verse 19 is not the usual word in the New Testament to describe the preaching of the gospel. It literally means to herald a message. Jesus suffered and died on the Cross, His body being put to death, and His spirit died when He was made sin. But His spirit was made alive and He yielded it to the Father. According to Peter, sometime between His

death and His resurrection Jesus made a special proclamation to "the spirits in prison."

To begin with, Peter referred to people as "souls" and not "spirits" (3:20). In the New Testament, the word "spirits" is used to describe angels or demons, not human beings, and verse 22 seems to bear out this meaning. Also, nowhere in the Bible are we told that Jesus visited hell. Acts 2:31 says that He went to "Hades" (New American Standard Bible), but "Hades" is not hell. The word "Hades" refers to the realm of the dead, a temporary place where they await the resurrection. Revelation 20:11-15 in the NASB or the New International Version give a clear distinction between the two. Hell is the permanent and final place of judgment for the lost. Hades is a temporary place.

Our Lord yielded His spirit to the Father, died, and at some time between death and resurrection, visited the realm of the dead where He delivered a message to spirit beings (probably fallen angels; see Jude 6) who were somehow related to the period before the flood in Noah's time.

Verse 20 makes this clear. Peter did not tell us what He proclaimed to these imprisoned spirits, but it could not be a message of redemption since angels cannot be saved (Hebrews 2:16). It was probably a declaration of victory over Satan and his hosts (1 Peter 3:22; Colossians 2:15). Ephesians 4:8-10 also seems to indicate that Christ went to "paradise" (Luke 16:20; 23:43) and took to heaven all those who had believed in Him prior to His death. The passage doesn't give a great amount of detail about what occurred, but most Bible scholars agree that this is what is meant by "led captivity captive."

So, all that to say, the Bible isn't entirely clear what exactly Christ did for the three days between His death and

resurrection. It does seem, though, that He was preaching victory over the fallen angels and/or unbelievers. What we can know for sure is that Jesus was not giving people a second chance for salvation. The Bible tells us that we face judgment after death (Hebrews 9:27), not a second chance. There isn't really any definitively clear answer for what Jesus was doing for the time between His death and resurrection. Perhaps this is one of the mysteries we will understand once we reach glory.

BestBibleScience.Org

WHAT DOES THE BIBLE SAY ABOUT WOMEN IN MINISTRY?

There is perhaps no more hotly debated issue in the church today than the issue of women serving as pastors/preachers. As a result, it is very important to not see this issue as men versus women. There are women who believe women should not serve as pastors and that the Bible places restrictions on the ministry of women, and there are men who believe women can serve as preachers and that there are no restrictions on women in ministry. This is not an issue of chauvinism or discrimination. It is an issue of biblical interpretation.

The Word of God proclaims, "A woman should learn in quietness and full submission. I do not permit a woman to teach or to have authority over a man; she must be silent" (1 Timothy 2:11-12). In the church, God assigns different roles to men and women. This is a result of the way mankind was created and the way in which sin entered the world (1 Timothy 2:13-14). God, through the apostle Paul, restricts women from serving in roles of teaching and/or having spiritual authority over men. This precludes women from serving as pastors over men, which definitely includes preaching to, teaching, and having spiritual authority.

There are many "objections" to this view of women in ministry. A common one is that Paul restricts women from teaching because in the first century, women were typically uneducated. However, 1 Timothy 2:11-14 nowhere mentions educational status. If education were a qualification for ministry, the majority of Jesus' disciples would not have been qualified. A second common

objection is that Paul only restricted the women of Ephesus from teaching (1 Timothy was written to Timothy, who was the pastor of the church in Ephesus). The city of Ephesus was known for its temple to Artemis, a false Greek/Roman goddess. Women were the authority in the worship of Artemis. However, the book of 1 Timothy nowhere mentions Artemis, nor does Paul mention Artemis worship as a reason for the restrictions in 1 Timothy 2:11-12.

A third common objection is that Paul is only referring to husbands and wives, not men and women in general. The Greek words in the passage could refer to husbands and wives; however, the basic meaning of the words refers to men and women. Further, the same Greek words are used in verses 8-10. Are only husbands to lift up holy hands in prayer without anger and disputing (verse 8)? Are only wives to dress modestly, have good deeds, and worship God (verses 9-10)? Of course not. Verses 8-10 clearly refer to all men and women, not only husbands and wives. There is nothing in the context that would indicate a switch to husbands and wives in verses 11-14.

Yet another frequent objection to this interpretation of women in ministry is in relation to women who held positions of leadership in the Bible, specifically Miriam, Deborah, and Huldah in the Old Testament. This objection fails to note some significant factors. First, Deborah was the only female judge among 13 male judges. Huldah was the only female prophet among dozens of male prophets mentioned in the Bible. Miriam's only connection to leadership was being the sister of Moses and Aaron.

The two most prominent women in the times of the Kings were Athaliah and Jezebel—hardly examples of godly female leadership. Most significantly, though, the authority

of women in the Old Testament is not relevant to the issue. The book of 1 Timothy and the other Pastoral Epistles present a new paradigm for the church—the body of Christ—and that paradigm involves the authority structure for the church, not for the nation of Israel or any other Old Testament entity.

Similar arguments are made using Priscilla and Phoebe in the New Testament. In Acts 18, Priscilla and Aquila are presented as faithful ministers for Christ. Priscilla's name is mentioned first, perhaps indicating that she was more "prominent" in ministry than her husband. However, Priscilla is nowhere described as participating in a ministry activity that is in contradiction to 1 Timothy 2:11-14. Priscilla and Aquila brought Apollos into their home and they both discipled him, explaining the Word of God to him more accurately (Acts 18:26).

In Romans 16:1, even if Phoebe is considered a "deaconess" instead of a "servant," that does not indicate that Phoebe was a teacher in the church. "Able to teach" is given as a qualification for elders, but not deacons (1 Timothy 3:1-13; Titus 1:6-9). Elders/bishops/deacons are described as the "husband of one wife," "a man whose children believe," and "men worthy of respect." Clearly the indication is that these qualifications refer to men. In addition, in 1 Timothy 3:1-13 and Titus 1:6-9; masculine pronouns are used exclusively to refer to elders/bishops/deacons.

The structure of 1 Timothy 2:11-14 makes the "reason" perfectly clear. Verse 13 begins with "for" and gives the "cause" of Paul's statement in verses 11-12. Why should women not teach or have authority over men? Because "Adam was created first, then Eve. And Adam was not the one deceived; it was the woman who was deceived." God

created Adam first and then created Eve to be a "helper" for Adam. This order of creation has universal application in the family (Ephesians 5:22-33) and the church.

The fact that Eve was deceived is also given as a reason for women not serving as pastors or having spiritual authority over men. This leads some to believe that women should not teach because they are more easily deceived. That concept is debatable, but if women are more easily deceived, why should they be allowed to teach children (who are easily deceived) and other women (who are supposedly more easily deceived)? That is not what the text says. Women are not to teach men or have spiritual authority over men because Eve was deceived. As a result, God has given men the primary teaching authority in the church. Many women excel in gifts of hospitality, mercy, teaching, evangelism, and helps. Much of the ministry of the local church depends on women. Women in the church are not restricted from public praying or prophesying (1 Corinthians 11:5), only from having spiritual teaching authority over men. The Bible nowhere restricts women from exercising the gifts of the Holy Spirit (1 Corinthians 12). Women, just as much as men, are called to minister to others, to demonstrate the fruit of the Spirit (Galatians 5:22-23), and to proclaim the gospel to the lost (Matthew 28:18-20; Acts 1:8; 1 Peter 3:15).

God has ordained that only men are to serve in positions of spiritual teaching authority in the church. This is not because men are necessarily better teachers, or because women are inferior or less intelligent (which is not the case). It is simply the way God designed the church to function. Men are to set the example in spiritual leadership—in their lives and through their words. Women are to take a less authoritative role. Women are encouraged to teach other women (Titus 2:3-5).

The Bible also does not restrict women from teaching children. The only activity women are restricted from is teaching or having spiritual authority over men. This logically would preclude women from serving as pastors to men. This does not make women less important, by any means, but rather gives them a ministry focus more in agreement with God's plan and His gifting of them.

BestBibleScience.Org

WHAT DOES THE BIBLE SAY ABOUT DRINKING ALCOHOL?

Scripture has much to say regarding the drinking of alcohol (Leviticus 10:9; Numbers 6:3; Deuteronomy 29:6; Judges 13:4, 7, 14; Proverbs 20:1; 31:4; Isaiah 5:1122, 24:9; 28:7; 29:9; 56:12). However, Scripture does not necessarily forbid a Christian from drinking beer, wine, or any other drink containing alcohol. In fact, some Scriptures discuss alcohol in positive terms. Ecclesiastes 9:7 instructs, "Drink your wine with a merry heart." Psalm 104:14-15 states that God gives wine "that makes glad the heart of men." Amos 9:14 discusses drinking wine from your own vineyard as a sign of God's blessing. Isaiah 55:1 encourages, "Yes, come buy wine and milk…"

What God commands Christians regarding alcohol is to avoid drunkenness (Ephesians 5:18). The Bible condemns drunkenness and its effects (Proverbs 23:29-35). Christians are also commanded to not allow their bodies to be "mastered" by anything (1 Corinthians 6:12; 2 Peter 2:19). Drinking alcohol in excess is undeniably addictive. Scripture also forbids a Christian from doing anything that might offend other Christians or encourage them to sin against their conscience (1 Corinthians 8:9-13). In light of these principles, it would be extremely difficult for any Christian to say he is drinking alcohol in excess to the glory of God (1 Corinthians 10:31).

Jesus changed water into wine. It even seems that Jesus drank wine on occasion (John 2:1-11; Matthew 26:29). In New Testament times, the water was not very clean. Without modern sanitation, the water was often filled with

bacteria, viruses, and all kinds of contaminants. The same is true in many third-world countries today. As a result, people often drank wine (or grape juice) because it was far less likely to be contaminated. In 1 Timothy 5:23, Paul was instructing Timothy to stop drinking the water (which was probably causing his stomach problems) and instead drink wine. In that day, wine was fermented (containing alcohol), but not necessarily to the degree it is today. It is incorrect to say that it was grape juice, but it is also incorrect to say that it was the same thing as the wine commonly used today.

Again, Scripture does not forbid Christians from drinking beer, wine, or any other drink containing alcohol. Alcohol is not, in and of itself, tainted by sin. It is drunkenness and addiction to alcohol that a Christian must absolutely refrain from (Ephesians 5:18; 1 Corinthians 6:12).

Alcohol, consumed in small quantities, is neither harmful nor addictive. In fact, some doctors advocate drinking small amounts of red wine for its health benefits, especially for the heart. Consumption of small quantities of alcohol is a matter of Christian freedom.

Drunkenness and addiction are sin. However, due to the biblical concerns regarding alcohol and its effects, due to the easy temptation to consume alcohol in excess, and due to the possibility of causing offense and/or stumbling of others, it is usually best for a Christian to abstain entirely from drinking alcohol.

BestBibleScience.Org

DO ANIMALS GO TO HEAVEN? DO THEY HAVE SOULS?

The Bible does not give any explicit teaching on whether pets/animals have "souls" or whether pets/animals will be in heaven. However, we can use general biblical principles to develop some clarity on the subject. The Bible states that both man (Genesis 2:7) and animals (Genesis 1:30; 6:17; 7:15, 22) have the breath of life.

The primary difference between human beings and animals is that humanity is made in the image and likeness of God (Genesis 1:26-27), while animals are not. Being made in the image and likeness of God means that human beings are like God, capable of spirituality, with mind, emotion, and will, and they have a part of their being that continues after death. If pets/animals do have a "soul" or immaterial aspect, it must therefore be of a different and lesser "quality." This difference possibly means that pet/animal "souls" do not continue in existence after death.

Another factor to consider is that animals are a part of God's creative process in Genesis. God created the animals and said they were good (Genesis 1:25). Therefore, there is no reason why there could not be animals on the new earth (Revelation 21:1). There will most definitely be animals during the millennial kingdom (Isaiah 11:6; 65:25). It is impossible to say definitively whether some of these animals might be the pets we had while here on earth. We do know that God is just and that when we get to heaven we will find ourselves in complete agreement with His decision on this issue, whatever it may be.

WHAT IS THE IMPORTANCE OF CHRISTIAN BAPTISM?

Christian baptism is, according to the Bible, an outward testimony of what has occurred inwardly in a believer's life. Christian baptism illustrates a believer's identification with Christ's death, burial, and resurrection.

The Bible declares, "Or don't you know that all of us who were baptized into Christ Jesus were baptized into his death? We were therefore buried with Him through baptism into death in order that, just as Christ was raised from the dead through the glory of the Father, we too may live a new life" (Romans 6:3-4). In Christian baptism, the action of being immersed in the water symbolizes dying and being buried with Christ. The action of coming out of the water pictures Christ's resurrection.

In Christian baptism, there are two requirements before a person is baptized: 1) the person being baptized must have trusted in Jesus Christ as Savior, and 2) the person must understand what baptism signifies. If a person knows the Lord Jesus as Savior, understands that Christian baptism is a step of obedience in publicly proclaiming his faith in Christ, and desires to be baptized, then there is no reason to prevent the believer from being baptized.

According to the Bible, Christian baptism is important because it is a step of obedience—publicly declaring faith in Christ and commitment to Him—an identification with Christ's death, burial, and resurrection.

BestBibleScience.Org

FUNNY QUOTES

"Sometimes I lie awake at night, and I ask, 'Where have I gone wrong?' Then a voice says to me, 'This is going to take more than one night."
Charlie Brown

"God heals and the doctor takes the fee.
Benjamin Franklin

If you want to make God laugh, tell him your future plans."
Woody Allen

"I believe there is something out there watching over us. Unfortunately, it's the government."
Woody Allen

"You can safely assume that you've created God in your own image when it turns out that God hates all the same people you do."
Anne Lamott

"When I was young, I said to God, 'God, tell me the mystery of the universe.' But God answered, 'That knowledge is for me alone. 'So I said, 'God, tell me the mystery of the peanut.' Then God said, 'Well George, that's more nearly your size.' And he told me."
George Washington Carver

"And God said, 'Let there be light' and there was light, but the Electricity Board said he would have to wait until Thursday to be connected."
Unknown

"One with God is a majority."
Billy Graham

"Had I been present at the creation, I would have given some useful hints for the better ordering of the universe."
Alphonso

"I have never made but one prayer to God, a very short one: 'O Lord, make my enemies ridiculous.' And God granted it."
Voltaire

"To surrender to ignorance and call it God has always been pre- mature, and it remains premature today."
Issac Asimov

"Before God we are all equally wise—and equally foolish."
Albert Einstein

"In the first place God made idiots; that was for practice; then he made school boards."
Mark Twain

"If I'm on the course and lightning starts, I get inside fast. If God wants to play through, let him."
Bob Hope

"Why attack God? He may be as miserable as we are."
Erik Satie

They say God has existed from the beginning of time and will exist beyond the end of time. Can you imagine trying to sit through his home movies?"
Scott Roeben

"God is a comedian playing to an audience too afraid to laugh."
Unknown

"I am convinced that He (God) does not play dice."
Albert Einstein

"If God has cable, we are the 24-hour doofus network."
Unknown

I hear Glenn Hoddle has found God. That must have been one hell of a pass."
Bob Davies

"God writes a lot of comedy... the trouble is, he's stuck with so many bad actors who don't know how to play funny."
Garrison Keillor

"Is man one of God's blunders or is God one of man's blunders."
Friedrich Nietzsche

"As the post said, 'Only God can make a tree,' probably because it's so hard to figure out how to get the bark on."
Woody Allen

"God don't make no mistakes. That's how He got to be God." *Archie Bunker*

"It was God who made me so beautiful. If I weren't, then I'd be a teacher."
Linda Evangelista

"I'm Jewish. I don't work out. If God had wanted us to bend over, He would have put diamonds on the floor."
Joan Rivers

"I don't pray because I don't want to bore God."
Orson Welles

IN THE BEGINNING

In the beginning God created the heavens and the Earth. And the Earth was without form, and void, and darkness was upon the face of the deep.

And Satan said, "It doesn't get any better than this."

And God said, "Let there be light," and there was light.

And God said, "Let the earth bring forth grass, the herb yielding seed, and the fruit tree yielding fruit," and God saw that it was good.

And Satan said, "There goes the neighborhood."

And God said, "Let us make Man in our image, after our likeness, and let them have dominion over the fish of the sea, and over the fowl of the air and over the cattle, and over all the Earth, and over every creeping thing that creepeth upon the Earth."

And so God created Man in his own image; male and female created he them. And God looked upon Man and Woman and saw that they were lean and fit.

And Satan said, "I know how I can get back in this game."

And God populated the earth with broccoli and cauliflower and spinach, green and yellow vegetables of all kinds, so Man and Woman would live long and healthy lives.

And Satan created McDonald's. And McDonald's brought forth the 99-centdouble cheeseburger.

And Satan said to Man, "You want fries with that?"

And Man said, "Supersize them." And Man gained 5 pounds.

And God created the healthful yoghurt, that woman might keep her figure that man found so fair.

And Satan brought forth chocolate. And Woman gained 5 pounds. And God said, "Try my crispy fresh salad."

And Satan brought forth Ben and Jerry's. And Woman gained 10 pounds.

And God said, "I have sent thee heart-healthy vegetables and olive oil with which to cook them."

And Satan brought forth chicken-fried steak so big it needed its own platter.

And Man gained 10 pounds and his bad cholesterol went through the roof.

And God brought forth running shoes and Man resolved to lose those extra pounds.

And Satan brought forth cable TV with remote control so Man would not have to toil to change channels between ESPN and ESPN2.

And Man gained another 20 pounds.

And God said, "You're running up the score, Devil." And God brought forth the potato, a vegetable naturally low in fat and brimming with nutrition.

And Satan peeled off the healthful skin and sliced the starchy center into chips and deep-fat fried them. And he created sour cream dip also.

And Man clutched his remote control and ate the potato chips swaddled in cholesterol. And Satan saw and said, "It is good."

And Man went into cardiac arrest.

And God sighed and created quadruple bypass surgery.

And Satan created HMO's.

GOSPEL OF JUDAS

A 62-page codex, dated to the third or fourth century and written in the Sahidic dialect of Coptic, was found in the Egyptian desert in the 1970's. It was passed around for several years and eventually sold and acquired by *National Geographic* in 2001. After four years of restoration and translation, the "Gospel of Judas" was revealed in a much-hyped *National Geographic Channel* special on Palm Sunday, April 9, 2006. The "gospel" reported an interesting twist on the events surrounding the crucifixion of Jesus of Nazareth. Judas Iscariot, instead of being the evil one controlled by Satan, who betrayed Jesus for 30 pieces of silver, is portrayed as the obedient one who did Jesus' bidding by turning Jesus into the Sanhedrin, the council of Jewish leaders. Reportedly, Jesus wanted to escape from his human body and return to the spiritual realm by being executed. So, Jesus conspired with Judas and ordered him to betray Him, so that the Old Testament prophecies might be fulfilled. According to the "Gospel of Judas", Judas was actually the hero of the world!

The timing of the release
The timing of the *National Geographic* special with the beginning of Christianity's Holy Week was not by accident. What better way to hype their anti-Christian message then run their "Gospel of Judas" special on the high Christian holiday of Palm Sunday. This technique has been used previously to attempt to discredit Christianity's founder at a time of the year when popular interest focuses on His death and resurrection.

Does the dating make it a "gospel"?
The "Gospel of Judas" manuscript was carbon dated at 220-340 A.D. In addition the ink was analyzed, confirming

the radiocarbon date of the manuscript. However early the date, it is still at least two centuries after the actual events. In contrast, the biblical manuscripts date as early as 125 A.D., with most scholars agreeing they were all written in the first century. However, *National Geographic*-hired scholars claimed that the manuscript found represents a translation of an earlier second century Greek document. However, there is no physical evidence to back up this belief. There is circumstantial evidence for the existence of "Christian" Gnostic writings from the writings of leaders early Christian church, such as Irenaeus, who wrote *Against Heresies* in 180 A.D These Christian leaders strongly denounced the Gnostic writings, which were attempting to cash in on the growing popularity of Christianity, as factually untrue and heretical in their theology.

Promotion of the *National Geographic* program and book ignores such evidence and makes claims that are obviously untrue. For example, their website claims the gospel of Judas comes from "the earliest days of Christianity":

"Dramatic recreations portray and clarify the complex story of intrigue and politics of the earliest days of Christianity, and reveal the contents of the Gospel itself."

There is no way that writings, optimistically be assigned to a period at least 150 years after the ministry and death of Jesus, can be called "the earliest days of Christianity." Even the title, "gospel", given to the manuscript, is misleading, since all the truly Christian gospels were written by eyewitnesses to the events in the first century (with the possible except of Luke, who composed his gospel by interviewing eyewitnesses). Such obvious bias by the *National Geographic* demonstrates their desire to smear Christianity and make a buck in the process.

Who wrote the "Gospel of Judas"?

Obviously, since the "Gospel of Judas" cannot be attributed to Judas Iscariot, because its earliest possible dating is late second century, it must have been written by someone else. The content of the document tells us exactly who wrote the "Gospel of Judas" and for what purpose. Besides the question of whose idea the betrayal of Jesus was, the manuscript clearly presents a Gnostic distortion of fundamental Christian and Judaic theology. Gnosticism combined Greek mythology with Christian theology and Far East religions. According to Gnostic "Christianity", the self-generated one was the goddess Barbelo, who created the goddess Sophia, a virgin deity who gave birth to god Jehovah (Yahweh), who created the Earth and became the god of the Hebrews. In Gnostic theology, he was portrayed as being jealous, uncompassionate, and likely to commit genocide.

The Gnostics believed that they were given special hidden, knowledge that was given only to them. In accordance with this idea, the "Gospel of Judas" indicates that Jesus revealed this special knowledge only to Judas Iscariot: "Knowing that Judas was reflecting upon something that was exalted, Jesus said to him: 'Step away from the others and I shall tell you the mysteries of the kingdom.'"
An excerpt from the "Gospel of Judas" reveals how the Gnostic deities were created:

"A great angel, the enlightened divine Self-Generated, emerged from the cloud. Because of him, four other angels came into being from another cloud, and they became attendants for the angelic Self-Generated. The Self-Generated said, 'Let [...] come into being [...] and it came into being. And he created the first luminary to reign over him. He said, 'Let angels come into being to serve him, and

myriads without number came into being.' He said, 'let an enlightened aeon come into being,' and he came into being. He created the second luminary to reign over him, together with myriads of angels without number, to offer service. That is how he created the rest of the enlightened aeons. He made them reign over them...The multitude of those immortals is called the cosmos—that is, perdition—by the Father of the seven-two luminaries who are with the Self-Generated and his seventy-two aeons. In him the first human appeared with his incorruptible powers. And the aeon that appeared with his generation, the aeon in whom are the cloud of knowledge and the angel, is called [...] after that [...] said, 'Let twelve angels come into being to rule over chaos and the underworld.' And look, from he cloud there appeared an angel whose face flashed with fire and whose appearance was defiled with blood. His name was Nabro, which means rebel. Others call him Yaldabaoth. Another angel, Saklas, also came from the cloud. So Nabro created six angels—as well as Saklas—to be assistants, and these produced twelve angels in the heavens, with each one receiving a portion in the heavens."

Gnosticism's roots in Greek mythology and philosophy are evident in their belief in multiple minor deities (called "aeons" in the example above). The idea that there are multiple gods and goddesses is abhorrent to Christianity and also Judaism, from which it was derived. Since all the apostles of Jesus were Jewish, it is clear that the "Gospel of Judas" was not written by a real disciple of Jesus.

Conclusion
The "Gospel of Judas" and similar Gnostic texts were rejected by the early Christian Church not because of their unfavorable portrayal of Jesus of Nazareth, but because Church leaders knew they were not written by the original disciples, but fabricated much later by splinter groups, who

incorporated heretical teachings and false historical claims into those documents. The content of the "Gospel of Judas" clearly indicates that its origin derives from second or third century Gnostic teachings, which incorporate both Greek mythology and Far East philosophy in an attempt to hijack Christianity's rising popularity. The theology in the "Gospel of Judas" is polytheistic, which is why it was labeled as heretical by early church leaders. Such aberrant theology was clearly outside the mainstream of both Christianity and Old Testament writings. The fact that the *National Geographic* promoted the "Gospel of Judas" manuscript as an authentic early Christian document testifies to their unscholarly attempt to discredit Jesus of Nazareth as worthy of worship.

GodandScience.Org

YOUR TIME IS NOT UP YET!

A middle-aged woman had a heart attack and was taken to the hospital. While on the operating table, she had a near death experience. Seeing God, she asked "Is my time up?"

God said, "No, you have another 43 years, 2 months, and 8 days to live."

Upon recovery, the woman decided to stay in the hospital and have a facelift, liposuction, and a tummy tuck. She even had someone come in and change her hair color. Since she had so much more time to live, she figured she might as well make the most of it.

After her last operation, she was released from the hospital. While crossing the street on her way home, she was killed by an ambulance.

Arriving in front of God, she demanded, "I thought you said I had another 40 years? Why didn't you pull me from out of the path of the ambulance?"

God replied, "I didn't recognize you!"

FALSE TEACHINGS AND CONTRADICTIONS IN THE BIBLE?

Atheists claim that the Bible teaches many false things about the nature of our world - things that have been disproved by science. Others claim that the Bible contradicts itself. This page is a somewhat random collection of such allegations and their rebuttals. Most of the "false teachings" are based upon selected translations of the Bible (atheists love to use the KJV, since the archaic language had different meanings in the past) that are often taken out of context.

The Earth is flat
Many atheists claim that the Bible says that the earth is flat. Specific examples are seldom given - for good reason - they don't exist. The word "flat" occurs only a few times in the Bible, none of which is associated with the Earth. Synonyms, such as level, plain, plane, even, or horizontal are never used in reference to the entire Earth, but only to specific geographic areas. In addition, the Bible indicates in several places that the earth is a sphere suspended in space, with day and night existing. If a flat earth were a doctrine of the Bible, it would have to rank as one of the most obscure.

The Earth is covered by a dome
Atheists claim that the firmament (KJV) or expanse (NASB, NIV) was a solid dome in which the stars and sun were placed. However, the Hebrew word, *raqia*, translated "firmament" is definitely not a solid structure, as indicated in Genesis 1:20, since birds cannot fly through solid material. The only verse in which the word "dome" is used

is an obscure verse from the book of Amos, only in the NASB translation. The Hebrew word in question is *aguddah*, meaning a band:- band(1), bands(1), bunch(1). The other translations use the word "foundation" (NIV) and troop" (KJV). A Hebrew colleague indicated that the word refers to human beings (His gathering).

1. He who builds his lofty palace in the heavens and sets its foundation [aguddah] on the earth, who calls for the waters of the sea and pours them out over the face of the land-- the LORD is his name. (*Amos 9:6, NIV*)

- It is he that buildeth his stories in the heaven, and hath founded his troop [aguddah] in the earth; he that calleth for the waters of the sea, and poureth them out upon the face of the earth: The LORD is his name. (*Amos 9:6, KJV*)

- He builds His chambers (layers) in the heavens and established His beings (gathering) [aguddah] on earth. (*Amos 9:6*)

Here are the other three verses in which the word *aguddah* appears:

- "And you shall take a bunch [*aguddah*] of hyssop and dip it in the blood which is in the basin, and apply some of the blood that is in the basin to the lintel and the two doorposts; and none of you shall go outside the door of his house until morning." (*Exodus 12:22*)

- And the sons of Benjamin gathered together behind Abner and became one band [*aguddah*], and they stood on the top of a certain hill. (*2 Samuel 2:25*)

- "Is this not the fast which I choose, To loosen the bonds of wickedness, To undo the bands [*aguddah*] of the

yoke, And to let the oppressed go free, And break every yoke?" (*Isaiah 58:6*)

It is obvious that the NASB translation of Amos 9:6 is off base. This example is typical of the kind of objections raised by atheists. Their MO is to find an unusual translation (usually found in only one translation) and use this as "proof" that the Bible is inaccurate.

Another example given for the claim that the Bible teaches there is a dome that holds the stars comes from the book of Job:

"Can you, with Him, spread out the skies, Strong as a molten mirror?" (*Job 37:18*)

Out of context, it seems like an open and shut case that the Bible teaches that the skies are solid. What the atheists don't want to tell you is who was talking (Elihu, one of Job's "friends") and what was God's response to these teachings. In fact, in the next chapter, God answers Job's "friends" teachings with this comment:

"Who is this that darkens counsel By words without knowledge?" (*Job 38:2*)

In other words, God tells Job that his friends don't know what they are talking about. So much for the claim that the Bible endorses the idea that the skies are a solid dome. Since God Himself answered Job in the next 5 chapters, atheists would have a valid point if they found an error in any of those chapters. However, you won't find any complaints about the content of chapters 38-42. In fact, chapter 38 accurately establishes the initial conditions of the earth (covered with a thick layer of clouds):

"Where were you when I laid the foundation of the earth? When I made a cloud its garment And thick darkness its swaddling band" (*Job 38:4, 9*)

For more information, please see The Bible Teaches That the Heavens Were a Solid Dome, Embedded with Stars?

Stars were created in the sky
Related to the dome question is where the Bible says God created the Sun, moon, and stars. Here is what the Bible says:

God made the two great lights, the greater light to govern the day, and the lesser light to govern the night; He made the stars also. God placed them in the **expanse** of the **heavens** to give light on the earth, (*Genesis 1:16-17, NASBNASB*) God made two great lights--the greater light to govern the day and the lesser light to govern the night. He also made the stars. God set them in the **expanse** of the **sky** to give light on the earth, (*Genesis 1:16-17, NIV*) And God made two great lights; the greater light to rule the day, and the lesser light to rule the night: he made the stars also. And God set them in the **firmament** of the **heaven** to give light upon the earth, (*Genesis 1:16-17, KJV*)
One word is "expanse" (or "firmament" in the KJV) which is the Hebrew word "râqîya". The other two English words are "sky" and "heaven" (or "heavens"). In the Hebrew, these words are actually the same. There is no specific word that differentiates "sky" from "heaven," since they are all the same Hebrew word, "shâmayim." Essentially, it was the translators choice whether to use the word "sky" or "heaven." So, there is no differentiation whether the stars were created in the sky or heaven. Secondly, God defines the râqîya as being equal to the shâmayim:

God called the expanse [râqîya] heaven [shâmayim]. And there was evening and there was morning, a second day. (Genesis 1:8)

So, contrary to the claim, the Bible does not say that the sun, moon and stars were created in the sky or atmosphere.

Heaven consists of water
Atheists claim that the Hebrews thought that heaven (Hebrew word is *shamayin*) consisted of water. However, the word *shamayin* occurs 39 times in conjunction with birds flying through *shamayin* (no, these verses are not referring to diving water fowl!). Obviously, *shamayin* means more than heaven, and often refers to the atmosphere, or sky. One needs to be careful in looking at the context to determine the true English meaning.

The Earth was created from water
A verse from 2 Peter makes the statement that "the earth was formed out of water and by water." In reading the English translation, one would think that the verse states that planet Earth was created from water. Let us look at the verse 2 Peter 3:5 from the context in which it appears:

For when they maintain this, it escapes their notice that by the word of God the heavens existed long ago and the earth was formed out of water and by water, through which the world at that time was destroyed, being flooded with water. But the present heavens and earth by His word are being reserved for fire, kept for the day of judgment and destruction of ungodly men. (*2 Peter 3:5-7*)

This chapter is talking about judgment. It is clear from the context the Greek word, *gay*, translated "earth" in the NASB is better translated as "land," "soil" or "ground," since this verse refers to this same "earth" being destroyed

in the judgment of mankind at the flood. It is obvious that the planet earth was not destroyed by water, but the land was covered with water. The Greek word, *sunistaymi*, is only in this instance translated "formed" and is, in every other instance, translated "to commend" or "to establish" and does not have the meaning "create." This verse is an obvious reference to the formation of continents mentioned in Genesis 1:9-10.9 Therefore, the concept of the earth being created out of water is supported by neither the context of the verse nor the original language. It is obvious that the NASB translation of 2 Peter 3:5 is a very misleading and a poor rendering of the original. Although the meaning of the original language of this verse is clear, a lack of understanding of science allowed scholars to translate the verse into something that makes no sense scientifically.

Hell is under the Earth
Atheist claim that the Bible says that Hell is under the Earth. The Greek word for hell, *genna*, occurs only 11 times in the Bible, none of which refer to a place under the Earth. In fact, all the references to under the Earth refer to either Sheol (Hebrew) or its Greek equivalent (Hades), both of which refer to the grave, which *is* under the Earth. Obviously, all people end up in the grave at death. Here are the verses commonly cited:

"The LORD kills and makes alive; He brings down to Sheol and raises up. (*1 Samuel 2:6*) (refers to death and resurrection)

that at the name of Jesus EVERY KNEE SHOULD BOW, of those who are in heaven, and on earth, and under the earth, (*Philippians 2:10*) (at Jesus' second coming all will acknowledge Him, the Angels, those still alive, and those in the grave.)

Here is a list of all verses that refer to Hell:

- "But I say to you that everyone who is angry with his brother shall be guilty before the court; and whoever shall say to his brother, 'Raca,' shall be guilty before the supreme court; and whoever shall say, 'You fool,' shall be guilty *enough to go* into the fiery hell." (*Matthew 5:22*)

- "And if your right eye makes you stumble, tear it out, and throw it from you; for it is better for you that one of the parts of your body perish, than for your whole body to be thrown into hell." (*Matthew 5:29*)

- "And if your right hand makes you stumble, cut it off, and throw it from you; for it is better for you that one of the parts of your body perish, than for your whole body to go into hell." (*Matthew 5:30*)

- "And do not fear those who kill the body, but are unable to kill the soul; but rather fear Him who is able to destroy both soul and body in hell." (*Matthew 10:28*)

- "And if your eye causes you to stumble, pluck it out, and throw it from you. It is better for you to enter life with one eye, than having two eyes, to be cast into the fiery hell." (*Matthew 18:9*)

- "Woe to you, scribes and Pharisees, hypocrites, because you travel about on sea and land to make one proselyte; and when he becomes one, you make him twice as much a son of hell as yourselves." (*Matthew 23:15*)

- "You serpents, you brood of vipers, how shall you escape the sentence of hell?" (*Matthew 23:33*)

- "And if your hand causes you to stumble, cut it off; it is

better for you to enter life crippled, than having your two hands, to go into hell, into the unquenchable fire," (*Mark 9:43*)

- "And if your foot causes you to stumble, cut it off; it is better for you to enter life lame, than having your two feet, to be cast into hell," (*Mark 9:45*)

- "And if your eye causes you to stumble, cast it out; it is better for you to enter the kingdom of God with one eye, than having two eyes, to be cast into hell," (*Mark 9:47*)

- "But I will warn you whom to fear: fear the One who after He has killed has authority to cast into hell; yes, I tell you, fear Him!" (*Luke 12:5*)

- And the tongue is a fire, the *very* world of iniquity; the tongue is set among our members as that which defiles the entire body, and sets on fire the course of *our* life, and is set on fire by hell. (*James 3:6*)

As noted before, none of these verses says that Hell is under the Earth. In fact, the Bible says that the Earth will be destroyed[10] and that Hades (or the grave) will be thrown into Hell (Lake of Fire). It would be rather difficult for Hell to be thrown into itself, or for Hades to be thrown into the Earth when the Earth was already destroyed.

John would not die before Christ returned
Atheists claim that there are false prophesies in the Bible, such as the one that predicts that the early saints would be there for Christ's glorious (2nd) coming, and that John would not taste death. This is the specific prophecy that they are referring to:

"Truly I say to you, there are some of those who are standing here who shall not taste death until they see the Son of Man coming in His kingdom." (*Matthew 16:28*)

This prophecy was actually fulfilled in its entirety in the late first century. If you read the book of Revelation, you will see that John, the apostle to whom the prophecy was directed, saw Jesus coming in His glory to establish His kingdom. This is what the entire book of revelation describes - the second coming of Jesus Christ. John saw it all in a vision, as it will happen. The prophecy was fulfilled! The prophecy does not say that John would not die before Christ returned. It said that he would not die before *seeing* the return of Jesus Christ. What is awesome about the vision reported by John is that he did not understand what he was seeing, but reported it as he saw it. As such, he includes descriptions of a giant meteor collision with the earth, battles with mechanized machines that sound like tanks, and huge armies (200,000,000 men), which would not even be possible until at least the 20th century.

Stars cannot fall on the Earth
Atheist claim that the Bible describes an impossible event - the falling of stars onto the Earth. Revelation 6:13-14 is talking about an event yet to come, and as such cannot be proven or disproved from science. In fact the book indicates that the events are *not* natural, but supernatural.

To say that they describe something that is not naturally possible is to state what the book already tells us. Revelation is the book of the Bible, which the apostle John received in a vision. As in many visions given to men by God, the receiver was not always able to explain or understand exactly what he saw. The description of the events are those as *perceived* by John. The Greek word,

astayr, besides being translated "star" can also have the meaning "comet," "meteor" or "asteroid", since there is no Greek word having this meaning. Even our English language refers to meteorites as "falling stars."

The description of the "star" Wormwood seems to be that of a large meteorite or comet.[13] The impact of one or a number of large meteorites on the earth will have the effect of a several thousand to hundreds of thousands megaton or larger nuclear explosions. It would appear to the observer that the sky was split apart by the large amount of ejecta thrown into the atmosphere. This interpretation makes sense from the description by John. An article in *Scientific American* (August, 1995, page 86) described the result of a collision of a large meteor with the earth:

"Sixty-five million years ago an object somewhat larger than Haley's comet slammed into what is now the coast of Mexico's Yucatan peninsula. The impact gouged a crater 170 kilometers across and launched debris world-wide. As the multitude of tiny ballistic missiles fell beck to earth, meteors filled the sky, and the atmosphere became red-hot. Fires erupted over the earth's surface, but the global inferno was soon followed by persistent darkness."

This seems to be the scenario described in Revelation and by Peter, who stated that this world will be judged by fire. The impact of a comet would specifically address the issue of the poisoning of the waters as nitric acid rain poured down near the comet's impact.

First rainbow did not appear until the flood
Atheists claim that God did not create the first rainbow until the flood, implying that the laws concerning the refraction of light were not in effect until then. However,

the Bible does not make this statement at all. Here are the relevant verses:

And God said, "This is the sign of the covenant I am making between me and you and every living creature with you, a covenant for all generations to come: I have set my rainbow in the clouds, and it will be the sign of the covenant between me and the earth." (*Genesis 9:12-13*)

The Hebrew states that the setting of the rainbow in the clouds was something accomplished in the past (notice the English translation. "I *have* set"). Nowhere does the Bible state that this was the first time a rainbow was visible on the earth.

Fire consumes wet wood, stones, and dust and licks up water
This is a reference to the "contest" between Elijah and the prophets of Baal. Here is the relevant verse:

Then the fire of the LORD fell, and consumed the burnt offering and the wood and the stones and the dust, and licked up the water that was in the trench. (*1 Kings 18:38*)
Presumably, no fire could be hot enough to burn wet wood, stone, and dust. However, the verse makes it clear that this is no ordinary fire. The fire was called for by a prayer from Elijah, and answered by the Creator of the universe. Obviously, if God exists, He would be capable of creating a fire hot enough to burn wet wood, and stones and evaporate water.

The earth is square and has four corners
There are some verses in the Bible that suggest (from the English translations) that the earth has four corners. An example is from Isaiah:

And He will lift up a standard for the nations, And will assemble the banished ones of Israel, And will gather the dispersed of Judah from the four corners of the earth. (*Isaiah 11:12, NASBNASB*)

Actually, what these four "corners" refer to are the points of the compass - north, south, east, and west. In reality, the Hebrew word has nothing to do with corners at all. In fact, the word *kanaph* refers to the wing or extremity of birds. The word is translated as a form of "wing" in nearly every instance. It is also used to refer to the wing of an army. However, it would sound rather strange to refer to the wings of the earth, so the English translators used the word "corners." Some of the newer translations use the word "quarters."[17] It certainly has nothing to do with squares, but refers to the uttermost parts of the earth. By the way, this prophecy was fulfilled in 1948 with the establishment of the nation of Israel following nearly 2,000 years of dispersion. Jews from literally the uttermost parts of the earth were reunited in that new nation.

The earth can be turned upside down scattering the inhabitants
This is a typical example of the deceptive atheists practice of taking verses from archaic English translations (KJV) and making conclusions that are completely unsupported. Here is the verse from the KJV translation:

Behold, the LORD maketh the earth empty, and maketh it waste, and turneth it upside down, and scattereth abroad the inhabitants thereof. (*Isaiah 24:1, KJV*)

Of course, the other English translations are never cited for this verse, since they obviously do not show that the Bible is errant:

Behold, the LORD lays the earth waste, devastates it, distorts its surface, and scatters its inhabitants. (*Isaiah 24:1, NASBNASB*)

The Hebrew verb used in this verse is avah, which means to "bend" or "twist" or "distort." The noun to which it refers is panim, which is most often translated face, in this instance referring to the face (or surface) of the earth. The verse seems to be an obvious reference to earthquakes. It has nothing to do with turning the earth upside down.

Plants created before the sun?
Sun was created "in the beginning". The Bible says, "In the beginning God created the heavens and the earth." The Hebrew construction "heavens and the earth" refer to the entire created universe. The light of the Sun first fell on the surface of the earth on the first "day," since the Bible describes day and night on the first "day" (*Genesis 1:2-3*). In contrast, the plants were not created until the third "day." For more information, see Day-Age Genesis One Interpretation.

The sun orbits the earth
Atheists claim that the Bible teaches geocentrism, the idea that earth is the center of the universe and that everything orbits around it. One example given is the long day of Joshua, where the sun stood still to provide more daylight. The Bible says that Joshua prayed to God and God performed a miracle. The text makes it clear that Sun "stopped in the middle of the sky". We still use phrases like the "Sun rose", "Sun set". There is no English (or Hebrew) phrase indicating that the earth rotates until the horizon covers the Sun.

Rabbits chew the cud

The Bible does say that rabbits chew the cud. As most people know, ruminant animals eat their food, swallow it, then regurgitate it and chew it a second time. This process is called "chewing the cud." Rabbits don't regurgitate their food, but they do eat it a second time. The process is called "coprophagy." The rabbit sends its food through the intestines, then produces soft fecal pellets at night that it eats. Because the process resembles that of ruminants, it has been called pseudorumination.

Insects have four legs

There are several verses that are translated in our English Bibles to imply that insects have four legs. In reality, the Hebrew word *sherets*, translated as "insect" is not nearly as specific as the term "insect" would imply. The word really refers to crawling or swimming creatures that tend to swarm together. For example, in Genesis, *sherets* refers to swarming sea creatures, in the flood account (Genesis 7) *sherets* refers to rodents, and in Leviticus, *sherets* refers to crustaceans, insects, rodents, and reptiles. The term *sherets* was never intended as a biological classification system, so to say that it specifically refers to "insects" is deceptive.

What is common among all the creatures mentioned is that they have short legs and often travel together in groups. In fact, the Bible defines *sherets* as "crawling on its belly" and "whatever walks on all fours." What is common in this group of crustaceans, insects, rodents, and reptiles is that they all crawl on "all four" legs. Some from this group actually have more than four legs. However, the Hebrew idiom "on all fours" refers to any creature that crawls low to the ground on *at least* four legs. Were the writers of the Bible unaware that insects have six legs? This statement would seem rather silly, but atheists actually make this

claim. However, one of the verses clearly indicates that these "four-legged" insects have six legs:
'Yet these you may eat among all the winged insects [*sherets*] which walk on all fours: those which have above their feet jointed legs with which to jump on the earth. (*Leviticus 11:21*)

The key part of the verse is the phrase "above their feet jointed legs." The Hebrew uses two different words to describe the "feet" (*regel*) and "legs" (*kera*). What the verse says is that these insects walk on four "feet" (their anterior four short legs), with an additional two "legs" that are used for jumping. Therefore, all six appendages are described.

Snakes, donkeys can talk
Critics of the Bible claim that it says that a snake came to Eve and had a conversation with her to tempt her to eat the forbidden fruit.   However, the Bible describes that this "snake" was none other than Satan, who, being an angel, took on the form of an animal. As such, this event is clearly a description of a supernatural, rather than a naturalistic event. Another example is when a donkey talked to Balaam. However, the passage clearly states that it was God who caused the donkey to talk.   This, likewise was a supernatural event.

Striped sticks cause livestock to become genetically altered
In the story of Jacob, Laban, his father-in-law, cheated him out of his pledged wife. Jacob had offered to work for Laban seven years to be married to Rachel. However, on the wedding night, Laban switched daughters and gave him Leah. In the light of the next day, Jacob discovered the switch, but Laban would not offer Jacob Rachel as his wife unless he agreed to work another seven years for him. After the second seven years were completed, Jacob asked to be

allowed to leave, but Laban did not want him to leave, since Jacob had greatly increased Laban's flocks and herds. Laban offered Jacob to take some of his animals, so Jacob chose the black, spotted, and striped ones for himself. Jacob separate the spotted and striped animals and kept them separated from Laban's flocks. Jacob believed that by putting striped rods in front of where the animals mated that more striped and spotted animals would be born. Atheists claim that the Bible says that doing this would actually produce more animals that have altered genetics. However, what they fail to mention is that the Bible clearly states in the verses following that the reason for the increase of striped and spotted animals is due to a miracle from God:

"Then the angel of God said to me in the dream, 'Jacob,' and I said, 'Here I am.' "And he said, 'Lift up, now, your eyes and see that all the male goats which are mating are striped, speckled, and mottled; for I have seen all that Laban has been doing to you. 'I am the God of Bethel, where you anointed a pillar, where you made a vow to Me; now arise, leave this land, and return to the land of your birth.'" (*Genesis 31:11-13*)

God caused the animals to have altered genetics, although Jacob thought that it was due to his little trick of putting the striped rods in front of where the animals mated. As such, this is an example of a supernatural rather than a naturalistic event.

Stephen contradicts Moses on the death of Terah
According to atheists:
Acts 7:4--Stephen tells us that Abraham departed from Haran "after his father died." Had he studied the Book of Genesis (11:26,32; 12:4), he would have realized his error: Abraham departed from Haran at age 75, at a time when his

father Terah was 145; since Terah lived for 205 years, he still had another 60 years of life remaining.

However, what does Genesis really say about Abraham and Terah?

After Terah had lived 70 years, he became the father of Abram, Nahor and Haran. (*Genesis 11:26*)

Unless he had triplets, all three of these sons were *not* born when Terah was 70 years old. One cannot assume from the order in the text that this was the order in which the sons were born. The text tells us that Haran became the father of Lot, but died before Terah died. It is possible, maybe even likely that Haran was the oldest son, and was born when Terah was 70 years old. What you do notice is that the order of sons in Genesis 11:26 is given by order of importance, with Abram being first and Nahor second with Haran third.40 However, in discussing the sons, Haran is discussed first (Genesis 11:27-28), indicating that he was, most likely, the firstborn. Nahor and Abram could have been born after Haran, maybe even 60 years after Haran was born. This would solve any kind of contradiction.

Did Jesse have seven or eight sons?
1 Chronicles says that David was the seventh son of Jesse, whereas 1 Samuel says that Jesse paraded the first seven of his sons in front of Samuel, with David still in the fields (making eight sons). It appears to be a direct contradiction - but is it?

Here is the list from 1 Chronicles:
and Jesse became the father of Eliab his first-born, then Abinadab the second, Shimea the third, (1 Chronicles 2:13)

Nethanel the fourth, Raddai the fifth, (1 Chronicles 2:14)

Ozem the sixth, David the seventh; (1 Chronicles 2:15)

Here is the list from 1 Samuel:
And he said, "In peace; I have come to sacrifice to the LORD. Consecrate yourselves and come with me to the sacrifice." He also consecrated Jesse and his sons, and invited them to the sacrifice. (1 Samuel 16:5)

Then it came about when they entered, that he looked at Eliab and thought, "Surely the LORD'S anointed is before Him." (1 Samuel 16:6)

But the LORD said to Samuel, "Do not look at his appearance or at the height of his stature, because I have rejected him; for God *sees* not as man sees, for man looks at the outward appearance, but the LORD looks at the heart." (1 Samuel 16:7)

Then Jesse called Abinadab, and made him pass before Samuel. And he said, "Neither has the LORD chosen this one." (1 Samuel 16:8)

Next Jesse made Shammah pass by. And he said, "Neither has the LORD chosen this one." (1 Samuel 16:9)
Thus Jesse made seven of his sons pass before Samuel. But Samuel said to Jesse, "The LORD has not chosen these." (1 Samuel 16:10)

And the three older sons of Jesse had gone after Saul to the battle. And the names of his three sons who went to the battle were Eliab the first-born, and the second to him Abinadab, and the third Shammah. (1 Samuel 17:13)

It seems that there is a discrepancy between 1 Chronicles and 1 Samuel. In 1 Chronicles, the third son is "Shimea,"

whereas in 1 Samuel it is "Shammah." These are different Hebrew words that have different origins, so they seem to represent two different sons. 1 Samuel gives only the first three sons of Jesse (Eliab, Abinadab, and Shammah). The 1 Chronicles account gives the 4th-6th sons, none of which appear anywhere else in scripture. So, if we add up all the names that we have, we end up with 8 sons. It seems that one of JesseÃ-s sons (Shammah) shown to Samuel at Bethlehem might have died while young and without posterity.

Thus, at one time David was the youngest of **eight** sons (at the time of 1 Samuel), and at another time he was the youngest of **seven** sons (after the death of Shammah). If we keep in mind that Hebrew genealogies often included only the names of those who have some significance for future generations, it makes sense that Shammah would have been left out of the later genealogy in 1 Chronicles.

False Prophecy by Joshua?
There are a number of prophecies that remain unfulfilled. For example, God's promise to Abraham that his descendants would possess the land between the Euphrates and Nile Rivers has not yet occurred (Genesis 15:18-21). However, not every prophecy in the Bible has been fulfilled in the past. Revelation suggests that this Genesis prophecy (along with Joshua prophecy41) will not be fulfilled until the Millennial kingdom rule of Christ.

Shortly before the Israelites entered Canaan, God instructed Israel, through Moses, concerning the conquering of these territories, as related in Deuteronomy 20:16-18:

However, in the cities of the nations the LORD your God is giving you as an inheritance, do not leave alive anything that breathes. Completely destroy them the Hittites,

Amorites, Canaanites, Perizzites, Hivites and Jebusites as the LORD your God has commanded you. Otherwise, they will teach you to follow all the detestable things they do in worshiping their gods, and you will sin against the LORD your God. (Deuteronomy 20:16-18)

Yes, God was going to drive the other people groups out, but it was the responsibility of the people to follow God's instructions. Joshua began by destroying certain peoples, but did not continue with the destruction of Jebusites, Canaanites and the Amorites listed in Genesis 15:18-21, Deuteronomy 20:16-18, and Joshua 3:9-10. If Joshua had followed the instructions completely, the prophecy would have been fulfilled in his lifetime. Instead, the latter part of the prophecy, "they will teach you to follow all the detestable things," was fulfilled in the days of Israel's kings.

Egypt, an uninhabited wasteland for forty years?
Ezekiel 29 is clearly a future prophecy. The reason why they don't continue the prophecy beyond chapter 29 is that three verses later it says that all this will happen in the day of the Lord, which is still in the future:

The word of the LORD came to me: "Son of man, prophesy and say: 'This is what the Sovereign LORD says: "'Wail and say, "Alas for that day! For the day is near, the day of the LORD is near a day of clouds, a time of doom for the nations. A sword will come against Egypt, and anguish will come upon Cush. When the slain fall in Egypt, her wealth will be carried away and her foundations torn down." (Ezekiel 30:4)

GodandScience.Org

GARDEN OF EDEN

Adam was walking around the Garden of Eden feeling very lonely, so
God asked Adam, "What is wrong with you?"

Adam said, "I don't have anyone to talk to."

God said, "I will give you a companion and it will be a woman." He said, "This person will cook for you and wash your clothes, she will always agree with every decision you make, she will bear your children and never ask you to get up in the middle of the night to take care of them.

"She will not nag," God continued, "and will always be the first to admit she was wrong. When you've had a disagreement, she will never have a headache and will freely give you love and passion whenever needed."

Adam asked God, "What will a woman like this cost?"

God said, "An arm and a leg!"

Adam said, "What can I get for just a rib?"

AND THE REST IS HISTORY.

E-MAIL

It's wise to remember how easily this wonderful technology can be misused, sometimes unintentionally, with serious consequences.

Consider the case of the Illinois man who left the snow-filled streets of Chicago for a vacation in Florida. His wife was on a business trip and was planning to meet him there the next day.

When he reached his hotel, he decided to send his wife a quick e-mail. Unable to find the scrap of paper on which he had written her e-mail address, he did his best to type it in from memory.

Unfortunately, he missed one letter, and his note was directed instead to an elderly preacher's wife, whose husband had passed away only the day before. When the grieving widow checked her e-mail, she took one look at the monitor, let out a piercing scream, and fell to the floor in a dead faint.

At the sound, her family rushed into the room and saw this note on the screen:

Dearest Wife,

Just got checked in. Everything prepared for your arrival tomorrow.

PS. Sure is hot down here.

THE ATHEIST, A BEAR AND GOD

An atheist was walking through the woods, admiring all that the "accidents" that evolution had created.

"What majestic trees! What powerful rivers! What beautiful animals!" he said to himself.

As he was walking alongside the river he heard a rustling in the bushes behind him. Turning to look, he saw a 7-foot grizzly bear charge towards him.

He ran as fast as he could up the path. He looked over his shoulder and saw the grizzly was closing.

Somehow, he ran even faster, so scared that tears came to his eyes. He looked again and the bear was even closer.

His heart was pounding and he tried to run faster. He tripped and fell to the ground. He rolled over to pick himself up but the bear was right over him, reaching for him with its left paw and raising its right paw strike him.

At that instant the atheist cried, "Oh my God...!"

Time stopped. The bear froze. The forest was silent. Even the river stopped moving.

As a bright light shone upon the man, a voice came out of the sky, "You deny my existence for all these years, teach others that I don't exist and even credit creation to a cosmic accident. Do you expect me to help you out of this predicament? Am I to count you as a believer?"

The atheist looked directly into the light, "It would be hypocritical to ask to be religious after all these years, but perhaps you could make the bear religious?"

"Very well" said the voice.

The light went out. The river ran. The sounds of the forest resumed.

…and then the bear dropped his right paw, brought both paws together and bowed its head and spoke: "Lord, for this food which I am about to receive, I am truly thankful..."

GOD'S KIDS

Whenever your children are out of control, you can take comfort from the thought that even God's omnipotence did not extend to His own children.

After creating heaven and earth, God created Adam and Eve.
The first thing he said was, "Don't."

"Don't what?" Adam replied.

"Don't eat the forbidden fruit," God said.

"Forbidden fruit? We have forbidden fruit?
Hey, Eve...we have forbidden fruit!"

"No way!"

"Yes, way!"

"Do NOT eat the fruit!" said God.

"Why?"

"Because I am your Father and I said so!" God replied, wondering why he stopped creation after making the elephants.

A few minutes later, God saw his children having an apple break and he was ticked! "Didn't I tell you not to eat the fruit?"
God, as our first parent, asked.

"Uh huh," Adam replied.

"Then why did you?" said the Father.

"I don't know," said Eve.

"She started it!" Adam said.

"Did not!"

"Did too!"

"DID NOT!"

Having had it with the two of them, God's punishment was that Adam and Eve should have children of their own.

Thus, the pattern was set and it has never changed! But there is reassurance in this story. If you have persistently and lovingly tried to give children wisdom and they haven't taken it, don't be hard on yourself. If God had trouble raising children, what made you think it would be a piece of cake for you?

CHILDREN'S MORNING PRAYERS

1.

Now I awake and see the light;
Lord, Thou hast kept me through the night.
To Thee I lift my voice and pray
That Thou wilt keep me through the day.
If I should die before 'tis done,
O God, accept me through Thy Son!
Amen.

2.

The morning bright
With rosy light
Has waked me from my sleep;
Father, I own
Thy love alone
Thy little one doth keep.

All through the day,
I humbly pray,
Be Thou my Guard and Guide;
My sins forgive
And let me live,
Blest Jesus, near Thy side. Amen.

3.

Now I raise me up from sleep,
I thank the Lord who did me keep,
All through the night; and to Him pray
That He may keep me through the day.
All which for Jesus' sake, I say.
Amen.

4.

O help me, Lord, this day to be
Thy own dear child and follow Thee;
And lead me, Savior, by Thy hand
Until I reach the heavenly land.
Amen.

5.

O Lord, my God, to Thee pray
While from my bed I rise
That all I do and all I say
Be pleasing to Thine eyes. Amen.

6.

Jesus, Lord, to Thee I pray,
Guide and guard me through this day.
As the shepherd tends his sheep.
Lord, me safe from evil keep.
Keep my feet from every snare,
Keep me with Thy watchful care.

All my little wants supply
If I live or if I die.
And when life, O Lord, is past,
Take me to Thyself at last. Amen.

7.

In the early morning,
With the sun's first rays.
All God's little children
Thank and pray and praise.

I, too, thanks would offer,
Jesus, Shepherd dear,
For Thy tender pasture,
For Thy guiding care.

And I would implore Thee,
Be with me this day,
Lest I from Thee wander,
Into danger stray. Amen.

8.

For this new morning with its light,
For rest and shelter of the night,
For health and food, for love and friends.
For everything Thy goodness sends,

We thank Thee, dearest Lord. Amen.

9.
I thank Thee, Lord, for sleep and rest,
For all the things that I love best,
Now guide me through another day
And bless my work and bless my play.
Lord, make me strong for noble ends,
Protect and bless my loving friends;
Of all mankind good Christians make.
All this I ask for Jesus' sake. Amen.

10.
Jesus, gentle Shepherd,
Bless Thy lamb to-day;
Keep in Thy footsteps,
Never let me stray.
Guard me through the daytime.
Every hour, I pray;
Keep my feet from straying
From the narrow way. Amen.

11.
Keep my little tongue to-day,
Keep it gentle while I play;
Keep my hands from doing wrong.
Keep my feet the whole day long;
Keep me all, O Jesus mild,
Keep me ever Thy dear child. Amen.

12.
Jesus, keep me all this day.
When at school and when at play;
May I do all things I ought,
May I hate each evil thought;
Help me love and trust in Thee
Now and through eternity. Amen.

13.
O blessed Lord, protect Thou me
And my dear parents graciously;
With Thy strong arm be ever near
To brothers and to sisters dear.
And all our loved ones in the land,
Protect them with Thine own right hand.

From sin defend and keep me free;
Help me a Christlike child to be.
Amen.

14.
My Father, for another night
Of quiet sleep and rest.
For all the joys of morning light,
Thy holy name be blest. Amen.

15.
Now with the new-born day I give
Myself anew to Thee,
That as Thou willest, I may live,
And what Thou willest, be. Amen.

16.
Lord, for the mercies of this night
My humble thanks I pay
And unto Thee I give myself
To-day and every day. Amen.

17.
Whate'er I do, things great or small
Whate'er I speak or frame.
Thy glory may I seek in all,
Do all in Jesus' name.

My Father, for His sake I pray.
Thy child accept and bless
And lead me by Thy grace to-day
In paths of righteousness. Amen.

18.
I thank Thee, my heavenly Father,
through Jesus Christ, Thy dear Son,
that Thou hast kept me this night
from all harm and danger; and I pray
Thee that Thou wouldst keep me this
day also from sin and every evil, that
all my doings and life may please
Thee. For into Thy hands I commend
myself, my body and soul, and all
things. Let Thy holy angel lie with
me, that the wicked Foe may have no
power over me. Amen.

Evening Prayers.

19.

Savior, lay Thy hand on me,
Bless me, and remember me. Amen.

20.

Now I lay me down to sleep;
I pray Thee, Lord, my soul to keep.
If I should die before I wake.
I pray Thee, Lord, my soul to take;
And this I ask for Jesus' sake. Amen.

21.

Dear Father in heaven,
Look down from above;
Bless papa and mama,
And those whom I love.

May angels guard over
My slumbers, and when
The morning is breaking,
Awake me. Amen.

22.

Now the light has gone away;
Savior, listen while I pray.
Asking Thee to watch and keep
And to send me quiet sleep.

Jesus, Savior, wash away
All that has been wrong to-day;
Help me every day to be
Good and gentle, more like Thee.

Let my near and dear ones be
Always near and dear to Thee.
O bring me and all I love
To Thy happy home above. Amen.

23.

In my little bed I lie:
Heavenly Father, hear my cry;
Lord, keep Thou me through this
night.
Bring me safe to morning light.
Amen.

24.

The day is past and over,
All thanks, O Lord, to Thee!
O Jesus, keep me in Thy sight
And save me through the coming
night.
Amen.

25.

The day is done;
O God the Son,
Look down upon
Thy little one!

O Light of Light,
Keep me this night,
And shed round me
Thy presence bright.

I need not fear
If Thou art near;
Thou art my Savior
Kind and dear. Amen.

26.

Forgive, O Lord, for Thy dear Son
The ill that I this day have done.
That with the world, myself, and
Thee
I, ere I sleep, at peace may be. Amen.

27.

Watch o'er a little child to-night,
Blest Savior from above,
And keep me till the morning light
Within Thine arms of love. Amen.

28.

Jesus, tender Shepherd, hear me:
Bless Thy little child to-night;
Through the darkness be Thou near
me,
Keep me safe till morning light.

All this day Thy hand has led me,
And I thank Thee for Thy care;
Thou hast warmed me, clothed me,
fed me;
Listen to my evening prayer.

May my sins be all forgiven;
Bless the friends I love so well;
Take me, Lord, at last to heaven.
Happy there with Thee to dwell.
Amen.

29.
Lord, send me sleep that I may live;
The wrongs I've done this day
forgive.
Bless every deed and thought and
word
I've rightly done, or said, or heard.
Bless relatives and friends alway;
Teach all the world to watch and
pray.
My thanks for all my blessings take
And hear my prayer for Jesus' sake.
Amen.

30.
Abide with me! Fast falls the
eventide,
The darkness deepens; Lord, with me
abide!
When other helpers fail and comforts
flee,
Help of the helpless, O abide with
me! Amen.

31.
At the close of every day,
Lord, to Thee I kneel and pray.
Look upon Thy little child,
Look in love and mercy mild.
O forgive and wash away
All my naughtiness this day,
And both when I sleep and wake
Bless me for my Savior's sake.
Amen.

32.
Lord, I have passed another day
And come to thank Thee for Thy
care.
Forgive my faults in work or play
And listen to my evening prayer.
Thy favor gives me daily bread
And friends, who all my wants

supply:
And safely now I rest my head,
Preserved and guarded by Thine eye.
Amen.

33.
All praise to Thee, my God, this night
For all the blessings of the light:
Keep me, O keep me, King of kings,
Beneath Thine own almighty wings.
Amen.

34.
I fall asleep in Jesus' wounds,
There pardon for my sins abounds;
Yea, Jesus' blood and righteousness
My jewels are, my glorious dress,
Wherein before my God I'll stand
When I shall reach the heavenly land.
Amen.

35.
The toils of day are over;
I lift my heart to Thee
And ask that free from peril
The hours of night may be.
O Jesus, make their darkness light
And guard me through the coming
night. Amen.

36.
O Lord God, I pray Thee, for Christ's
sake, forgive me whatsoever I have
done wrong this day and keep me
safe all the night while I am asleep.
Amen.

37.
I thank Thee, my heavenly Father,
through Jesus Christ, Thy dear Son,
that Thou hast graciously kept me
this day; and I pray Thee that Thou
wouldst forgive me all my sins where
I have done wrong, and graciously
keep me this night. For into Thy
hands I commend myself, my body
and soul, and all things. Let Thy holy
angel be with me, that the wicked

Foe may have no power over me.
Amen.

Table Prayers.
Before Meals.
38.
Abba, Jesus! Amen.

39.
Abba, Father, bless this food
For our everlasting good. Amen.

40.
Come, Lord Jesus, be our Guest
And let Thy gifts to us be blest.
Amen.

41.
O Bread of Life, from day to day
Be Thou our Comfort, Food, and
Stay.
Amen.

42.
Be present at our table, Lord,
Be here and everywhere adored.
Thy creatures bless and grant that we
May feast in paradise with Thee.
Amen.

43.
Great God, Thou Giver of all good,
Accept our praise and bless our food.
Grace, health, and strength to us
afford
Through Jesus Christ, our blessed
Lord.
Amen.

44.
Jesus, bless what Thou hast given,
Feed our souls with bread from
heaven;
Guide and lead us all the way
In all that we may do and say. Amen.

45.
Lord God, heavenly Father, bless us
and these Thy gifts which we receive
from Thy bountiful goodness,
through Jesus Christ, our Lord.
Amen.

46.
The eyes of all wait upon Thee, O
Lord, and Thou givest them their
meat in due season: Thou openest
Thine hand and satisfiest the desire of
every living thing. Amen.

47.
Grant us Thy grace, O Lord, that,
whether we eat or drink, or
whatsoever we do, we may do it all in
Thy name and to Thy glory. Amen.

After Meals.
48.
Thanks, Lord Jesus! Amen.

49.
Thanks be unto Thee, O God! Amen.

50.
The Lord is my Shepherd, I shall not
want. Amen.

51.
We thank the Lord
For meat and drink
Through Jesus Christ. Amen.

52.
We thank Thee, dear Lord Jesus.
That Thou our Guest hast been;
O be Thou with us ever
And save us from all sin. Amen.

53.
We thank Thee for those gifts, O
Lord;
Pray feed our souls, too, with Thy
Word.
Amen.

54.
O give thanks unto the Lord, for He is good; for His mercy endureth forever. Amen.

55.
Bless the Lord, O my soul; and all that is within me bless His holy name. Bless the Lord, O my soul, and forget not all His benefits. Amen.

56.
Heavenly Father, accept our thanks for this and for all Thy blessings, through Jesus Christ. Amen.

57.
O God, who givest unto all their food, make us thankful and provide for all the needy, now and evermore. Amen.

58.
Accept, O Lord, our thankful praises
For all Thy goodness did bestow;
May it increase our faith and lead us
Our praise by godly lives to show,
That every deed and word may prove
We trust and own our Father's love.
Amen.

59.
We thank Thee, Lord God, heavenly Father, through Jesus Christ, our Lord, for all Thy benefits, who livest and reignest forever and ever. Amen.

60.
O Lord, we thank Thee for our daily bread. May it strengthen and refresh our bodies! And we pray Thee, nourish our souls with Thy heavenly grace, through Jesus Christ, our Lord. Amen.

61.
The Lord is good to all, and His tender mercies are over all His works. Bless the Lord, O my soul, and all that is within me, bless His holy name. Bless the Lord, O my soul, and forget not all His benefits. Amen.

Prayers in Sickness.
62.
Lord, help me! Amen.

63.
Jesus, Redeemer, have mercy upon me! Amen.

64.
Tender Jesus, meek and mild,
Look on me, a little child;
Help me, if it is Thy will,
To recover from all ill. Amen.

65.
I am weak, but Thou art mighty. Help me, O my God! Amen.

66.
Dear Father, help me believe that all things work together for good to them that love God. Amen.

67.
O Thou, from whom all blessings flow,
I lift my heart to Thee;
In all my sorrows, conflicts, woes,
Dear Lord, remember me. Amen.

68.
Dear Father, Thy child is sick. Look upon me in tender mercy, and if it be Thy will, raise me up and grant me health and strength. Amen.

69.
Heavenly Father, it hath pleased Thee to visit me with sickness, I know that Thou art too kind and good to send me anything but for my blessing.

Help me to bear my illness and grant that I may soon recover, through Jesus Christ, my Lord and Savior. Amen.

70.
Other refuge have I none;
Hangs my helpless soul on Thee:
Leave, ah! leave me not alone,
Still support and comfort me.
All my trust on Thee is stayed,
All my help from Thee I bring;
Cover my defenseless head
With the shadow of Thy wing!
Amen.

71.
Lord, gracious God, I cry to Thee,
Still bless me with Thy favor,
Forgive my sins, and let me live,
Thy child remain forever.

Thou hast redeemed me with Thy blood,
Thou art my only Trust and God
In every need, my Savior. Amen.

72.
Nearer, my God, to Thee,
Nearer to Thee!
E'en though it be a cross
That raiseth me;
Still all my song shall be,
Nearer, my God, to Thee,
Nearer, my God, to Thee,
Nearer to Thee. Amen.

73.
Lord Jesus Christ, my best Physician,
I come to Thee in this my sickness. I pray Thee to look upon me in tender mercy. Send Thy guardian angel to watch over me and soon make me well. Amen.

74.
Lord Jesus, look down from heaven upon my mama (papa, brother, sister) and soon make her (him) well again. Thou canst do all things; hear my prayer! Amen.

Birthday.
75.
Holy Jesus, every day
Keep us in the narrow way,
And when earthly things are past,
Bring our ransomed souls at last
Where they need no star to guide.
Where no clouds Thy glory hide.
Amen.

76.
As a little child relies
On a care beyond his own;
Knows he's neither strong nor wise,
Fears to stir a step alone,—
Let me thus with Thee abide
As my Father, Guard, and Guide!
Amen.

77.
Faithful Shepherd, feed me
In the pastures green;
Faithful Shepherd, lead me
Where Thy steps are seen.

Hold me fast and guide me
In the narrow way;
So, with Thee beside me,
I shall never stray.

Daily bring me nearer
To the heavenly shore;
May my faith grow clearer.
May I love Thee more!

Hallow every pleasure,
Every gift and pain;
Be Thyself my Treasure.
Though none else I gain. Amen.

78.
We thank Thee, heav'nly Father,
For ev'ry earthly good,
For life, and health, and clothing,
And for our daily food.

O give us hearts to thank Thee,
For ev'ry blessing sent,
And whatsoe'er Thou sendest
Make us therewith content. Amen.

79.
Holy Jesus, be my Light,
Shine upon my way;
Through this tempting, changing life
Lead me day by day. Amen.

80.
Lord, be Thou my constant Guide,
Lead me all the way,
Till I reach Thy home at last,
Nevermore to stray. Amen.

81.
O God, Thou faithful God,
Thou Fount that ever flowest,
Without whom nothing is,
Who all good gifts bestowest:
A pure and healthy frame
O give me and within
A conscience free from blame,
A soul unhurt by sin. Amen.

For School and Church.
82.
Lord Jesus Christ, to us attend.
Thy Holy Spirit to us send. Amen.

83.
Lord, teach us how to keep Thy day
And lead and bless us all the way.
Amen.

84.
Lord, open Thou my heart to hear
And by Thy Word to me draw near;
Let me Thy Word still pure retain,
Let me Thy child and heir remain.
Amen.

85.
Direct me now, O gracious Lord,
To hear aright Thy holy Word;
Assist Thy minister to preach,
And let Thy Holy Spirit teach,
And let eternal life be found

By all who hear the joyful sound.
Amen.
86.
On what has now been sown
Thy blessing, Lord, bestow;
The power is Thine alone
To make it spring and grow. Amen.

87.
Blessed Lord, let Thy blessing go
with me to-day and grant that I may
be obedient to my teachers and may
learn with pleasure whatever I am
taught, to Thy great honor and glory.
Amen.

88.
O most gracious God, let me never
forget the many good things that I
have heard this day; but let them
abide in my heart, so that I may
amend my life, that I may be able to
give a good account of them to Jesus
Christ, our Lord and Savior, when He
comes to judge the world at the Last
Day, for whose sake I ask all
blessings, and to whom be glory
forever and ever! Amen.

89.
Almighty God, Thy Word is cast
Like seed into the ground;
Now let the dew of heaven descend
And righteous fruits abound. Amen.

90.
May the grace of Christ, our Savior,
And the Father's boundless love,
With the Holy Spirit's favor,
Rest upon us from above.

Thus may we abide in union
With each other and the Lord
And possess, in sweet communion,
Joys which earth cannot afford.
Amen.

91.

O give me Samuel's ear,
The open ear, O Lord,
Alive and quick to hear
Each whisper of Thy Word,
Like him to answer at Thy call,
And to obey Thee first of all. Amen.

92.

Abide, O dear Redeemer,
Among us with Thy Word
And thus now and hereafter
True peace and joy afford. Amen.

93.

Now our worship sweet is o'er—
Singing, praying, teaching, hearing:
Let us gladly God adore
For His gracious strength and
cheering.
Blest His name, who fain would save
us,
For the rich repast He gave us.

Let our going out be blest,
Bless our entrance in like measure;
Bless, O Lord, our toil and rest,
Bless our bread, our grief and
pleasure;
Be in death Thy blessing given,
And make us blest heirs of heaven.
Amen.

94.

My God, accept my heart this day
And make it always Thine,
That I from Thee no more may stray,
No more from Thee decline.

Anoint me with Thy heavenly grace,
Adopt me for Thine own,
That I may see Thy glorious face
And worship at Thy throne.

Let every thought and work and word
To Thee be ever given;
Then life shall be Thy service, Lord,
And death the gate of heaven. Amen.

95.

Dismiss us with Thy blessing, Lord;
Help us to feed upon Thy Word;
All that has been amiss forgive
And let Thy truth within us live.
Amen.

Christmas.
96.

Let us all with gladsome voice
Praise the God of heaven,
Who, to bid our hearts rejoice,
His own Son hath given. Amen.

97.

O Lord Christ, our Savior dear,
Be Thou ever near us;
Grant us now a glad New Year.
Amen, Jesus, hear us! Amen.

98.

O holy Child of Bethlehem,
Descend to us, we pray;
Cast out our sin and enter in.
Be born in us to-day. Amen.

99.

O welcome, little Christmas Guest,
Dear Jesus, from above;
Upon Thy face, so pure and mild,
We see God's smile of love. Amen.

100.

Precious Babe of Bethlehem,
Gift of love to sinful men,
Thou, our Savior, Lord, and King—
May we all Thy praises sing! Amen.

101.

Ah! dearest Jesus, holy Child,
Make Thee a bed, soft, undefiled,
Within my heart, that it may be
A quiet chamber kept for Thee.
Amen.

General Prayers.
102.

Come, dearest Savior, take my heart
And let me ne'er from Thee depart.

Amen.

103.

Jesus, tender Savior,
Thou hast died for me;
Make me very thankful
In my heart to Thee.
When the sad, sad story
Of Thy grief I read,
Make me very sorry
For my sins indeed.

Now, I know Thou livest,
And dost plead for me;
Make me very thankful
In my prayers to Thee.
Soon I hope in glory
At Thy side to stand;
Make me fit to meet Thee
In that happy land! Amen.

104.

Lamb of God, I look to Thee;
Thou shalt my example be;
Thou art gentle, meek, and mild,
Thou wast once a little child.

Fain I would be as Thou art:
Give me Thy obedient heart.
Thou art pitiful and kind:
Let me have Thy loving mind.

Loving Jesus, gentle Lamb,
In Thy gracious hands I am;
Make me, Savior, what Thou art,
Live Thyself within my heart.

I shall then show forth Thy praise,
Serve Thee all my happy days;
Then the world shall always see
Christ, the holy Child, in me. Amen.

105.

Jesus, help my eyes to see
All the good Thou sendest me.
Jesus, help my ears to hear
Calls for help from far and near.
Jesus, help my feet to go

In the way that Thou wilt show.
Jesus, help my hands to do
All things loving, kind, and true.
Jesus, may I helpful be,
Growing every day like Thee. Amen.

106.

Be near me, Lord Jesus!
I ask Thee to stay
Close by me forever
And love me, I pray.
Bless all the dear children
In Thy tender care
And take us to heaven
To live with Thee there. Amen.

107.

Holy Spirit, give us
Each a lowly mind;
Make us more like Jesus,
Gentle, pure, and kind.

Holy Spirit, brighten
Little deeds of toil,
And our playful pastimes
Let no folly spoil.

Holy Spirit, help us
Daily by Thy might
What is wrong to conquer
And to choose the right. Amen.

108.

Jesus, from Thy throne on high,
Far above the bright blue sky,
Look on us with loving eye;
Hear us, holy Jesus!

Be Thou with us every day,
In our work and in our play,
When we learn and when we pray;
Hear us, holy Jesus!

May we grow from day to day,
Glad to learn each holy way,

Ever ready to obey;
Hear us, holy Jesus!

May we ever try to be
From our sinful tempers free,
Pure and gentle, Lord, like Thee;
Hear us, holy Jesus!

Jesus, Son of God most high,
Who didst in the manger lie,
Who upon the cross didst die—
Hear us, holy Jesus! Amen.

Special Prayers.
For Parents.

109.
Almighty and most merciful God,
who in Thy infinite goodness hast
committed us unto the charge of
loving parents, who are to watch over
us and provide for all our wants of
body and soul, we pray Thee, protect
and prolong their life, that we may
continue to enjoy their loving care,
and strengthen us that as obedient
children we may be subject to their
will and hold them in love and
esteem; through Jesus Christ, our
Lord Amen.

For the Teacher.
110.
Dear Father in heaven, who in Thy
goodness hast given us teachers that
they may instruct and train us in all
useful knowledge, we pray Thee,
bless them with strength and patience
so to guide our feeble footsteps that,
being warned, nurtured, comforted,
and strengthened, we may do all
things well-pleasing to Thee and
profitable to us; through Jesus Christ,
our Lord. Amen.

For the Pastor.
111.
O almighty God, who by Thy Son

Jesus Christ didst give to Thy holy
apostles many excellent gifts and
commandedst them faithfully to feed
Thy flock, bless, we beseech Thee,
our pastor that he may diligently
preach Thy holy Word, and grant us
grace to believe Thy saving Gospel
and obediently to follow the
teachings of Thy Word, that we may
receive the crown of everlasting
glory; through Jesus Christ, our Lord.
Amen.

For a Blessed End.
112.
While life's paths we still are
pressing,
Grant us, Father, steadfast faith
And for Christ's sake grant the
blessing
Of a peaceful, Christian death. Amen.

The Lord's Prayer.
113.
Our Father who art in heaven;
Hallowed be Thy Name; Thy
kingdom come; Thy will be done on
earth as it is in heaven; Give us this
day our daily bread; And forgive us
our trespasses as we forgive those
who trespass against us; And lead us
not into temptation; But deliver us
from evil; For Thine is the kingdom,
and the power, and the glory, forever
and ever. Amen.

Psalm 23.
114.
1. The Lord is my Shepherd; I shall
not want.

2. He maketh me to lie down in green
pastures; He leadeth me beside the
still waters.

3. He restoreth my soul; He leaded
me in the paths of righteousness for
His name's sake.

4. Yea, though I walk through the valley of the shadow of death, I will fear no evil; for Thou art with me; Thy rod and Thy staff, they comfort me.

5. Thou preparest a table before me in the presence of mine enemies; Thou anointest my head with oil; my cup runneth over.

6. Surely goodness and mercy shall follow me all the days of my life, and I will dwell in the house of the Lord forever.

THIS IS HEAVEN

This 85-year-old couple, having been married almost 60 years, died in a car crash. They had been in good health the last 10 years, mainly due to her interest in health food and exercise.

When they reached the pearly gates, St. Peter took them to their mansion, which was decked out with a beautiful kitchen, master bath suite and Jacuzzi.

As they oohed and ached, the old man asked Peter how much all this was going to cost. "It's free," Peter replied. "This is Heaven."

Next they went out back to survey the championship golf course in the backyard. They would have golfing privileges every day, and each week the course would change to a new one, representing the great golf courses on Earth.

The old man asked, "What are the greens fees?"

Peter's reply, "This is Heaven -- you play for free."

Next they went to the clubhouse and saw the lavish buffet lunch with the cuisines of the world laid out.

"How much to eat?" asked the old man.

"Don't you understand yet? This is Heaven, it's FREE!" Peter replied with some exasperation.

"Well, where are the low-fat and low-cholesterol tables?" the old man asked timidly.

Peter lectured, "That's the best part -- you can eat as much as you like of whatever you like and you never get fat and you never get sick. This is Heaven."

With that the old man went into a fit of anger, throwing down his hat and stomping on it, and shrieking wildly.

Peter and his wife both tried to calm him down, asking him what was wrong. The old man looked at his wife and said, "This is all your fault. If it weren't for your blasted bran muffins, I could have been here 10 years ago!"

GOD'S SOLUTION

One day in the Garden of Eden, Eve calls out to God:

"Lord, I have a problem."

"What's the problem, Eve?"

"Lord, you've created me and provided this beautiful spot, these wonderful animals, and that comedic snake, but I'm just not happy."

"Why is that, Eve?" came the voice from above.

"Lord, I am lonely. And I'm sick to death of apples."

"Well, I have a solution. I shall create a man for you."

"What's a man, Lord?"

"Man will be a flawed creature, with aggressive tendencies, an enormous ego and an inability to empathize. All in all, he'll give you a hard time. But he'll be bigger, faster, and stronger than you. And while he'll need your advice to think properly, he'll be good at fighting, kicking a ball around and hunting fleet-footed ruminants.

"Sounds good to me," says Eve. "But isn't there a catch, Lord?" "Yeah, well, there is one."

"What's that, Lord?"

"You'll have to let him believe that I made him first."

GOLF, BY GOD!

Moses, Jesus and another guy were out playing golf one day. Moses pulled up to the tee and drove a long one. It landed in the fairway but rolled directly toward a water trap. Quickly Moses raised his club, the water parted and it rolled to the other side, safe and sound.

Next, Jesus strolled up to the tee and hit a nice long one directly toward the same water trap. It landed directly in the center of the pond and kind of hovered over the water. Jesus casually walked out on the pond and chipped it up onto the green.

The third guy got up and sort of randomly whacked the ball. It headed out over the fence and into on-coming traffic on a nearby street. It bounced off a truck and hit a nearby tree.

From there it bounced onto the roof of a nearby shack and rolled down into the gutter, down the downspout, out onto the fairway and right toward the aforementioned pond. On the way to the pond, it hit a little stone and bounced out over the water and onto a lily pad where it rested quietly.

Suddenly, a very large bullfrog jumped up on the lily pad and snatched the ball into his mouth. Just then, an eagle swooped down and grabbed the frog and flew away. As they passed over the green, the frog squealed with fright and dropped the ball, which bounced right into the hole for a beautiful hole in one.

Moses then turned to Jesus and said, "I hate playing with your Dad."

GATES GETS HIS PUNISHMENT

Bill Gates suddenly dies and finds himself face to face with God.

God stood over Bill Gates and said, "Well Bill, I'm really confused on this one. It's a tough decision; I'm not sure whether to send you to Heaven or Hell. After all, you helped society enormously by putting a computer in almost every home in America, yet you also created that ghastly Windows '95 among other indiscretions. I believe I'll do something I've never done before; I'll let you decide where you want to go."

Bill pushed up his glasses, looked up at God and replied, "Could you briefly explain the difference between the two?"

Looking slightly puzzled, God said, "Better yet, why don't I let you visit both places briefly, then you can make your decision. Which do you choose to see first, Heaven or Hell?"

Bill played with his pocket protector for a moment, then looked back at God and said, "I think I'll try Hell first." So, with a flash of lightning and a cloud of smoke, Bill Gates went to Hell.

When he materialized in Hell, Bill looked around. It was a beautiful and clean place, a bit warm, with sandy beaches and tall mountains, clear skies, pristine water, and beautiful women frolicking about. A smile came across Bill's face as he took in a deep breath of the clean air. "This is great," he thought, "if this is Hell, I can't wait to see heaven."

Within seconds of his thought, another flash of lightning and a cloud of smoke appeared, and Bill was off to Heaven. Heaven was a place high above the clouds, where angels were drifting about playing their harps and singing in a beautiful chorus.

It was a very nice place, Bill thought, but not as enticing as Hell.

Bill looked up, cupped his hands around his mouth and yelled for God and Bill Gates was sent to Hell for eternity.

Time passed, and God decided to check on the late billionaire to see how he was progressing in Hell. When he got there, he found Bill Gates shackled to a wall in a dark cave amid bone thin men and tongues of fire, being burned and tortured by demons.

"So, how is everything going?" God asked.

Bill responded with a crackling voice filled with anguish and disappointment, "This is awful! It's nothing like the Hell I visited the first time!! I can't believe this is happening!

What happened to the other place....with the beaches and the mountains and the beautiful women?

"That was the demo," replied God.

THE REQUEST

A little boy wanted $100 badly and prayed for two weeks but nothing happened.

Then he decided to write GOD a letter requesting the $100. When the postal authorities received the letter addressed to GOD USA, they decided to send it to President Obama.

The President was so impressed, touched, and amused that he instructed his secretary to send the little boy a $5.00 bill. President Obama thought this would appear to be a lot of money to a little boy.

The little boy was delighted with the $5.00 and sat down to write a thank you note to GOD, which read:

Dear GOD,

Thank you very much for sending the money, however, I noticed that for some reason you had to send it through Washington D.C. and, as usual, those idiots deducted $95.00!

RANDOM QUOTES

"Moral indignation is jealousy with a halo."
H. G. Wells (1866-1946)

"Glory is fleeting, but obscurity is forever."
Napoleon Bonaparte (1769-1821)

"The fundamental cause of trouble in the world is that the stupid are cocksure while the intelligent are full of doubt."
Bertrand Russell (1872-1970)

"Victory goes to the player who makes the next-to-last mistake."
Chessmaster Savagely Grigorievitch Tartakower (1887-1956)

"Don't be so humble - you are not that great."
Golda Meir (1898-1978) to a visiting diplomat

"His ignorance is encyclopedic"
Abba Eban (1915-2002)

"If a man does his best, what else is there?"
General George S. Patton (1885-1945)

"Political correctness is tyranny with manners."
Charlton Hesston (1924-2008)

"You can avoid reality, but you cannot avoid the consequences of avoiding reality."
Ayn Rand (1905-1982)

"When one person suffers from a delusion it is called insanity; when many people suffer from a delusion it is called religion."
Robert Pirsig (1948)

"Sex and religion are closer to each other than either might prefer."
Saint Thomas More (1478-1535)

"I can write better than anybody who can write faster, and I can write faster than anybody who can write better."
A. J. Libeling (1904-1963)

"People demand freedom of speech to make up for the freedom of thought which they avoid."
Siren Aabye Kierkegaard (1813-1855)

"Give me chastity and continence, but not yet."
Saint Augustine (354-430)

"Not everything that can be counted counts, and not everything that counts can be counted."
Albert Einstein (1879-1955)

"Only two things are infinite, the universe and human stupidity, and I'm not sure about the former."
Albert Einstein (1879-1955)

"A lie gets halfway around the world before the truth has a chance to get its pants on."
Sir Winston Churchill (1874-1965)

"You may not be interested in war, but war is interested in you."
Leon Trotsky (1879-1940)

"I do not feel obliged to believe that the same God who has
endowed us with sense, reason, and intellect
has intended us to forgo their use."
Galileo Galilee (1564-1642)

"We are all atheists about most of the gods humanity has
ever believed in. Some of us just go one god further."
Richard Dawkins (1941)

"The artist is nothing without the gift, but the gift is
nothing without work."
Emile Zola (1840-1902)

"This book fills a much-needed gap."
Moses Hades (1900-1966) in a review

"The full use of your powers along lines of excellence."
definition of "happiness" by John F. Kennedy (1917-1963)

"I'm living so far beyond my income that we may almost
be said to be living apart."
e e Cummings (1894-1962)

"Give me a museum and I'll fill it."
Pablo Picasso (1881-1973)

"Assassins!"
Arturo Toscanini (1867-1957) to his orchestra

"I'll moider da bum."
*Heavyweight boxer Tony Galento, when asked what he
thought of William Shakespeare*

"In theory, there is no difference between theory and
practice. But in practice, there is."
Yogi Berra

"I find that the harder I work, the more luck I seem to have." *Thomas Jefferson (1743-1826)*

"Each problem that I solved became a rule which served after- wards to solve other problems."
Rene Descartes (1596-1650), "Discours de la Methode"

"In the End, we will remember not the words of our enemies, but the silence of our friends."
Martin Luther King Jr. (1929-1968)

"Whether you think that you can, or that you can't, you are usually right."
Henry Ford (1863-1947)

"Do, or do not. There is no 'try'."
Yoda ('The Empire Strikes Back')

"The only way to get rid of a temptation is to yield to it."
Oscar Wilde (1854-1900)

"Don't stay in bed, unless you can make money in bed."
George Burns (1896-1996)

"I don't know why we are here, but I'm pretty sure that it is not in order to enjoy ourselves."
Ludwig Wittgenstein (1889-1951)

"There are no facts, only interpretations."
Friedrich Nietzsche (1844-1900)

"Nothing in the world is more dangerous than sincere ignorance and conscientious stupidity."
Martin Luther King Jr. (1929-1968)

"The use of COBOL cripples the mind; its teaching should, there- fore, be regarded as a criminal offense."
Edsgar Dijkstra (1930-2002)

"C makes it easy to shoot yourself in the foot; C++ makes it harder, but when you do, it blows away your whole leg."
Bjarne Stroustrup

"A mathematician is a device for turning coffee into theorems."
Paul Erdos (1913-1996)

"Problems worthy of attack prove their worth by fighting back."
Paul Erdos (1913-1996)

"Try to learn something about everything and everything about something."
Thomas Henry Huxley (1825-1895)

"Dancing is silent poetry."
Simonides (556-468bc)

"The only difference between me and a madman is that I'm not mad."
Salvador Dali (1904-1989)

"If you can't get rid of the skeleton in your closet, you'd best teach it to dance."
George Bernard Shaw (1856-1950)

"But at my back I always hear Time's winged chariot hurrying near."
Andrew Marvell (1621-1678)

"Good people do not need laws to tell them to act
responsibly, while bad people will find a
way around the laws."
Plato (427-347 B.C.)

"The power of accurate observation is frequently called
cynicism by those who don't have it."
George Bernard Shaw (1856-1950)

"Whenever I climb I am followed by a dog called 'Ego'."
Friedrich Nietzsche (1844-1900)

"Everybody pities the weak; jealousy you have to earn."
Arnold Schwarzenegger (1947-)

"Against stupidity, the gods themselves contend in vain."
Friedrich von Schiller (1759-1805)

"We have art to save ourselves from the truth."
Friedrich Nietzsche (1844-1900)

"Never interrupt your enemy when he is making a
mistake." *Napoleon Bonaparte (1769-1821)*

"I think 'Hail to the Chief' has a nice ring to it."
*John F. Kennedy (1917-1963) when asked what is his
favorite song*

"I have nothing to declare except my genius."
*Oscar Wilde (1854-1900) upon arriving at U.S. customs
1882*

"Human history becomes more and more a race between
education and catastrophe."
H. G. Wells (1866-1946)

"Talent does what it can; genius does what it must."
Edward George Bulwer-Lytton (1803-1873)

"The difference between 'involvement' and 'commitment' is like an eggs-and-ham breakfast: the chicken was 'involved' the pig was 'committed'."
unknown

"Women might be able to fake orgasms. But men can fake a whole relationship."
Sharon Stone

"If you are going through hell, keep going."
Sir Winston Churchill (1874-1965)

"He who has a 'why' to live, can bear with almost any 'how'." *Friedrich Nietzsche (1844-1900)*

"Many wealthy people are little more than janitors of their pos- sessions."
Frank Lloyd Wright (1868-1959)

"I'm all in favor of keeping dangerous weapons out of the hands of fools. Let's start with typewriters."
Frank Lloyd Wright (1868-1959)

"Some cause happiness wherever they go; others, whenever they go."
Oscar Wilde (1854-1900)

"God is a comedian playing to an audience too afraid to laugh."
Voltaire (1694-1778)

"He is one of those people who would be enormously
improved by death."
H. H. Munro (Saki) (1870-1916)

"I am ready to meet my Maker. Whether my Maker is
prepared for the great ordeal of meeting
me is another matter."
Sir Winston Churchill (1874-1965)

"I shall not waste my days in trying to prolong them."
Ian L. Fleming (1908-1964)

"If you can count your money, you don't have a billion
dollars."
J. Paul Getty (1892-1976)

"Facts are the enemy of truth."
Don Quixote - "Man of La Mancha"

"When you do the common things in life in an uncommon
way, you will command the attention of the world."
George Washington Carver (1864-1943)

"How wrong it is for a woman to expect the man to build
the world she wants, rather than to create it herself."
Anais Nin (1903-1977)

"I have not failed. I've just found 10,000
ways that won't work."
Thomas Alva Edison (1847-1931)

"I begin by taking. I shall find scholars later to
demonstrate my perfect right."
- Frederick (II) the Great

"Maybe this world is another planet's Hell."
Aldous Huxley (1894-1963)

"Blessed is the man, who having nothing to say, abstains
from giving wordy evidence of the fact."
George Eliot (1819-1880)

"Once you eliminate the impossible, whatever remains, no
mat- ter how improbable, must be the truth."
Sherlock Holmes (by Sir Arthur Conan Doyle, 1859-1930)

"Black holes are where God divided by zero."
Steven Wright

"I've had a wonderful time, but this wasn't it."
Groucho Marx (1895-1977)

"It's kind of fun to do the impossible."
Walt Disney (1901-1966)

"We didn't lose the game; we just ran out of time."
Vince Lombardi

"The optimist proclaims that we live in the best of all
possible worlds, and the pessimist fears this is true."
James Branch Cabell

"A friendship founded on business is better than a business
founded on friendship."
John D. Rockefeller (1874-1960)

"All are lunatics, but he who can analyze his delusion is
called a philosopher."
Ambrose Bierce (1842-1914)

"You can only find truth with logic if you have already found truth without it."
Gilbert Keith Chesterton (1874-1936)

"An inconvenience is only an adventure wrongly considered; an adventure is an inconvenience rightly considered."
Gilbert Keith Chesterton (1874-1936)

"I have come to believe that the whole world is an enigma, a harmless enigma that is made terrible by our own mad attempt to interpret it as though it had an underlying truth."
Umberto Eco

"The true measure of a man is how he treats someone who can do him absolutely no good."
Samuel Johnson (1709-1784)

"A people that values its privileges above its principles soon loses both."
Dwight D. Eisenhower (1890-1969),
Inaugural Address, January 20, 1953

"The significant problems we face cannot be solved at the same level of thinking we were at when we created them."
Albert Einstein (1879-1955)

"Basically, I no longer work for anything but the sensation I have while working."
Albert Giacometti (sculptor)

"There's a limit to how many times you can read how great you are and what an inspiration you are, but I'm not there yet."
Randy Pausch (1960-2008)

"It is far better to grasp the Universe as it really is than to persist in delusion, however satisfying and reassuring."
Carl Sagan (1934-1996)

"All truth passes through three stages. First, it is ridiculed. Sec- ond, it is violently opposed. Third, it is accepted as being self- evident."
Arthur Schopenhauer (1788-1860)

"Many a man's reputation would not know his character if they met on the street."
Elbert Hubbard (1856-1915)

"There is more stupidity than hydrogen in the universe, and it has a longer shelf life."
Frank Zappa

"Perfection is achieved, not when there is nothing more to add, but when there is nothing left to take away."
Antoine de Saint Exupery

"Life is pleasant. Death is peaceful. It's the transition that's troublesome."
Isaac Asimov

"If you want to make an apple pie from scratch, you must first create the universe."
Carl Sagan (1934-1996)

"It is much more comfortable to be mad and know it, than to be sane and have one's doubts."
G. B. Burgin

"Once is happenstance. Twice is coincidence. Three times is enemy action."
Auric Goldfinger, in "Goldfinger" by Ian L. Fleming (1908-1964)

"To love oneself is the beginning of a lifelong romance"
Oscar Wilde (1854-1900)

"Knowledge speaks, but wisdom listens."
Jimi Hendrix

"A clever man commits no minor blunders."
Goethe (1749-1832)

"Argue for your limitations, and sure enough
they're yours."
Richard Bach

"A witty saying proves nothing."
Voltaire (1694-1778)

"Sleep is an excellent way of listening to an opera."
James Stephens (1882-1950)

"The nice thing about being a celebrity is that if you bore
people they think it's their fault."
Henry Kissinger (1923-)

"Education is a progressive discovery of
our own ignorance."
Will Durant

"I have often regretted my speech, never my silence."
Xenocrates (396-314 B.C.)

"It was the experience of mystery even if mixed with fear
that engendered religion."
Albert Einstein (1879-1955)

"If everything seems under control, you're
just not going fast enough."
Mario Andretti

"I do not consider it an insult, but rather a compliment to be
called an agnostic. I do not pretend to know where many
ignorant men are sure that is all that agnosticism means."
Clarence Darrow, Scopes trial, 1925.

"Obstacles are those frightful things you see
when you take your eyes off your goal."
Henry Ford (1863-1947)

"I'll sleep when I'm dead."
Warren Zevon (1947-2003)

"There are people in the world so hungry, that God cannot
appear to them except in the form of bread."
Mahatma Gandhi (1869-1948)

"When you gaze long into the abyss, the abyss
also gazes into you."
Friedrich Nietzsche (1844-1900)

"The instinct of nearly all societies is to lock up anybody
who is truly free. First, society begins by trying to beat you
up. If this fails, they try to poison you. If this fails too, they
finish by load- ing honors on your head."
Jean Cocteau (1889-1963)

"Everyone is a genius at least once a year; a real genius has
his original ideas closer together."
Georg Lichtenberg (1742-1799)

"Success usually comes to those who are too busy to be looking for it"
Henry David Thoreau (1817-1862)

"While we are postponing, life speeds by."
Seneca (3BC - 65AD)

"Where are we going, and why am I in this handbasket?"
Bumper Sticker

"God, please save me from your followers!"
Bumper Sticker

"Fill what's empty, empty what's full, and scratch where it itches."
the Duchess of Windsor, when asked what is the secret of a long and happy life

"First they ignore you, then they laugh at you, then they fight you, then you win."
Mahatma Gandhi (1869-1948)

"Luck is the residue of design."
Branch Rickey - former owner of the Brooklyn Dodger Baseball Team

"Tragedy is when I cut my finger. Comedy is when you walk into an open sewer and die."
Mel Brooks

"Most people would sooner die than think; in fact, they do so."
Bertrand Russell (1872-1970)

"Wit is educated insolence."
Aristotle (384-322 B.C.)

"My advice to you is get married: if you find a good wife you'llbe happy; if not, you'll become a philosopher.
Socrates (470-399 B.C.)

"Advice is what we ask for when we already know the answer but wish we didn't"
Erica Jong (1942-)

"Show me a woman who doesn't feel guilty and I'll show you a man."
Erica Jong (1942-)

"I've learned that people will forget what you said, people will forget what you did, but people will never forget how you made them feel."
Maya Angelou (1928-)

"Egotist: a person more interested in himself than in me."
Ambrose Bierce (1842-1914)

"A narcissist is someone better looking than you are."
Gore Vidal

"Wise men make proverbs, but fools repeat them."
Samuel Palmer (1805-80)

"It has become appallingly obvious that our technology has ex- ceeded our humanity."
Albert Einstein (1879-1955)

"The secret of success is to know something nobody else knows."
Aristotle Onassis (1906-1975)

"Sometimes when reading Goethe I have the paralyzing suspi- cion that he is trying to be funny."
Guy Davenport

"When you have to kill a man, it costs nothing to be polite." *Sir Winston Churchill (1874-1965)*

"Any man who is under 30, and is not a liberal, has no heart; and any man who is over 30, and is not a conservative, has no brains."
Sir Winston Churchill (1874-1965)

"The opposite of a correct statement is a false statement. The opposite of a profound truth may well be another profound truth."
Niels Bohr (1885-1962)

"We all agree that your theory is crazy, but is it crazy enough?"
Niels Bohr (1885-1962)

"When I am working on a problem I never think about beauty. I only think about how to solve the problem. But when I have fin- ished, if the solution is not beautiful, I know it is wrong."
Buckminster Fuller (1895-1983)

"In science one tries to tell people, in such a way as to be under- stood by everyone, something that no one ever knew before. But in poetry, it's the exact opposite."
Paul Dirac (1902-1984)

"I would have made a good Pope."
Richard M. Nixon (1913-1994)

"In any contest between power and
patience, bet on patience."
W.B. Prescott

"Anyone who considers arithmetical methods of producing
random digits is, of course, in a state of sin."
John von Neumann (1903-1957)

"The mistakes are all waiting to be made."
*chessmaster Savielly Grigorievitch Tartakower (1887-
1956) on the game's opening position*

"It is unbecoming for young men to utter maxims."
Aristotle (384-322 B.C.)

"Grove giveth and Gates taketh away."
*Bob Metcalfe (inventor of Ethernet) on the trend of
hardware speedups not being able to keep up
with software demands*

"Reality is merely an illusion, albeit a very persistent one."
Albert Einstein (1879-1955)

"One of the symptoms of an approaching nervous
breakdown is the belief that one's work is
terribly important."
Bertrand Russell (1872-1970)

"A little inaccuracy sometimes saves a ton of explanation."
H. H. Munro (Saki) (1870-1916)

"There are two ways of constructing a software design; one
way is to make it so simple that there are obviously no
deficiencies, and the other way is to make it so complicated
that there are no obvious deficiencies. The first method is
far more difficult."
C. A. R. Hoare

"Make everything as simple as possible, but not simpler."
Albert Einstein (1879-1955)

"What do you take me for, an idiot?"
General Charles de Gaulle (1890-1970), when a journalist asked him if he was happy

"I heard someone tried the monkeys-on-typewriters bit trying for the plays of W. Shakespeare, but all they got was the collected works of Francis Bacon."
Bill Hirst

"Three o'clock is always too late or too early for anything you want to do."
Jean-Paul Sartre (1905-1980)

"A doctor can bury his mistakes but an architect can only advise his clients to plant vines."
Frank Lloyd Wright (1868-1959)

"It is dangerous to be sincere unless you are also stupid."
George Bernard Shaw (1856-1950)

"If you haven't got anything nice to say about anybody, come sit next to me."
Alice Roosevelt Longworth (1884-1980)

"A man can't be too careful in the choice of his enemies."
Oscar Wilde (1854-1900)

"Forgive your enemies, but never forget their names."
John F. Kennedy (1917-1963)

"Logic is in the eye of the logician." - Gloria Steinem
"No one can earn a million dollars honestly."
William Jennings Bryan (1860-1925)

"Everything has been figured out, except how to live."
Jean-Paul Sartre (1905-1980)

"Well-timed silence hath more eloquence than speech."
Martin Fraquhar Tupper

"Thank you for sending me a copy of your
book - I'll waste no time reading it."
Moses Hadas (1900-1966)

"From the moment I picked your book up until I laid it
down I was convulsed with laughter. Some day I intend
reading it."
Groucho Marx (1895-1977)

"It is better to have a permanent income
than to be fascinating."
Oscar Wilde (1854-1900)

"When ideas fail, words come in very handy."
Goethe (1749-1832)

"In the end, everything is a gag."
Charlie Chaplin (1889-1977)

"The nice thing about egotists is that they don't talk about
other people."
Lucille S. Harper

"You got to be careful if you don't know where you're
going, because you might not get there."
Yogi Berra

"I love Mickey Mouse more than any woman
I have ever known."
Walt Disney (1901-1966)

"He who hesitates is a damned fool."
Mae West (1892-1980)

"Good teaching is one-fourth preparation
and three-fourths theater."
Gail Godwin

"University politics are vicious precisely because
the stakes are so small."
Henry Kissinger (1923-)

"The graveyards are full of indispensable men."
Charles de Gaulle (1890-1970)

"You can pretend to be serious; you can't
pretend to be witty."
Sacha Guitry (1885-1957)

"Behind every great fortune there is a crime."
Honore de Balzac (1799-1850)

"If women didn't exist, all the money in the
world would have no meaning."
Aristotle Onassis (1906-1975)

"I am not young enough to know everything."
Oscar Wilde (1854-1900)

"Bigamy is having one wife too many.
Monogamy is the same."
Oscar Wilde (1854-1900)

"The object of war is not to die for your country but to
make the other bastard die for his."
General George Patton (1885-1945)

"Sometimes a scream is better than a thesis."
Ralph Waldo Emerson (1803-1882)

"There is no sincerer love than the love of food."
George Bernard Shaw (1856-1950)

"I don't even butter my bread; I consider that cooking." -
Katherine Cebrian

"I have an existential map; it has 'you are
here' written all over it."
Steven Wright

"Mr. Wagner has beautiful moments but bad
quarters of an hour."
Gioacchino Rossini (1792-1868)

"Manuscript: something submitted in haste
and returned at lei- sure."
Oliver Herford (1863-1935)

"I have read your book and much like it."
Moses Hadas (1900-1966)

"The covers of this book are too far apart."
Ambrose Bierce (1842-1914)

"Everywhere I go I'm asked if I think the university stifles
writers. My opinion is that they don't
stifle enough of them."
Flannery O'Connor (1925-1964)

"Too many pieces of music finish too long after the end."
Igor Stravinsky (1882-1971)

"Anything that is too stupid to be spoken is sung."
Voltaire (1694-1778)

"When choosing between two evils, I always like to try the one I've never tried before."
Mae West (1892-1980)

"I don't know anything about music. In my line you don't have to."
Elvis Presley (1935-1977)

"No Sane man will dance."
Cicero (106-43 B.C.)

"Hell is a half-filled auditorium."
Robert Frost (1874-1963)

"Show me a sane man and I will cure him for you."
Carl Gustav Jung (1875-1961)

"Vote early and vote often."
Al Capone (1899-1947)

FAITH QUOTES

"I would rather walk with God in the dark than
go alone in the light."
Mary Gardiner Brainard

"Live as though Christ died yesterday, rose from the grave
today, and is coming back tomorrow."
Theodore Epp

"I believe in the sun even if it isn't shining. I believe in love
even when I am alone. I believe in God even
when He is silent."
Unknown

"A man can no more diminish God's glory by refusing to
worship Him than a lunatic can put out the sun by
scribbling the word, 'darkness' on the walls of his cell."
C. S. Lewis

"The safest place to be is within the will of God."
Anonymous

"Wishing will never be a substitute for prayer."
Ed Cole

"Here, then, is the real problem of our negligence. We fail
in our duty to study God's Word not so much because it is
difficult to understand, not so much because it is dull and
boring, but because it is work. Our problem is not a lack of
intelligence or a lack of passion. Our problem
is that we are lazy."
R. C. Sproul

"Never underestimate Jesus, because He will
just prove you wrong."
Brian Gurney

"When life knocks you on your knees, your in the perfect
position to pray!"
Unknown

"Any fool can count the seeds in an apple. Only God can
count all the apples in one seed."
Robert H. Schuller

"Be assured, if you walk with Him and look to Him, and
expect help from Him, He will never fail you."
George Mueller

"If you are not as close to God as you used to be, who
moved?"
Unknown

"I am sure that never was a people, who had more reason to
acknowledge a Divine interposition in their affairs, than
those of the United States; and I should be pained to
believe that they have forgotten that agency, which was so
often mani- fested during our Revolution, or that they
failed to consider the omnipotence of that God
who is alone able to protect them."
George Washington

"God's last name is not Dammit."
Unknown

"No two Christians will ever meet for the last time."
"God understands our prayers even when we can't find the
words to say them."
Unknown

"Every evening I turn my worries over to God. He's going
to be up all night anyway."
Mary C. Crowley

"Trials are medicines which our gracious and wise
Physician prescribes because we need them; and he
proportions the frequency and weight of them to what the
case requires. Let us trust his skill and
thank him for his prescription."
Isaac Newton

"Sometimes God has to put us flat on our back before we
are looking up to Him."
Jack Graham

"You do well to believe in God. Satan
also believes...and trembles".
James 2:19

"We turn to God for help when our foundations are shaking
only to learn that it is God shaking them."
Charles West

"Darkness cannot put out the Light. It can
only make God brighter."
Unknown

"Prayer is when you talk to God; meditation
is when you listen to God."
Diana Robinson

"Some people talk about finding God as
if He could get lost."
Unknown

"The Bible is a compass, pointing
you in the right direction."
Anonymous

"If a man cannot be a Christian in the place he is, he cannot
be a Christian anywhere."
Henry Ward Beecher

"Unless we rely on God's power within us, we will yield to
the pressures around us."
Anonymous

"It is a great consolation for me to remember that the Lord,
to whom I had drawn near in humble and child-like faith,
has suffered and died for me, and that He
will look on me in love and compassion."
Wolfgang Amadeus Mozart

"God's answers are wiser than our prayers."
Anonymous

"Satan, the Hinderer, may build a barrier about us, but he
can never roof us in, so that we cannot look up."
J. Hudson Taylor

"God loves you, whether you like it or not."
Anonymous

"I cannot imagine how the clockwork of the universe can
exist without a clockmaker."
Voltaire

"Everyman's life is a fairy tale written by God's fingers."
Hans Christian Anderson

"I could not say I believe. I know! I have had the experience of being gripped by something that is stronger than myself, something that people call God."
Carl Jung

"We have this day restored the Sovereign to Whom all men ought to be obedient. He reigns in heaven and from the rising to the setting of the sun, let His kingdom come."
Samuel Adams

"The next moment is as much beyond our grasp, and as much in God's care, as that a hundred years away. Care for the next minute is as foolish as care for a day in the next thousand years. In neither can we do anything, in both God is doing everything."
C. S. Lewis

"But I always think that the best way to know God is to love many things."
Vincent Van Gogh

"It always strikes me, and it is very peculiar, that when we see the image of indescribable and unutterable desolation - of loneliness, of poverty and misery, the end of all things, or their extreme then rises in our mind the thought of God."
Vincent Van Gogh

"God is not what you imagine or what you think you under- stand. If you understand you have failed."
St. Augustine

"You can tell the size of your God by looking at the size of your worry list. The longer your list, the smaller your God."
Unknown

"Do unto others as you would have them do unto you."
Christian Proverbs

"How else but through a broken heart
may Lord Christ enter in."
Oscar Wilde

"God is a verb, not a noun proper or improper."
R. Buckminster Fuller

"The Christian ideal has not been tried and found wanting.
It has been found difficult and left untried."
Gilbert Keith Chesterton

"We can stand affliction better than we can prosperity, for
in prosperity we forget God."
Dwight L. Moody

"Discretion is the salt, and fancy the sugar of life; the one
pre- serves, the other sweetens it."
John Christian Bovee

"It is in the ordinary duties and labors of life that the
Christian can and should develop his
spiritual union with God."
Thomas Merton

"Spirit is the real and eternal; matter
is the unreal and temporal."
Mary Baker Eddy

"We believe that all men are created equal because they are
created in the image of God."
Harry S. Truman

"The winds of God are always blowing,
but you must set the sails."
Anonymous

"Before me, even as behind, God is, and all is well."
John Greenleaf Whittier

"Depend on it. Gods work done in Gods way will never
lack Gods supply. He is too wise a God to frustrate His
purposes for lack of funds, and He can just as easily supply
them ahead of time as afterwards, and
He much prefers doing so."
J. Hudson Taylor

"We're all in the same garden. I hope you're not eating
from the wrong tree."
Justin Holland

"A man who is eating or lying with his wife or preparing to
go to sleep in humility, thankfulness and temperance, is, by
Christian standards, in an infinitely higher state than one
who is listening to Bach or reading
Plato in a state of pride."
Clive Staples Lewis

"God is not a cosmic bellboy for whom we can press a
button to get things done."
Harry Emerson Fosdick

"The soul can split the sky in two and let the face of God
shine through."
Edna St. Vincent Millay

'The light in the eyes of him whose heart is joyful,
rejoices the heart of others."
Proverbs 15:30

"Every morning I spend fifteen minutes filling my mind
full of God; and so there's no room left for worry
thoughts."
Howard Chandler Christy

"Young man, young man, your arm's too
short to box with God."
James Weldon Johnson

"When I saw others straining toward God, I did not understand it, for though I may have had him less than they did,
there was no one blocking the way between him and me,
and I could reach his heart easily. It is up to him, after all,
to have us, our part consists of almost solely
in letting him grasp us."
Rainer Maria Rilke

101 SCIENTIFIC FACTS AND FOREKNOWLEDGE

1. The earth free-floats in space (Job 26:7), affected only by gravity. While other sources declared the earth sat on the back of an elephant or turtle, or was held up by Atlas, the Bible alone states what we now know to be true – "He hangs the earth on nothing."

2. Creation is made of particles, indiscernible to our eyes (Hebrews 11:3). Not until the 19th century was it discovered that all visible matter consists of invisible elements.

3. The Bible specifies the perfect dimensions for a stable water vessel (Genesis 6:15). Ship builders today are well aware that the ideal dimension for ship stability is a length six times that of the width. Keep in mind, God told Noah the ideal dimensions for the ark 4,500 years ago.

4. When dealing with disease, clothes and body should be washed under *running water* (Leviticus 15:13). For centuries people naively washed in standing water. Today we recognize the need to wash away germs with fresh water.

5. Sanitation industry birthed (Deuteronomy 23:12-13). Some 3,500 years ago God commanded His people to have a place outside the camp where they could relieve themselves. They were to each carry a shovel so that they could dig a hole (latrine) and cover their waste. Up until World War I, more soldiers died from disease than war because they did not isolate human waste.

6. Oceans contain springs (Job 38:16). The ocean is very

deep. Almost all the ocean floor is in total darkness and the pressure there is enormous. It would have been impossible for Job to have explored the "springs of the sea." Until recently, it was thought that oceans were fed only by rivers and rain. Yet in the 1970s, with the help of deep diving research submarines that were constructed to withstand 6,000 pounds-per-square-inch pressure, oceanographers discovered springs on the ocean floors!

7. There are mountains on the bottom of the ocean floor (Jonah 2:5-6). Only in the last century have we discovered that there are towering mountains and deep trenches in the depths of the sea.

8. Joy and gladness understood (Acts 14:17). Evolution cannot explain emotions. Matter and energy do not feel. Scripture explains that God places gladness in our hearts (Psalm 4:7), and ultimate joy is found only in our Creator's presence – "in Your presence is fullness of joy" (Psalm 16:11).

9. Blood is the source of life and health (Leviticus 17:11; 14). Up until 120 years ago, sick people were "bled" and many died as a result (e.g. George Washington). Today we know that healthy blood is necessary to bring life-giving nutrients to every cell in the body. God declared that "the life of the flesh is in the blood" long before science understood its function.

10. The Bible states that God created life according to *kinds* (Genesis 1:24). The fact that God distinguishes *kinds*, agrees with what scientists observe – namely that there are horizontal genetic boundaries beyond which life cannot vary. Life produces after its own kind. Dogs produce dogs, cats produce cats, roses produce roses. Never have we witnessed one kind changing into another kind as evolution

supposes. There are truly natural *limits* to biological change.

11. Noble behavior understood (John 15:13; Romans 5:7-8). The Bible and history reveal that countless people have endangered or even sacrificed their lives for another. This reality is completely at odds with Darwin's theory of the survival of the fittest.

12. Chicken or egg dilemma solved (Genesis 1:20-22). Which came first, the chicken or the egg? This question has plagued philosophers for centuries. The Bible states that God created birds with the ability to reproduce after their kind. Therefore the chicken was created first with the ability to make eggs! Yet, evolution has no solution for this dilemma.

13. Which came first, proteins or DNA (Revelation 4:11)? For evolutionists, the chicken or egg dilemma goes even deeper. Chickens consist of proteins. The code for each protein is contained in the DNA/RNA system. However, proteins are required in order to manufacture DNA. So which came first: proteins or DNA? The ONLY explanation is that they were *created* together.

14. Our bodies are made from the dust of the ground (Genesis 2:7; 3:19). Scientists have discovered that the human body is comprised of some 28 base and trace elements – all of which are found in the earth.

15. The First Law of Thermodynamics established (Genesis 2:1-2). The First Law states that the total quantity of energy and matter in the universe is a constant. One form of energy or matter may be converted into another, but the total quantity always remains the same. Therefore the creation is *finished*, exactly as God said way back in

Genesis.

16. The first three verses of Genesis accurately express all known aspects of the creation (Genesis 1:1-3). Science expresses the universe in terms of: time, space, matter, and energy. In Genesis chapter one we read: "In the beginning (time) God created the heavens (space) and the earth (matter)...Then God said, "Let there be light (energy)." No other creation account agrees with the observable evidence.

17. The universe had a beginning (Genesis 1:1; Hebrews 1:10-12). Starting with the studies of Albert Einstein in the early 1900s and continuing today, science has confirmed the biblical view that the universe had a beginning. When the Bible was written most people believed the universe was eternal. Science has proven them wrong, but the Bible correct.

18. The earth is a sphere (Isaiah 40:22). At a time when many thought the earth was flat, the Bible told us that the earth is spherical.

19. Scripture assumes a revolving (spherical) earth (Luke 17:34-36). Jesus said that at His return some would be asleep at night while others would be working at day time activities in the field. This is a clear indication of a revolving earth, with day and night occurring simultaneously.

20. Origin of the rainbow explained (Genesis 9:13-16). Prior to the Flood there was a different environment on the earth (Genesis 2:5-6). After the Flood, God set His rainbow "in the cloud" as a sign that He would never again judge the earth by water. Meteorologists now understand that a rainbow is formed when the sun shines through water droplets – which act as a prism – separating white light into

its color spectrum.

21. Light can be divided (Job 38:24). Sir Isaac Newton studied light and discovered that white light is made of seven colors, which can be "parted" and then recombined. Science confirmed this four centuries ago – God declared this four millennia ago!

22. Ocean currents anticipated (Psalm 8:8). Three thousand years ago the Bible described the "paths of the seas." In the 19th century Matthew Maury – the father of oceanography – after reading Psalm 8, researched and discovered ocean currents that follow specific paths through the seas! Utilizing Maury's data, marine navigators have since reduced by many days the time required to traverse the seas.

23. Sexual promiscuity is dangerous to your health (1 Corinthians 6:18; Romans 1:27). The Bible warns that "he who commits sexual immorality sins against his own body," and that those who commit homosexual sin would "receive in themselves" the penalty of their error. Much data now confirms that any sexual relationship outside of holy matrimony is unsafe.

24. Reproduction explained (Genesis 1:27-28; 2:24; Mark 10:6-8). While evolution has no mechanism to explain how male and female reproductive organs evolved at the same time, the Bible says that from the beginning God made them male and female in order to propagate the human race and animal kinds.

25. Incalculable number of stars (Jeremiah 33:22). At a time when less than 5,000 stars were visible to the human eye, God stated that the stars of heaven were innumerable. Not until the 17th century did Galileo glimpse the

immensity of our universe with his new telescope. Today, astronomers estimate that there are ten thousand billion trillion stars – that's a 1 followed by 25 zeros! Yet, as the Bible states, scientists admit this number may be woefully inadequate.

26. The number of stars, though vast, are finite (Isaiah 40:26). Although man is unable to calculate the exact number of stars, we now know their number is finite. Of course God knew this all along – "He counts the number of the stars; He calls them all by name" (Psalm 147:4). What an awesome God!

27. The Bible compares the number of stars with the number of grains of sand on the seashore (Genesis 22:17; Hebrews 11:12). Amazingly, gross estimates of the number of sand grains are comparable to the estimated number of stars in the universe. Visit: The Stars of Heaven (Institute For Creation Research)

28. Rejecting the Creator results in moral depravity (Romans 1:20-32). The Bible warns that when mankind rejects the overwhelming evidence for a Creator, lawlessness will result. Since the theory of evolution has swept the globe, abortion, pornography, genocide, etc., have all risen sharply.

29. The fact that God once flooded the earth (the Noahic Flood) would be denied (2 Peter 3:5-6). There is a mass of fossil evidence to prove this fact, yet it is flatly ignored by most of the scientific world because it was God's judgment on man's wickedness.

30. Vast fossil deposits anticipated (Genesis 7). When plants and animals die they decompose rapidly. Yet billions of life forms around the globe have been preserved as

fossils. Geologists now know that fossils only form if there is rapid deposition of life buried away from scavengers and bacteria. This agrees exactly with what the Bible says occurred during the global Flood.

31. The continents were created as one large land mass (Genesis 1:9-10). Many geologists agree there is strong evidence that the earth was originally one super continent – just as the Bible said way back in Genesis.

32. Continental drift inferred (Genesis 7:11). Today the study of the ocean floor indicates that the landmasses have been ripped apart. Scripture states that during the global Flood the "fountains of the great deep were broken up." This cataclysmic event apparently resulted in the continental plates breaking and shifting.

33. Ice Age inferred (Job 38:29-30). Prior to the global Flood the earth was apparently subtropical. However shortly after the Flood, the Bible mentions ice often – "By the breath of God ice is given, and the broad waters are frozen" (Job 37:10). Evidently the Ice Age occurred in the centuries following the Flood.

34. Life begins at fertilization (Jeremiah 1:5). God declares that He knew us before we were born. The biblical penalty for murdering an unborn child was death (Exodus 21:22-23). Today, it is an irrefutable biological fact that the fertilized egg is truly an entire human being. Nothing will be added to the first cell except nutrition and oxygen.

35. God fashions and knits us together in the womb (Job 10:8-12; 31:15). Science was ignorant concerning embryonic development until recently. Yet many centuries ago, the Bible accurately described God making us an "intricate unity" in the womb.

36. DNA anticipated (Psalm 139:13-16). During the 1950s, Watson and Crick discovered the genetic blueprint for life. Three thousand years ago the Bible seems to reference this written digital code in Psalm 139 – "Thine eyes did see my substance, yet being unperfect [unformed]; and in Thy book all my members were written, which in continuance were fashioned, when as yet there was none of them."

37. God has created all mankind from one blood (Acts 17:26; Genesis 5). Today researchers have discovered that we have all descended from one gene pool. For example, a 1995 study of a section of Y chromosomes from 38 men from different ethnic groups around the world was consistent with the biblical teaching that we all come from one man (Adam)

38. Origin of the major language groups explained (Genesis 11). After the rebellion at Babel, God scattered the people by confounding the one language into many languages. Evolution teaches that we all evolved from a common ancestor, yet offers no mechanism to explain the origin of the thousands of diverse languages in existence today.

39. Origin of the different "races" explained (Genesis 11). As Noah's descendants migrated around the world after Babel, each language group developed distinct features based on environment and genetic variation. Those with a genetic makeup suitable to their new environment survived to reproduce. Over time, certain traits (such as dark skin color for those closer to the equator) dominated. Genesis alone offers a reasonable answer to the origin of the races and languages.

40. God has given us the leaves of the trees as medicine (Ezekiel 47:12; Revelation 22:2). Ancient cultures utilized

many herbal remedies. Today, modern medicine has rediscovered what the Bible has said all along – there are healing compounds found in plants.

41. Healthy dietary laws (Leviticus 11:9-12). Scripture states that we should avoid those sea creatures which do not have fins or scales. We now know that bottom-feeders (those with no scales or fins) tend to consume waste and are likely to carry disease.

42. The Bible warns against eating birds of prey (Leviticus 11:13-19). Scientists now recognize that those birds which eat carrion (putrefying flesh), often spread disease.

43. Avoid swine (Deuteronomy 14:8). Not so long ago, science learned that eating undercooked pork causes an infection of parasites called trichinosis. Now consider this: the Bible forbid the eating of swine more than 3,000 years before we learned how to cook pork safely.

44. Radical environmentalism foreseen (Romans 1:25). Two thousand years ago, God's Word stated that many would worship and serve creation rather than the Creator. Today, nature is revered as "Mother" and naturalism is enshrined.

45. Black holes and dark matter anticipated (Matthew 25:30; Jude 1:13; Isaiah 50:3). Cosmologists now speculate that over 98% of the known universe is comprised of dark matter, with dark energy and black holes. A black hole's gravitational field is so strong that nothing, not even light, escapes. Beyond the expanding universe there is no measured radiation and therefore only outer darkness exists. These theories paint a seemingly accurate description of what the Bible calls "outer darkness" or "the blackness of darkness forever."

46. The Second Law of Thermodynamics (Entropy) explained (Psalm 102:25-26). This law states that everything in the universe is running down, deteriorating, constantly becoming less and less orderly. Entropy (disorder) entered when mankind rebelled against God – resulting in the curse (Genesis 3:17; Romans 8:20-22). Historically most people believed the universe was unchangeable. Yet modern science verifies that the universe is "grow(ing) old like a garment" (Hebrews 1:11). Evol Cain's wife discovered (Genesis 5:4). Skeptics point out that Cain had no one to marry – therefore the Bible must be false. However, the Bible states plainly that Adam and Eve had other sons and daughters. Cain married his sister.

48. Incest laws established (Leviticus 18:6). To marry near of kin in the ancient world was common. Yet, beginning about 1500 B.C., God forbid this practice. The reason is simple – the genetic mutations (resulting from the curse) had a cumulative effect. Though Cain could safely marry his sister because the genetic pool was still relatively pure at that time, by Moses' day the genetic errors had swelled. Today, geneticists confirm that the risk of passing on a genetic abnormality to your child is much greater if you marry a close relative because relatives are more likely to carry the same defective gene. If they procreate, their offspring are more apt to have this defect expressed.

49. Genetic mixing of different seeds forbidden (Leviticus 19:19; Deuteronomy 22:9). The Bible warns against mixing seeds – as this will result in an inferior or dangerous crop. There is now growing evidence that unnatural, genetically engineered crops may be harmful.

50. Hydrological cycle described (Ecclesiastes 1:7; Jeremiah 10:13; Amos 9:6). Four thousand years ago the

Bible declared that God "draws up drops of water, which distill as rain from the mist, which the clouds drop down and pour abundantly on man" (Job 36:27-28). The ancients observed mighty rivers flowing into the ocean, but they could not conceive why the sea level never rose. Though they observed rainfall, they had only quaint theories as to its origin. Meteorologists now understand that the hydrological cycle consists of evaporation, atmospheric transportation, distillation, and precipitation.

51. The sun goes in a circuit (Psalm 19:6). Some scientists scoffed at this verse thinking that it taught geocentricity – the theory that the sun revolves around the earth. They insisted the sun was stationary. However, we now know that the sun is traveling through space at approximately 600,000 miles per hour. It is literally moving through space in a huge circuit – just as the Bible stated 3,000 years ago!

52. Circumcision on the eighth day is ideal (Genesis 17:12; Leviticus 12:3; Luke 1:59). Medical science has discovered that the blood clotting chemical prothrombin peaks in a newborn on the eighth day. This is therefore the safest day to circumcise a baby. How did Moses know?!

53. God has given us just the right amount of water to sustain life (Isaiah 40:12). We now recognize that if there was significantly more or less water, the earth would not support life as we know it.

54. The earth was designed for biological life (Isaiah 45:18). Scientists have discovered that the most fundamental characteristics of our earth and cosmos are so finely tuned that if just one of them were even slightly different, life as we know it couldn't exist. This is called the Anthropic Principle and it agrees with the Bible which states that God formed the earth to be inhabited.

55. The universe is expanding (Job 9:8; Isaiah 42:5; Jeremiah 51:15; Zechariah 12:1). Repeatedly God declares that He stretches out the heavens. During the early 20th century, most scientists (including Einstein) believed the universe was static. Others believed it should have collapsed due to gravity. Then in 1929, astronomer Edwin Hubble showed that distant galaxies were receding from the earth, and the further away they were, the faster they were moving. This discovery revolutionized the field of astronomy. Eisntein admitted his mistake, and today most astronomers agree with what the Creator told us millennia ago – the universe is expanding!

56. Law of Biogenesis explained (Genesis 1). Scientists observe that life only comes from existing life. This law has *never* been violated under observation or experimentation (as evolution imagines). Therefore life, God's life, created all life.

57. Animal and plant extinction explained (Jeremiah 12:4; Hosea 4:3). According to evolution, occasionally we should witness a new kind springing into existence. Yet, this has never been observed. On the contrary, as Scripture explains, since the curse on all creation, we observe death and extinction (Romans 8:20-22).

58. Light travels in a path (Job 38:19). Light is said to have a "way" [Hebrew: derek, literally a traveled path or road]. Until the 17th century it was believed that light was transmitted instantaneously. We now know that light is a form of energy that travels at ~186,000 miles per second in a straight line. Indeed, there is a "way" of light.

59. Air has weight (Job 28:25). It was once thought that air was weightless. Yet 4,000 years ago Job declared that God established "a weight for the wind." In recent years,

meteorologists have calculated that the average thunderstorm holds thousands of tons of rain. To carry this load, air must have mass.

60. Jet stream anticipated (Ecclesiastes 1:6). At a time when it was thought that winds blew straight, the Bible declares "The wind goes toward the south, and turns around to the north; The wind whirls about continually, and comes again on its circuit." King Solomon wrote this 3,000 years ago. Now consider this: it was not until World War II that airmen discovered the jet stream circuit.

61. Medical quarantine instituted (Leviticus 13:45-46; Numbers 5:1-4). Long before man understood the principles of quarantine, God commanded the Israelites to isolate those with a contagious disease until cured.

62. Each star is unique (1 Corinthians 15:41). Centuries before the advent of the telescope, the Bible declared what only God and the angels knew – each star varies in size and intensity!

63. The Bible says that light can be sent, and then manifest itself in speech (Job 38:35). We now know that radio waves and light waves are two forms of the same thing – electromagnetic waves. Therefore, radio waves are a form of light. Today, using radio transmitters, we can send "lightnings" which indeed speak when they arrive.

64. Laughter promotes physical healing (Proverbs 17:22). Recent studies confirm what King Solomon was inspired to write 3,000 years ago, "A merry heart does good, like medicine." For instance, laughter reduces levels of certain stress hormones. This brings balance to the immune system, which helps your body fight off disease.

65. Intense sorrow or stress is harmful to your health (Proverbs 18:14; Mark 14:34). Researchers have studied individuals with no prior medical problems who showed symptoms of stress cardiomyopathy including chest pain, difficulty breathing, low blood pressure, and even heart failure – following a stressful incident.

66. Microorganisms anticipated (Exodus 22:31). The Bible warns "Whatever dies naturally or is torn by beasts he shall not eat, to defile himself with it: I am the LORD" (Leviticus 22:8). Today we understand that a decaying carcass is full of disease causing germs.

67. The Bible cautions against consuming fat (Leviticus 7:23). Only in recent decades has the medical community determined that fat clogs arteries and contributes to heart disease.

68. Do not consume blood (Leviticus 17:12). A common ritual in many religions in the ancient world was to drink blood. However, the Creator repeatedly told His people to abstain from blood (Genesis 9:4; Leviticus 3:17; Acts 15:20; 21:25). Of course, modern science reveals that consuming raw blood is dangerous.

69. The Bible describes dinosaurs (Job 40:15-24). In 1842, Sir Richard Owen coined the word dinosaur, meaning "terrible lizard," after discovering large reptilian-like fossils. However in the Book of Job, written 4,000 years earlier, God describes the behemoth as: the largest of all land creatures, plant eating (herbivore), with great strength in its hips and legs, powerful stomach muscles, a tail like a cedar tree, and bones like bars of iron. This is an accurate description of sauropods – the largest known dinosaur family.

70. Pleasure explained (Psalm 36:8). Evolution cannot explain pleasure – even the most complex chemicals do not experience bliss. However, the Bible states that God "gives us richly all things to enjoy" (1 Timothy 6:17). Pleasure is a gift from God.

71. Life is more than matter and energy (Genesis 2:7; Job 12:7-10). We know that if a creature is denied air it dies. Even though its body may be perfectly intact, and air and energy are reintroduced to spark life, the body remains dead. Scripture agrees with the observable evidence when it states that only God can give the breath of life. Life cannot be explained by raw materials, time, and chance alone – as evolutionists would lead us to believe.

72. Origin of music explained (Psalm 40:3). Evolution cannot explain the origin of music. The Bible says that every good gift comes from God (James 1:17). This includes joyful melodies. God has given both man and angels the gift of music-making (Genesis 4:21; Ezekiel 28:13). Singing is intended to express rejoicing in and worship of the Lord (Job 38:7; Psalm 95:1-2).

73. Our ancestors were not primitive (Genesis 4:20-22; Job 8:8-10; 12:12). Archeologists have discovered that our ancestors mined, had metallurgical factories, created air-conditioned buildings, designed musical instruments, studied the stars, and much more. This evidence directly contradicts the theory of evolution, but agrees completely with God's Word.

74. Cavemen described in the Bible (Job 30:1-8). Four thousand years ago, Job describes certain "vile men" who were driven from society to forage "among the bushes" for survival and who "live in the clefts of the valleys, (and) in caves of the earth and the rocks." Therefore "cavemen"

were simply outcasts and vagabounds – not our primitive ancestors as evolutionists speculate.

75. Environmental devastation of the planet foreseen (Revelation 11:18). Though evolution imagines that things should be getting better, the Bible foresaw what is really occurring today: pollution, destruction and corrupt dominion.

76. The seed of a plant contains its life (Genesis 1:11; 29). As stated in the Book of Genesis, we now recognize that inside the humble seed is life itself. Within the seed is a tiny factory of amazing complexity. No scientist can build a synthetic seed and no seed is simple!

77. A seed must die to produce new life (1 Corinthians 15:36-38). Jesus said, "unless a grain of wheat falls into the ground and dies, it remains alone; but if it dies, it produces much grain." (John 12:24). In this verse is remarkable confirmation of two of the fundamental concepts in biology: 1) Cells arise only from existing cells. 2) A grain must die to produce more grain. The fallen seed is surrounded by supporting cells from the old body. These supporting cells "give their lives" to provide nourishment to the inner kernel. Once planted, this inner kernel germinates resulting in much grain.

78. The order of creation agrees with true science (Genesis 1). Plants require sunlight, water, and minerals in order to survive. In the first chapter of Genesis we read that God created light first (v.3), then water (v. 6), then soil (v. 9), and *then* He created plant life (v. 11).

79. God created "lights" in the heavens "for signs and seasons, and for days and years" (Genesis 1:14-16). We now know that a year is the time required for the earth to

travel once around the sun. The seasons are caused by the changing position of the earth in relation to the sun. The moon's phases follow one another in clock-like precision – constituting the lunar calendar Evolution teaches that the cosmos evolved by random chance, yet the Bible agrees with the observable evidence.

80. The Bible speaks of "heaven and the highest heavens" (Deuteronomy 10:14). Long before the Hubble Space Telescope, Scripture spoke of the "heaven of heavens" and the "third heaven" (1 Kings 8:27; 2 Corinthians 12:2). We now know that the heavens consist of our immediate atmosphere and the vast reaches of outer space – as well as God's wonderful abode.

81. Olive oil and wine useful on wounds (Luke 10:34). Jesus told of a Samaritan man, who when he came upon a wounded traveler, he bandaged him – pouring upon his wounds olive oil and wine. Today we know that wine contains ethyl alcohol and traces of methyl alcohol. Both are good disinfectants. Olive oil is also a good disinfectant, as well as a skin moisturizer, protector, and soothing lotion. This is common knowledge to us today. However, did you know that during the Middle Ages and right up till the early 20th century, millions died because they did not know to treat and protect open wounds?

82. Man is "fearfully and wonderfully made" (Psalm 139:14). We are only beginning to probe the complexity of the DNA molecule, the eye, the brain, and all the intricate components of life. No human invention compares to the marvelous wonders of God's creation.

83. Beauty understood (Genesis 1:31; 2:9; Job 40:10; Ecclesiastes 3:11; Matthew 6:28-30). Beauty surrounds us: radiant sunsets, majestic mountains, brightly colored

flowers, glowing gems, soothing foliage, brilliantly adorned birds, etc. Beauty is a mystery to the evolutionist. However, Scripture reveals that God creates beautiful things for our benefit and His glory.

84. Strong and weak nuclear force explained (Colossians 1:17; Hebrews 1:3). Physicists do not understand what binds the atom's nucleus together. Yet, the Bible states that "all things consist" – or are held together by the Creator – Jesus Christ.

85. Atomic fission anticipated (2 Peter 3:10-12). Scripture states that "the elements will melt with fervent heat" when the earth and the heavens are "dissolved" by fire. Today we understand that if the elements of the atom are loosed, there would be an enormous release of heat and energy (radiation).

86. The Pleiades and Orion star clusters described (Job 38:31). The Pleiades star cluster is gravitationally bound, while the Orion star cluster is loose and disintegrating because the gravity of the cluster is not enough to bind the group together. 4,000 years ago God asked Job, "Can you bind the cluster of the Pleiades, or loose the belt of Orion?" Yet, it is only recently that we realized that the Pleiades is gravitationally bound, but Orion's stars are flying apart.

87. Safe drinking water (Leviticus 11:33-36). God forbade drinking from vessels or stagnant water that had been contaminated by coming into contact with a dead animal. It is only in the last 100 years that medical science has learned that contaminated water can cause typhoid and cholera.

88. Pest control (Leviticus 25:1-24). Farmers are plagued today with insects. Yet God gave a sure-fire remedy to

control pests centuries ago. Moses commanded Israel to set aside one year in seven when no crops were raised. Insects winter in the stalks of last year's harvest, hatch in the spring, and are perpetuated by laying eggs in the new crop. If the crop is denied one year in seven, the pests have nothing to subsist upon, and are thereby controlled.

89. Soil conservation (Leviticus 23:22). Not only was the land to lay fallow every seventh year, but God also instructed farmers to leave the gleanings when reaping their fields, and not to reap the corners (sides) of their fields. This served several purposes: 1) Vital soil minerals would be maintained. 2) The hedge row would limit wind erosion. 3) The poor could eat the gleanings. Today, approximately four billion metric tons of soil are lost from U.S. crop lands each year. Much of this soil depletion could be avoided if God's commands were followed.

90. Animal instincts understood (Job 39; Proverbs 30:24-28; Jeremiah 8:7). A newly hatched spider weaves an intricate web without being taught. A recently emerged butterfly somehow knows to navigate a 2,500-mile migration route without a guide. God explains that He has endowed each creature with specific knowledge. Scripture, not evolution, explains animal instincts.

91. Animals do not have a conscience (Psalm 32:9). A parrot can be taught to swear and blaspheme, yet never feel conviction. Many animals steal, but they do not experience guilt. If man evolved from animals, where did our conscience come from? The Bible explains that man alone was created as a moral being in God's image.

92. Pseudo-science anticipated (1 Timothy 6:20). The theory of evolution contradicts the observable evidence. The Bible warned us in advance that there would be those

who would profess: "profane and idle babblings and contradictions of what is falsely called knowledge (science)." True science agrees with the Creator's Word.

93. Science confirms the Bible (Colossians 2:3). These insights place the Bible far above every manmade theory and all other so-called inspired books. In contrast, the Koran states that the sun sets in a muddy pond (Surah 18:86). The Hadith contains many myths. The Book of Mormon declares that Native Americans descended from Jews – which has been disproven by DNA research. The Eastern writings also contradict true science.

94. Human conscience understood (Romans 2:14-15). The Bible reveals that God has impressed His moral law onto every human heart. *Con* means *with* and *science* means *knowledge*. We know it is wrong to murder, lie, steal, etc. Only the Bible explains that each human has a God-given knowledge of right and wrong.

95. Love explained (Matthew 22:37-40; 1 John 4:7-12). Evolution cannot explain love. Yet, God's Word reveals that the very purpose of our existence is to know and love God and our fellow man. God is love, and we were created in His image to reflect His love.

96. The real you is spirit (Numbers 16:22; Zechariah 12:1). Personality is non-physical. For example, after a heart transplant the recipient does not receive the donor's character. An amputee is not half the person he was before loosing his limbs. Our eternal nature is spirit, heart, soul, mind. The Bible tells us that "man looks at the outward appearance, but the Lord looks at the heart" (1 Samuel 16:7).

97. The cause of suffering revealed (Genesis 3; Isaiah 24:5-

6). The earth is subject to misery, which appears at odds with our wonderfully designed universe. However, the Bible, not evolution, explains the origin of suffering. When mankind rebelled against God, the curse resulted – introducing affliction, pain and death into the world.

98. Death explained (Romans 6:23). All eventually die. The Bible alone explains why we die – "The soul who sins shall die" (Ezekiel 18:20). Sin is transgression of God's Law. To see if you will die, please review God's Ten Commandments (Exodus 20). Have you ever lied? (White lies and fibs count.) Ever stolen? (Cheating on a test or taxes is stealing.) Jesus said that "whoever looks at a woman to lust for her has already committed adultery with her in his heart" (Matthew 5:28). Have you ever looked with lust? Then you're an adulterer at heart. Have you ever hated someone or called someone a fool? If so, the Bible says you are guilty of murder (Matthew 5:21-22; 1 John 3:15). Have you ever used your Creator's name (Lord, God, Jesus, or Christ) in vain? This is called blasphemy – and God hates it. If you have broken these commandments at any time, then by your own admission, you are a blasphemer, a murderer, an adulterer, a thief, and a liar at heart. And we have only looked at five of the Ten Commandments. This is why we die.

99. Justice understood (Acts 17:30-31). Our God-given conscience reveals that all sin will be judged. Down deep we know that He who created the eyes sees every secret sin (Romans 2:16). He who formed our mind remembers our past offense as if it just occurred. God has declared that the penalty for sin is death. Physical death comes first, then the second death – which is eternal separation from God in the lake of fire (Revelation 21:8). God cannot lie. Every sin will be judged. His justice demands it. But God is also rich in mercy to all who call upon His name. He has made a

way for justice to be served and mercy to be shown.

100. Eternal life revealed (John 3:16). Scientists search in vain for the cure for aging and death. Yet, the good news is that God, who is the source of all life, has made a way to freely forgive us so that we may live forever with Him in heaven. "But God demonstrates His own love toward us, in that while we were still sinners, Christ died for us" (Romans 5:8). "For God so loved the world that He gave His only begotten Son, that whoever believes in Him should not perish but have everlasting life" (John 3:16). God desires a loving, eternal relationship with each person – free from sin, fear, and pain. Therefore, He sent His Son to die as our substitute on the cross. "The wages of sin is death, but the gift of God is eternal life in Christ Jesus our Lord" (Romans 6:23). Jesus never sinned, therefore He alone qualified to pay the penalty for our sins on the cross. He died in our place. He then rose from the grave defeating death. All who turn from their sins and trust Him will be saved. To repent and place your trust in Jesus Christ, make Psalm 51 your prayer. Then read your Bible daily, obeying what you read. God will never let you down.

101. The solution to suffering (Revelation 21). Neither evolution nor religion offers a solution to suffering. But God offers heaven as a gift to all who trust in His Son. In heaven, "God will wipe away every tear from their eyes; there shall be no more death, nor sorrow, nor crying. There shall be no more pain, for the former things have passed away" (Revelation 21:4).

www.eternal-productions.org

CHURCH BULLETIN BLOOPERS

The Scouts are saving aluminum cans, bottles and other items to be recycled. Proceeds will be used to cripple children.

The pastor would appreciate it if the ladies of the congregation would lend him their electric girdles for the pancake breakfast next Sunday morning.

Our youth basketball team is back in action Wednesday at 8 PM in the recreation hall. Come out and watch us kill Christ the King.

The peacemaking meeting scheduled for today has been canceled due to a conflict.

Remember in prayer the many who are sick of our community. Smile at someone who is hard to love. Say "Hell" to someone who doesn't care much about you.

For those of you who have children and don't know it, we have a nursery downstairs.

Next Thursday there will be tryouts for the choir. They need all the help they can get.

Irving Benson and Jessie Carter were married on October 24 in the church. So ends a friendship that began in their school days.

At the evening service tonight, the sermon topic will be "What Is Hell?" Come early and listen to our choir practice.

This evening at 7 PM there will be a hymn singing in the park across from the Church. Bring a blanket and come prepared to sin.

Weight Watchers will meet at 7 PM at the First Presbyterian Church. Please use large double door at the side entrance.

The Associate Minister unveiled the church's new tithing campaign slogan last Sunday: "I Upped My Pledge--Up Yours"

The Fasting and Prayer Conference includes meals.

The sermon this morning: 'Jesus Walks on the Water.' The sermon tonight: 'Searching for Jesus.'

Ladies, don't forget the rummage sale. It's a chance to get rid of those things not worth keeping around the house. Bring your husbands.

Don't let worry kill you off - let the Church help.

Miss Charlene Mason sang 'I will not pass this way again,' giving obvious pleasure to the congregation.

Eight new choir robes are currently needed due to the addition of several new members and to the deterioration of some older ones.

Please place your donation in the envelope along with the deceased person you want remembered.

The church will host an evening of fine dining, super entertainment and gracious hostility.

Potluck supper Sunday at 5:00 PM - prayer and medication to follow.

The ladies of the Church have cast off clothing of every kind. They may be seen in the basement on Friday afternoon.

Ladies Bible Study will be held Thursday morning at 10 AM. All ladies are invited to lunch in the Fellowship Hall after the B. S. Is done.

Low Self Esteem Support Group will meet Thursday at 7 PM. Please use the back door.

The eighth-graders will be presenting Shakespeare's Hamlet in the Church basement Friday at 7 PM. The congregation is invited to attend this tragedy.

Weight Watchers will meet at 7 PM at the First Presbyterian Church.. Please use large double door at the side entrance.

Coming Up—Theological Open House. We discuss thought-provoking topics. Your opinions are hardly welcome.

All singles are invited to join us Friday at 7 p.m. for the annula Christmas Sing-alone."

Thursday night – potluck supper. Prayer and medication to follow.

Remember in prayer the many who are sick of our church and the community.

For those of you who have children and don't know it, we have a nursery downstairs.

The rosebud on the altar this morning is to announce the birth of David Alan Belzer, the sin of Rev. and Mrs. Julius Belzer.

This afternoon there will be a meeting in the south and north ends of the church. Children will be baptized at both ends.

Tuesday at 4:00 p.m. there will be an ice cream social. All ladies giving milk will please come early.

Wednesday, the Ladies Liturgy Society will meet. Mrs. Jones will sing "Put Me In My Little Bed" accompanied by the pastor.

Thursday at 5:00 p.m. there will be a meeting of the Little Mothers Club. All wishing to become little mothers, please see the minister in his study.

This being Easter Sunday, we will ask Mrs. Lewis to come forward and lay an egg on the altar.

The service will close with "Little Drops Of Water." One of the ladies will start quietly, and the rest of the congregation will join in.

Next Sunday, a special collection will be taken to defray the cost of the new carpet. All those wishing to do something on the new carpet will come forward and get a piece of paper.

The ladies of the church have cast off clothing of every kind and they may be seen in the church basement Friday.

A bean supper will be held on Tuesday evening in the church hall. Music will follow.

At the evening service tonight, the sermon topic will be "What Is Hell?" – come early and listen to our choir practice.

Our youth basketball team is back in action Wednesday at 8:00 p.m. in the recreation hall. Come out and watch us kill Christ the King.

Miss Charlene Mason sang, "I will not pass this way again," giving obvious pleasure to the congregation.

"Ladies, don't forget the rummage sale. It's a chance to get rid of those things not worth keeping around the house. Don't forget your husbands."

The sermon this morning: "Jesus Walks on the Water." The sermon tonight: "Searching for Jesus."

Next Thursday there will be tryouts for the choir. They need all the help they can get.

Barbara remains in the hospital and needs blood donors for more transfusions. She is also having trouble sleeping and requests tapes of Pastor Jack's sermons.

The Rector will preach his farewell message after which the choir will sing "Break Forth into Joy."

Irving Benson and Jessie Carter were married on October 24 in the church. So ends a friendship that began in their school days.

Eight new choir robes are currently needed, due to the addition of several new members and to the deterioration of some older ones.

Scouts are saving aluminum cans, bottles, and other items to be recycled. Proceeds will be used to cripple children.

Please place your donation in the envelope along with the deceased person(s) you want remembered.

The church will host an evening of fine dining, superb entertainment, and gracious hostility.

The pastor would appreciate it if the ladies of the congregation would lend him their electric girdles for the pancake breakfast next Sunday morning.

Low Self Esteem Support Group will meet Thursday. Please use the back door.

The eighth-graders will be presenting Shakespeare's Hamlet in the Church basement Friday at 7:00 p.m. The Congregation is invited to attend this tragedy.

Weight Watchers will meet at 7:00 p.m. at the First Presbyterian Church. Please use large double door at the side entrance.

The outreach committee has enlisted 25 visitors to make calls on people who are not afflicted with any church.

The Rev. Merriwether spoke briefly, much to the delight of the audience.

Next Sunday Mrs. Vinson will be soloist for the morning service. The pastor will then speak on "It's a Terrible Experience."

The music for today's service was all composed by George Friedrich Handel in celebration of the 300th anniversary of his birth.

Remember in prayer the many who are sick of our church and community.

The concert held in Fellowship Hall was a great success. Special thanks are due to the minister's daughter, who labored the whole evening at the piano, which as usual fell upon her.

Today's Sermon: HOW MUCH CAN A MAN DRINK? with hymns from a full choir.

Pastor is on vacation. Massages can be given to church secretary.

Bertha Belch, a missionary from Africa, will be speaking tonight at Calvary Methodist. Come hear Bertha Belch all the way from Africa.

Attend and you will hear an excellent speaker and heave a healthy lunch.

This evening at 7 pm there will be a hymn sing in the park across from the Church. Bring a blanket and come prepared to sin.

Ladies Bible Study will be held Thursday morning at 10. All ladies are invited to lunch in the Fellowship Hall after the B.S. is done.

The Associate Minister unveiled the church's new tithing campaign slogan last Sunday "I Upped My Pledge - Up Yours."

WHEN GOD LAUGHS BY
JACK LONDON

"The gods, the gods are stronger; time Falls down before them, all men's knees Bow, all men's prayers and sorrows climb Like incense toward them; yea, for these Are gods, Felise."

Carquinez had relaxed finally. He stole a glance at the rattling windows, looked upward at the beamed roof, and listened for a moment to the savage roar of the south-easter as it caught the bungalow in its bellowing jaws. Then he held his glass between him and the fire and laughed for joy through the golden wine.

"It is beautiful," he said. "It is sweetly sweet. It is a woman's wine, and it was made for gray-robed saints to drink."

"We grow it on our own warm hills," I said, with pardonable Califor- nia pride. "You rode up yesterday through the vines from which it was made."

It was worth while to get Carquinez to loosen up. Nor was he ever really himself until he felt the mellow warmth of the vine singing in his blood. He was an artist, it is true, always an artist; but somehow, sober, the high pitch and lilt went out of his thought-processes and he was prone to be as deadly dull as a British Sunday—not dull as other men are dull, but dull when measured by the sprightly wight that Monte Car- quinez was when he was really himself.

From all this it must not be inferred that Carquinez, who is my dear friend and dearer comrade, was a sot. Far from it. He rarely erred. As I have said, he was an artist. He knew when he had enough, and enough, with him, was equilibrium—the equilibrium that is yours and mine when we are sober.

His was a wise and instinctive temperateness that savoured of the Greek. Yet he was far from Greek. "I am Aztec, I am Inca, I am Spaniard," I have heard him say. And in truth he looked it, a compound of strange and ancient races, what with his swarthy skin and the asymmetry and primitiveness of his features. His eyes, under massively arched brows, were wide apart and black with the blackness that is barbaric, while before them was perpetually falling down a great black mop of hair through which he gazed like a roguish satyr from a thicket. He invari- ably wore a soft flannel shirt under his velvet-corduroy jacket, and his necktie was red. This latter stood for the red flag (he had once lived with the socialists of Paris), and it symbolized the blood and brotherhood of man. Also, he had never been known to wear anything on his head save a leather-banded sombrero. It was even rumoured that he had been born

with this particular piece of headgear. And in my experience it was provocative of nothing short of sheer delight to see that Mexican sombrero

hailing a cab in Piccadilly or storm-tossed in the crush for the New York Elevated.

As I have said, Carquinez was made quick by wine—"as the clay was made quick when God breathed the breath of life into it," was his way of saying it. I confess that he was blasphemously intimate with God; and I must add that there was no blasphemy in him. He was at all times hon- est, and, because he was compounded of paradoxes, greatly misunder- stood by those who did not know him. He could be as elementally raw at times as a screaming savage; and at other times as delicate as a maid, as subtle as a Spaniard. And—well, was he not Aztec? Inca? Spaniard?

And now I must ask pardon for the space I have given him. (He is my friend, and I love him.) The house was shaking to the storm, as he drew closer to the fire and laughed at it through his wine. He looked at me, and by the added lustre of his eye, and by the alertness of it, I knew that at last he was pitched in his proper key.

"And so you think you've won out against the gods?" he demanded.
"Why the gods?"
"Whose will but theirs has put satiety upon man?" he cried.
"And whence the will in me to escape satiety?" I asked triumphantly.
"Again the gods," he laughed. "It is their game we play. They deal and

shuffle all the cards ... and take the stakes. Think not that you have es-caped by fleeing from the mad cities. You with your vine-clad hills, your sunsets and your sunrises, your

homely fare and simple round of living!

"I've watched you ever since I came. You have not won. You have sur-rendered. You have made terms with the enemy. You have made confes-sion that you are tired. You have flown the white flag of fatigue. You have nailed up a notice to the effect that life is ebbing down in you. You have run away from life. You have played a trick, shabby trick. You have balked at the game. You refuse to play. You have thrown your cards un- der the table and run away to hide, here amongst your hills."

He tossed his straight hair back from his flashing eyes, and scarcely in-terrupted to roll a long, brown, Mexican cigarette.

"But the gods know. It is an old trick. All the generations of man have tried it ... and lost. The gods know how to deal with such as you. To pur- sue is to possess, and to possess is to be sated. And so you, in your wis- dom, have refused any longer to pursue. You have elected surcease. Very well. You will become sated with surcease. You say you have escaped satiety! You have merely bartered it for senility. And senility is another name for satiety. It is satiety's masquerade. Bah!"

"But look at me!" I cried.

Carquinez was ever a demon for haling ones soul out and making rags and tatters of it.

He looked me witheringly up and down.
"You see no signs," I challenged.
"Decay is insidious," he retorted.

"You are rotten ripe."
I laughed and forgave him for his very deviltry. But he refused to be

forgiven.
"Do I not know?" he asked. "The gods always win. I have watched men

play for years what seemed a winning game. In the end they lost."
"Don't you ever make mistakes?" I asked.
He blew many meditative rings of smoke before replying.
"Yes, I was nearly fooled, once. Let me tell you. There was Marvin

Fiske. You remember him? And his Dantesque face and poet's soul, singing his chant of the flesh, the very priest of Love? And there was Ethel Baird, whom also you must remember."

"A warm saint," I said.

"That is she! Holy as Love, and sweeter! Just a woman, made for love; and yet—how shall I say?—drenched through with holiness as your own air here is with the perfume of flowers. Well, they married. They played a hand with the gods—"

"And they won, they gloriously won!" I broke in.
Carquinez looked at me pityingly, and his voice was like a funeral bell.
"They lost. They supremely, colossally lost."
"But the world believes otherwise," I ventured coldly.
"The world conjectures. The world sees only the face of things. But I

know. Has it ever entered your mind to wonder why she took the veil, buried herself in that dolorous convent of the living dead?"

"Because she loved him so, and when he died ... "
Speech was frozen on my lips by Carquinez's sneer.
"A pat answer," he said, "machine-made like a piece of cotton-drill.

The world's judgment! And much the world knows about it. Like you, she fled from life. She was beaten. She flung out the white flag of fatigue. And no beleaguered city ever flew that flag in such bitterness and tears.

"Now I shall tell you the whole tale, and you must believe me, for I know. They had pondered the problem of satiety. They loved Love. They knew to the uttermost farthing the value of Love. They loved him so well

that they were fain to keep him always, warm and a-thrill in their hearts. They welcomed his coming; they feared to have him depart.

"Love was desire, they held, a delicious pain. He was ever seeking easement, and when he found that for which he sought, he died. Love denied was Love alive; Love granted was Love deceased. Do you follow me? They saw it was not the way of life to be hungry for what it has. To eat and still be hungry—man has never accomplished that feat. The problem of satiety. That is it. To have and to keep the sharp famine-edge of appetite at the groaning board. This was their problem, for they loved Love. Often did they discuss it, with all Love's sweet ardours brimming in their eyes; his ruddy blood spraying their cheeks; his voice playing in and out with their voices, now hiding as a tremolo in their throats, and again

shading a tone with that ineffable tenderness which he alone can utter.

"How do I know all this? I saw— much. More I learned from her diary. This I found in it, from Fiona Macleod: 'For, truly, that wandering voice, that twilight-whisper, that breath so dewy-sweet, that flame-winged lute- player whom none sees but for a moment, in a rainbow-shimmer of joy, or a sudden lightning-flare of passion, this exquisite mystery we call Amor, comes, to some rapt visionaries at least, not with a song upon the lips that all may hear, or with blithe viol of public music, but as one wrought by ecstasy, dumbly eloquent with desire.'

"How to keep the flame-winged lute-player with his dumb eloquence of desire? To feast him was to lose him. Their love for each other was a great love. Their granaries were overflowing with plenitude; yet they wanted to keep the sharp famine-edge of their love undulled.

"Nor were they lean little fledglings theorizing on the threshold of Love. They were robust and realized souls. They had loved before, with others, in the days before they met; and in those days they had throttled Love with caresses, and killed him with kisses, and buried him in the pit of satiety.

"They were not cold wraiths, this man and woman. They were warm human. They had no Saxon soberness in their blood. The colour of it was sunset- red. They glowed with it. Temperamentally theirs was the French joy in the flesh. They were idealists, but their idealism was Gallic. It was not tempered by the chill and sombre fluid that for the English serves as blood. There was no stoicism about them. They were Americans, descen- ded out of the English, and yet the refraining and self-denying of the English spirit-groping were not theirs.

"They were all this that I have said, and they were made for joy, only they achieved a concept. A curse on concepts! They played with logic, and this was their logic.—But first let me tell you of a talk we had one night. It was of Gautier's Madeline de Maupin. You remember the maid? She kissed once, and once only, and kisses she would have no more. Not that she found kisses were not sweet, but that she feared with repetition they would cloy. Satiety again! She tried to play without stakes against the gods. Now this is contrary to a rule of the game the gods themselves have made. Only the rules are not posted over the table. Mortals must play in order to learn the rules.

"Well, to the logic. The man and the woman argued thus: Why kiss once only? If to kiss once were wise, was it not wiser to kiss not at all? Thus could they keep Love alive. Fasting, he would knock forever at their hearts.

"Perhaps it was out of their heredity that they achieved this unholy concept. The breed will out and sometimes most fantastically. Thus in them did cursed Albion array herself a scheming wanton, a bold, cold-calculating, and artful hussy. After all, I do not know. But this I know: it was out of their inordinate desire for joy that they forewent joy.

"As he said (I read it long afterward in one of his letters to her): 'To hold you in my arms, close, and yet not close. To yearn for you, and nev- er to have you, and so always to have you.' And she: 'For you to be al- ways just beyond my reach. To be ever attaining you, and yet never at- taining you, and for this to last forever, always fresh and new, and al- ways with the first flush upon us.

"That is not the way they said it. On my lips their love-philosophy is mangled. And who am I to delve into their soul-stuff? I am a frog, on the dank edge of a great darkness, gazing goggle-eyed at the mystery and wonder of their flaming souls.

"And they were right, as far as they went. Everything is good ... as long as it is unpossessed. Satiety and possession are Death's horses; they run in span.

"'And time could only tutor us to eke Our rapture's warmth with custom's afterglow.'

"They got that from a sonnet of Alfred Austin's. It was called 'Love's Wisdom.' It was the one kiss of Madeline de Maupin. How did it run?

"'Kiss we and part; no further can we go; And better death than we from high to low Should dwindle, or decline from strong to weak.'

"But they were wiser. They would not kiss and part. They would not kiss at all, and thus they planned to stay at Love's topmost peak. They married. You were in England at the time. And never was there such a marriage. They kept their secret to themselves. I did not know, then.

Their rapture's warmth did not cool. Their love burned with increasing brightness. Never was there anything like it. The time passed, the months, the years, and ever the flame-winged lute-player grew more resplendent.

"Everybody marvelled. They became the wonderful lovers, and they were greatly envied. Sometimes women pitied her because she was childless; it is the form the envy of such creatures takes.

"And I did not know their secret. I pondered and I marvelled. As first I had expected, subconsciously I imagine, the passing of their love. Then I became aware that it was Time that passed and Love that remained. Then I became curious. What was their secret? What were the magic fet- ters with which they bound Love to them? How did they hold the grace- less elf? What elixir of eternal love had they drunk together as had Tris- tram and Iseult of old time? And whose hand had brewed the fairy drink?

"As I say, I was curious, and I watched them. They were love-mad. They lived in an unending revel of Love. They made a pomp and cere- monial of it. They saturated themselves in the art and poetry of Love. No, they were not neurotics. They were sane and healthy, and they were artists. But they had accomplished the impossible. They had achieved deathless desire.

"And I? I saw much of them and their everlasting miracle of Love. I puzzled and wondered, and then one day—"

Carquinez broke off abruptly and

asked, "Have you ever read, 'Love's Waiting Time'?"

I shook my head.

"Page wrote it—Curtis Hidden Page, I think. Well, it was that bit of verse that gave me the clue. One day, in the window-seat near the big pi- ano—you remember how she could play? She used to laugh, sometimes, and doubt whether it was for them I came, or for the music. She called me a 'music-sot' once, a 'sound-debauchee.' What a voice he had! When he sang I believed in immortality, my regard for the gods grew almost patronizing and I devised ways and means whereby I surely could out- wit them and their tricks.

"It was a spectacle for God, that man and woman, years married, and singing love-songs with a freshness virginal as new-born Love himself, with a ripeness and wealth of ardour that young lovers can never know. Young lovers were pale and anaemic beside that long-married pair. To

see them, all fire and flame and tenderness, at a trembling distance, lav- ishing caresses of eye and voice with every action, through every si- lence—their love driving them toward each other, and they withholding like fluttering moths, each to the other a candle-flame, and revolving each about the other in the mad gyrations of an amazing orbit-flight! It seemed, in obedience to some great law of physics, more potent than gravitation and more subtle, that they must corporeally melt each into each there before my very eyes. Small wonder they were called the won- derful lovers.

"I have wandered. Now to the clue. One day in the window-seat I found a book of verse. It opened of itself, betraying long habit, to 'Love's Waiting Time.' The page was thumbed and limp with overhandling, and there I read:—

"'So sweet it is to stand but just apart, To know each other better, and to keep The soft, delicious sense of two that touch ...

O love, not yet! ... Sweet, let us keep our love Wrapped round with sacred mystery awhile, Waiting the secret of the coming years, That come not yet, not yet ... sometime ... not yet ...

Oh, yet a little while our love may grow! When it has blossomed it will haply die. Feed it with lipless kisses, let it sleep, Bedded in dead denial yet some while ... Oh, yet a little while, a little while.'

"I folded the book on my thumb and sat there silent and without mov- ing for a long time. I was stunned by the clearness of vision the verse had imparted to me. It was illumination. It was like a bolt of God's lightning in the Pit. They would keep Love, the fickle sprite, the forerunner of young life—young life that is imperative to be born!

"I conned the lines over in my mind—'Not yet, sometime'—'O Love, not yet'—'Feed it with lipless kisses, let it sleep.' And I laughed aloud, ha, ha! I saw with white vision their blameless souls. They were children. They did not understand. They played with Nature's fire and bedded with a naked sword. They laughed at the gods. They would stop the cos- mic sap. They had invented a

system, and brought it to the gaming-table of life, and expected to win out. 'Beware!' I cried. 'The gods are behind the table. They make new rules for every system that is devised. You have no chance to win.'

"But I did not so cry to them. I waited. They would learn that their sys- tem was worthless and throw it away. They would be content with whatever happiness the gods gave them and not strive to wrest more away.

"I watched. I said nothing. The months continued to come and go, and still the famine-edge of their love grew the sharper. Never did they dull it with a permitted love-clasp. They ground and whetted it on self-deni-al, and sharper and sharper it grew. This went on until even I doubted. Did the gods sleep? I wondered. Or were they dead? I laughed to myself. The man and the woman had made a miracle. They had outwitted God. They had shamed the flesh, and blackened the face of the good Earth Mother. They had played with her fire and not been burned. They were immune. They were themselves gods, knowing good from evil and tast- ing not. 'Was this the way gods came to be?' I asked myself. 'I am a frog,' I said. 'But for my mud- lidded eyes I should have been blinded by the brightness of this wonder I have witnessed. I have puffed myself up with my wisdom and passed judgment upon gods.'

"Yet even in this, my latest wisdom, I was wrong. They were not gods. They were man and woman—soft clay that sighed and thrilled, shot through with desire, thumbed with strange weaknesses which the gods have not."

Carquinez broke from his narrative to roll another cigarette and to laugh harshly. It was not a pretty laugh; it was like the mockery of a dev- il, and it rose over and rode the roar of the storm that came muffled to our ears from the crashing outside world.

"I am a frog," he said apologetically. "How were they to understand? They were artists, not biologists. They knew the clay of the studio, but they did not know the clay of which they themselves were made. But this I will say—they played high. Never was there such a game before, and I doubt me if there will ever be such a game again.

"Never was lovers' ecstasy like theirs. They had not killed Love with kisses. They had quickened him with denial. And by denial they drove him on till he was all aburst with desire. And the flame-winged lute- player fanned them with his warm wings till they were all but swooning. It was the very delirium of Love, and it continued undiminished and in-creasing through the weeks and months.

"They longed and yearned, with all the fond pangs and sweet deli- cious agonies, with an intensity never felt by lovers before nor since.

"And then one day the drowsy gods ceased nodding. They aroused and looked at the man and woman who had made a mock of them. And the man and woman looked into each other's eyes one morning and knew that something was gone. It was the flame-winged one. He had fled, silently, in the night, from their

anchorites' board.

"They looked into each other's eyes and knew that they did not care. Desire was dead. Do you understand? Desire was dead. And they had never kissed. Not once had they kissed. Love was gone. They would never yearn and burn again. For them there was nothing left—no more tremblings and flutterings and delicious anguishes, no more throbbing and pulsing, and sighing and song. Desire was dead. It had died in the night, on a couch cold and unattended; nor had they witnessed its passing. They learned it for the first time in each other's eyes.

"The gods may not be kind, but they are often merciful. They had twirled the little ivory ball and swept the stakes from the table. All that remained was the man and woman gazing into each other's cold eyes. And then he died. That was the mercy. Within the week Marvin Fiske was dead— you remember the accident. And in her diary, written at this time, I long afterward read Mitchell Kennerly's:—

"'There was not a single hour We might have kissed and did not kiss.'"
"Oh, the irony of it!" I cried out. And Carquinez, in the firelight a veritable Mephistopheles in velvet

jacket, fixed me with his black eyes. "And they won, you said? The world's judgment! I have told you, and

I know. They won as you are winning, here in your hills."
"But you," I demanded hotly; "you with your orgies of sound and sense, with your mad cities and madder frolics—bethink you that you

win?"
He shook his head slowly. "Because you with your sober bucolic re-

gime, lose, is no reason that I should win. We never win. Sometimes we think we win. That is a little pleasantry of the gods."

THE ANGEL OF ODD
BY EDGAR ALLAN POE (1809-1849)

It was a chilly November afternoon. I had just consummated an unusually hearty dinner, of which the dyspeptic *truffe* formed not the least important item, and was sitting alone in the dining-room with my feet upon the fender and at my elbow a small table which I had rolled up to the fire, and upon which were some apologies for dessert, with some miscellaneous bottles of wine, spirit, and *liqueur*. In the morning I had been reading Glover's *Leonidas*, Wilkie's *Epigoniad*, Lamartine's *Pilgrimage*, Barlow's *Columbiad*, Tuckerman's *Sicily*, and Griswold's *Curiosities*, I am willing to confess, therefore, that I now felt a little stupid. I made effort to arouse myself by frequent aid of Lafitte, and all failing, I betook myself to a stray newspaper in despair. Having carefully perused the column of "Houses to let," and the column of "Dogs lost," and then the columns of "Wives and apprentices runaway," I attacked with great resolution the editorial matter, and reading it from beginning to end without understanding a syllable, conceived the possibility of its being Chinese, and so re-read it from the end to the beginning, but with no more satisfactory result. I was about throwing away in disgust

This folio of four pages, happy work.
Which not even critics criticise,

when I felt my attention somewhat aroused by the paragraph which follows:

"The avenues to death are numerous and strange. A London paper mentions the decease of a person from a singular cause. He was playing at 'puff the dart,' which is played with a long needle inserted in some worsted, and blown at a target through a tin tube. He placed the needle at the wrong end of the tube, and drawing his breath strongly to puff the dart forward with force, drew the needle into his throat. It entered the lungs, and in a few days killed him."

Upon seeing this I fell into a great rage, without exactly knowing why. "This thing," I exclaimed, "is a contemptible falsehood—a poor hoax—the lees of the invention of some pitiable penny-a-liner, of some wretched concocter of accidents in Cocaigne. These fellows knowing the extravagant gullibility of the age set their wits to work in the imagination of improbable possibilities, of odd accidents as they term them, but to a reflecting intellect (like mine, I added, in parenthesis, putting my forefinger unconsciously to the side of my nose), to a contemplative understanding such as I myself possess, it seems evident at once that the marvelous increase of late in these 'odd accidents' is by far the oddest accident of all. For my own part, I intend to believe nothing henceforward that has anything of the 'singular' about it."

"Mein Gott, den, vat a vool you bees for dat!" replied one of the most remarkable voices I ever heard. At first I took it for a rumbling in my

ears—such as a man sometimes experiences when getting very drunk—but upon second thought, I considered the sound as more nearly resembling that which proceeds from an empty barrel beaten with a big stick; and, in fact, this I should have concluded it to be, but for the articulation of the syllables and words. I am by no means naturally nervous, and the very few glasses of Lafitte which I had sipped served to embolden me a little, so that I felt nothing of trepidation, but merely uplifted my eyes with a leisurely movement and looked carefully around the room for the intruder. I could not, however, perceive any one at all.

"Humph!" resumed the voice as I continued my survey, "you mus pe so dronk as de pig den for not zee me as I zit here at your zide."

Hereupon I bethought me of looking immediately before my nose, and there, sure enough, confronting me at the table sat a personage nondescript, although not altogether indescribable. His body was a wine-pipe or a rum puncheon, or something of that character, and had a truly Falstaffian air. In its nether extremity were inserted two kegs, which seemed to answer all the purposes of legs. For arms there dangled from the upper portion of the carcass two tolerably long bottles with the necks outward for hands. All the head that I saw the monster possessed of was one of those Hessian canteens which resemble a large snuff-box with a hole in the middle of the lid. This canteen (with a funnel on its top like a cavalier cap slouched over the eyes) was set on edge upon the puncheon, with the hole toward myself; and

through this hole, which seemed puckered up like the mouth of a very precise old maid, the creature was emitting certain rumbling and grumbling noises which he evidently intended for intelligible talk.

"I zay," said he, "you mos pe dronk as de pig, vor zit dare and not zee me zit ere; and I zay, doo, you mos pe pigger vool as de goose, vor to dispelief vat iz print in de print. 'Tiz de troof—dat it iz—ebery vord ob it."

"Who are you, pray?" said I with much dignity, although somewhat puzzled; "how did you get here? and what is it you are talking about?"

"As vor ow I com'd ere," replied the figure, "dat iz none of your pizziness; and as vor vat I be talking apout, I be talk apout vat I tink proper; and as vor who I be, vy dat is de very ting I com'd here for to let you zee for yourself."

"You are a drunken vagabond," said I, "and I shall ring the bell and order my footman to kick you into the street."

"He! he! he!" said the fellow, "hu! hu! hu! dat you can't do."

"Can't do!" said I, "what do you mean? I can't do what?"

"Ring de pell," he replied, attempting a grin with his little villainous mouth.

Upon this I made an effort to get up in order to put my threat into execution, but the ruffian just reached across the table very deliberately, and hitting me a tap on the forehead with the neck of one of the long bottles, knocked me back into the armchair

from which I had half arisen. I was utterly astounded, and for a moment was quite at a loss what to do. In the meantime he continued his talk.

"You zee," said he, "it iz te bess vor zit still; and now you shall know who I pe. Look at me! zee! I am te *Angel ov te Odd.*"

"And odd enough, too," I ventured to reply; "but I was always under the impression that an angel had wings."

"Te wing!" he cried, highly incensed, "vat I pe do mit te wing? Mein Gott! do you take me for a shicken?"

"No—oh, no!" I replied, much alarmed; "you are no chicken— certainly not."

"Well, den, zit still and pehabe yourself, or I'll rap you again mid me vist. It iz te shicken ab te wing, und te owl ab te wing, und te imp ab te wing, und te head-teuffel ab te wing. Te angel ab *not* te wing, and I am te *Angel ov te Odd.*"

"And your business with me at present is—is——"

"My pizziness!" ejaculated the thing, "vy vat a low-bred puppy you mos pe vor to ask a gentleman und an angel apout his pizziness!"

This language was rather more than I could bear, even from an angel; so, plucking up courage, I seized a salt-cellar which lay within reach, and hurled it at the head of the intruder. Either he dodged, however, or my aim was inaccurate; for all I accomplished was the demolition of the crystal which protected the dial of the clock upon the mantelpiece. As

for the Angel, he evinced his sense of my assault by giving me two or three hard, consecutive raps upon the forehead as before. These reduced me at once to submission, and I am almost ashamed to confess that, either through pain or vexation, there came a few tears into my eyes.

"Mein Gott!" said the Angel of the Odd, apparently much softened at my distress; "mein Gott, te man is eder ferry dronk or ferry zorry. You mos not trink it so strong—you mos put te water in te wine. Here, trink dis, like a good veller, and don't gry now— don't!"

Hereupon the Angel of the Odd replenished my goblet (which was about a third full of port) with a colorless fluid that he poured from one of his hand-bottles. I observed that these bottles had labels about their necks, and that these labels were inscribed "Kirschenwässer."

The considerate kindness of the Angel mollified me in no little measure; and, aided by the water with which he diluted my port more than once, I at length regained sufficient temper to listen to his very extraordinary discourse. I cannot pretend to recount all that he told me, but I gleaned from what he said that he was a genius who presided over the *contretemps* of mankind, and whose business it was to bring about the *odd accidents* which are continually astonishing the skeptic. Once or twice, upon my venturing to express my total incredulity in respect to his pretensions, he grew very angry indeed, so that at length I considered it the wiser policy to say nothing at all, and let him have his own way. He talked on, therefore, at

great length, while I merely leaned back in my chair with my eyes shut, and amused myself with munching raisins and filiping the stems about the room. But, by and by, the Angel suddenly construed this behavior of mine into contempt. He arose in a terrible passion, slouched his funnel down over his eyes, swore a vast oath, uttered a threat of some character, which I did not precisely comprehend, and finally made me a low bow and departed, wishing me, in the language of the archbishop in "Gil Bias," *beaucoup de bonheur et un peu plus de bon sens.*

His departure afforded me relief. The *very* few glasses of Lafitte that I had sipped had the effect of rendering me drowsy, and I felt inclined to take a nap of some fifteen or twenty minutes, as is my custom after dinner. At six I had an appointment of consequence, which it was quite indispensable that I should keep. The policy of insurance for my dwelling-house had expired the day before; and some dispute having arisen it was agreed that, at six, I should meet the board of directors of the company and settle the terms of a renewal. Glancing upward at the clock on the mantelpiece (for I felt too drowsy to take out my watch), I had the pleasure to find that I had still twenty-five minutes to spare. It was half-past five; I could easily walk to the insurance office in five minutes; and my usual siestas had never been known to exceed five-and-twenty. I felt sufficiently safe, therefore, and composed myself to my slumbers forthwith.

Having completed them to my satisfaction, I again looked toward the timepiece, and was half inclined to believe in the possibility of odd accidents when I found that, instead of my ordinary fifteen or twenty minutes, I had been dozing only three; for it still wanted seven-and-twenty of the appointed hour. I betook myself again to my nap, and at length a second time awoke, when, to my utter amazement, it still wanted twenty-seven minutes of six. I jumped up to examine the clock, and found that it had ceased running. My watch informed me that it was half-past seven; and, of course, having slept two hours, I was too late for my appointment. "It will make no difference," I said: "I can call at the office in the morning and apologize; in the meantime what can be the matter with the clock?" Upon examining it I discovered that one of the raisin stems which I had been filiping about the room during the discourse of the Angel of the Odd had flown through the fractured crystal, and lodging, singularly enough, in the keyhole, with an end projecting outward, had thus arrested the revolution of the minute hand.

"Ah!" said I, "I see how it is. This thing speaks for itself. A natural accident, such as will happen now and then!"

I gave the matter no further consideration, and at my usual hour retired to bed. Here, having placed a candle upon a reading stand at the bed head, and having made an attempt to peruse some pages of the *Omnipresence of the Deity*, I unfortunately fell asleep in less than twenty seconds, leaving the light burning as it was.

My dreams were terrifically disturbed by visions of the Angel of the Odd.

Methought he stood at the foot of the couch, drew aside the curtains, and in the hollow, detestable tones of a rum puncheon, menaced me with the bitterest vengeance for the contempt with which I had treated him. He concluded a long harangue by taking off his funnel-cap, inserting the tube into my gullet, and thus deluging me with an ocean of Kirschenwässer, which he poured in a continuous flood, from one of the long-necked bottles that stood him instead of an arm. My agony was at length insufferable, and I awoke just in time to perceive that a rat had run off with the lighted candle from the stand, but *not* in season to prevent his making his escape with it through the hole, Very soon a strong, suffocating odor assailed my nostrils; the house, I clearly perceived, was on fire. In a few minutes the blaze broke forth with violence, and in an incredibly brief period the entire building was wrapped in flames. All egress from my chamber, except through a window, was cut off. The crowd, however, quickly procured and raised a long ladder. By means of this I was descending rapidly, and in apparent safety, when a huge hog, about whose rotund stomach, and indeed about whose whole air and physiognomy, there was something which reminded me of the Angel of the Odd—when this hog, I say, which hitherto had been quietly slumbering in the mud, took it suddenly into his head that his left shoulder needed scratching, and could find no more convenient rubbing-post than that afforded by the foot of the ladder. In an instant I was precipitated, and had the misfortune to fracture my arm.

This accident, with the loss of my insurance, and with the more serious loss of my hair, the whole of which had been singed off by the fire, predisposed me to serious impressions, so that finally I made up my mind to take a wife. There was a rich widow disconsolate for the loss of her seventh husband, and to her wounded spirit I offered the balm of my vows. She yielded a reluctant consent to my prayers. I knelt at her feet in gratitude and adoration. She blushed and bowed her luxuriant tresses into close contact with those supplied me temporarily by Grandjean. I know not how the entanglement took place but so it was. I arose with a shining pate, wigless; she in disdain and wrath, half-buried in alien hair. Thus ended my hopes of the widow by an accident which could not have been anticipated, to be sure, but which the natural sequence of events had brought about.

Without despairing, however, I undertook the siege of a less implacable heart. The fates were again propitious for a brief period, but again a trivial incident interfered. Meeting my betrothed in an avenue thronged with the elite of the city, I was hastening to greet her with one of my best considered bows, when a small particle of some foreign matter lodging in the corner of my eye rendered me for the moment completely blind. Before I could recover my sight, the lady of my love had disappeared—irreparably affronted at what she chose to consider my premeditated rudeness in passing her by ungreeted. While I stood bewildered at the suddenness of this accident (which might have happened, nevertheless, to any one under the sun), and while I still continued incapable of sight, I was

accosted by the Angel of the Odd, who proffered me his aid with a civility which I had no reason to expect. He examined my disordered eye with much gentleness and skill, informed me that I had a drop in it, and (whatever a "drop" was) took it out, and afforded me relief.

I now considered it high time to die (since fortune had so determined to persecute me), and accordingly made my way to the nearest river. Here, divesting myself of my clothes (for there is no reason why we cannot die as we were born), I threw myself headlong into the current; the sole witness of my fate being a solitary crow that had been seduced into the eating of brandy-saturated corn, and so had staggered away from his fellows. No sooner had I entered the water than this bird took it into his head to fly away with the most indispensable portion of my apparel. Postponing, therefore, for the present, my suicidal design, I just slipped my nether extremities into the sleeves of my coat, and betook myself to a pursuit of the felon with all the nimbleness which the case required and its circumstances would admit. But my evil destiny attended me still. As I ran at full speed, with my nose up in the atmosphere, and intent only upon the purloiner of my property, I suddenly perceived that my feet rested no longer upon *terra firma*; the fact is, I had thrown myself over a precipice, and should inevitably have been dashed to pieces but for my good fortune in grasping the end of a long guide-rope, which depended from a passing balloon.

As soon as I sufficiently recovered my senses to comprehend the terrific predicament in which I stood, or rather hung, I exerted all the power of my lungs to make that predicament known to the aeronaut overhead. But for a long time I exerted myself in vain. Either the fool could not, or the villain would not perceive me. Meanwhile the machine rapidly soared, while my strength even more rapidly failed. I was soon upon the point of resigning myself to my fate, and dropping quietly into the sea, when my spirits were suddenly revived by hearing a hollow voice from above, which seemed to be lazily humming an opera air. Looking up, I perceived the Angel of the Odd. He was leaning, with his arms folded, over the rim of the car; and with a pipe in his mouth, at which he puffed leisurely, seemed to be upon excellent terms with himself and the universe. I was too much exhausted to speak, so I merely regarded him with an imploring air.

For several minutes, although he looked me full in the face, he said nothing. At length, removing carefully his meerschaum from the right to the left corner of his mouth, he condescended to speak.

"Who pe you," he asked, "und what der teuffel you pe do dare?"

To this piece of impudence, cruelty, and affectation, I could reply only by ejaculating the monosyllable "Help!"

"Elp!" echoed the ruffian, "not I. Dare iz te pottle—elp yourself, und pe tam'd!"

With these words he let fall a heavy bottle of Kirschenwässer, which, dropping precisely upon the crown of my head, caused me to imagine that my brains were entirely knocked out.

Impressed with this idea I was about to relinquish my hold and give up the ghost with a good grace, when I was arrested by the cry of the Angel, who bade me hold on.

"'Old on!" he said: "don't pe in te 'urry—don't. Will you pe take de odder pottle, or 'ave you pe got zober yet, and come to your zenzes?"

I made haste, hereupon, to nod my head twice—once in the negative, meaning thereby that I would prefer not taking the other bottle at present; and once in the affirmative, intending thus to imply that I *was* sober and *had* positively come to my senses. By these means I somewhat softened the Angel.

"Und you pelief, ten," he inquired, "at te last? You pelief, ten, in te possibility of te odd?"

I again nodded my head in assent.

"Und you ave pelief in *me*, te Angel of te Odd?"

I nodded again.

"Und you acknowledge tat you pe te blind dronk und te vool?"

I nodded once more.

"Put your right hand into your left preeches pocket, ten, in token ov your vull zubmizzion unto te Angel ov te Odd."

This thing, for very obvious reasons, I found it quite impossible to do. In the first place, my left arm had been broken in my fall from the ladder, and therefore, had I let go my hold with the right hand I must have let go altogether. In the second place, I

could have no breeches until I came across the crow. I was therefore obliged, much to my regret, to shake my head in the negative, intending thus to give the Angel to understand that I found it inconvenient, just at that moment, to comply with his very reasonable demand! No sooner, however, had I ceased shaking my head than—

"Go to der teuffel, ten!" roared the Angel of the Odd.

In pronouncing these words he drew a sharp knife across the guide-rope by which I was suspended, and as we then happened to be precisely over my own house (which, during my peregrinations, had been handsomely rebuilt), it so occurred that I tumbled headlong down the ample chimney and alit upon the dining-room hearth.

Upon coming to my senses (for the fall had very thoroughly stunned me) I found it about four o'clock in the morning. I lay outstretched where I had fallen from the balloon. My head groveled in the ashes of an extinguished fire, while my feet reposed upon the wreck of a small table, overthrown, and amid the fragments of a miscellaneous dessert, intermingled with a newspaper, some broken glasses and shattered bottles, and an empty jug of the Schiedam Kirschenwässer. Thus revenged himself the Angel of the Odd.

DISPUTATION OF DOCTOR MARTIN LUTHER ON THE POWER AND EFFICACY OF INDULGENCES

by Dr. Martin Luther, 1517** Out of love for the truth and the desire to bring it to light, the following propositions will be discussed at Wittenberg, under the presidency of the Reverend Father Martin Luther, Master of Arts and of Sacred Theology, and Lecturer in Ordinary on the same at that place. Wherefore he requests that those who are unable to be present and debate orally with us, may do so by letter.

In the Name our Lord Jesus Christ. Amen.

1. Our Lord and Master Jesus Christ, when He said Poenitentiam agite, willed that the whole life of believers should be repentance.

- This word cannot be understood to mean sacramental penance, i.e., confession and satisfaction, which is administered by the priests.

- Yet it means not inward repentance only; nay, there is no inward repentance which does not outwardly work divers mortifications of the flesh.

- The penalty [of sin], therefore, continues so long as hatred of self continues; for this is the true inward repentance, and continues until our entrance into the kingdom of heaven.

- The pope does not intend to remit, and cannot remit any penalties other than those which he has imposed either by his own authority or by that of the Canons.

- The pope cannot remit any guilt, except by declaring that it has been remitted by God and by assenting to God's remission; though, to be sure, he may grant remission in cases reserved to his judgment. If his right to grant remission in such cases were despised, the guilt would remain entirely unforgiven.

- God remits guilt to no one whom He does not, at the same time, humble in all things and bring into subjection to His vicar, the priest.

- The penitential canons are imposed only on the living, and, according to them, nothing should be imposed on the dying.

- Therefore the Holy Spirit in the pope is kind to us, because in his decrees he always makes exception of the article of death and of necessity.

- Ignorant and wicked are the doings of those priests who, in the case of the dying, reserve canonical penances for purgatory.

- This changing of the canonical penalty to the penalty of purgatory is quite evidently one of the tares that were sown while the bishops slept.

- In former times the canonical penalties were imposed not after, but before absolution, as tests of true contrition.

- The dying are freed by death from all penalties; they are already dead to canonical rules, and have a right to be released from them.

- The imperfect health [of soul], that is to say, the imperfect love, of the dying brings with it, of necessity, great fear; and the smaller the love, the greater is the

fear.

- This fear and horror is sufficient of itself alone (to say nothing of other things) to constitute the penalty of purgatory, since it is very near to the horror of despair.

- Hell, purgatory, and heaven seem to differ as do despair, almost-despair, and the assurance of safety.

- With souls in purgatory it seems necessary that horror should grow less and love increase.

- It seems unproved, either by reason or Scripture, that they are outside the state of merit, that is to say, of increasing love.

- Again, it seems unproved that they, or at least that all of them, are certain or assured of their own blessedness, though we may be quite certain of it.

- Therefore by "full remission of all penalties" the pope means not actually "of all," but only of those imposed by himself.

- Therefore those preachers of indulgences are in error, who say that by the pope's indulgences a man is freed from every penalty, and saved;

- Whereas he remits to souls in purgatory no penalty which, according to the canons, they would have had to pay in this life.

- If it is at all possible to grant to any one the remission of all penalties whatsoever, it is certain that this remission can be granted only to the most perfect, that is, to the very fewest.

- It must needs be, therefore, that the greater part of the

people are deceived by that indiscriminate and highsounding promise of release from penalty.

- The power which the pope has, in a general way, over purgatory, is just like the power which any bishop or curate has, in a special way, within his own diocese or parish.

- The pope does well when he grants remission to souls [in purgatory], not by the power of the keys (which he does not possess), but by way of intercession.

- They preach man who say that so soon as the penny jingles into the money-box, the soul flies out [of purgatory].

- It is certain that when the penny jingles into the money-box, gain and avarice can be increased, but the result of the intercession of the Church is in the power of God alone.

- Who knows whether all the souls in purgatory wish to be bought out of it, as in the legend of Sts. Severinus and Paschal.

- No one is sure that his own contrition is sincere; much less that he has attained full remission.

- Rare as is the man that is truly penitent, so rare is also the man who truly buys indulgences, i.e., such men are most rare.

- They will be condemned eternally, together with their teachers, who believe themselves sure of their salvation because they have letters of pardon.

- Men must be on their guard against those who say that the pope's pardons are that inestimable gift of God by

which man is reconciled to Him;

- For these "graces of pardon" concern only the penalties of sacramental satisfaction, and these are appointed by man.

- They preach no Christian doctrine who teach that contrition is not necessary in those who intend to buy souls out of purgatory or to buy confessionalia.

- Every truly repentant Christian has a right to full remission of penalty and guilt, even without letters of pardon.

- Every true Christian, whether living or dead, has part in all the blessings of Christ and the Church; and this is granted him by God, even without letters of pardon.

- Nevertheless, the remission and participation [in the blessings of the Church] which are granted by the pope are in no way to be despised, for they are, as I have said, the declaration of divine remission.

- It is most difficult, even for the very keenest theologians, at one and the same time to commend to the people the abundance of pardons and [the need of] true contrition.

- True contrition seeks and loves penalties, but liberal pardons only relax penalties and cause them to be hated, or at least, furnish an occasion [for hating them].

- Apostolic pardons are to be preached with caution, lest the people may falsely think them preferable to other good works of love.

- Christians are to be taught that the pope does not intend the buying of pardons to be compared in any way to

works of mercy.

- Christians are to be taught that he who gives to the poor or lends to the needy does a better work than buying pardons;

- Because love grows by works of love, and man becomes better; but by pardons man does not grow better, only more free from penalty.

- Christians are to be taught that he who sees a man in need, and passes him by, and gives [his money] for pardons, purchases not the indulgences of the pope, but the indignation of God.

- Christians are to be taught that unless they have more than they need, they are bound to keep back what is necessary for their own families, and by no means to squander it on pardons.

- Christians are to be taught that the buying of pardons is a matter of free will, and not of commandment.

- Christians are to be taught that the pope, in granting pardons, needs, and therefore desires, their devout prayer for him more than the money they bring.

- Christians are to be taught that the pope's pardons are useful, if they do not put their trust in them; but altogether harmful, if through them they lose their fear of God.

- Christians are to be taught that if the pope knew the exactions of the pardon-preachers, he would rather that St. Peter's church should go to ashes, than that it should be built up with the skin, flesh and bones of his sheep.

- Christians are to be taught that it would be the pope's

wish, as it is his duty, to give of his own money to very many of those from whom certain hawkers of pardons cajole money, even though the church of St. Peter might have to be sold.

- The assurance of salvation by letters of pardon is vain, even though the commissary, nay, even though the pope himself, were to stake his soul upon it.

- They are enemies of Christ and of the pope, who bid the Word of God be altogether silent in some Churches, in order that pardons may be preached in others.

- Injury is done the Word of God when, in the same sermon, an equal or a longer time is spent on pardons than on this Word.

- It must be the intention of the pope that if pardons, which are a very small thing, are celebrated with one bell, with single processions and ceremonies, then the Gospel, which is the very greatest thing, should be preached with a hundred bells, a hundred processions, a hundred ceremonies.

- The "treasures of the Church," out of which the pope grants indulgences, are not sufficiently named or known among the people of Christ.

- That they are not temporal treasures is certainly evident, for many of the vendors do not pour out such treasures so easily, but only gather them.

- Nor are they the merits of Christ and the Saints, for even without the pope, these always work grace for the inner man, and the cross, death, and hell for the outward man.

- St. Lawrence said that the treasures of the Church were the Church's poor, but he spoke according to the usage

of the word in his own time.

- Without rashness we say that the keys of the Church, given by Christ's merit, are that treasure;

- For it is clear that for the remission of penalties and of reserved cases, the power of the pope is of itself sufficient.

- The true treasure of the Church is the Most Holy Gospel of the glory and the grace of God.

- But this treasure is naturally most odious, for it makes the first to be last.

- On the other hand, the treasure of indulgences is naturally most acceptable, for it makes the last to be first.

- Therefore the treasures of the Gospel are nets with which they formerly were wont to fish for men of riches.

- The treasures of the indulgences are nets with which they now fish for the riches of men.

- The indulgences which the preachers cry as the "greatest graces" are known to be truly such, in so far as they promote gain.

- Yet they are in truth the very smallest graces compared with the grace of God and the piety of the Cross.

- Bishops and curates are bound to admit the commissaries of apostolic pardons, with all reverence.

- But still more are they bound to strain all their eyes and attend with all their ears, lest these men preach their

own dreams instead of the commission of the pope.

- He who speaks against the truth of apostolic pardons, let him be anathema and accursed!

- But he who guards against the lust and license of the pardon-preachers, let him be blessed!

- The pope justly thunders against those who, by any art, contrive the injury of the traffic in pardons.

- But much more does he intend to thunder against those who use the pretext of pardons to contrive the injury of holy love and truth.

- To think the papal pardons so great that they could absolve a man even if he had committed an impossible sin and violated the Mother of God -- this is madness.

- We say, on the contrary, that the papal pardons are not able to remove the very least of venial sins, so far as its guilt is concerned.

- It is said that even St. Peter, if he were now Pope, could not bestow greater graces; this is blasphemy against St. Peter and against the pope.

- We say, on the contrary, that even the present pope, and any pope at all, has greater graces at his disposal; to wit, the Gospel, powers, gifts of healing, etc., as it is written in I. Corinthians xii.

- To say that the cross, emblazoned with the papal arms, which is set up [by the preachers of indulgences], is of equal worth with the Cross of Christ, is blasphemy.

- The bishops, curates and theologians who allow such talk to be spread among the people, will have an account

to render.

- This unbridled preaching of pardons makes it no easy matter, even for learned men, to rescue the reverence due to the pope from slander, or even from the shrewd questionings of the laity.

- To wit: -- "Why does not the pope empty purgatory, for the sake of holy love and of the dire need of the souls that are there, if he redeems an infinite number of souls for the sake of miserable money with which to build a Church? The former reasons would be most just; the latter is most trivial."

- Again: -- "Why are mortuary and anniversary masses for the dead continued, and why does he not return or permit the withdrawal of the endowments founded on their behalf, since it is wrong to pray for the redeemed?"

- Again: -- "What is this new piety of God and the pope, that for money they allow a man who is impious and their enemy to buy out of purgatory the pious soul of a friend of God, and do not rather, because of that pious and beloved soul's own need, free it for pure love's sake?"

- Again: -- "Why are the penitential canons long since in actual fact and through disuse abrogated and dead, now satisfied by the granting of indulgences, as though they were still alive and in force?"

- Again: -- "Why does not the pope, whose wealth is to-day greater than the riches of the richest, build just this one church of St. Peter with his own money, rather than with the money of poor believers?"

- Again: -- "What is it that the pope remits, and what participation does he grant to those who, by perfect

contrition, have a right to full remission and participation?"

- Again: -- "What greater blessing could come to the Church than if the pope were to do a hundred times a day what he now does once, and bestow on every believer these remissions and participations?"

- "Since the pope, by his pardons, seeks the salvation of souls rather than money, why does he suspend the indulgences and pardons granted heretofore, since these have equal efficacy?"

- To repress these arguments and scruples of the laity by force alone, and not to resolve them by giving reasons, is to expose the Church and the pope to the ridicule of their enemies, and to make Christians unhappy.

- If, therefore, pardons were preached according to the spirit and mind of the pope, all these doubts would be readily resolved; nay, they would not exist.

- Away, then, with all those prophets who say to the people of Christ, "Peace, peace," and there is no peace!

- Blessed be all those prophets who say to the people of Christ, "Cross, cross," and there is no cross!

- Christians are to be exhorted that they be diligent in following Christ, their Head, through penalties, deaths, and hell;

And thus be confident of entering into heaven rather through many tribulations, than through the assurance of peace.

CONCERNING CHRISTIAN LIBERTY

LETTER OF MARTIN LUTHER TO POPE LEO X

Among those monstrous evils of this age with which I have now for three years been waging war, I am sometimes compelled to look to you and to call you to mind, most blessed father Leo. In truth, since you alone are everywhere considered as being the cause of my engaging in war, I cannot at any time fail to remember you; and although I have been compelled by the causeless raging of your impious flatterers against me to appeal from your seat to a future council--fearless of the futile decrees of your predecessors Pius and Julius, who in their foolish tyranny prohibited such an action--yet I have never been so alienated in feeling from your Blessedness as not to have sought with all my might, in diligent prayer and crying to God, all the best gifts for you and for your see. But those who have hitherto endeavoured to terrify me with the majesty of your name and authority, I have begun quite to despise and triumph over. One thing I see remaining which I cannot despise, and this has been the reason of my writing anew to your Blessedness: namely, that I find that blame is cast on me, and that it is imputed to me as a great offence, that in my rashness I am judged to have spared not even your person.

Now, to confess the truth openly, I am conscious that, whenever I have had to mention your person, I have said nothing of you but what was honourable and good. If I had done otherwise, I could by no means have approved my own conduct, but should have supported with all my power the judgment of those men concerning me, nor would anything have pleased me better, than to recant such rashness and impiety. I have called you Daniel in Babylon; and every reader thoroughly knows with what distinguished zeal I defended your conspicuous innocence against Silvester, who tried to stain it. Indeed, the published opinion of so many great men and the repute of your blameless life are too widely famed and too much reverenced throughout the world to be assailable by any man, of however great name, or by any arts. I am not so foolish as to attack one whom everybody praises; nay, it has been and always will be my desire not to attack even those whom public repute disgraces. I am not delighted at the faults of any man, since I am very conscious myself of the great beam in my own eye, nor can I be the first to cast a stone at the adulteress.

I have indeed inveighed sharply against impious doctrines, and I have not been slack to censure my adversaries on account, not of their bad morals, but of their impiety. And for this I am so far from being sorry that I have brought my mind to despise the judgments of men and to

persevere in this vehement zeal, according to the example of Christ, who, in His zeal, calls His adversaries a generation of vipers, blind, hypocrites, and children of the devil. Paul, too, charges the sorcerer with being a child of the devil, full of all subtlety and all malice; and defames certain persons as evil workers, dogs, and deceivers. In the opinion of those delicate-eared persons, nothing could be more bitter or intemperate than Paul's language. What can be more bitter than the words of the prophets? The ears of our generation have been made so delicate by the senseless multitude of flatterers that, as soon as we perceive that anything of ours is not approved of, we cry out that we are being bitterly assailed; and when we can repel the truth by no other pretence, we escape by attributing bitterness, impatience, intemperance, to our adversaries. What would be the use of salt if it were not pungent, or of the edge of the sword if it did not slay? Accursed is the man who does the work of the Lord deceitfully.

Wherefore, most excellent Leo, I beseech you to accept my vindication, made in this letter, and to persuade yourself that I have never thought any evil concerning your person; further, that I am one who desires that eternal blessing may fall to your lot, and that I have no dispute with any man concerning morals, but only concerning the word of truth. In all other things I will yield to any one, but I neither can nor will forsake and deny the word. He who thinks otherwise of me, or has taken in my words in another sense, does not think rightly, and has not taken in the truth.

Your see, however, which is called the Court of Rome, and which neither you nor any man can deny to be more corrupt than any Babylon or Sodom, and quite, as I believe, of a lost, desperate, and hopeless impiety, this I have verily abominated, and have felt indignant that the people of Christ should be cheated under your name and the pretext of the Church of Rome; and so I have resisted, and will resist, as long as the spirit of faith shall live in me. Not that I am striving after impossibilities, or hoping that by my labours alone, against the furious opposition of so many flatterers, any good can be done in that most disordered Babylon; but that I feel myself a debtor to my brethren, and am bound to take thought for them, that fewer of them may be ruined, or that their ruin may be less complete, by the plagues of Rome. For many years now, nothing else has overflowed from Rome into the world--as you are not ignorant--than the laying waste of goods, of bodies, and of souls, and the worst examples of all the worst things. These things are clearer than the light to all men; and the Church of Rome, formerly the most holy of all Churches, has become the most lawless den of thieves, the most shameless of all brothels, the very kingdom of sin, death, and hell; so that not even antichrist, if he were to come, could devise any addition to its wickedness.

Meanwhile you, Leo, are sitting like a lamb , like Daniel in the midst of lions, and, with Ezekiel, you dwell among scorpions. What opposition can you alone make to these monstrous evils? Take to yourself three or four of the most learned and best of the cardinals. What are these among so many? You would all perish by poison before you could undertake to decide on a remedy. It is all over

with the Court of Rome; the wrath of God has come upon her to the uttermost. She hates councils; she dreads to be reformed; she cannot restrain the madness of her impiety; she fills up the sentence passed on her mother, of whom it is said, "We would have healed Babylon, but she is not healed; let us forsake her." It had been your duty and that of your cardinals to apply a remedy to these evils, but this gout laughs at the physician's hand, and the chariot does not obey the reins. Under the influence of these feelings, I have always grieved that you, most excellent Leo, who were worthy of a better age, have been made pontiff in this. For the Roman Court is not worthy of you and those like you, but of Satan himself, who in truth is more the ruler in that Babylon than you are.

Oh, would that, having laid aside that glory which your most abandoned enemies declare to be yours, you were living rather in the office of a private priest or on your paternal inheritance! In that glory none are worthy to glory, except the race of Iscariot, the children of perdition. For what happens in your court, Leo, except that, the more wicked and execrable any man is, the more prosperously he can use your name and authority for the ruin of the property and souls of men, for the multiplication of crimes, for the oppression of faith and truth and of the whole Church of God? Oh, Leo! in reality most unfortunate, and sitting on a most perilous throne, I tell you the truth, because I wish you well; for if Bernard felt compassion for Eugenius III, formerly abbot of St. Anastasius his Anastasius at a time when the Roman see, though even then most corrupt, was as yet ruling with better hope than now, why

should not we lament, to whom so much further corruption and ruin has been added in three hundred years?

Is it not true that there is nothing under the vast heavens more corrupt, more pestilential, more hateful, than the Court of Rome? She incomparably surpasses the impiety of the Turks, so that in very truth she, who was formerly the gate of heaven, is now a sort of open mouth of hell, and such a mouth as, under the urgent wrath of God, cannot be blocked up; one course alone being left to us wretched men: to call back and save some few, if we can, from that Roman gulf.

Behold, Leo, my father, with what purpose and on what principle it is that I have stormed against that seat of pestilence. I am so far from having felt any rage against your person that I even hoped to gain favour with you and to aid you in your welfare by striking actively and vigorously at that your prison, nay, your hell. For whatever the efforts of all minds can contrive against the confusion of that impious Court will be advantageous to you and to your welfare, and to many others with you. Those who do harm to her are doing your office; those who in every way abhor her are glorifying Christ; in short, those are Christians who are not Romans.

But, to say yet more, even this never entered my heart: to inveigh against the Court of Rome or to dispute at all about her. For, seeing all remedies for her health to be desperate, I looked on her with contempt, and, giving her a bill of divorcement, said to her, "He that is unjust, let him be unjust still; and he that is filthy, let him be filthy still," giving myself up to the peaceful and quiet study of sacred literature,

that by this I might be of use to the brethren living about me.

While I was making some advance in these studies, Satan opened his eyes and goaded on his servant John Eccius, that notorious adversary of Christ, by the unchecked lust for fame, to drag me unexpectedly into the arena, trying to catch me in one little word concerning the primacy of the Church of Rome, which had fallen from me in passing. That boastful Thraso, foaming and gnashing his teeth, proclaimed that he would dare all things for the glory of God and for the honour of the holy apostolic seat; and, being puffed up respecting your power, which he was about to misuse, he looked forward with all certainty to victory; seeking to promote, not so much the primacy of Peter, as his own pre-eminence among the theologians of this age; for he thought it would contribute in no slight degree to this, if he were to lead Luther in triumph. The result having proved unfortunate for the sophist, an incredible rage torments him; for he feels that whatever discredit to Rome has arisen through me has been caused by the fault of himself alone.

Suffer me, I pray you, most excellent Leo, both to plead my own cause, and to accuse your true enemies. I believe it is known to you in what way Cardinal Cajetan, your imprudent and unfortunate, nay unfaithful, legate, acted towards me. When, on account of my reverence for your name, I had placed myself and all that was mine in his hands, he did not so act as to establish peace, which he could easily have established by one little word, since I at that time promised to be silent and to make an end of my case, if he would command my adversaries

to do the same. But that man of pride, not content with this agreement, began to justify my adversaries, to give them free licence, and to order me to recant, a thing which was certainly not in his commission. Thus indeed, when the case was in the best position, it came through his vexatious tyranny into a much worse one. Therefore whatever has followed upon this is the fault not of Luther, but entirely of Cajetan, since he did not suffer me to be silent and remain quiet, which at that time I was entreating for with all my might. What more was it my duty to do?

Next came Charles Miltitz, also a nuncio from your Blessedness. He, though he went up and down with much and varied exertion, and omitted nothing which could tend to restore the position of the cause thrown into confusion by the rashness and pride of Cajetan, had difficulty, even with the help of that very illustrious prince the Elector Frederick, in at last bringing about more than one familiar conference with me. In these I again yielded to your great name, and was prepared to keep silence, and to accept as my judge either the Archbishop of Treves, or the Bishop of Naumburg; and thus it was done and concluded. While this was being done with good hope of success, lo! that other and greater enemy of yours, Eccius, rushed in with his Leipsic disputation, which he had undertaken against Carlstadt, and, having taken up a new question concerning the primacy of the Pope, turned his arms unexpectedly against me, and completely overthrew the plan for peace. Meanwhile Charles Miltitz was waiting, disputations were held, judges were being chosen, but no decision was arrived at. And no wonder! for by the falsehoods,

pretences, and arts of Eccius the whole business was brought into such thorough disorder, confusion, and festering soreness, that, whichever way the sentence might lean, a greater conflagration was sure to arise; for he was seeking, not after truth, but after his own credit. In this case too I omitted nothing which it was right that I should do.

I confess that on this occasion no small part of the corruptions of Rome came to light; but, if there was any offence in this, it was the fault of Eccius, who, in taking on him a burden beyond his strength, and in furiously aiming at credit for himself, unveiled to the whole world the disgrace of Rome.

Here is that enemy of yours, Leo, or rather of your Court; by his example alone we may learn that an enemy is not more baneful than a flatterer. For what did he bring about by his flattery, except evils which no king could have brought about? At this day the name of the Court of Rome stinks in the nostrils of the world, the papal authority is growing weak, and its notorious ignorance is evil spoken of. We should hear none of these things, if Eccius had not disturbed the plans of Miltitz and myself for peace. He feels this clearly enough himself in the indignation he shows, too late and in vain, against the publication of my books. He ought to have reflected on this at the time when he was all mad for renown, and was seeking in your cause nothing but his own objects, and that with the greatest peril to you. The foolish man hoped that, from fear of your name, I should yield and keep silence; for I do not think he presumed on his talents and learning. Now, when he sees that I am very confident

and speak aloud, he repents too late of his rashness, and sees--if indeed he does see it--that there is One in heaven who resists the proud, and humbles the presumptuous.

Since then we were bringing about by this disputation nothing but the greater confusion of the cause of Rome, Charles Miltitz for the third time addressed the Fathers of the Order, assembled in chapter, and sought their advice for the settlement of the case, as being now in a most troubled and perilous state. Since, by the favour of God, there was no hope of proceeding against me by force, some of the more noted of their number were sent to me, and begged me at least to show respect to your person and to vindicate in a humble letter both your innocence and my own. They said that the affair was not as yet in a position of extreme hopelessness, if Leo X., in his inborn kindliness, would put his hand to it. On this I, who have always offered and wished for peace, in order that I might devote myself to calmer and more useful pursuits, and who for this very purpose have acted with so much spirit and vehemence, in order to put down by the strength and impetuosity of my words, as well as of my feelings, men whom I saw to be very far from equal to myself--I, say, not only gladly yielded, but even accepted it with joy and gratitude, as the greatest kindness and benefit, if you should think it right to satisfy my hopes.

Thus I come, most blessed Father, and in all abasement beseech you to put to your hand, if it is possible, and impose a curb to those flatterers who are enemies of peace, while they pretend peace. But there is no reason, most blessed Father, why any one should

assume that I am to utter a recantation, unless he prefers to involve the case in still greater confusion. Moreover, I cannot bear with laws for the interpretation of the word of God, since the word of God, which teaches liberty in all other things, ought not to be bound. Saving these two things, there is nothing which I am not able, and most heartily willing, to do or to suffer. I hate contention; I will challenge no one; in return I wish not to be challenged; but, being challenged, I will not be dumb in the cause of Christ my Master. For your Blessedness will be able by one short and easy word to call these controversies before you and suppress them, and to impose silence and peace on both sides--a word which I have ever longed to hear.

Therefore, Leo, my Father, beware of listening to those sirens who make you out to be not simply a man, but partly a god, so that you can command and require whatever you will. It will not happen so, nor will you prevail. You are the servant of servants, and more than any other man, in a most pitiable and perilous position. Let not those men deceive you who pretend that you are lord of the world; who will not allow any one to be a Christian without your authority; who babble of your having power over heaven, hell, and purgatory. These men are your enemies and are seeking your soul to destroy it, as Isaiah say, "My people, they that call thee blessed are themselves deceiving thee." They are in error who raise you above councils and the universal Church; they are in error who attribute to you alone the right of interpreting Scripture. All these men are seeking to set up their own impieties in the Church under your name, and alas! Satan has gained

much through them in the time of your predecessors.

In brief, trust not in any who exalt you, but in those who humiliate you. For this is the judgment of God: "He hath cast down the mighty from their seat, and hath exalted the humble." See how unlike Christ was to His successors, though all will have it that they are His vicars. I fear that in truth very many of them have been in too serious a sense His vicars, for a vicar represents a prince who is absent. Now if a pontiff rules while Christ is absent and does not dwell in his heart, what else is he but a vicar of Christ? And then what is that Church but a multitude without Christ? What indeed is such a vicar but antichrist and an idol? How much more rightly did the Apostles speak, who call themselves servants of a present Christ, not the vicars of an absent one!

Perhaps I am shamelessly bold in seeming to teach so great a head, by whom all men ought to be taught, and from whom, as those plagues of yours boast, the thrones of judges receive their sentence; but I imitate St. Bernard in his book concerning *Considerations* addressed to Eugenius, a book which ought to be known by heart by every pontiff. I do this, not from any desire to teach, but as a duty, from that simple and faithful solicitude which teaches us to be anxious for all that is safe for our neighbours, and does not allow considerations of worthiness or unworthiness to be entertained, being intent only on the dangers or advantage of others. For since I know that your Blessedness is driven and tossed by the waves at Rome, so that the depths of the sea press on you with infinite perils, and that you are

labouring under such a condition of misery that you need even the least help from any the least brother, I do not seem to myself to be acting unsuitably if I forget your majesty till I shall have fulfilled the office of charity. I will not flatter in so serious and perilous a matter; and if in this you do not see that I am your friend and most thoroughly your subject, there is One to see and judge.

In fine, that I may not approach you empty-handed, blessed Father, I bring with me this little treatise, published under your name, as a good omen of the establishment of peace and of good hope. By this you may perceive in what pursuits I should prefer and be able to occupy myself to more profit, if I were allowed, or had been hitherto allowed, by your impious flatterers. It is a small matter, if you look to its exterior, but, unless I mistake, it is a summary of the Christian life put together in small compass, if you apprehend its meaning. I, in my poverty, have no other present to make you, nor do you need anything else than to be enriched by a spiritual gift. I commend myself to your Paternity and Blessedness, whom may the Lord Jesus preserve for ever. Amen.

Wittenberg, 6th September, 1520.

FOUNDING FATHERS
QUOTES

George Washington, 1st U.S. President "While we are zealously performing the duties of good citizens and soldiers, we certainly ought not to be inattentive to the higher duties of religion. To the distinguished character of Patriot, it should be our highest glory to add the more distinguished character of Christian."

--The Writings of Washington, pp. 342-343.

John Adams 2nd U.S. President and Signer of the Declaration of Independence "Suppose a nation in some distant Region should take the Bible for their only law Book, and every member should regulate his conduct by the precepts there exhibited! Every member would be obliged in conscience, to temperance, frugality, and industry; to justice, kindness, and charity towards his fellow men; and to piety, love, and reverence toward Almighty God ... What a Eutopia, what a Paradise would this region be."

--Diary and Autobiography of John Adams, Vol. III, p. 9.

"The general principles on which the fathers achieved independence were the general principles of Christianity. I will avow that I then believed, and now believe, that those general principles of Christianity are as eternal and immutable as the existence and attributes of God."

--Adams wrote this on June 28, 1813, in a letter to Thomas Jefferson.

"The second day of July, 1776, will be the most memorable epoch in the history of America. I am apt to believe that it will be celebrated by succeeding generations as the great anniversary Festival. It ought to be commemorated, as the

Day of Deliverance, by solemn acts of devotion to God Almighty. It ought to be solemnized with pomp and parade, with shows, games, sports, guns, bells, bonfires and illuminations, from one end of this continent to the other, from this time forward forever."

--Adams wrote this in a letter to his wife, Abigail, on July 3, 1776.

Thomas Jefferson 3rd U.S. President, Drafter and Signer of the Declaration of Independence "God who gave us life gave us liberty. And can the liberties of a nation be thought secure when we have removed their only firm basis, a conviction in the minds of the people that these liberties are of the Gift of God? That they are not to be violated but with His wrath? Indeed, I tremble for my country when I reflect that God is just; that His justice cannot sleep forever; That a revolution of the wheel of fortune, a change of situation, is among possible events; that it may become probable by Supernatural influence! The Almighty has no attribute which can take side with us in that event."

--Notes on the State of Virginia, Query XVIII, p. 237.

"I am a real Christian – that is to say, a disciple of the doctrines of Jesus Christ."

--The Writings of Thomas Jefferson, p. 385.

John Hancock 1st Signer of the Declaration of Independence "Resistance to tyranny becomes the Christian and social duty of each individual. ... Continue steadfast and, with a proper sense of your dependence on God, nobly defend those rights which heaven gave, and no man ought to take from us."

--History of the United States of America, Vol. II, p. 229.

Benjamin Franklin Signer of the Declaration of Independence and Unites States Constitution "Here is my

Creed. I believe in one God, the Creator of the Universe.
That He governs it by His Providence. That He ought to be
worshipped.

That the most acceptable service we render to him is in
doing good to his other children. That the soul of man is
immortal, and will be treated with justice in another life
respecting its conduct in this. These I take to be the
fundamental points in all sound religion, and I regard them
as you do in whatever sect I meet with them.

As to Jesus of Nazareth, my opinion of whom you
particularly desire, I think the system of morals and his
religion, as he left them to us, is the best the world ever
saw, or is likely to see;

But I apprehend it has received various corrupting changes,
and I have, with most of the present dissenters in England,
some doubts as to his divinity; though it is a question I do
not dogmatize upon, having never studied it, and think it
needless to busy myself with it now, when I expect soon an
opportunity of knowing the truth with less trouble. I see no
harm, however, in its being believed, if that belief has the
good consequence, as probably it has, of making his
doctrines more respected and more observed; especially as
I do not perceive, that the Supreme takes it amiss, by
distinguishing the unbelievers in his government of the
world with any peculiar marks of his displeasure."
    *--Benjamin Franklin wrote this in a letter to Ezra Stiles,
    President of Yale University on March 9, 1790.*

Samuel Adams Signer of the Declaration of Independence
and Father of the American Revolution "And as it is our
duty to extend our wishes to the happiness of the great
family of man, I conceive that we cannot better express
ourselves than by humbly supplicating the Supreme Ruler

of the world that the rod of tyrants may be broken to pieces, and the oppressed made free again; that wars may cease in all the earth, and that the confusions that are and have been among nations may be overruled by promoting and speedily bringing on that holy and happy period when the kingdom of our Lord and Saviour Jesus Christ may be everywhere established, and all people everywhere willingly bow to the sceptre of Him who is Prince of Peace."

--As Governor of Massachusetts,
Proclamation of a Day of Fast, March 20, 1797.

James Madison 4th U.S. President "Cursed be all that learning that is contrary to the cross of Christ."
--America's Providential History, p. 93.

James Monroe 5th U.S. President "When we view the blessings with which our country has been favored, those which we now enjoy, and the means which we possess of handing them down unimpaired to our latest posterity, our attention is irresistibly drawn to the source from whence they flow. Let us then, unite in offering our most grateful acknowledgements for these blessings to the Divine Author of All Good."
--Monroe made this statement in his 2nd Annual Message to Congress, November 16, 1818.

John Quincy Adams 6th U.S. President "The hope of a Christian is inseparable from his faith. Whoever believes in the divine inspiration of the Holy Scriptures must hope that the religion of Jesus shall prevail throughout the earth. Never since the foundation of the world have the prospects of mankind been more encouraging to that hope than they appear to be at the present time. And may the associated distribution of the Bible proceed and prosper till the Lord

shall have made 'bare His holy arm in the eyes of all the nations, and all the ends of the earth shall see the salvation of our God' (Isaiah 52:10)."

--Life of John Quincy Adams, p. 248.

William Penn Founder of Pennsylvania "I do declare to the whole world that we believe the Scriptures to contain a declaration of the mind and will of God in and to those ages in which they were written; being given forth by the Holy Ghost moving in the hearts of holy men of God; that they ought also to be read, believed, and fulfilled in our day; being used for reproof and instruction, that the man of God may be perfect. They are a declaration and testimony of heavenly things themselves, and, as such, we carry a high respect for them. We accept them as the words of God Himself."

--Treatise of the Religion of the Quakers, p. 355.

Roger Sherman Signer of the Declaration of Independence and United States Constitution "I believe that there is one only living and true God, existing in three persons, the Father, the Son, and the Holy Ghost, the same in substance equal in power and glory. That the scriptures of the old and new testaments are a revelation from God, and a complete rule to direct us how we may glorify and enjoy him. That God has foreordained whatsoever comes to pass, so as thereby he is not the author or approver of sin. That he creates all things, and preserves and governs all creatures and all their actions, in a manner perfectly consistent with the freedom of will in moral agents, and the usefulness of means. That he made man at first perfectly holy, that the first man sinned, and as he was the public head of his posterity, they all became sinners in consequence of his first transgression, are wholly indisposed to that which is good and inclined to evil, and

on account of sin are liable to all the miseries of this life, to death, and to the pains of hell forever.

I believe that God having elected some of mankind to eternal life, did send his own Son to become man, die in the room and stead of sinners and thus to lay a foundation for the offer of pardon and salvation to all mankind, so as all may be saved who are willing to accept the gospel offer: also by his special grace and spirit, to regenerate, sanctify and enable to persevere in holiness, all who shall be saved; and to procure in consequence of their repentance and faith in himself their justification by virtue of his atonement as the only meritorious cause.

I believe a visible church to be a congregation of those who make a credible profession of their faith in Christ, and obedience to him, joined by the bond of the covenant.

I believe that the souls of believers are at their death made perfectly holy, and immediately taken to glory: that at the end of this world there will be a resurrection of the dead, and a final judgement of all mankind, when the righteous shall be publicly acquitted by Christ the Judge and admitted to everlasting life and glory, and the wicked be sentenced to everlasting punishment."
            --*The Life of Roger Sherman*, pp. 272-273.

Benjamin Rush   Signer of the Declaration of Independence and Ratifier of the U.S. Constitution "The Gospel of Jesus Christ prescribes the wisest rules for just conduct in every situation of life. Happy they who are enabled to obey them in all situations!"
            --*The Autobiography of Benjamin Rush*, pp. 165-166.

"Christianity is the only true and perfect religion, and that in proportion as mankind adopts its principles and obeys its precepts, they will be wise and happy."

--*Essays, Literary, Moral, and Philosophical*,
published in 1798.

"I know there is an objection among many people to teaching children doctrines of any kind, because they are liable to be controverted. But let us not be wiser than our Maker.

If moral precepts alone could have reformed mankind, the mission of the Son of God into all the world would have been unnecessary. The perfect morality of the Gospel rests upon the doctrine which, though often controverted has never been refuted: I mean the vicarious life and death of the Son of God."

--*Essays, Literary, Moral, and Philosophical*,
published in 1798.

John Witherspoon Signer of the Declaration of Independence, Clergyman and President of Princeton University "While we give praise to God, the Supreme Disposer of all events, for His interposition on our behalf, let us guard against the dangerous error of trusting in, or boasting of, an arm of flesh ... If your cause is just, if your principles are pure, and if your conduct is prudent, you need not fear the multitude of opposing hosts.

What follows from this? That he is the best friend to American liberty, who is most sincere and active in promoting true and undefiled religion, and who sets himself with the greatest firmness to bear down profanity and immorality of every kind.

Whoever is an avowed enemy of God, I scruple not to call
him an enemy of his country."
    --*Sermon at Princeton University, "The Dominion of
    Providence over the Passions of Men," May 17, 1776.*

Alexander Hamilton   Signer of the Declaration of
Independence and Ratifier of the U.S. Constitution

"I have carefully examined the evidences of the Christian
religion, and if I was sitting as a juror upon its authenticity
I would unhesitatingly give my verdict in its favor. I can
prove its truth as clearly as any proposition ever submitted
to the mind of man."
    --*Famous American Statesmen*, p. 126.

Patrick Henry Ratifier of the U.S. Constitution
"It cannot be emphasized too strongly or too often that this
great nation was founded, not by religionists, but by
Christians; not on religions, but on the Gospel of Jesus
Christ. For this very reason peoples of other faiths have
been afforded asylum, prosperity, and freedom of worship
here."
    --*The Trumpet Voice of Freedom:
    Patrick Henry of Virginia*, p. iii.

"The Bible ... is a book worth more than all the other books
that were ever printed."
    --*Sketches of the Life and Character of
    Patrick Henry*, p. 402.

John Jay 1st Chief Justice of the U.S. Supreme Court and
President of the American Bible Society "By conveying the
Bible to people thus circumstanced, we certainly do them a
most interesting kindness. We thereby enable them to learn
that man was originally created and placed in a state of
happiness, but, becoming disobedient, was subjected to the

degradation and evils which he and his posterity have since experienced.

The Bible will also inform them that our gracious Creator has provided for us a Redeemer, in whom all the nations of the earth shall be blessed; that this Redeemer has made atonement "for the sins of the whole world," and thereby reconciling the Divine justice with the Divine mercy has opened a way for our redemption and salvation; and that these inestimable benefits are of the free gift and grace of God, not of our deserving, nor in our power to deserve."
--In God We Trust—The Religious Beliefs and Ideas of the American Founding Fathers, p. 379.

"In forming and settling my belief relative to the doctrines of Christianity, I adopted no articles from creeds but such only as, on careful examination, I found to be confirmed by the Bible."
--American Statesman Series, p. 360.

The First Charter of Virginia (granted by King James I, on April 10, 1606) • We, greatly commending, and graciously accepting of, their Desires for the Furtherance of so noble a Work, which may, by the Providence of Almighty God, hereafter tend to the Glory of his Divine Majesty, in propagating of Christian Religion to such People, as yet live in Darkness and miserable Ignorance of the true Knowledge and Worship of God... Instructions for the Virginia Colony (1606) Lastly and chiefly the way to prosper and achieve good success is to make yourselves all of one mind for the good of your country and your own, and to serve and fear God the Giver of all Goodness, for every plantation which our Heavenly Father hath not planted shall be rooted out.

William Bradford • wrote that they [the Pilgrims] were seeking: • 1) "a better, and easier place of living"; and that "the children of the group were being drawn away by evil examples into extravagance and dangerous courses [in Holland]" •2) "The great hope, and for the propagating and advancing the gospel of the kingdom of Christ in those remote parts of the world" **The Mayflower Compact** (authored by William Bradford) 1620 | **Signing of the Mayflower painting** | **Picture of Compact**"Having undertaken, for the glory of God, and advancement of the Christian faith, and honor of our King and Country, a voyage to plant the first colony in the northern parts of Virginia, do by these presents solemnly and mutually, in the presence of God, and one of another, covenant and combine our selves together..."

John Adams and John Hancock: We Recognize No Sovereign but God, and no King but *Jesus*! [April 18, 1775]

John Adams: " The general principles upon which the Fathers achieved independence were the general principals of Christianity... I will avow that I believed and now believe that those general principles of Christianity are as eternal and immutable as the existence and attributes of God." • "[July 4th] ought to be commemorated as the day of deliverance by solemn acts of devotion to God Almighty."
–John Adams in a letter written to Abigail on the day the Declaration was approved by Congress

"We have no government armed with power capable of contending with human passions unbridled by morality and religion. Avarice, ambition, revenge, or gallantry, would break the strongest cords of our Constitution as a whale

goes through a net. **Our Constitution was made only for a moral and religious people. It is wholly inadequate to the government of any other.**"

--October 11, 1798

"I have examined all religions, as well as my narrow sphere, my straightened means, and my busy life, would allow; and the result is that the Bible is the best Book in the world. It contains more philosophy than all the libraries I have seen."

-- December 25, 1813 letter to Thomas Jefferson

"Without Religion this World would be Something not fit to be mentioned in polite Company, I mean Hell."

-- John Adams to Thomas Jefferson, April 19, 1817

Samuel Adams: | **Portrait of Sam Adams:** He who made all men hath made the truths necessary to human happiness obvious to all… Our forefathers opened the Bible to all." "American Independence,"

-- August 1, 1776. Speech delivered at the State House in Philadelphia

"Let divines and philosophers, statesmen and patriots, unite their endeavors to renovate the age by impressing the minds of men with the importance of educating their little boys and girls, inculcating in the minds of youth the fear and love of the Deity… and leading them in the study and practice of the exalted virtues of the Christian system."

-- October 4, 1790

John Quincy Adams: • "Why is it that, next to the birthday of the Savior of the world, your most joyous and most venerated festival returns on this day [the Fourth of July]?" "Is it not that, in the chain of human events, the birthday of the nation is indissolubly linked with the

birthday of the Savior? That it forms a leading event in the progress of the Gospel dispensation? Is it not that the Declaration of Independence first organized the social compact on the foundation of the Redeemer's mission upon earth? That it laid the cornerstone of human government upon the first precepts of Christianity"?

--1837, at the age of 69, when he delivered a Fourth of July speech at Newburyport, Massachusetts.

"The Law given from Sinai [The Ten Commandments] was a civil and municipal as well as a moral and religious code."

--John Quincy Adams. Letters to his son. p. 61

Elias Boudinot: | **Portrait of Elias Boudinot** " Be religiously careful in our choice of all public officers . . . and judge of the tree by its fruits."

Charles Carroll - *signer of the Declaration of Independence* | **Portrait of Charles Carroll** " Without morals a republic cannot subsist any length of time; they therefore who are decrying the Christian religion, whose morality is so sublime and pure...are undermining the solid foundation of morals, the best security for the duration of free governments."

-- Source: To James McHenry on November 4, 1800.

Benjamin Franklin: | **Portrait of Ben Franklin** " God governs in the affairs of man. And if a sparrow cannot fall to the ground without his notice, is it probable that an empire can rise without His aid? We have been assured in the Sacred Writings that except the Lord build the house, they labor in vain that build it. I firmly believe this. I also believe that, without His concurring aid, we shall succeed

in this political building no better than the builders of Babel"
-- Constitutional Convention of 1787 | original manuscript of this speech

"In the beginning of the contest with Britain, when we were sensible of danger, we had daily prayers in this room for Divine protection. Our prayers, Sir, were heard, and they were graciously answered... do we imagine we no longer need His assistance?"
-- Constitutional Convention, Thursday June 28, 1787

In Benjamin Franklin's **1749 plan of education for public schools in Pennsylvania**, he insisted that schools teach "the excellency of the Christian religion above all others, ancient or modern."

In 1787 when Franklin helped found Benjamin Franklin University, it was dedicated as "a nursery of religion and learning, built on Christ, the Cornerstone."

Alexander Hamilton: • Hamilton began work with the Rev. James Bayard to form the Christian Constitutional Society to help spread over the world the two things which Hamilton said made America great: (1) Christianity (2) a Constitution formed under Christianity. "The Christian Constitutional Society, its object is first: The support of the Christian religion. Second: The support of the United States."

On July 12, 1804 at his death, Hamilton said, "I have a tender reliance on the mercy of the Almighty, through the merits of the Lord Jesus Christ. I am a sinner. I look to Him for mercy; pray for me."

"For my own part, I sincerely esteem it [the Constitution] a system which without the finger of God, never could have been suggested and agreed upon by such a diversity of interests." [1787 after the Constitutional Convention]

"I have carefully examined the evidences of the Christian religion, and if I was sitting as a juror upon its authenticity I would unhesitatingly give my verdict in its favor. I can prove its truth as clearly as any proposition ever submitted to the mind of man."

John Hancock: • "In circumstances as dark as these, it becomes us, as Men and Christians, to reflect that whilst every prudent measure should be taken to ward off the impending judgments, …at the same time all confidence must be withheld from the means we use; and reposed only on that God rules in the armies of Heaven, and without His whole blessing, the best human counsels are but foolishness… Resolved; …Thursday the 11th of May…to humble themselves before God under the heavy judgments felt and feared, to confess the sins that have deserved them, to implore the Forgiveness of all our transgressions, and a spirit of repentance and reformation …and a Blessing on the … Union of the American Colonies in Defense of their Rights [for which hitherto we desire to thank Almighty God]…That the people of Great Britain and their rulers may have their eyes opened to discern the things that shall make for the peace of the nation…for the redress of America's many grievances, the restoration of all her invaded liberties, and their security to the latest generations. *"A Day of Fasting, Humiliation and Prayer, with a total abstinence from labor and recreation. Proclamation on April 15, 1775"*

Patrick Henry: *"Orator of the Revolution."* • This is all the inheritance I can give my dear family. The religion of Christ can give them one which will make them rich indeed."

-- The Last Will and Testament of Patrick Henry

"It cannot be emphasized too clearly and too often that this nation was founded, not by religionists, but by Christians; not on religion, but on the gospel of Jesus Christ. For this very reason, peoples of other faiths have been afforded asylum, prosperity, and freedom of worship here." [May 1765 Speech to the House of Burgesses]

"The Bible is worth all other books which have ever been printed."

John Jay: " Providence has given to our people the choice of their rulers, and it is the duty, as well as the privilege and interest of our Christian nation to select and prefer Christians for their rulers." Source: October 12, 1816. The Correspondence and Public Papers of John Jay, Henry P. Johnston, ed., (New York: Burt Franklin, 1970), Vol. IV, p. 393.

"Whether our religion permits Christians to vote for infidel rulers is a question which merits more consideration than it seems yet to have generally received either from the clergy or the laity. It appears to me that what the prophet said to Jehoshaphat about his attachment to Ahab ["Shouldest thou help the ungodly and love them that hate the Lord?" 2 Chronicles 19:2] affords a salutary lesson."

-- The Correspondence and Public Papers of John Jay, 1794-1826, Henry P. Johnston, editor (New York: G.P. Putnam's Sons, 1893), Vol. IV, p.365

Thomas Jefferson: " The doctrines of Jesus are simple, and tend to all the happiness of man." "Of all the systems of morality, ancient or modern which have come under my observation, none appears to me so pure as that of Jesus."

"I am a real Christian, that is to say, a disciple of the doctrines of Jesus."

"God who gave us life gave us liberty. And can the liberties of a nation be thought secure when we have removed their only firm basis, a conviction in the minds of the people that these liberties are a gift from God? That they are not to be violated but with His wrath? Indeed I tremble for my country when I reflect that God is just, and that His justice cannot sleep forever." (excerpts are inscribed on the walls of the Jefferson Memorial in the nations capital) [Source: Merrill . D. Peterson, ed., Jefferson Writings, (New York: Literary Classics of the United States, Inc., 1984), Vol. IV, p. 289. From Jefferson's Notes on the State of Virginia, Query XVIII, 1781.]

Samuel Johnston: • "It is apprehended that Jews, Mahometans (Muslims), pagans, etc., may be elected to high offices under the government of the United States. Those who are Mahometans, or any others who are not professors of the Christian religion, can never be elected to the office of President or other high office, [unless] first the people of America lay aside the Christian religion altogether, it may happen. Should this unfortunately take place, the people will choose such men as think as they do themselves. [Elliot's Debates, Vol. IV, pp 198-199, Governor Samuel Johnston, July 30, 1788 at the North Carolina Ratifying Convention]

James Madison " We've staked our future on our ability to follow the Ten Commandments with all of our heart." "We have staked the whole future of American civilization, not upon the power of government, far from it. We've staked the future of all our political institutions upon our capacity…to sustain ourselves according to the Ten Commandments of God." [1778 to the General Assembly of the State of Virginia]   • I have sometimes thought there could not be a stronger testimony in favor of religion or against temporal enjoyments, even the most rational and manly, than for men who occupy the most honorable and gainful departments and [who] are rising in reputation and wealth, publicly to declare the unsatisfactoriness [of temportal enjoyments] by becoming fervent advocates in the cause of Christ; and I wish you may give in your evidence in this way.   Letter by Madison to William Bradford (September 25, 1773) • In 1812, President Madison signed a federal bill which economically aided the Bible Society of Philadelphia in its goal of the mass distribution of the Bible.   " An Act for the relief of the Bible Society of Philadelphia" Approved February 2, 1813 by Congress

"It is the mutual duty of all to practice Christian forbearance, love, and charity toward each other."

A watchful eye must be kept on ourselves lest, while we are building ideal monuments of renown and bliss here, we neglect to have our names enrolled in the Annals of Heaven. [Letter by Madison to William Bradford [urging him to make sure of his own salvation] November 9, 1772]

At the Constitutional Convention of 1787, James Madison proposed the plan to divide the central government into three branches. He discovered this model of government

from the Perfect Governor, as he read *Isaiah 33:22*; "For the LORD is our judge, the LORD is our lawgiver, the LORD is our king; He will save us." [**Baron Charles Montesquieu**, *wrote in 1748;* "Nor is there liberty if the power of judging is not separated from legislative power and from executive power. If it [the power of judging] were joined to legislative power, the power over life and liberty of the citizens would be arbitrary, for the judge would be the legislature if it were joined to the executive power, the judge could have the force of an oppressor. All would be lost if the same ... body of principal men ... exercised these three powers." Madison claimed Isaiah 33:22 as the source of division of power in government See also: pp.241-242 in *Teaching and Learning America's Christian History: The Principle approach* by Rosalie Slater]

James McHenry – *Signer of the Constitution* Public utility pleads most forcibly for the general distribution of the Holy Scriptures. The doctrine they preach, the obligations they impose, the punishment they threaten, the rewards they promise, the stamp and image of divinity they bear, which produces a conviction of their truths, can alone secure to society, order and peace, and to our courts of justice and constitutions of government, purity, stability and usefulness. In vain, without the Bible, we increase penal laws and draw entrenchments around our institutions. Bibles are strong entrenchments. Where they abound, men cannot pursue wicked courses, and at the same time enjoy quiet conscience.

Jedediah Morse: "To the kindly influence of Christianity we owe that degree of civil freedom, and political and social happiness which mankind now enjoys. . . . Whenever the pillars of Christianity shall be overthrown, our present

republican forms of government, and all blessings which flow from them, must fall with them."

John Peter Gabriel Muhlenberg In a sermon delivered to his Virginia congregation on Jan. 21, 1776, he preached from Ecclesiastes 3. Arriving at verse 8, which declares that there is a time of war and a time of peace, Muhlenberg noted that this surely was not the time of peace; this was the time of war. Concluding with a prayer, and while standing in full view of the congregation, he removed his clerical robes to reveal that beneath them he was wearing the uniform of an officer in the Continental army! He marched to the back of the church; ordered the drum to beat for recruits and over three hundred men joined him, becoming the Eighth Virginia Brigade. John Peter Muhlenberg finished the Revolution as a Major-General, having been at Valley Forge and having participated in the battles of Brandywine, Germantown, Monmouth, Stonypoint, and Yorktown.

Thomas Paine: " It has been the error of the schools to teach astronomy, and all the other sciences, and subjects of natural philosophy, as accomplishments only; whereas they should be taught theologically, or with reference to the Being who is the author of them: for all the principles of science are of divine origin. Man cannot make, or invent, or contrive principles: he can only discover them; and he ought to look through the discovery to the Author." " The evil that has resulted from the error of the schools, in teaching natural philosophy as an accomplishment only, has been that of generating in the pupils a species of atheism. Instead of looking through the works of creation to the Creator himself, they stop short, and employ the knowledge they acquire to create doubts of his existence. They labour with studied ingenuity to ascribe every thing

they behold to innate properties of matter, and jump over all the rest by saying, that matter is eternal."

"The Existence of God--1810"

Benjamin Rush: • "I lament that we waste so much time and money in punishing crimes and take so little pains to prevent them…we neglect the only means of establishing and perpetuating our republican forms of government; that is, the universal education of our youth in the principles of Christianity by means of the Bible; for this Divine Book, above all others, constitutes the soul of republicanism." "By withholding the knowledge of [the Scriptures] from children, we deprive ourselves of the best means of awakening moral sensibility in their minds." [Letter written (1790's) in Defense of the Bible in all schools in America] • "Christianity is the only true and perfect religion." • "If moral precepts alone could have reformed mankind, the mission of the Son of God into our world would have been unnecessary."

"Let the children who are sent to those schools be taught to read and write and above all, let both sexes be carefully instructed in the principles and obligations of the Christian religion. This is the most essential part of education" Letters of Benjamin Rush, "To the citizens of Philadelphia: A Plan for Free Schools", March 28, 1787

Justice Joseph Story: " I verily believe Christianity necessary to the support of civil society. One of the beautiful boasts of our municipal jurisprudence is that Christianity is a part of the Common Law. . . There never has been a period in which the Common Law did not recognize Christianity as lying its foundations." [Commentaries on the Constitution of the United States p. 593] " Infidels and pagans were banished

from the halls of justice as unworthy of credit." [Life and letters of Joseph Story, Vol. II 1851, pp. 8-9.] " At the time of the adoption of the constitution, and of the amendment to it, now under consideration [i.e., the First Amendment], the general, if not the universal sentiment in America was, that Christianity ought to receive encouragement from the state, so far as was not incompatible with the private rights of conscience, and the freedom of religious worship." [Commentaries on the Constitution of the United States p. 593]

Noah Webster: " The duties of men are summarily comprised in the Ten Commandments, consisting of two tables; one comprehending the duties which we owe immediately to God-the other, the duties we owe to our fellow men."

"In my view, the Christian religion is the most important and one of the first things in which all children, under a free government ought to be instructed...No truth is more evident to my mind than that the Christian religion must be the basis of any government intended to secure the rights and privileges of a free people." [Source: 1828, in the preface to his American Dictionary of the English Language]

Let it be impressed on your mind that God commands you to choose for rulers just men who will rule in the fear of God [Exodus 18:21]. . . . If the citizens neglect their duty and place unprincipled men in office, the government will soon be corrupted . . . If our government fails to secure public prosperity and happiness, it must be because the citizens neglect the Divine commands, and elect bad men to make and administer the laws. [Noah Webster, The

History of the United States (New Haven: Durrie and Peck, 1832), pp. 336-337, 49]

"All the miseries and evils which men suffer from vice, crime, ambition, injustice, oppression, slavery and war, proceed from their despising or neglecting the precepts contained in the Bible." [Noah Webster. History. p. 339]

"The Bible was America's basic textbook in all fields." [Noah Webster. Our Christian Heritage p.5] "Education is useless without the Bible" [Noah Webster. Our Christian Heritage p.5]

George Washington:
Farewell Address: The name of American, which belongs to you, in your national capacity, must always exalt the just pride of Patriotism, more than any appellation derived from local discriminations. **With slight shades of difference, you have the same religion"** ...and later: ***"...reason and experience both forbid us to expect, that national morality can prevail in exclusion of religious principle..."***

" It is impossible to rightly govern the world without God and Bible."

"What students would learn in American schools above all is the religion of Jesus Christ." [speech to the Delaware Indian Chiefs May 12, 1779]

"To the distinguished character of patriot, it should be our highest glory to add the more distinguished character of Christian" [May 2, 1778, at Valley Forge]

During his inauguration, Washington took the oath as prescribed by the Constitution but added several religious

components to that official ceremony. Before taking his oath of office, he summoned a Bible on which to take the oath, added the words "So help me God!" to the end of the oath, then leaned over and kissed the Bible. *Nelly Custis-Lewis (Washington's adopted daughter):* Is it necessary that any one should [ask], "Did General Washington avow himself to be a believer in Christianity?" As well may we question his patriotism, his heroic devotion to his country. His mottos were, "Deeds, not Words"; and, "For God and my Country." " O Most Glorious God, in Jesus Christ, my merciful and loving Father; I acknowledge and confess my guilt in the weak and imperfect performance of the duties of this day. I have called on Thee for pardon and forgiveness of my sins, but so coldly and carelessly that my prayers are become my sin, and they stand in need of pardon." " I have sinned against heaven and before Thee in thought, word, and deed. I have contemned Thy majesty and holy laws. I have likewise sinned by omitting what I ought to have done and committing what I ought not. I have rebelled against the light, despising Thy mercies and judgment, and broken my vows and promise. I have neglected the better things. My iniquities are multiplied and my sins are very great. I confess them, O Lord, with shame and sorrow, detestation and loathing and desire to be vile in my own eyes as I have rendered myself vile in Thine. I humbly beseech Thee to be merciful to me in the free pardon of my sins for the sake of Thy dear Son and only Savior Jesus Christ who came to call not the righteous, but sinners to repentance. Thou gavest Thy Son to die for me." [George Washington; from a 24 page authentic handwritten manuscript book dated April 21-23, 1752 William J. Johnson *George Washington, the Christian* (New York: The Abingdon Press, New York & Cincinnati, 1919), pp. 24-35.]

"Although guided by our excellent Constitution in the discharge of official duties, and actuated, through the whole course of my public life, solely by a wish to promote the best interests of our country; *yet, without the beneficial interposition of the Supreme Ruler of the Universe, we could not have reached the distinguished situation which we have attained* with such unprecedented rapidity. To HIM, therefore, should we bow with gratitude and reverence, and endeavor to merit a continuance of HIS special favors". [1797 letter to John Adams]

James Wilson: *Signer of the Declaration of Independence and the Constitution Supreme Court Justice appointed by George Washington Spoke 168 times during the Constitutional Convention*

"Christianity is part of the common law" [Sources: James Wilson, Course of Lectures [vol 3, p.122]; and quoted in Updegraph v. The Commonwealth, 11 Serg, & R. 393, 403 (1824).]

Public Institutions Liberty Bell Inscription: " Proclaim liberty throughout the land and to all the inhabitants thereof" [Leviticus 25:10]

Proposals for the seal of the United States of America • "Moses lifting his wand and dividing the Red Sea" –Ben Franklin • "The children of Israel in the wilderness, led by a cloud by day and a pillar of fire by night." --Thomas Jefferson

On July 4, 1776, Congress appointed Benjamin Franklin, Thomas Jefferson and John Adams "to bring in a device for a seal for the United States of America." Franklin's proposal adapted the biblical story of the parting of the Red

Sea. Jefferson first recommended the "Children of Israel in the Wilderness, led by a Cloud by Day, and a Pillar of Fire by night. . . ." He then embraced Franklin's proposal and rewrote it Jefferson's revision of Franklin's proposal was presented by the committee to Congress on August 20, 1776.

Another popular proposal to the Great Seal of the United States was: " Rebellion to Tyrants is Obedience to God"; with Pharoah's army drowning in the Red Sea **The three branches of the U.S. Government: Judicial, Legislative, Executive** • At the Constitutional Convention of 1787, James Madison proposed the plan to divide the central government into three branches. He discovered this model of government from the Perfect Governor, as he read Isaiah 33:22; "For the LORD is our judge, the LORD is our lawgiver, the LORD is our king; He will save us."

Article 22 of the constitution of Delaware (1776)

Required all officers, besides taking an oath of allegiance, to make and subscribe to the following declaration: • "I, [name], do profess faith in God the Father, and in Jesus Christ His only Son, and in the Holy Ghost, one God, blessed for evermore; and I do acknowledge the Holy Scriptures of the Old and New Testament to be given by divine inspiration."

New York Spectator. August 23, 1831 "The court of common pleas of Chester county [New York] rejected a witness who declared his disbelief in the existence of God. The presiding judge remarked that he had not before been aware that there was a man living who did not believe in the existence of God; that this belief constituted the sanction of all testimony in a court of justice: and that he

knew of no cause in a Christian country where a witness had been permitted to testify without such belief.

THE UNITED STATES CONSTITUTION

Preamble

We the People of the United States, in Order to form a more perfect Union, establish Justice, insure domestic Tranquility, provide for the common defence, promote the general Welfare, and secure the Blessings of Liberty to ourselves and our Posterity, do ordain and establish this Constitution for the United States of America.

Article 1 - The Legislative Branch

Section 1 - The Legislature

All legislative Powers herein granted shall be vested in a Congress of the United States, which shall consist of a Senate and House of Representatives.

Section 2 - The House

The House of Representatives shall be composed of Members chosen every second Year by the People of the several States, and the Electors in each State shall have the Qualifications requisite for Electors of the most numerous Branch of the State Legislature.

No Person shall be a Representative who shall not have attained to the Age of twenty five Years, and been seven Years a Citizen of the United States, and who shall not, when elected, be an Inhabitant of that State in which he shall be chosen.

(Representatives and direct Taxes shall be apportioned among the several States which may be included within this Union, according to their respective Numbers, which shall be determined by adding to the whole Number of free Per- sons, including those bound to Service for a Term of Years, and excluding Indians not taxed, three fifths of all other Persons.) (The previous sentence in parentheses was modified by the 14th Amendment, section 2.) The actual Enumeration shall be made within three Years after the first Meeting of the Congress of the United States, and within every subsequent Term of ten Years, in such Manner as they shall by Law direct. The Number of Representatives shall not exceed one for every thirty Thousand, but each State shall have at Least one Representative; and until such enumeration shall be made, the State of New Hampshire shall be entitled to chuse three, Massachusetts eight, Rhode Island and Providence Plantations one, Connecticut five, New York six, New Jersey four, Pennsylvania eight, Delaware one, Maryland six, Virginia ten, North Carolina five, South Carolina five and Georgia three.

When vacancies happen in the Representation from any State, the Executive Authority thereof shall issue Writs of Election to fill such Vacancies.

The House of Representatives shall chuse their Speaker and other Officers; and shall have the sole Power of Impeachment.

Section 3 - The Senate

The Senate of the United States shall be composed of two Senators from each State, (chosen by the Legislature thereof,) (The preceding words in parentheses superseded by the17th Amendment, section 1.)for six Years; and each Senator shall have one Vote.

Immediately after they shall be assembled in Consequence of the first Election, they shall be divided as equally as may be into three Classes. The Seats of the Senators of the first Class shall be vacated at the Expiration of the second Year, of the second Class at the Expiration of the fourth Year, and of the third Class at the Expiration of the sixth Year, so that one third may be chosen every second Year; (and if Vacancies happen by Resignation, or otherwise, during the Recess of the Legislature of any State, the Executive thereof may make temporary Appointments until the next Meeting of the Legislature, which shall then fill such Vacancies.) (The preceding words in parentheses were superseded by the 17th Amendment, section 2.)

No person shall be a Senator who shall not have attained to the Age of thirty Years, and been nine Years a Citizen of the United States, and who shall not, when elected, be an Inhabitant of that State for which he shall be chosen.

The Vice President of the United States shall be President of the Senate, but shall have no Vote, unless they be equally divided.

The Senate shall chuse their other Officers, and also a President pro tempore, in the absence of the Vice President, or when he shall exercise the Office of President of the United States.

The Senate shall have the sole Power to try all Impeachments. When sitting for that Purpose, they shall be on Oath or Affirmation. When the President of the United States is tried, the Chief Justice shall preside: And no Person shall be convicted without the Concurrence of two thirds of the Members present.

Judgment in Cases of Impeachment shall not extend further than to removal from Office, and disqualification to hold and enjoy any Office of honor, Trust or Profit under the United States: but the Party convicted shall nevertheless be liable and subject to Indictment, Trial, Judgment and Punishment, according to Law.

Section 4 - Elections, Meetings
The Times, Places and Manner of holding Elections for Senators and Representatives, shall be prescribed in each State by the Legislature thereof; but the Congress may at any time by Law make or alter such Regulations, except as to the Place of Chusing Senators.

The Congress shall assemble at least once in every Year, and such Meeting shall (be on the first Monday in December,) (The preceding words in parentheses were superseded by the20th Amendment, section 2.) unless they shall by Law appoint a different Day.

Section 5 - Membership, Rules, Journals, Adjournment
Each House shall be the Judge of the Elections, Returns and Qualifications of its own Members, and a Majority

of each shall constitute a Quorum to do Business; but a smaller number may adjourn from day to day, and may be authorized to compel the Attendance of absent Members, in such Manner, and under such Penalties as each House may provide.

Each House may determine the Rules of its Proceedings, punish its Members for disorderly Behavior, and, with the Concurrence of two-thirds, expel a Member.

Each House shall keep a Journal of its Proceedings, and from time to time publish the same, excepting such Parts as may in their Judgment re- quire Secrecy; and the Yeas and Nays of the Members of either House on any question shall, at the Desire of one fifth of those Present, be entered on the Journal.

Neither House, during the Session of Congress, shall, without the Con-sent of the other, adjourn for more than three days, nor to any other Place than that in which the two Houses shall be sitting.

Section 6 - Compensation
(The Senators and Representatives shall receive a Compensation for their Ser- vices, to be ascertained by Law, and paid out of the Treasury of the United States.)(The preceding words in parentheses were modified by the 27th Amendment.) They shall in all Cases, except Treason, Felony and Breach of the Peace, be privileged from Arrest during their Attendance at the Session of their respective Houses, and in going to and re- turning from the same; and for any Speech or Debate in either House, they shall not be questioned in any other Place.

No Senator or Representative shall, during the Time for which he was elected, be appointed to any civil Office under the Authority of the United States which shall have been created, or the Emoluments whereof shall have been increased during such time; and no Person holding any Office under the United States, shall be a Member of either House during his Continuance in Office.

Section 7 - Revenue Bills, Legislative Process, Presidential Veto
All bills for raising Revenue shall originate in the House of Representatives; but the Senate may propose or concur with Amendments as on other Bills.

Every Bill which shall have passed the House of Representatives and the Senate, shall, before it become a Law, be presented to the President of the United States; If he approve he shall sign it, but if not he shall return it, with his Objections to that House in which it shall have originated, who shall enter the Objections at large on their Journal, and proceed to reconsider it. If after such Reconsideration two thirds of that House shall agree to pass the Bill, it shall be sent, together with the Objections, to the other House, by which it shall likewise be reconsidered, and if approved by two thirds of that House, it shall become a Law. But in all such Cases the Votes of both Houses shall be determined by Yeas and Nays, and the Names of the Persons voting for and against the Bill shall be entered on the Journal of each House respectively. If any Bill shall not be returned by the President within ten Days (Sundays excepted) after it shall have been presented to

him, the Same shall be a Law, in like Manner as if he had signed it, unless the Congress by their Adjournment prevent its Return, in which Case it shall not be a Law.

Every Order, Resolution, or Vote to which the Concurrence of the Senate and House of Representatives may be necessary (except on a question of Adjournment) shall be presented to the President of the United States; and before the Same shall take Effect, shall be approved by him, or being disapproved by him, shall be repassed by two thirds of the Senate and House of Representatives, according to the Rules and Limitations prescribed in the Case of a Bill.

Section 8 - Powers of Congress
The Congress shall have Power To lay and collect Taxes, Du- ties, Imposts and Excises, to pay the Debts and provide for the common Defence and general Welfare of the United States; but all Du- ties, Imposts and Excises shall be uniform throughout the United States;

To borrow money on the credit of the United States;

To regulate Commerce with foreign Nations, and among the several States, and with the Indian Tribes;

To establish an uniform Rule of Naturalization, and uniform Laws on the subject of Bankruptcies throughout the United States;

To coin Money, regulate the Value thereof, and of foreign Coin, and fix the Standard of Weights and Measures;

To provide for the Punishment of counterfeiting the Securities and cur- rent Coin of the United States;

To establish Post Offices and Post Roads;

To promote the Progress of Science and useful Arts, by securing for limited Times to Authors and Inventors the exclusive Right to their respective Writings and Discoveries;

To constitute Tribunals inferior to the supreme Court;

To define and punish Piracies and Felonies committed on the high Seas, and Offenses against the Law of Nations;

To declare War, grant Letters of Marque and Reprisal, and make Rules concerning Captures on Land and Water;

To raise and support Armies, but no Appropriation of Money to that Use shall be for a longer Term than two Years;

To provide and maintain a Navy;

To make Rules for the Government and Regulation of the land and naval Forces;

To provide for calling forth the Militia to execute the Laws of the Union, suppress Insurrections and repel Invasions;

To provide for organizing, arming, and disciplining the Militia, and for governing such Part of them as may be employed in the Service of the United States, reserving to the States respectively, the Appointment of the Officers, and the Authority of

training the Militia according to the discipline prescribed by Congress;

To exercise exclusive Legislation in all Cases whatsoever, over such District (not exceeding ten Miles square) as may, by Cession of particular States, and the acceptance of Congress, become the Seat of the Government of the United States, and to exercise like Authority over all Places

purchased by the Consent of the Legislature of the State in which the Same shall be, for the Erection of Forts, Magazines, Arsenals, dock-Yards, and other needful Buildings; And

To make all Laws which shall be necessary and proper for carrying into Execution the foregoing Powers, and all other Powers vested by this Constitution in the Government of the United States, or in any Department or Officer thereof.

Section 9 - Limits on Congress

The Migration or Importation of such Persons as any of the States now existing shall think proper to admit, shall not be prohibited by the Congress prior to the Year one thousand eight hundred and eight, but a tax or duty may be imposed on such Importation, not exceeding ten dollars for each Person.

The privilege of the Writ of Habeas Corpus shall not be suspended, unless when in Cases of Rebellion or Invasion the public Safety may require it.

No Bill of Attainder or ex post facto Law shall be passed.

(No capitation, or other direct, Tax shall be laid, unless in Proportion to the Census or Enumeration herein before directed to be taken.) (Section in parentheses clarified by the 16th Amendment.)

No Tax or Duty shall be laid on Articles exported from any State.

No Preference shall be given by any Regulation of Commerce or Revenue to the Ports of one State over those of another: nor shall Vessels bound to, or from, one State, be obliged to enter, clear, or pay Duties in another.

No Money shall be drawn from the Treasury, but in Consequence of Appropriations made by Law; and a regular Statement and Account of the Receipts and Expenditures of all public Money shall be published from time to time.

No Title of Nobility shall be granted by the United States: And no Per- son holding any Office of Profit or Trust under them, shall, without the Consent of the Congress, accept of any present, Emolument, Office, or Title, of any kind whatever, from any King, Prince or foreign State.

Section 10 - Powers Prohibited of States

No State shall enter into any Treaty, Alliance, or Confederation; grant Letters of Marque and Reprisal; coin Money; emit Bills of Credit; make any Thing but gold and silver Coin a Tender in Payment of Debts; pass any Bill of Attainder, ex post facto Law, or Law impairing the Obligation of Contracts, or grant any Title of Nobility.

No State shall, without the Consent

of the Congress, lay any Imposts or Duties on Imports or Exports, except what may be absolutely necessary for executing it's inspection Laws: and the net Produce of all Duties and Imposts, laid by any State on Imports or Exports, shall be for the Use of the Treasury of the United States; and all such Laws shall be subject to the Revision and Controul of the Congress.

No State shall, without the Consent of Congress, lay any duty of Tonnage, keep Troops, or Ships of War in time of Peace, enter into any Agreement or Compact with another State, or with a foreign Power, or engage in War, unless actually invaded, or in such imminent Danger as will not admit of delay.

Article 2 - The Executive Branch
Section 1 - The President
The executive Power shall be vested in a President of the United States of America. He shall hold his Office during the Term of four Years, and, together with the Vice-President chosen for the same Term, be elected, as follows:

Each State shall appoint, in such Manner as the Legislature thereof may direct, a Number of Electors, equal to the whole Number of Senators and Representatives to which the State may be entitled in the Congress: but no Senator or Representative, or Person holding an Office of Trust or Profit under the United States, shall be appointed an Elector.

(The Electors shall meet in their respective States, and vote by Ballot for two persons, of whom one at least shall not lie an Inhabitant of the same State with themselves. And they shall make a List of all the Persons voted for, and of the Number of Votes for each; which List they shall sign and certify, and transmit sealed to the Seat of the Government of the United States, directed to the Presid- ent of the Senate. The President of the Senate shall, in the Presence of the Senate and House of Representatives, open all the Certificates, and the Votes shall then be counted. The Person having the greatest Number of Votes shall be the President, if such Number be a Majority of the whole Number of Electors appointed; and if there be more than one who have such Majority, and have an equal Number of Votes, then the House of Representatives shall immediately chuse by Bal- lot one of them for President; and if no Person have a Majority, then from the five highest on the List the said House shall in like Manner chuse the President. But in chusing the President, the Votes shall be taken by States, the Representation from each State having one Vote; a quorum for this Purpose shall consist of a Member or Members from two-thirds of the States, and a Majority of all the States shall be necessary to a Choice. In every Case, after the Choice of the President, the Person having the greatest Number of Votes of the Electors shall be the Vice President. But if there should remain two or more who have equal Votes, the Senate shall chuse from them by Ballot the Vice-President.) (This clause in parentheses was superseded by the 12th Amendment.)

The Congress may determine the Time of chusing the Electors, and the Day on which they shall give their

Votes; which Day shall be the same throughout the United States.

No person except a natural born Citizen, or a Citizen of the United States, at the time of the Adoption of this Constitution, shall be eligible to the Office of President; neither shall any Person be eligible to that Office who shall not have attained to the Age of thirty-five Years, and been fourteen Years a Resident within the United States.

(In Case of the Removal of the President from Office, or of his Death, Resignation, or Inability to discharge the Powers and Duties of the said Office, the same shall devolve on the Vice President, and the Congress may by Law provide for the Case of Removal, Death, Resignation or Inability, both of the President and Vice President, declaring what Officer shall then act as President, and such Officer shall act accordingly, until the Disability be removed, or a President shall be elected.)(This clause in parentheses has been modified by the 20th and 25th Amendments.)

The President shall, at stated Times, receive for his Services, a Compensation, which shall neither be increased nor diminished during the Period for which he shall have been elected, and he shall not receive within that Period any other Emolument from the United States, or any of them.

Before he enter on the Execution of his Office, he shall take the following Oath or Affirmation:

"I do solemnly swear (or affirm) that I will faithfully execute the Office of President of the United States, and will to the best of my Ability, pre-serve, protect and defend the Constitution of the United States."

Section 2 - Civilian Power Over Military, Cabinet, Pardon Power, Appointments

The President shall be Commander in Chief of the Army and Navy of the United States, and of the Militia of the several States, when called into the actual Service of the United States; he may require the Opinion, in writing, of the principal Officer in each of the executive Departments, upon any subject relating to the Duties of their respective Offices, and he shall have Power to Grant Reprieves and Pardons for Offenses against the United States, except in Cases of Impeachment.

He shall have Power, by and with the Advice and Consent of the Senate, to make Treaties, provided two thirds of the Senators present concur; and he shall nominate, and by and with the Advice and Consent of the Senate, shall appoint Ambassadors, other public Ministers and Consuls, Judges of the supreme Court, and all other Officers of the United States, whose Appointments are not herein otherwise provided for, and which shall be established by Law: but the Congress may by Law vest the Appointment of such inferior Officers, as they think proper, in the President alone, in the Courts of Law, or in the Heads of Departments.

Section 3 - State of the Union, Convening Congress

He shall from time to time give to the Congress Information of the State of the Union, and recommend to their

Consideration such Measures as he shall judge necessary and expedient; he may, on extraordinary Occasions, convene both Houses, or either of them, and in Case of Disagreement between them, with Respect to the Time of Adjournment, he may adjourn them to such Time as he shall think proper; he shall receive Ambassadors and other public Ministers; he shall take Care that the Laws be faithfully executed, and shall Commission all the Officers of the United States.

Section 4 - Disqualification

The President, Vice President and all civil Officers of the United States, shall be removed from Office on Impeachment for, and Conviction of, Treason, Bribery, or other high Crimes and Misdemeanors.

Article 3 - The Judicial Branch

Section 1 - Judicial Powers

The judicial Power of the United States, shall be vested in one supreme Court, and in such inferior Courts as the Congress may from time to time ordain and establish. The Judges, both of the supreme and inferior Courts, shall hold their Offices during good Behavior, and shall, at stated Times, receive for their Services a Compensation which shall not be diminished during their Continuance in Office.

Section 2 - Trial by Jury, Original Jurisdiction, Jury Trials

(The judicial Power shall extend to all Cases, in Law and Equity, arising under this Constitution, the Laws of the United States, and Treaties made, or which shall be made, under their Authority; to all Cases affecting Ambassadors, other public Ministers and Consuls; to all Cases of admiralty and maritime Jurisdiction; to Controversies to which the United States shall be a Party; to Controversies between two or more States; between a State and Citizens of an- other State; between Citizens of different States; between Citizens of the same State claiming Lands under Grants of different States, and between a State, or the Citizens thereof, and foreign States, Citizens or Subjects.) (This section in parentheses is modified by the 11th Amendment.)

In all Cases affecting Ambassadors, other public Ministers and Consuls, and those in which a State shall be Party, the supreme Court shall have original Jurisdiction. In all the other Cases before mentioned, the supreme Court shall have appellate Jurisdiction, both as to Law and Fact, with such Exceptions, and under such Regulations as the Congress shall make.

The Trial of all Crimes, except in Cases of Impeachment, shall be by Jury; and such Trial shall be held in the State where the said Crimes shall have been committed; but when not committed within any State, the Trial shall be at such Place or Places as the Congress may by Law have directed.

Section 3 - Treason

Treason against the United States, shall consist only in levying War against them, or in adhering to their Enemies, giving them Aid and Comfort. No Person shall be convicted of Treason unless on the Testimony of two Witnesses to the same overt Act, or on Confession in open Court.

The Congress shall have power to

declare the Punishment of Treason, but no Attainder of Treason shall work Corruption of Blood, or Forfeiture except during the Life of the Person attainted.

Article 4 - The States
Section 1 - Each State to Honor all Others
Full Faith and Credit shall be given in each State to the public Acts, Records, and judicial Proceedings of every other State. And the Congress may by general Laws prescribe the Manner in which such Acts, Records and Proceedings shall be proved, and the Effect thereof.

Section 2 - State Citizens, Extradition
The Citizens of each State shall be entitled to all Privileges and Immunities of Citizens in the several States.

A Person charged in any State with Treason, Felony, or other Crime, who shall flee from Justice, and be found in another State, shall on demand of the executive Authority of the State from which he fled, be de- livered up, to be removed to the State having Jurisdiction of the Crime.

(No Person held to Service or Labour in one State, under the Laws thereof, escaping into another, shall, in Consequence of any Law or Regulation therein, be discharged from such Service or Labour, But shall be delivered up on Claim of the Party to whom such Service or Labour may be due.) (This clause in parentheses is superseded by the 13th Amendment.)

Section 3 - New States
New States may be admitted by the Congress into this Union; but no new States shall be formed or erected within the Jurisdiction of any other State; nor any State be formed by the Junction of two or more States, or parts of States, without the Consent of the Legislatures of the States concerned as well as of the Congress.

The Congress shall have Power to dispose of and make all needful Rules and Regulations respecting the Territory or other Property belonging to the United States; and nothing in this Constitution shall be so construed as to Prejudice any Claims of the United States, or of any particular State.

Section 4 - Republican Government
The United States shall guarantee to every State in this Union a Republican Form of Government, and shall protect each of them against Invasion; and on Application of the Legislature, or of the Executive (when the Legislature cannot be convened) against domestic Violence.

Article 5 - Amendment
The Congress, whenever two thirds of both Houses shall deem it necessary, shall propose Amendments to this Constitution, or, on the Application of the Legislatures of two thirds of the several States, shall call a Convention for proposing Amendments, which, in either Case, shall be valid to all Intents and Purposes, as part of this Constitution, when ratified by the Legislatures of three fourths of the several States, or by Conventions in three fourths thereof, as the one or the other Mode of Ratific- ation may be proposed by the Congress; Provided that no

Amendment which may be made prior to the Year One thousand eight hundred and eight shall in any Manner affect the first and fourth Clauses in the Ninth Section of the first Article; and that no State, without its Consent, shall be deprived of its equal Suffrage in the Senate.

Article 6 - Debts, Supremacy, Oaths

All Debts contracted and Engagements entered into, before the Adoption of this Constitution, shall be as valid against the United States under this Constitution, as under the Confederation.

This Constitution, and the Laws of the United States which shall be made in Pursuance thereof; and all Treaties made, or which shall be made, under the Authority of the United States, shall be the supreme Law of the Land; and the Judges in every State shall be bound thereby, any Thing in the Constitution or Laws of any State to the Contrary notwithstanding.

The Senators and Representatives before mentioned, and the Members of the several State Legislatures, and all executive and judicial Officers, both of the United States and of the several States, shall be bound by Oath or Affirmation, to support this Constitution; but no religious Test shall ever be required as a Qualification to any Office or public Trust under the United States.

Article 7 - Ratification

The Ratification of the Conventions of nine States, shall be sufficient for the Establishment of this Constitution between the States so ratifying the Same.

Signatories

Done in Convention by the Unanimous Consent of the States present the Seventeenth Day of September in the Year of our Lord one thousand seven hundred and Eighty seven and of the Independence of the United States of America the Twelfth. In Witness whereof We have hereunto subscribed our Names.

Go Washington - President and deputy from Virginia New Hampshire - John Langdon, Nicholas Gilman Massachusetts - Nathaniel Gorham, Rufus King Connecticut - Wm Saml Johnson, Roger Sherman New York - Alexander Hamilton

New Jersey - Wil Livingston, David Brearley, Wm Paterson, Jona. Dayton

Pensylvania - B Franklin, Thomas Mifflin, Robt Morris, Geo. Clymer, Thos FitzSimons, Jared Ingersoll, James Wilson, Gouv Morris

Delaware - Geo. Read, Gunning Bedford jun, John Dickinson, Richard Bassett, Jaco. Broom

Maryland - James McHenry, Dan of St Tho Jenifer, Danl Carroll Virginia - John Blair, James Madison Jr. North Carolina - Wm Blount, Richd Dobbs Spaight, Hu Williamson South Carolina - J. Rutledge, Charles Cotesworth Pinckney, Charles

Pinckney, Pierce Butler Georgia - William Few, Abr Baldwin Attest: William Jackson, Secretary

Amendments
Amendment 1 - Freedom of Religion, Press, Expression
Congress shall make no law

respecting an establishment of religion, or prohibiting the free exercise thereof; or abridging the freedom of speech, or of the press; or the right of the people peaceably to assemble, and to petition the Government for a redress of grievances.

Amendment 2 - Right to Bear Arms

A well regulated Militia, being necessary to the security of a free State, the right of the people to keep and bear Arms, shall not be infringed.

Amendment 3 - Quartering of Soldiers

No Soldier shall, in time of peace be quartered in any house, without the consent of the Owner, nor in time of war, but in a manner to be pre-scribed by law.

Amendment 4 - Search and Seizure

The right of the people to be secure in their persons, houses, papers, and effects, against unreasonable searches and seizures, shall not be violated, and no Warrants shall issue, but upon probable cause, supported by Oath or affirmation, and particularly describing the place to be searched, and the persons or things to be seized.

Amendment 5 - Trial and Punishment, Compensation for Takings

No person shall be held to answer for a capital, or otherwise infamous crime, unless on a presentment or indictment of a Grand Jury, except in cases arising in the land or naval forces, or in the Militia, when in actual service in time of War or public danger; nor shall any person be subject for the same offense to be twice put in jeopardy of life or limb; nor shall be compelled in any criminal case to be a witness against himself, nor be deprived of life, liberty, or property, without due process of law; nor shall private property be taken for public use, without just compensation.

Amendment 6 - Right to Speedy Trial, Confrontation of Witnesses

In all criminal prosecutions, the accused shall enjoy the right to a speedy and public trial, by an impartial jury of the State and district wherein the crime shall have been committed, which district shall have been previously ascertained by law, and to be informed of the nature and cause of the accusation; to be confronted with the witnesses against him; to have compulsory process for obtaining witnesses in his favor, and to have the Assistance of Counsel for his defence.

Amendment 7 - Trial by Jury in Civil Cases

In Suits at common law, where the value in controversy shall exceed twenty dollars, the right of trial by jury shall be preserved, and no fact tried by a jury, shall be otherwise re-examined in any Court of the United States, than according to the rules of the common law.

Amendment 8 - Cruel and Unusual Punishment

Excessive bail shall not be required, nor excessive fines imposed, nor cruel and unusual punishments inflicted.

Amendment 9 - Construction of Constitution

The enumeration in the Constitution, of certain rights, shall not be

construed to deny or disparage others retained by the people.

Amendment 10 - Powers of the States and People

The powers not delegated to the United States by the Constitution, nor prohibited by it to the States, are reserved to the States respectively, or to the people.

Amendment 11 - Judicial Limits

The Judicial power of the United States shall not be construed to extend to any suit in law or equity, commenced or prosecuted against one of the United States by Citizens of another State, or by Citizens or Subjects of any Foreign State.

Amendment 12 - Choosing the President, Vice-President

The Electors shall meet in their respective states, and vote by ballot for President and Vice-President, one of whom, at least, shall not be an in-habitant of the same state with themselves; they shall name in their bal- lots the person voted for as President, and in distinct ballots the person voted for as Vice-President, and they shall make distinct lists of all per- sons voted for as President, and of all persons voted for as Vice-President and of the number of votes for each, which lists they shall sign and certify, and transmit sealed to the seat of the government of the United States, directed to the President of the Senate;

The President of the Senate shall, in the presence of the Senate and House of Representatives, open all the certificates and the votes shall then be counted;

The person having the greatest

Number of votes for President, shall be the President, if such number be a majority of the whole number of Elect- ors appointed; and if no person have such majority, then from the per- sons having the highest numbers not exceeding three on the list of those voted for as President, the House of Representatives shall choose immediately, by ballot, the President. But in choosing the President, the votes shall be taken by states, the representation from each state having one vote; a quorum for this purpose shall consist of a member or members from two-thirds of the states, and a majority of all the states shall be necessary to a choice. And if the House of Representatives shall not choose a President whenever the right of choice shall devolve upon them, before the fourth day of March next following, then the Vice-President shall act as President, as in the case of the death or other constitutional disability of the President.

The person having the greatest number of votes as Vice-President, shall be the Vice-President, if such number be a majority of the whole number of Electors appointed, and if no person have a majority, then from the two highest numbers on the list, the Senate shall choose the Vice-President; a quorum for the purpose shall consist of two-thirds of the whole number of Senators, and a majority of the whole number shall be necessary to a choice. But no person constitutionally ineligible to the office of President shall be eligible to that of Vice-President of the United States.

Amendment 13 - Slavery Abolished

1. Neither slavery nor involuntary

servitude, except as a punishment for crime whereof the party shall have been duly convicted, shall exist within the United States, or any place subject to their jurisdiction.

2. Congress shall have power to enforce this article by appropriate legislation.

Amendment 14 - Citizenship Rights

1. All persons born or naturalized in the United States, and subject to the jurisdiction thereof, are citizens of the United States and of the State wherein they reside. No State shall make or enforce any law which shall abridge the privileges or immunities of citizens of the United States; nor shall any State deprive any person of life, liberty, or property, without due process of law; nor deny to any person within its jurisdiction the equal protection of the laws.

2. Representatives shall be apportioned among the several States according to their respective numbers, counting the whole number of persons in each State, excluding Indians not taxed. But when the right to vote at any election for the choice of electors for President and Vice-President of the United States, Representatives in Congress, the Executive and Judicial officers of a State, or the members of the Legislature thereof, is denied to any of the male inhabitants of such State, being twenty-one years of age, and citizens of the United States, or in any way abridged, except for participation in rebellion, or other crime, the basis of representation therein shall be reduced in the proportion which the number of such male citizens shall bear to the whole number of male citizens twenty-one years of age in such State.

3. No person shall be a Senator or Representative in Congress, or elector of President and Vice-President, or hold any office, civil or military, under the United States, or under any State, who, having previously taken an oath, as a member of Congress, or as an officer of the United States, or as a member of any State legislature, or as an executive or judicial officer of any State, to support the Constitution of the United States, shall have engaged in insurrection or rebellion against the same, or given aid or comfort to the enemies thereof. But Congress may by a vote of two- thirds of each House, remove such disability.

4. The validity of the public debt of the United States, authorized by law, including debts incurred for payment of pensions and bounties for services in suppressing insurrection or rebellion, shall not be questioned. But neither the United States nor any State shall assume or pay any debt or obligation incurred in aid of insurrection or rebellion against the Un-ted States, or any claim for the loss or emancipation of any slave; but all such debts, obligations and claims shall be held illegal and void.

5. The Congress shall have power to enforce, by appropriate legislation, the provisions of this article.

Amendment 15 - Race No Bar to Vote

1. The right of citizens of the United States to vote shall not be denied or abridged by the United States or by any State on account of race, color, or previous condition of servitude.

2. The Congress shall have power to enforce this article by appropriate legislation.

Amendment 16 - Status of Income Tax Clarified

The Congress shall have power to lay and collect taxes on incomes, from whatever source derived, without apportionment among the several States, and without regard to any census or enumeration.

Amendment 17 - Senators Elected by Popular Vote

The Senate of the United States shall be composed of two Senators from each State, elected by the people thereof, for six years; and each Senator shall have one vote. The electors in each State shall have the qualifications requisite for electors of the most numerous branch of the State legislatures.

When vacancies happen in the representation of any State in the Senate, the executive authority of such State shall issue writs of election to fill such vacancies: Provided, That the legislature of any State may empower the executive thereof to make temporary appointments until the people fill the vacancies by election as the legislature may direct.

This amendment shall not be so construed as to affect the election or term of any Senator chosen before it becomes valid as part of the Constitution.

Amendment 18 - Liquor Abolished

1. After one year from the ratification of this article the manufacture, sale, or transportation of intoxicating liquors within, the importation thereof into, or the exportation thereof from the United States and all territory subject to the jurisdiction thereof for beverage purposes is hereby prohibited.

2. The Congress and the several States shall have concurrent power to enforce this article by appropriate legislation.

3. This article shall be inoperative unless it shall have been ratified as an amendment to the Constitution by the legislatures of the several States, as provided in the Constitution, within seven years from the date of the submission hereof to the States by the Congress.

Amendment 19 - Women's Suffrage

The right of citizens of the United States to vote shall not be denied or abridged by the United States or by any State on account of sex.

Congress shall have power to enforce this article by appropriate legislation.

Amendment 20 - Presidential, Congressional Terms

1. The terms of the President and Vice President shall end at noon on the 20th day of January, and the terms of Senators and Representatives at noon on the 3d day of January, of the years in which such terms would have ended if this article had not been ratified; and the terms of their successors shall then begin.

2. The Congress shall assemble at least once in every year, and such meeting shall begin at noon on the 3d day of January, unless they shall by law appoint a different day.

3. If, at the time fixed for the beginning of the term of the President, the President elect shall have died, the Vice President elect shall become President. If a President shall not have been chosen before the time fixed for the beginning of his term, or if the President elect shall have failed to qualify, then the Vice President elect shall act as President until a President shall have qualified; and the Congress may by law provide for the case wherein neither a President elect nor a Vice President elect shall have qualified, declaring who shall then act as President, or the manner in which one who is to act shall be selected, and such person shall act accordingly until a President or Vice President shall have qualified.

4. The Congress may by law provide for the case of the death of any of the persons from whom the House of Representatives may choose a President whenever the right of choice shall have devolved upon them, and for the case of the death of any of the persons from whom the Senate may choose a Vice President whenever the right of choice shall have devolved upon them.

5. Sections 1 and 2 shall take effect on the 15th day of October following the ratification of this article.

6. This article shall be inoperative unless it shall have been ratified as an amendment to the Constitution by the legislatures of three-fourths of the several States within seven years from the date of its submission.

Amendment 21 - 18th Amendment Repealed

1. The eighteenth article of amendment to the Constitution of the United States is hereby repealed.

2. The transportation or importation into any State, Territory, or possession of the United States for delivery or use therein of intoxicating liquors, in violation of the laws thereof, is hereby prohibited.

3. The article shall be inoperative unless it shall have been ratified as an amendment to the Constitution by conventions in the several States, as provided in the Constitution, within seven years from the date of the submission hereof to the States by the Congress.

Amendment 22 - Presidential Term Limits

1. No person shall be elected to the office of the President more than twice, and no person who has held the office of President, or acted as President, for more than two years of a term to which some other person was elected President shall be elected to the office of the President more than once. But this Article shall not apply to any person holding the office of President, when this Article was proposed by the Congress, and shall not prevent any person who may be holding the office of President, or acting as President, during the term within which this Article becomes operative from holding the office of President or acting as President during the remainder of such term.

2. This article shall be inoperative unless it shall have been ratified as an amendment to the Constitution by the legislatures of three-fourths of the several States within seven years

from the date of its submission to the States by the Congress.

Amendment 23 - Presidential Vote for District of Columbia

1. The District constituting the seat of Government of the United States shall appoint in such manner as the Congress may direct: A number of electors of President and Vice President equal to the whole number of Senators and Representatives in Congress to which the District would be entitled if it were a State, but in no event more than the least populous State; they shall be in addition to those appointed by the States, but they shall be considered, for the purposes of the election of President and Vice President, to be electors appointed by a State; and they shall meet in the District and perform such duties as provided by the twelfth article of amendment.

2. The Congress shall have power to enforce this article by appropriate legislation.

Amendment 24 - Poll Tax Barred

1. The right of citizens of the United States to vote in any primary or other election for President or Vice President, for electors for President or Vice President, or for Senator or Representative in Congress, shall not be denied or abridged by the United States or any State by reason of failure to pay any poll tax or other tax.

2. The Congress shall have power to enforce this article by appropriate legislation.

Amendment 25 - Presidential Disability and Succession

1. In case of the removal of the President from office or of his death or resignation, the Vice President shall become President.

2. Whenever there is a vacancy in the office of the Vice President, the President shall nominate a Vice President who shall take office upon confirmation by a majority vote of both Houses of Congress.

3. Whenever the President transmits to the President pro tempore of the Senate and the Speaker of the House of Representatives his written declaration that he is unable to discharge the powers and duties of his office, and until he transmits to them a written declaration to the contrary, such powers and duties shall be discharged by the Vice President as Acting President.

4. Whenever the Vice President and a majority of either the principal officers of the executive departments or of such other body as Congress may by law provide, transmit to the President pro tempore of the Senate and the Speaker of the House of Representatives their written declaration that the President is unable to discharge the powers and duties of his office, the Vice President shall immediately assume the powers and duties of the office as Acting President.

Thereafter, when the President transmits to the President pro tempore of the Senate and the Speaker of the House of Representatives his written declaration that no inability exists, he shall resume the powers and du- ties of his office unless the Vice President and a majority of either the principal officers of the executive department

or of such other body as Congress may by law provide, transmit within four days to the President pro tempore of the Senate and the Speaker of the House of Representatives their written declaration that the President is unable to discharge the powers and duties of his office. Thereupon Congress shall decide the is- sue, assembling within forty eight hours for that purpose if not in session. If the Congress, within twenty one days after receipt of the latter written declaration, or, if Congress is not in session, within twenty one days after Congress is required to assemble, determines by two thirds vote of both Houses that the President is unable to discharge the powers and duties of his office, the Vice President shall continue to discharge the same as Acting President; otherwise, the President shall resume the powers and duties of his office.

Amendment 26 - Voting Age Set to 18 Years

1. The right of citizens of the United States, who are eighteen years of age or older, to vote shall not be denied or abridged by the United States or by any State on account of age.

2. The Congress shall have power to enforce this article by appropriate legislation.

Amendment 27 - Limiting Congressional Pay Increases

No law, varying the compensation for the services of the Senators and Representatives, shall take effect, until an election of Representatives shall have intervened.

DAYS OF HEAVEN UPON EARTH
A YEAR BOOK OF
SCRIPTURE TEXTS
AND LIVING TRUTHS

By

Rev. A. B. Simpson

The Days Of Heaven
The days of heaven are peaceful days,
Still as yon glassy sea;
So calm, so still in God, our days,
As the days of heaven would be.
The days of heaven are holy days,
From sin forever free;
So cleansed and kept our days, O Lord,
As the days of heaven would be.
The days of heaven are happy days.
Sorrow they never see;
So full of gladness all our days,
As the days of heaven would be.
The days of heaven are healthful days,
They feed on life's fair tree;
So feeding on Thy strength, O Christ,
Our days as heaven may be.
Walk with us, Lord, thro' all the days,
And let us walk with Thee;
Till as Thy will is done in heaven,
On earth so shall it be.

January 1

"Redeeming the time" (Eph. v. 16).

Two little words are found in the Greek version here. They are translated "*ton kairon*" in the revised version, "Buying up for yourselves the opportunity." The two words *ton kairon* mean, literally, the opportunity.

They do not refer to time in general, but to a special point of time, a juncture, a crisis, a moment full of possibilities and quickly passing by, which we must seize and make the best of before it has passed away.

It is intimated that there are not many such moments of opportunity, because the days are evil; like a barren desert, in which, here and there, you find a flower, pluck it while you can; like a business opportunity which comes a few times in a life-time; buy it up while you have the chance. Be spiritually alert; be not unwise, but understanding what the will of God is. "Walk circumspectly, not as fools, but as wise, buying up for yourselves the opportunity."

Sometimes it is a moment of time to be saved; sometimes a soul to be led to Christ; sometimes it is an occasion for love; sometimes for patience: sometimes for victory over temptation and sin. Let us redeem it.

January 2.

"I will cause you to walk in My statutes" (Eze. xxxvi. 27).

The highest spiritual condition is one where life is spontaneous and flows without effort, like the deep floods of Ezekiel's river, where the struggles of the swimmer ceased, and he was borne by the current's resistless force.

So God leads us into spiritual conditions and habits which become the spontaneous impulses of our being, and we live and move in the fulness of the divine life.

But these spiritual habits are not the outcome of some transitory impulse, but are often slowly acquired and established. They begin, like every true habit, in a definite act of will, and they are confirmed by the repetition of that act until it becomes a habit. The first stages always involve effort and choice. We have to take a stand and hold it steadily, and after we have done so a certain time, it becomes second nature, and carries us by its own force.

The Holy Spirit is willing to form such habits in every direction of our Christian life, and if we will but obey Him in the first steppings of faith, we will soon become established in the attitude of obedience, and duty will be delight.

January 3.

"Watch and pray" (Matt. xxvi. 41).

We need to watch for prayers as well as for the answers to our prayers. It needs as much wisdom to pray rightly as it does faith to receive the answers to our prayers.

We met a friend the other day, who had been in years of darkness because God had failed to answer certain prayers, and the result had been a state bordering on infidelity.

A very few moments were sufficient to convince this friend that these prayers had been entirely unauthorized, and that God had never promised to answer such prayers, and they were for things which this friend should have accomplished himself, in the exercise of ordinary wisdom.

The result was deliverance from a cloud of unbelief which was almost wrecking a Christian life. There are some things about which we do not need to pray, as much as to take the light which God has already given.

Many persons are asking God to give them peculiar signs, tokens and supernatural intimations of His will. Our business is to use the light He has given, and then He will give whatever more we need.

January 4.

"Blessed is the man that walketh not" (Ps. i. 1).

Three things are notable about this man:

1. His company. "He walketh not in the counsel of the ungodly, nor standeth in the way of sinners, nor sitteth in the seat of the scornful."

2. His reading and thinking. "His delight is in the law of the Lord, and in His law doth he meditate day and night."

3. His fruitfulness. "And he shall be like a tree planted by the rivers of water, that bringeth forth his fruit in his season; his leaf also shall not wither, and whatsoever he doeth shall prosper."

The river is the Holy Ghost; the planting, the deep, abiding life in which, not occasionally, but habitually, we absorb the Holy Spirit; and the fruit is not occasional, but continual, and appropriate to each changing season.

His life is also prosperous, and his spirit fresh, like the unfading leaf. Such a life must be happy. Indeed, happiness is a matter of spiritual conditions. Put a sunbeam in a cellar and it must be bright. Put a nightingale in the darkest midnight, and it must sing.

January 5.

"I know him that he will do the law" (Gen. xviii. 19).

God wants people that He can depend upon. He could say of Abraham, "I know him, that the Lord may bring upon Abraham all that He hath spoken." God can be depended upon; He wants us to be just as decided, as reliable, as stable. This is just what faith means. God is looking for men on whom He can put the weight of all His love, and power, and faithful promises. When God finds such a soul there is nothing He will not do for him. God's engines are strong enough to draw any weight we attach to them. Unfortunately the cable which we fasten to the engine is often too weak to hold the weight of our prayer, therefore God is drilling us, disciplining us, and training us to stability and certainty in the life of faith. Let us learn our lessons, and let us stand fast.

God has His best things for the few

Who dare to stand the test;

God has his second choice for those

Who will not have His best.

Give me, O Lord, Thy highest choice,

Let others take the rest.

Their good things have no charm for me,

For I have got Thy best.

January 6.

"The body is not one member, but many" (I. Cor. xii. 14).

We have a friend who has a phonograph for his correspondence. It consists of two parts. One is a simple and wonderful apparatus, whose sensitive cylinders receive the tones and then give them out again, word for word, through the hearing tube. The other part is a common little box that stands under the table, and does nothing but supply the power through connecting wires.

Now, the little box might insist upon being the phonograph, and doing the talking; but if it should, it would not only waste its own life but destroy the life of its partner.

Its sole business is to supply power to the phonograph, while the latter is to do the talking. So some of us are called to be voices to speak for God to our fellow-men, others are forces to sustain them, by our holy sympathy and silent prayer. (Some of us are little dynamos under the table, while others are phonographs that speak aloud the messages of heaven.)

Let each of us be true to our God-given ministry, and when the day comes our work will be weighed and the rewards distributed.

January 7.

"Now unto Him that is able to keep you from stumbling" (Jude 24).

This is a most precious promise. The revised translation is both accurate and suggestive. It is not merely from falling that He wants to keep us, but from even the slightest stumbling.

We are told of Abraham that he staggered not at the promise. God wants us to walk so steadily that there will not even be a quiver in the line of His regiments as they face the foe. It is the little stumblings of life that most

discourage and hinder us, and most of these stumblings are over trifles. Satan would much rather knock us down with a feather than with an Armstrong gun. It is much more to his honor and keen delight to defeat a child of God by some flimsy trifle than by some great temptation.

Beloved, let us watch, in these days, against the orange peels that trip us on our pathway, the little foxes that destroy the vines, and the dead flies that mar, sometimes, a whole vessel of precious ointment. "Trifles make perfection," and as we get farther on, in our Christian life, God will hold us much more closely to obedience in things that seem insignificant.

January 8.

"It is I, be not afraid" (Mark vi. 50).

Someone tells of a little child with some big story of sorrow upon its little heart, flying to its mother's arms for comfort, and intending to tell her the story of its trouble; but as that mother presses it to her bosom and pours out her love, it soon becomes so occupied with her and the sweetness of her affection that it forgets to tell its story, and in a little while even the memory of the trouble is forgotten. It has just been loved away, and she has taken its place in the heart of the little one.

This is the way God comforts us Himself. "It is I, be not afraid," is His reassuring word. The circumstances are not altered, but He Himself comes in their place, and satisfies every need of our being, and we forget all things in His sweet presence, as He becomes our all in all.

I am breathing out my sorrow

On Thy kind and loving breast;

Breathing in Thy joy and comfort,

Breathing in Thy peace and rest.
I am breathing out my longings
In Thy listening, loving ear;
I am breathing in Thy answer,
Stilling every doubt and fear.

January 9.

"Not as I will, but as Thou wilt" (Matt. xxvi. 39).

"To will and do of His good pleasure" (Phil. ii. 13).

There are two attitudes in which our will should be given to God.

First. We should have the surrendered will. This is where we must all begin, by yielding up to God our natural will, and having Him possess it.

But next, He wants us to have the victorious will. As soon as He receives our will in honest surrender, He wants to put His will into it and make it stronger than ever for Him. It is henceforth no longer our will, but His will. And having yielded to His choice and placed itself under His direction, He wants to put into it all the strength and intensity of His own great will and make us positive, forceful, victorious and unmovable, even as Himself. "Not My will, but Thine be done." That is the first step. "Father, I will that they whom Thou hast given Me, be with Me." That is the second attitude. Both are divine; both are right; both are necessary to our right living and successful working for God.

January 10.

"Charity doth not behave itself unseemly" (I. Cor. xiii. 5).

In the dress of a Hindu woman, her graceful robe is fastened upon her person entirely by means of a single knot. The long strip of cloth is wound around her person so as to fall in graceful folds like a made garment, and the end is fastened by a little knot, and the whole thing hangs by that single fastening. If that were loosed the robe would fall. And so in the spiritual life, our habits of grace are likened unto garments; and it is also true that the garment of love, which is the beautiful adorning of the child of God, is entirely fastened by little *nots*.

If you will read with care the thirteenth chapter of I. Corinthians, you will find that most of the qualities of love are purely negative. "Love envieth not, love vaunteth not itself, is not puffed up, doth not behave herself rudely, seeketh not her own, is not provoked, thinketh no evil." Here are *"nots"* enough to hold on our spiritual wardrobe. Here are reasons enough to explain the failure of so many, and the reason why they walk naked, or with rent garments, and others see their shame. Let us look after the *nots*.

January 11.

"Hold fast till I come" (Rev. ii. 25).

The other day we asked a Hebrew friend how it was that his countrymen were so successful in acquiring wealth. "Ah," said he, "we do not make more money than other people, but we keep more." Beloved, let us look out this day for spiritual pickpockets and spiritual leakage. Let us "lose nothing of what we have wrought, but receive a full reward"; and, as each day comes and goes, let us put away in the savings bank of eternity its treasures of grace and victory, and so be conscious from day to day that something real and everlasting is being added to our

eternal fortune.

It may be but a little, but if we only economize all that God gives us, and pass it on to His keeping, when the close shall come we shall be amazed to see how much the accumulated treasures of a well spent life have laid up on high, and how much more He has added to them by His glorious investment of the life committed to His keeping.

Oh, how the days are telling! Oh, how precious these golden hours will seem sometime! God help us to make the most of them now.

January 12.

"Ask and it shall be given you" (Matt. vii. 7).

We must receive, as well as ask. We must take the place of believing, and recognize ourselves as in it. A friend was saying, "I want to get into the will of God," and this was the answer: "Will you step into the will of God? And now, are you in the will of God?" The question aroused a thought that had not come before.

The gentleman saw that he had been straining after, but not receiving the blessing he sought.

Jesus has said, "Ask and ye shall receive." The very strain keeps back the blessing. The intense tension of all your spiritual nature so binds you that you are not open to the blessing which God is waiting to give you. "Whosoever will, let him take the water of life freely."

He tells me there is cleansing

From every secret sin,

And a great and full salvation

To keep the heart within.

And I take Him in His fulness,

With all His glorious grace,

For He says it is mine by taking,

And I take just what He says.

January 13.

"Thou shalt be to him instead of God" (Ex. iv. 16).

Such was God's promise to Moses, and such the high character that Moses was to assume toward Aaron, his brother. May it not suggest a high and glorious place that each of us may occupy toward all whom we meet, instead of God?

What a dignity and glory it would give our lives, could we uniformly realize this high calling! How it would lead us to act toward our fellow-men! God can always be depended upon. God is without variableness or shadow of turning. God's word is unchangeable, and we can trust Him without reserve or question. Oh, that we might so live that men can trust us, even as God!

Again, God has no needs or wants to be supplied. He is always giving. "Rich unto all that call upon Him." The glory of His nature is love, unselfish love, and beneficence toward all His creatures. The Divine life is a self-forgetting life, a life that has nothing to do but love and bless.

Let us so live, representing our Master here, while He represents us before the Throne on high.

January 14.

"Unto the measure of the stature of the fulness of Christ" (Eph. iv. 13).

God loves us so well that He will not suffer us to take less than His highest will. Some day we shall bless our

faithful teacher, who kept the standard inflexibly rigid, and then gave us the strength and grace to reach it, and would not excuse us until we had accomplished all His glorious will.

Let us be inexorable with ourselves. Let us mean exactly what God means, and have no discounts upon His promises or commandments. Let us keep the standard up, and never rest until we reach it. "Let God be true and every man a liar." If we fail a hundred times don't let us accommodate God's ideal to our realization, but like the brave ensign who stood in front of his company waving the banner, and when the soldiers called him back he only waved it higher, and cried, "Don't bring the standard back to the regiment, but bring the regiment up to the colors."

Forward, forward, leave the past behind thee,

Reaching forth unto the things before;

All the Land of Promise lies before thee,

God has greater blessings yet in store.

January 15.

"As ye have received Christ Jesus so walk in Him" (Col. ii. 6).It is much easier to keep the fire burning than to rekindle it after it has gone out. Let us abide in Him. Let us not have to remove the cinders and ashes from our hearthstones every day and kindle a new flame; but let us keep it burning and never let it expire. Among the ancient Greeks the sacred fire was never allowed to go out; so, in a higher sense, let us keep the heavenly flame aglow upon the altar of the heart.

It takes very much less effort to maintain a good habit than to form it. A true spiritual habit once formed becomes a spontaneous tendency of our being, and we grow into delightful freedom in following it. "Let us not be ever laying again the foundation of repentance from dead works, but let us go on unto perfection; and whereto we have already attained, let us walk by the same rule, let us mind the same things."

Every spiritual habit begins with difficulty and effort and watchfulness, but if we will only let it get thoroughly established, it will become a channel along which currents of life will flow with divine spontaneousness and freedom.

January 16.

"Prove what is that good, and acceptable and perfect will of God" (Rom. xii. 2).

There are three conditions in which the water in that engine may be. First, the boiler may be full and the water clean and clear; or, secondly, the boiler may not only be full but the water may be hot, very hot, hot enough to scald you, almost boiling; thirdly, it may be just one degree hotter and at the boiling point, giving forth its vapor in clouds of steam, pressing through the valves and driving the mighty piston which turns the wheels and propels the train of cars across the country.

So there are three kinds of Christians. The first we will call cold water Christians, or, perhaps better, clean water Christians.

Secondly, there are hot water Christians. They are almost at the boiling point.

One degree more, we come to the third class of Christians, the boiling water Christians. The difference is a very

slight one; it simply takes one reservation out, drops one "if," eliminates a single touch, and yet it is all the difference in the world. That one degree changes that engine into a motive power, not now a thing to be looked at, but a thing to go.

January 17.

"It is God which worketh in you" (Phil. ii. 13).

God has not two ways for any of us; but one; not two things for us to do which we may choose between; but one best and highest choice. It is a blessed thing to find and fill the perfect will of God. It is a blessed thing to have our life laid out and our Christian work adjusted to God's plan. Much strength is lost by working at a venture. Much spiritual force is expended in wasted effort, and scattered, indefinite and inconstant attempts at doing good. There is spiritual force and financial strength enough in the hands and hearts of the consecrated Christians of to-day to bring the coming of Christ, to bring about the evangelization of the world in a generation, if it were only wisely directed and utilized according to God's plan.

Christ has laid down a definite plan of work for His Church, and He expects us to understand it, and to work up to it; and as we catch His thought, and obediently, loyally fulfil it, we shall work to purpose, and please Him far better than by our thoughtless, reckless, and indiscriminate attempts to carry out our ideas, and compel God to bless our work.

January 18.

"That take and give for Me and thee"

(Matt. xvii. 27).

There is a beautiful touch of loving thoughtfulness in the account of Christ's miracle at Capernaum in providing the tribute money. After the reference to Peter's interview with the tax collector, it is added, "When he came into the house Jesus prevented him," that is, anticipated him, as the old Saxon word means, by arranging for the need before Peter needed to speak about it at all, and He sent Peter down to the sea to find the piece of gold in the mouth of the fish.

So our dear Lord is always thinking in advance of our needs, and He loves to save us from embarrassment, and anticipate our anxieties and cares by laying up His loving acts and providing before the emergency comes. Then with exquisite tenderness the Master adds: "That take and give for Me and thee." He puts Himself first in the embarrassing need and bears the heavy end of the burden for His distressed and suffering child. He makes our cares His cares, our sorrows His sorrows, our shame His shame, and "He is able to be touched with the feeling of our infirmities."

January 19.

"Prove me now herewith" (Mal. iii. 10).

We once heard a simple old colored man say something that we have never forgotten. "When God tests You it is a good time for you to test Him by putting His promises to the proof, and claiming from Him just as much as your trials have rendered necessary."

There are two ways of getting out of a trial. One is to simply try to get rid of the trial, and be thankful when it is over. The other is to recognize the trial

as a challenge from God to claim a larger blessing than we have ever had, and to hail it with delight as an opportunity of obtaining a larger measure of Divine grace.

Thus even the adversary becomes an auxiliary, and the things that seem to be against us turn out to be for the furtherance of our way. Surely, this is to be more than conquerors through Him who loved us.

Blessed Rose of Sharon

Breathe upon our heart,

Fill us with Thy fragrance,

Keep us as Thou art.

Then Thy life will make us

Holy and complete;

In Thy grace triumphant,

In Thy sweetness, sweet.

January 20.

"Ye know not what manner of spirit ye are of" (Luke ix. 55).

Some one has said that the most spiritual people are the easiest to get along with. When one has a little of the Holy Ghost it is like "a little learning, a dangerous thing"; but a full baptism of the Holy Spirit, and a really disciplined, stablished and tested spiritual life, makes one simple, tender, tolerant, considerate of others, and like a little child.

James and John, in their early zeal, wanted to call down fire from heaven on the Samaritans. But John, the aged, allowed Demetrius to exclude him from the church, and suffered in Patmos for the kingdom and with the patience of Jesus. And aged Paul was willing to take back even Mark, whom he had refused as a companion in his early ministry, and to acknowledge

that he was profitable to him for the ministry.

I want the love that cannot help but love;

Loving, like God, for very sake of love.

A spring so full that it must overflow,

A fountain flowing from the throne above.

"Now abideth faith, hope, love; but the greatest of these is love."

January 21.

"Pray without ceasing" (I. Thess. v. 17).

An important help in the life of prayer is the habit of bringing everything to God, moment by moment, as it comes to us in life. This may be established as a habit on the principle on which all habits are formed, of repeated and constant attention, moment by moment, until that which is at first an act of will, becomes spontaneous and second nature.

If we will watch our lives we shall find that God meets the things that we commit to Him in prayer with special blessing, and often allows the best things that we have not committed to Him to be ineffectual, simply to remind us of our dependence upon Him for everything. It is very gracious and mindful of Him thus gently to compel us to remember Him and to hold us so close to Him that we cannot get away even the length of a single minute from His all-sustaining arm. "In everything ... let our requests be made known unto God."

Let us bring our least petitions,

Like the incense beaten small,

All our cares, complaints, conditions

Jesus loves to bear them all.

January 22.

"His wife hath made herself ready" (Rev. xix. 7).

There is danger in becoming morbid even in preparing for the Lord's coming. We remember a time in our life when we had devoted ourselves to spend a month in waiting upon the Lord for a baptism of the Holy Ghost, and before the end of the month, the Lord shook us out of our seclusion and compelled us to go out and carry His message to others; and as we went, He met us in the service.

There is a musty, monkish way of seeking a blessing, and there is a wholesome, practical holiness which finds us in the company of the Lord Himself not only in the closet and on the mountain-top of prayer, but among publicans and sinners, and in the practical duties of life.

It seems to us that the practical preparation for the Lord's coming consists, first, of a very full entering into fellowship with Him in our own spiritual life, and letting Him not only cleanse us, but perfect us in all the finer touches of the Spirit's deeper work, and then, secondly, getting out of ourselves and living for the help of others and the preparation of the world for His appearing.

January 23.

"I know a man in Christ" (II. Cor. xii. 2).

It is a great deliverance to lose one's self. There is no heavier millstone that one can be compelled to carry than self-consciousness. It is so easy to get introverted and coiled round one's self

in our spiritual consciousness. There is nothing that is so easy to fasten on as our misery; there is nothing that is more apt to produce self-consciousness than suffering, until it becomes almost a settled habit to hold on to our burden, and pray it unceasingly into the very face of God, until our very prayer saturates us with our own misery, instead of asking for power to drop ourselves altogether, and leave ourselves in His loving hands and know that we are free, and then rise into the blessed liberty of His higher thoughts and will, and His love and care for others.

The very act of letting go of ourselves really lifts us into a higher plane, and relieves us from the thing that is hurting. This habit of prayer for others, and especially for the world, brings its own recompense, and leaves upon our hearts a blessing like the fertility which the Nile deposits upon the soil of Egypt, as it flows through to its distant goal.

[

January 24.

"Freely ye have received, freely give" (Matt. x. 8).

When God does anything marked and special for our souls, or bodies, He intends it as a sacred trust for us to communicate to others. "Freely ye have received, freely give."

It has pleased the Master in these closing days of the dispensation to reveal Himself in peculiar blessing to the hearts of His chosen disciples in all parts of the Christian Church; but this is intended to be communicated to a still wider circle, and every one of us who has been brought into these intimate relations with God, becomes a trustee, or witness for these higher truths to every one we can influence.

If God has revealed Himself to us as our Sanctifier, it is that we may help others to know Him as a Sanctifier.

If He has become our Healer, it is because there are sick and suffering lives to whom we can bring some blessing.

In like manner, if the hope of the Lord's coming has become precious to us, it would be worse than ingratitude for us to hide our testimony to this truth, and hold it only for our own personal comfort.

January 25.

"Hold fast that which is good" (I. Thess. v. 21).

It is a great thing to be able to receive new truth and blessing without sacrificing the truths already proved, and abandoning foundations already laid.

Some persons are always laying the foundations, and they present at last, the appearance of a lot of abandoned sites and half constructed buildings, and nothing is ever brought to completion.

The fact that you are abandoning to-day for some new truth the things that a year ago you counted most precious and believed to be divinely true, should be sufficient evidence that you will probably a year from to-day abandon your present convictions for the next new light that comes to you.

God is ever wanting to add to us, to develop us, to enlarge us, to teach us more and more, but it is ever in the line of things which He has already taught us, and in which we have been established.

While we are to "prove all things," let us "hold fast that which is good," and "whereto we have already attained, let us walk by the same rule, let us mind the same thing."

January 26.

"I called him alone and blessed him" (Isa. li. 2).

When we were in the East we noticed the beautiful process of raising rice. The rice is sown on a morass of mud and water, ploughed up by great buffaloes, and after a few weeks it springs up and appears above the water with its beautiful pale green shoots. The seed has been sown very thickly and the plants are clustered together in great numbers, so that you can pull up a score at a single handful. But now comes the process of transplanting. He first plants us and lets us grow very close to some of His children, and in great clusters in the nursery or the hothouse, but when we reach a certain stage we must be transplanted, or come to nothing. He calls us out by His Spirit and Providence into situations where we have to lean directly on Him, where He puts upon us a weight of responsibility and service so great that we have an opportunity of developing and are thrown upon the great resources of His grace.

"Blessed is the man that trusteth in the Lord, and whose hope the Lord is; for he shall be like a tree planted by the waters and that spreadeth out her roots by the rivers."

January 27.

"This one thing I do" (Phil. iii. 13).

One of Satan's favorite employees is the switchman. He likes nothing better than to side-track one of God's express trains, sent on some blessed mission

and filled with the fire of a holy purpose.

Something will come up in the pathway of the earnest soul, to attract its attention and occupy its strength and thought. Sometimes it is a little irritation and provocation. Sometimes it is some petty grievance we stop to pursue or adjust. Sometimes it is somebody else's business in which we become interested, and which we feel bound to rectify, and before we know, we are absorbed in a lot of distracting cares and interests that quite turn us aside from the great purpose of our life.

Perhaps we do not do much harm, but we have missed our connection. We have got off the main line.

Let all these things alone. Let grievances come and go, but press forward steadily and irresistibly, crying, as you haste to the goal, "This one thing I do."

January 28.

"That my joy might remain in you, and that your joy might be full" (John xv. 11).

There is a joy that springs spontaneously in the heart without external or even rational cause. It is an artesian fountain. It rejoices because it cannot help it. It is the glory of God; it is the heart of Christ, it is the joy divine of which He says, "These things have I spoken unto you that My joy might remain in you, and that your joy might be full." And your joy no man taketh from you. He who possesses this fountain is not discouraged by surrounding circumstances, but is often surprised at the deep, sweet gladness that comes without any apparent cause, and even

comes most strongly when everything in our condition and circumstances is fitted to fill us with sorrow and depression.

It is the nightingale in the heart, which sings at night, and sings because it is its nature to sing.

It is the glorified and incorruptible joy which belongs to heaven, and anticipates already the everlasting song. Lord, give me Thy joy under all circumstances this day, and let my full heart overflow in blessing to others.

January 29.

"Send portions unto them for whom nothing is prepared" (Neh. viii. 10).

That was a fine picture in the days of Nehemiah, when they were celebrating their glorious Feast of Tabernacles. "Neither be ye sorry; for the joy of the Lord is your strength. Go your way, eat the fat, and drink the sweet, and send portions to them for whom nothing is prepared."

How many there are on every side for whom nothing is prepared! Let us find out some sad and needy heart for whom there is no one else to think or care. Let us pray for some one that has none to pray for him. Let us be like Him who, one Christmas Day, gave His life and His all, and came to those who would not appreciate His holy gift, but rejected His blessed Babe, and murdered His only Son.

Let us not be afraid to know something even of the love that is unrequited and is thrown away on the unworthy. That is the love of Christ, and God has for such love a rich recompense.

How Christ must almost weep over the selfishness that meets Him from those for whom He died.

January 30.

"Cast down but not destroyed" (II. Cor. iv. 9).

How did God bring about the miracle of the Red Sea? By shutting His people in on every side, so that there was no way out but the divine way. The Egyptians were behind them, the sea was in front of them, the mountains were on every side of them. There was no escape but from above.

Some one has said that the devil can wall us in, but he cannot roof us over. We can always get out at the top. Our difficulties are but God's challenges, and He makes them so hard, often, that we must go under or get above them.

In such an hour, if there is a divine element, it brings out the highest possibilities of faith and we are pushed by the very emergency into God's best.

Beloved, this is God's hour. If you will rise to meet it you will get such a hold upon Him that you will never be in extremities again, or if you are, you will learn to call them not extremities, but opportunities, and like Jacob, you will go forth from that night at Peniel, no longer Jacob, but victorious Israel. Let us bring to Him our need and prove Him true.

January 31.

"Jesus, who of God is made unto us wisdom, and righteousness and sanctification and redemption" (I. Cor. i. 30).

More and more we are coming to see the supreme importance of getting the right conception of sanctification, not as a blessing, but as a personal union with the personal Saviour and the indwelling Holy Spirit. Thousands of people get stranded after they have embarked on the great voyage of holiness.

They find themselves failing and falling, and are astonished and perplexed, and they conclude that they must have been mistaken in their experience, and so they make a new attempt at the same thing and again fall, until at last, worn out with the experiment, they conclude that the experience is a delusion, or, at least, that it was never intended for them, and so they fall back into the old way, and their last state is worse than their first.

What people need to-day to satisfy their deep hunger and to give them a permanent and Divine experience is to know, not sanctification as a state, but Christ as a living Person, who is waiting to enter the heart that is willing to receive Him.

February 1.

"A well of water springing up" (John iv. 14).

In the life overflowing in service for others, we find the deep fountain of life running over the spring and finding vent in rivers of living water that go out to bless and save the world around us. It is beautiful to notice that as the blessing grows unselfish it grows larger. The water in the heart is only a well, but when reaching out to the needs of others it is not only a river, but a delta of many rivers overflowing in majestic blessing. This overflowing love is connected with the Person and work of the Holy Spirit which was to be poured out upon the disciples after Jesus was glorified.

This is the true secret of power for service, the heart filled and satisfied with Jesus, and so baptized with the

Holy Ghost that it is impelled by the fulness of its joy and love to impart to others what it has so abundantly received; and yet each new ministry only makes room for a new filling and a deeper receiving of the life which grows by giving.

Letting go is twice possessing,

Would you double every blessing,

Pass it on.

February 2.

"And whosoever will be great among you, let him be your minister. And whosoever will be chief among you, let him be your servant" (Matt. xx. 26, 27).

Slave is the literal meaning of the word, *doulos*.

The first word used for service is *diakanos*, which means a minister to others in any usual way or work: but the word *doulos* means a bond slave, and the Lord here plainly teaches us that the highest service is that of a bond slave.

He Himself made Himself the servant of all, and he who would come nearest to Him and stand closest to Him at last, must likewise learn the spirit of the ministry that has utterly renounced selfish rights and claims forever.

It is quite possible to be entirely loyal to the Lord Jesus, and yet for Jesus' sake, a servant ourselves, and under the authority of those who are over us in the Lord.

The *doulos* spirit is the spirit of self-renunciation and glad submission to proper authority, service utterly disinterested, yielding our own preferences and interests unreservedly for the glory of the Master and the sake of our brethren. Lord, clothe us with humility and make us wholly Thine.

February 3.

"He went out, not knowing whither He went" (Heb. xi. 8).

It is faith without sight. When we can see, it is not faith but reasoning. In crossing the Atlantic we observed this very principle of faith. We saw no path upon the sea nor sign of the shore. And yet day by day we were marking our path upon the chart as exactly as if there had followed us a great chalk line upon the sea; and when we came within twenty miles of land we knew where we were as exactly as if we had seen it all three thousand miles ahead.

How had we measured and marked our course? Day by day our captain had taken his instruments, and looking up to the sky had fixed his course by the sun. He was sailing by the heavenly, not the earthly lights. So faith looks up and sails on, by God's great Sun, not seeing one shore line or earthly lighthouse or path upon the way. Often its steps seem to lead into utter uncertainty, and even darkness and disaster. But He opens the way, and often makes such midnight hours the very gates of day. Let us go forth this day, not knowing but trusting.

[

February 4.

"Lo, I am with you alway" (Matt. xxviii. 20).

This living Christ is not the person that was, but the person that still is, your living Lord. At Preston Pans, near Edinburgh, I looked on the field where in the olden days armies were engaged in contest. In the crisis of the battle the chieftain fell wounded. His men were

about to shrink away from the field when they saw their leader's form go down; their strong hands held the claymore with trembling grip, and they faltered for a moment. Then the old chieftain rallied strength enough to rise on his elbow and cry: "I am not dead, my children, I am only watching you—to see my clansmen do their duty." And so from the other side of Calvary He is speaking; we cannot see Him, but He says, "Lo, I am with you alway, even to the end of the world"; and He puts it, "I am"—an uninterrupted and continuous presence. Not "I will be," but the unbroken presence still is with us forevermore.

Soon the conflict shall be done,

Soon the battle shall be won;

Soon shall wave the victor's palm,

Soon shall sing the eternal Psalm;

Then our joyful song shall be,

I have overcome through Thee.

February 5.

"Rest in the Lord" (Ps. xxxvii.).

In the old creation the week began with work and ended with Sabbath rest. The resurrection week begins with the first day—first rest, then labor.

So we must first cease from our own works as God did from His, and enter into His rest, and then we will work, with rested hearts, His works with effectual power.

But why "labor to enter into rest"? See that ship—how restfully she sails over the waters, her sails swelling with the gale; and borne without an effort! And yet, look at that man at the helm. See how firmly he holds the rudder, bearing against the wind, and holding her steady to her position. Let him for a moment relax his steady hold and the ship will fall listlessly along the wind. The sails will flap, the waves will toss the vessel at their will, and all rest and power will have gone. It is the fixed helm that brings the steadying power of the wind. And so He has said, "Thou wilt keep him in perfect peace, whose mind is stayed on Thee, because he trusteth in Thee." The steady will and stayed heart are ours. The keeping is the Lord's. So let us labor to enter and abide in His rest.

February 6.

"Praying always for all saints" (Eph. vi. 18).

One good counsel will suffice just now. Stop praying so much for yourself; begin to ask unselfish things, and see if God won't give you faith. See how much easier it will be to believe for another than for your own petty self. Try the effect of praying for the world, for definite things, for difficult things, for glorious things, for things that will honor Christ and save mankind, and after you have received a few wonderful answers to prayer in this direction, see if you won't feel stronger to touch your own little burden with a Divine faith, and then go back again to the high place of unselfish prayer for others.

Have you ever learned the beautiful art of letting God take care of you, and giving all your thought and strength to pray for others and for the kingdom of God? It will relieve you of a thousand cares. It will lift you up into a noble and lofty sphere, and teach you to live and love like God. Lord save us from our selfish prayers and give us the faith that worketh by love, and the heart of Christ for a perishing world.

February 7.

"Faithful in that which is least" (Luke xvi. 10).

The man that missed his opportunity and met the doom of the faithless servant was not the man with five talents, or the man with two, but the man who had only one. The people who are in danger of missing life's great meaning are the people of ordinary capacity and opportunity, and who say to themselves, "There is so little I can do that I will not try to do anything." One of the finest windows in Europe was made from the remnants an apprentice boy collected from the cuttings of his master's great work. The sweepings of the British mint are worth millions. The little pivots on which the works of your watch turn are so important that they are actually made of jewels. And so God places a solemn value and responsibility on the humble workers, the people that try to hide behind their insignificance the trifling opportunities and the single talents; and our littleness will not excuse us in the reckoning day.

"Talk not of talents, what hast thou to do?

Thou hast sufficient, whether five or two.

Talk not of talents; is thy duty done?

This brings the blessing whether ten or one."

February 8.

"We are not sufficient of ourselves to think anything as of ourselves" (II. Cor. iii. 5).

Insufficient, "All sufficient." These two words form the complement of each other and together give the key to an efficient Christian life. The discovery and full conviction of our utter helplessness is the constant condition of spiritual supply. The aim of the Old Testament, therefore, is ever to show man's failure; that of the New, to reveal Christ's sufficiency. He has all things for us, but we cannot receive them till we know that we have nothing.

The very essence, therefore, of Christian perfection is the constant renunciation of our own perfection, and the continual acceptance of Christ's righteousness. And as we receive deeper views of our nothingness and evil, it is but a call to claim more of His rich grace. But it is possible fully to know our insufficiency and yet not take firmly hold of His "all things." This, too, must be done with a faith that will not accept less than ALL. The prophet was angry because the king of Israel had only smitten thrice upon the ground. He should have done it five or six times. He might have had all. So let us meet His greatness and grace.

February 9.

"None of these things move me" (Acts xx. 24).

The best evidence of God's presence is the devil's growl. So wrote good Mr. Spurgeon once in "The Sword and the Trowel," and that little sentence has helped many a tried and tired child Of God to stand fast and even rejoice under the fiercest attacks of the foe.

We read in the book of Samuel that the moment that David was crowned at Hebron, "All the Philistines came up to seek David." And the moment we get anything from the Lord worth contending for, then the devil comes to seek us.

When the enemy meets us at the threshold of any great work for God let us accept it as "a token of salvation," and claim double blessing, victory and power. Power is developed by resistance. The cannon carries twice as far because the exploding power has to find its way through resistance. The way electricity is produced in the power-house yonder is by the sharp friction of the revolving wheels. And so we shall find some day that even Satan has been one of God's agencies of blessing.

February 10.

"I am crucified with Christ; nevertheless I live" (Gal. ii. 20).

Christ life is in harmony with our nature. A lady asked me the other day—a thoughtful, intelligent woman who was not a Christian, but who had the deepest hunger for that which is right: "How can this be so, and we not lose our individuality! This will destroy our personality, and it violates our responsibility as individuals."

I said: "Dear sister, your personality is only half without Christ. Christ was made for you, and you were made for Christ, and until you meet you are not complete, and He needs you as you need Him." I said: "Suppose that gas-jet should say, 'If I take this fire in, the gas will lose its individuality.' Oh, no; it is only when the fire comes in that the gas fulfils its very purpose of being. Suppose the snowflake should say, 'What shall I do? If I drop on the ground I shall lose my individuality.' But it falls and is absorbed by the soil, and the snowflakes are seen by-and-by in the primroses and daisies. Let us lose ourselves and rise to a new life in Christ."

February 11.

"Strengthened with all might unto all patience" (Col. i. 11).

The apostle prays for the Colossians, that they may be "strengthened with all might, according to His glorious power, unto all patience and long-suffering with joyfulness." It is one thing to endure and show the strain on every muscle of your face, and seem to say with every wrinkle, "Why does not somebody sympathize with me?" It is another to endure the cross, "despising the shame" for the joy set before us.

There are some trees in the garden of the Lord which "shall not see when heat cometh"; and shall not be careful in the year of drought, nor cease from yielding fruit. Let us set our faces toward the sunrising and use the clouds that come, to make rainbows. Not much longer shall we have the glorious opportunity to rejoice in tribulation, and learn patience. In heaven we shall have nothing to teach long-suffering. If we do not learn it here, we shall be without our brightest crown forever, and wish ourselves back for a little while, in the very circumstances of which we are now trying so hard to get rid.

February 12.

"But seek ye first the Kingdom of God, and His righteousness, and all these things shall be added unto you" (Matt. vi. 33).

For every heart that is seeking anything from the Lord this is a good watchword. That very thing, or the desire for it, may unconsciously separate you from the Lord, or at least from the singleness of your purpose unto Him. The thing we desire may be

a right thing, but we may desire it in a distrusting and selfish spirit. Let us commit it to Him, and not cease to believe for it, but let us, at the same time, keep our purpose fixed on His will and glory, and claim even His promised blessings, not for themselves or ourselves, but for Him. Then shall it be true, "Delight thyself in the Lord, and He shall give thee the desires of thine heart." All other things but Himself God will "*add*." But they must be ever *added*, never *first*.

Then shall we be able to believe for them without doubt, when we claim them for Him and not for ourselves. It is only when "we are Christ's" that "all things are ours."

Lord, help me this day to seek Thee first, and be more desirous to please Thee and have Thy will than to possess any other blessing.

February 13.

"Thy prayers are come up for a memorial before God" (Acts x. 4).

What a beautiful expression the angel used to Cornelius, "Thy prayers are come up for a memorial." It would almost seem as if supplications of years had accumulated before the Throne, and at last the answer broke in blessings on the head of Cornelius, even as the accumulated evaporation of months at last bursts in floods of rain upon the parched ground. So God is represented as treasuring the prayers of His saints in vials; they are described as sweet odors. They are placed like fragrant flowers in the chambers of the King. And kept in sweet remembrance before Him. And later they are represented as poured out upon the earth; and lo, there are voices and thunderings and great providential movements fulfilling

God's purposes for His kingdom. We are called "the Lord's remembrancers," and are commanded to give Him no rest, day nor night, but crowd the heavens with our petitions and in due time the answer will come with its accumulated blessings.

No breath of true prayer is lost. The longer it waits, the larger it becomes.

February 14.

"He shall baptize you with fire" (Matt. iii. 11).

Fire is strangely intense and intrinsic. It goes into the very substance of things. It somehow blends with every particle of the thing it touches.

There are the severe trials that come to minds more sensitive, to the minds that have more points of contact with what hurts; so that the higher the nature the higher the joy, and the greater the avenues of pain that come.

And then there are deeper trials that come as we pass into the hands of God, as we pass from the physical and intellectual into the spiritual nature.

When they first come, we shrink back from their unnatural and fearful breath, and we say: "Oh, this cannot be from the hand of a loving Father! This cannot be necessary to me."

And then come the pains and sufferings from God's own hand, when He sits as a refiner and purifier of silver, when He lets it burn, until it seems that we must be burned to ashes, and we are, indeed, at last burned to ashes.

But we must get the victory through faith. The moment you cease to fear it, that moment it ceases to harm you. He says, "The flames shall not kindle upon you."

February 15.

"Be strong in the grace that is in Christ Jesus" (II. Tim. ii. 1).

How to enjoy this day. This will never come by trying to be happy and yet we are responsible for the conditions of real joy.

1. Be right with God; for "Gladness is sown for the upright in heart." "It is His joy that remains in us that makes our joy to be full."

2. Forget yourself and live for others; for "It is more blessed to give than to receive."

3. When you cannot rejoice in feelings, circumstances and states, "rejoice in the Lord," and "count it all joy, when ye fall into divers temptations."

Finally, obey the Lord and be faithful to your trust; and again and again will His blessed Spirit whisper to your heart, "Well done, good and faithful servant, enter into the joy of thy Lord."

"Not enjoyment and not sorrow
Is our destined end or way,
But to act that each to-morrow
Finds us farther than to-day.
"Let us then be up and doing
With a heart for any fate,
Still achieving, still pursuing,
Learn to labor and to wait."

February 16.

"We will give ourselves continually to prayer" (Acts vi. 4).

In the consecrated believer the Holy Spirit is pre-eminently a Spirit of prayer. If our whole being is committed to Him, and our thoughts are at His bidding, He will occupy every moment in communion and we shall bring every thing to Him as it comes, and pray it out in our spiritual consciousness before we act it out in our lives. We shall, therefore, find ourselves taking up the burdens of life and praying them out in a wordless prayer which we ourselves often cannot understand, but which is simply the unfolding of His thought and will within us, and which will be followed by the unfolding of His providence concerning us.

Want of faithfulness and obedience to the faintest whisper of His will will often hinder some blessing which He meant for us until after a while we may get so dull and negligent that He will not be able to trust us with His whispers and we shall thus stumble on in the darkness and miss His highest thoughts.

Lord, teach us to pray in the Spirit, to pray without ceasing and to lose nothing of Thy will.

February 17.

"Your life is hid" (Col. iii. 3).

Some Christians loom up in larger proportion than is becoming. They can tell, and others can tell, how many souls they bring to Christ. Their labor seems to crystallize and become its own memorial. Others again seem to blend so wholly with other workers that their own individuality can scarcely be traced. And yet, after all, this is the most Christ-like ministry of all, for the Master Himself does not even appear in the work of the church except as her hidden Life and ascended Head, and even the Holy Spirit is lost in the vessels that He uses. The vine does not bear the fruit, and even the sap is unseen in its ceaseless flow, and it is the little branches which bear all the clusters

and seem to have all the honor of the vintage. And so the nearer we come to Christ the more we are willing to be lost sight of in our fruit, and let others be more prominent, while we are the glad and willing witnesses of our testimony and hold up their hands by the silent ministry of love and prayer. Lord, let me be like the veiled seraphim before the throne, who cover their faces and their feet, and hide themselves and their service while they fly to obey Thee.

February 18.

"Christ in you" (Col. i. 27).

How great the difference between the old and the new way of deliverance! One touch of Christ is worth a lifetime of struggling. A sufferer in one of our hospitals was in danger of losing his sight from a small piece of broken needle that had entered his eye.

Operation after operation had only irritated it, and driven the foreign substance farther still into the delicate nerves of the sensitive organ. At length a skilful young physician thought of a new expedient. He came one day without lancet and probes, and holding in his hand a small but powerful magnet, which he kept before the wounded eye, as close as it could bear. Immediately the piece of steel began to move toward the powerful attraction, and soon flew up to meet it and left the suffering eye completely relieved, without an effort or a laceration. It was as simple as it was wonderful. By a single touch of power the organ was saved and a dangerous trouble completely cured.

It is thus that God delivers us, by the simple attraction of Christ's life and power.

February 19.

"As much as in me is I am ready" (Rom. i. 15).

Be earnest. Intense earnestness, a whole heart for Christ, the passion sign of the cross, the enthusiasm of our whole being for our Master and humanity—this is what the Lord expects, this is what His cross deserves, this is what the world needs, this is what the age has a right to look for. Everything around us is intensely alive. Life is earnest, death is earnest, sin is earnest, men are earnest, business is earnest, knowledge is earnest, the age is earnest; God forgive us if we alone are trifling in the white heat of this crisis time. Oh, for the baptism of fire! Oh, for the living coal upon the burning lips of love! Oh, for men God-possessed and self-surrendered grasping God's great idea and pressing forward "for the mark of the prize of the high calling of God in Christ Jesus."

All the world for Jesus

My prayer shall be,

And my watchword ever,

Himself for me.

All the world for Jesus,

Lord, quickly come,

Bring Thy promised kingdom,

And take us home.

February 20.

"Fear thou not, for I am with thee" (Isa. xli. 10).

Satan is always trying to weaken our faith by fear. He is a great metaphysician and knows the paralyzing effect of fear, that it is the great enemy of faith, and that faith is the great secret of help. If he can get

us fearing he will stop our trusting and hinder the very blessing we need. Job found the peril of fear and gives us the sorrowful testimony, "I feared a fear and it came upon me."

Fear is born of Satan, and if we would only take time to think a moment we would see that everything Satan says is founded upon a falsehood. He is the father of lies. Even his fears are falsehoods and his terrors ought rather be to us encouragements.

When Satan tells you, therefore, that some ill is going to come, you may quietly look in his face and tell him he is a liar, that instead of ill, goodness and mercy shall follow you all the days of your life, and then turn to your blessed Lord and say, "What time I am afraid, I will trust in Thee." Every fear is distrust and trust is the remedy for fear. "What time I am afraid I will *trust* in thee."

February 21.

"Be not dismayed, for I am thy God" (Isa. xli. 10).

How tenderly God is always comforting our fears! How sweetly He says in Isaiah xli. 10, "Fear not; for I am with thee: be not dismayed; for I am thy God: I will uphold thee with the right hand of My righteousness." And yet again with still tenderer thoughtfulness, "I, the Lord thy God, will hold thy right hand, saying unto thee, Fear not, I will help thee." Not only does He say it once, but He keeps holding our right hand and repeating such promises.

The blessed Lord has condensed it all into one sweet monogram of eternal comfort in His message to the disciples on the sea of Galilee, "It is I; be not afraid." He does not say, "It is

over," or "It is morning," or "It is fine weather," or "It is smooth water," but He says, "It is I, be not afraid." He is the antidote to fear; He is the remedy for trouble; He is the substance and the sum of deliverance. Therefore, we should rise above fear. Let us keep our eyes fastened upon Him; let us abide continually in Him; let us be content with Him; let us cling closely to Him and cry, "We will not fear though the earth be removed, though the mountains be carried into the midst of the sea."

February 22.

"He that hath entered into His rest hath ceased from his own works even as God did from His" (Heb. iv. 10).

What a rest it would be to many of us if we could but exchange burdens with Christ, and so utterly and forever transfer to Him all our cares and needs that we would not feel henceforth responsible for our burdens, but know that He has undertaken all the care, and that our faith is simply to carry His burdens, and that He prays, labors, and suffers only for us and our interests. This is what He truly invites us to do. "Come unto Me," He says, "all ye that labor and are heavy-laden and I will rest you," and then He adds, "Take My yoke upon you, and learn of Me." He takes our yoke and we take His and we find it a thousand times easier to carry one of His burdens than to carry our own. How much more delightful it is to spend an hour in supplication for another than five minutes in pleading for ourselves. Are we not weary of carrying our wretched loads?

'Twas for this His mercy sought you,

And to all His fulness brought you,

By the precious blood that bought you,
Pass it on.

February 23.

"For me to live is Christ and to die is gain" (Phil. i. 21).

The secret of a sound body is a sound heart, and the prayer of the Holy Ghost for us is, that we "may be in health and prosper even as our soul prospers."

We find Paul in the Epistles to the Philippians expressing a sublime and holy indifference to the question of life or death. Indeed he is in a real strait, whether he would prefer "to depart and be with Christ," or to remain still in the flesh.

The former would indeed be his sweetest preference, but the latter would be at the same time a joyful service. His only object in wanting to live is to be a blessing. "To abide in the flesh is more needful to you."

Having reached this state of heart, it is beautiful to notice how quickly he rises to the victorious faith necessary to claim perfect strength and health. Because it is more needful to you that I abide in the flesh, he adds, "I know that I shall continue with you all, for your furtherance and joy of faith." Lord, help me to-day to "count not my life dear unto myself that I may finish my course with joy and the ministry that I have received of Jesus."

February 24.

"Sin shall not have dominion over you, for ye are not under the law, but under grace" (Rom. vi. 14).

The secret of Moses' failures was this: "The law made nothing perfect, but the bringing in of a better hope did."

And this was why his life work also came short of full realization. He saw but entered not the Promised Land. The founder of the law had to be its victim, and his life and death might demonstrate the inability of the law to lead any man into the Promised Land. The very fact, that it was for so slight a fault that Moses lost his inheritance, makes all the more emphatic the solemn sentence of the law. "Cursed is every one that continueth not in all things that are written in the Book of the Law to do them."

But to the glory of the grace of God we can add that what the law could not do for Moses the Gospel did; and he who could not pass over the Jordan under the old dispensation is seen on the very heights of Hermon with the Son of Man, sharing His Transfiguration glory, and talking of that death on Calvary to which be owed his glorious destiny.

That grace we have inherited under the Gospel of Jesus Christ.

February 25.

"I am the vine, ye are the branches" (John xv. 5).

How can I take Christ as my Sanctifier, or Healer? is a question that we are constantly asked. It is necessary first of all that we get into the posture of faith. This has to be done by a definite and voluntary act, and then maintained by a uniform habit. It is just the same as the planting of a tree. You must put it in the soil by a definite act, and then you must let it stay put and remain settled in the ground until the little roots have time to fix themselves and begin to draw the sustenance from the soil. There are two stages, the definite planting and then the habitual absorbing of

moisture and nourishment from the ground. The root fibers must rest until they reach out their spongy pores and drink in the nutriment of the earth. After the habit is established, then by a certain uniform law, the plant draws its life from the ground without an effort, and it is just as natural for it to grow as it is for us to breathe.

Lord, help me this day to abide in Thee, and to grow into the habit of drawing all my life from Thine so that it shall be true for me, "In Him I live and move and have my being."

February 26.

"Make you perfect in every good work" (Heb. xiii. 21).

In that beautiful prayer at the close of the Epistle to the Hebrews, "Now the God of peace, that brought again from the dead, our Lord Jesus Christ, that great Shepherd of the sheep, through the blood of the everlasting covenant, make you perfect in every good work to do His will," the phrase, "make you perfect in every good work," literally means, it is said, "adjust you in every good work." It is a great thing to be adjusted, adjusted to our surroundings and circumstances rather than trying to have them adjusted to us, adjusted to the people we are thrown with, adjusted to the work God has for us, and not trying to get God to help us to do our work; adjusted to do the very will and plan of God for us in our whole life. This is the secret of rest, power and freedom in our life-work.

"Oh, fill me with Thy fulness, Lord.

Until my very heart o'erflow

In kindling thought and glowing word,

Thy love to tell, Thy praise to show.

Oh, use me, Lord, use even me,

Just as Thou wilt, and when, and where;

Until Thy blessed face I see,

Thy rest, Thy joy, Thy glory share."

February 27.

"Stablish, strengthen, settle you" (I. Peter v. 10).

In taking Christ in any new relationship, we must first have sufficient intellectual light to satisfy our mind that we are entitled to stand in this relationship. The shadow of a question here will wreck our confidence. Then, having seen this, we must make the venture, the committal, the choice, and take the place just as definitely as the tree is planted in the soil, or the bride gives herself away at the marriage altar. It must be once for all, without reserve, without recall.

Then there is a season of establishing, settling and testing, during which we must stay put until the new relationship gets so fixed as to become a permanent habit. It is just the same as when the surgeon sets the broken arm. He puts it in splints to keep it from vibration. So God has His spiritual splints that He wants to put upon His children and keep them quiet and unmoved until they pass the first stage of faith.

It is not always easy work for us, "but the God of all grace who hath called you unto His eternal glory by Christ Jesus after you have suffered awhile, stablish, strengthen, settle you."

February 28.

"Count it all joy" (James i. 2).

We do not always feel joyful, but we are to count it all joy. The word "reckon" is one of the key-words of

Scripture. It is the same word used about our being dead. We do not feel dead. We are painfully conscious of something that would gladly return to life. But we are to treat ourselves as dead, and neither fear nor obey the old nature.

So we are to reckon the thing that comes as a blessing. We are determined to rejoice, to say, "My heart is fixed, O God, I will sing and give praise." This rejoicing, by faith, will soon become a habit, and will ever bring speedily the spirit of gladness and the spontaneous overflow of praise.

Then, "although the fig-tree may wither and no fruit appear in the vines, the labor of the olive fail and the fields yield no increase, the herd be cut off from the stall, and the cattle from the field, yet we will rejoice in the Lord, and joy in the God of our salvation."

"Peace, perfect peace, with sorrows surging round,

On Jesus' bosom naught but calm is found;

Peace, perfect peace, our future all unknown,

Jesus we know, and He is on the throne."

March 1.

"Wait on the Lord" (Ps. xxvii. 14).

How often this is said in the Bible, how little understood! It is what the old monk calls the "practice of the presence of God." It is the habit of prayer. It is the continued communion that not only asks, but receives. People often ask us to pray for them and we have to say, "Why, God has answered our prayer for you, and you must now take the answer. It is awaiting you, and you must take it by waiting on the Lord."

This it is that renews the strength, until we mount up with wings as eagles, run and are not weary, walk and are not faint. Our hearts are too vast to take in His fulness at a single breath. We must live in the atmosphere of His presence till we absorb His very life. This is the secret of spiritual depth and rest, of power and fulness, of love and prayer, of hope and holy usefulness. "Wait, I say, on the Lord."

I am waiting in communion at the blessed mercy seat,

I am waiting, sweetly waiting, on the Lord;

I am drinking, of His fulness; I am sitting at His feet;

I am hearkening to the whispers of His word.

March 2.

"That good thing which was committed unto thee keep by the Holy Ghost" (II. Tim. i. 14).

God gives to us a power within which will hold our hearts in victory and purity. "That good thing which was committed unto thee, keep by the Holy Ghost which dwelleth in us." It is the Holy Ghost; and when any thought or suggestion of evil arises in our breast, the quick conscience can instantly call upon the Holy Ghost to drive it out, and He will expel it at the command of faith or prayer, and keep us as pure as we are willing to be kept. But when the will surrenders and consents to evil, the Holy Ghost will not expel it. God, then, requires us to stand in holy vigilance, and He will do exceeding abundantly for us as we hold fast that which is good, and He will also be in us a spirit of vigilance, showing us the

evil and enabling us to detect it, and to bring it to Him for expulsion and destruction.

"O Spirit of Jesus fill us until we shall have room only for Thee!"

O, come as the heart-searching fire,

O, come as the sin-cleansing flood;

Consume us with holy desire,

And fill with the fulness of God.

March 3.

"Now no chastening for the present seemeth to be joyous but grievous; nevertheless afterward" (Heb. xii. 11).

God seems to love to work by paradoxes and contraries. In the transformations of grace, the bitter is the base of the sweet, night is the mother of day, and death is the gate of life.

Many people are wanting power. Now, how is power produced? The other day we passed the great works where the trolley engines are supplied with electricity. We heard the hum and roar of countless wheels, and we asked our friend, "How do they make the power?" "Why," he said, "just by the revolution of those wheels and the friction they produce. The rubbing creates the electric current."

It is very simple, and a trifling experiment will prove it to any one.

And so when God wants to bring more power into your life, He brings more pressure. He is generating spiritual force by hard rubbing. Some of us don't like it. Some of us don't understand, and we try to run away from the pressure, instead of getting the power and using it to rise above the painful cause.

March 4.

"They were all filled with the Holy Ghost" (Acts ii. 4).

Blessed secret of spiritual purity, victory and joy, of physical life and healing, and all power for service. Filled with the Spirit there is no room for self or sin, for fret or care. Filled with the Spirit we repel the elements of disease that are in the air as the red-hot iron repels the water that touches it. Filled with the Spirit we are always ready for service, and Satan turns away when he finds the Holy Ghost enrobing us in His garments of holy flame. Not half-filled, but filled with the Spirit is the place of victory and power.

This is not only a privilege; it is a command, and He who gave it will enable us to fulfill it if we bring it to Him with an empty, honest, trusting heart, and claim our privilege in the name of Jesus and for the glory of God.

Holy Ghost, I bid Thee welcome;

Come and be my Holy Guest;

Heavenly Dove within my bosom,

Make Thy home and build Thy nest;

Lead me on to all Thy fulness,

Bring me to Thy Promised Rest,

Holy Ghost, I bid Thee welcome,

Come and be my Holy Guest.

March 5.

"I have overcome the world" (John xvi. 33).

Christ has overcome for us every one of our four terrible foes—Sin, Sickness, Sorrow, Satan. He has borne our Sin, and we may lay all, even down to our sinfulness itself, on Him.

"I have overcome for thee." He has borne our sickness, and we may detach ourselves from our old infirmities and rise into His glorious life and strength. He has borne our sorrows, and we must not even carry a care, but rejoice evermore, and even glory in tribulations also. And He has conquered Satan for us, too, and left him nailed to the cross, spoiled and dishonored and but a shadow of himself. And now we have but to claim His full atonement and assert our victory, and so "overcome him by the blood of the Lamb and the word of our testimony."

Beloved, are we overcoming sin? Are we overcoming sickness? Are we overcoming sorrow? Are we overcoming Satan?

Fear not, though the strife be long;

Faint not, though the foe be strong;

Trust thy glorious Captain's power;

Watch with Him one little hour,

Hear Him calling, "Follow me.

"I have overcome for thee."

March 6.

"Lean not unto thine own understanding" (Prov. iii. 5).

Faith is hindered by reliance upon human wisdom, whether our own or the wisdom of others. The devil's first bait to Eve was an offer of wisdom, and for this she sold her faith. "Ye shall be as gods," he said, "knowing good and evil," and from the hour she began to know she ceased to trust. It was the spies that lost the Land of Promise to Israel of old. It was their foolish proposition to search out the land, and find out by investigation whether God had told the truth or not, that led to the awful outbreak of

unbelief that shut the doors of Canaan to a whole generation. It is very significant that the names of these spies are nearly all suggestive of human wisdom, greatness and fame.

So in the days of Christ, it was the bondage of the Jews to the traditions of their fathers and the opinions of men, that kept them back from receiving Him. "How can ye believe," He asked, "which receive honor from men, and seek not that which cometh from God only?"

Let us trust Him with all our heart and lean not to our own understanding.

March 7.

"It is more blessed to give than to receive" (Acts xx. 35).

How shall we know the difference between the earthly and the heavenly love? The one terminates on ourselves and is partly ourself seeking its own gratification. The other reaches out to God and others, and finds its joy in glorifying Him and blessing them. Love is unselfishness, and the love that is not unselfish is not divine. How much do we pray for others, and how much for ourselves? What is the center of our being? Ourselves, or our Lord and His people and work? The Lord help us to know more fully the meaning of that great truth, "It is more blessed to give than to receive." "He that saveth his life shall lose it, and he that loseth his life for My sake and the Gospel, shall keep it unto life eternal."

Have you found some precious treasure,

Pass it on.

Have You found some holy pleasure,

Pass it on.

Giving out is twice possessing,

Love will double every blessing,

On to higher service pressing,

Pass it on.

March 8.

"Pray Ye therefore" (Luke x. 2).

Prayer is the mighty engine that is to move the missionary work. "Pray ye therefore the Lord of the harvest that He will send forth laborers into His harvest."

We are asking God to touch the hearts of men every day by the Holy Ghost, so that they shall be compelled to go abroad and preach the Gospel. We are asking Him to wake them up at night with the solemn conviction that the heathen are perishing, and that their blood will be upon their souls, and God is answering the prayer by sending persons to us every day who "feel that the King's business requireth haste."

Beloved, pray, pray, pray; and as the incense rises to the heavens, "there will be silence in heaven" by the space of more than half an hour, and the coals of fire will be emptied out upon the earth, and the coming of the Lord will begin to draw nearer. Pray till the Lord of the harvest shall thrust forth laborers into His harvest.

Send the coals of heavenly fire,

From the altar of the skies;

Fill our hearts with strong desire,

Till our pray'rs like incense rise.

March 9.

"How ye ought to walk and please God" (I. Thess. iv. 1).

How many dear Christians are in the place that the Lord has appointed them, and yet the devil is harassing their lives with a vague sense of not quite pleasing the Lord. Could they just settle down in the place that God has assigned them and fill it sweetly and lovingly for Him there would be more joy in their hearts and more power in their lives. God wants us all in various places, and the secret of accomplishing the most for Him is to recognize our places from Him and our service in it as pleasing Him. In the great factory and machine there is a place for the smallest screw and rivet as well as the great driving wheel and piston, and so God has His little screws whose business is simply to stay where He puts them and to believe that He wants them there and is making the most of their lives in the little spaces that they fill for Him.

There is something all can do,

Tho' you're neither wise nor strong;

You can be a helper true,

You can stand when friends are few,

Some lone heart has need of you,

You can help along.

March 10.

"The peace of God which passeth all understanding shall keep your hearts and minds" (Phil. iv. 7).

It is not peace with God, but the peace of God. "The peace that passes all understanding" is the very breath of God in the soul. He alone is able to keep it, and He can so keep it that "nothing shall offend us." Beloved, are you there?

God's rest did not come till after His work was over, and ours will not. We begin our Christian life by working, trying and struggling in the energy of the flesh to save ourselves. At last,

when we are able to cease from our own work, God comes in with His blessed rest, and works His own Divine works in us.

Oh! have you heard the glorious word
Of hope and holy cheer;
From heav'n above its tones of love
Are lingering on my ear;
The blessed Comforter has come,
And Christ will soon be here.
Oh, hearts that sigh there's succor nigh,
The Comforter is near;
He comes to bring us to our King,
And fit us to appear.
I'm glad the Comforter has come,
And Christ will soon be here.

March 11.

"But ye are a chosen generation, a peculiar people" (I. Peter ii. 9).

We have been thinking lately very much of the strange way in which God is calling a people out of a people already called. The word *ecclesia*, or church, means called out, but God is calling out a still more select body from the church to be His bride—the specially prepared ones for His coming.

We see a fine type of this in the story of Gideon. When first he sounded the trumpet of Abiezer there resorted to him more than thirty thousand men; but these had to be picked, so a first test was applied, appealing to their courage, and all but ten thousand went back; but there must be an election out of the election, and so a second test was applied, appealing to their prudence, caution and singleness of purpose, and all but three hundred were refused; and, with this little picked band, he raised the standard against the Midianites, and through the power of God won his glorious victory. So, again, in our days, the Master is choosing His three hundred, and by them He will yet win the world for Himself. Let us be sure that we belong to the "out and out" people.

March 12.

"They wandered in the wilderness in a solitary way" (Ps. cvii. 4).

All who fight the Lord's battles must be content to die to all the favorable opinions of men and all the flattery of human praise. You cannot make an exception in favor of the good opinions of the children of God. It is very easy for the insidious adversary to make this also all appeal to the flesh. It is all right when God sends us the approval of our fellow men, but we must never make it a motive in our life, but be content with the "solitary way" and the lonely "wilderness."

All such motives are poison and a taking away from you of the strength with which you are to give glory to God. It is not the fact that all that see the face of the Lord do see each other.

The man of God must walk alone with God. He must be contented that the Lord knoweth that God knows. It is such a relief to the natural man within us to fall back upon human countenances and human thoughts and sympathy, that we often deceive ourselves and think it "brotherly love," when we are just resting in the earthly sympathy of some fellow worm!

March 13.

"Keep yourselves in the love of God" (Jude 21).

Some time ago, we were enjoying a

surpassingly beautiful sunset. The western skies seemed like a great archipelago of golden islands, the masses in the distance rising up into vast mountains of glory. The hue of the sky was so gorgeous that it seemed to reflect itself upon the whole atmosphere, as we looked back from the west to the eastern horizon. The whole earth was radiant with glory. The fields had changed to strange, red richness, and the earth seemed bathed with the dews of heaven.

And so it is, when the love of God shines through all our celestial sky, it covers everything below, and life becomes radiant with its light. Things that were hard become easy. Things that were sharp become sweet. Labor loses its burden, and sorrow becomes silver-lined with hope and gladness.

There are two ways of living in His love. One is constant trust, and the other is constant obedience, and His own Word gives the message for both. "If ye keep My commandments ye shall live in My love, even as I keep My Father's, and live in His love."

March 14.

"We are His workmanship" (Eph. ii. 10).

Christ sends us to serve Him, not in our own strength, but in His resources and might. "We are His workmanship, created in Christ Jesus unto good works, which God hath prepared that we should walk in them." We do not have to prepare them; but to wear them as garments, made to order for every occasion of our life.

We must receive them by faith and go forth in His work, believing that He is with us, and in us, as our all sufficiency for wisdom, faith, love, prayer, power, and every grace and gift that our work requires. In this work of faith we shall have to feel weak and helpless, and even have little consciousness of power. But if we believe and go forward, He will be the power and send the fruits.

The most useful services we render are those which, like the sweet fruits of the wilderness, spring from hours of barrenness. "I will bring her into the wilderness and I will give her vineyards from thence." Let us learn to work by faith as well as walk by faith, then we shall receive even the end of our faith, the salvation of precious souls, and our lives will bear fruit which shall be manifest throughout all eternity.

March 15.

"Continue ye in My love" (John xv. 9).

Many atmospheres there are in which we may live. Some people live in an atmosphere of thought. Their faces are thoughtful, minds intellectual. They live in their ideas, their conceptions of truth, their tastes, and esthetic nature. Some people, again, live in their animal nature, in the lusts of the flesh and eye, the coarse, low atmosphere of a sensuous life, or something worse. Some, again, live in a world of duty. The predominating feature of their life is conscience, and it carries with it a certain shadowy fear that takes away the simple freedom and gladness of life, but there is a rectitude, and uprightness, a strictness of purpose, and of conduct which cannot be gainsaid or questioned.

But Christ bids us live in an atmosphere of love. "As My Father has loved Me, so have I loved you; continue ye in My love." In the

original it is, "Live in My love." Love is the atmosphere that He would have us ever live in, that is, believing that He ever loves us, and claiming His sweet approval and tender regard. This is a life of love.

March 16.

"The Lord will give grace and glory" (Ps. lxxxiv. 11).

The Lord will give grace and glory. This word *glory* is very difficult to translate, define and explain; but there is something in the spiritual consciousness of the quickened Christian that interprets it. It is the overflow of grace; it is the wine of life; it is the foretaste of heaven; it is a flash from the Throne and an inspiration from the heart of God which we may have and in which we may live. "The glory which Thou hast given Me I have given them," the Master prayed for us. Let us take it and live in it. David used to say, "Wake up my glory." Ask God to wake up your glory and enable you to mount up with wings as eagles, to dwell on high and sit with Christ in the heavenly places.

Mounting up with wings as eagles,

Waiting on the Lord we rise,

Strength exchanging, life renewing,

How our spirit heavenward flies.

Then our springing feet returning,

Tread the pathway of the saint,

We shall run and not be weary,

We shall walk and never faint.

March 17.

"He hath remembered His covenant forever" (Ps. cv. 8).

So long as you struggle under law, that is by your own effort, sin shall have dominion over you: but the moment you step from under the shadow of Sinai, throw yourself upon the simple grace of Christ and His free and absolute gift of righteousness, and take Him to be to you what He has pledged Himself to be, your righteousness of thought and feeling, and to keep you in spite of everything, that ever can be against you, in His perfect will and peace, the struggle is practically over. Beloved, do you really know and believe that this is the very promise of the Gospel, the very essence of the new covenant, that Christ pledges Himself to put His law in your heart, and to cause you to walk in His statutes, and to keep His judgments and do them? Do you know that this is the oath which He sware unto Abraham, that He would grant unto us. "That we being delivered from the hands of our enemies, and from all that hate us, might serve Him without fear, in righteousness and holiness before Him all the days of our life." He has sworn to do this for you, and He is faithful, that promised. Trust Him ever.

March 18.

"Neither shall any plague come near thy dwelling" (Ps. xci. 10).

We know what it is to be fireproof, to be waterproof: but it is a greater thing to be proof against sin. It is possible to be so filled with the Spirit and presence of Jesus that all the shafts of the enemy glance off our heavenly armor; that all the burrs and thistles which grow on the wayside fail to stick to our heavenly robes; that all the noxious vapors of the pit disappear before the warm breath of the Holy Ghost, and we walk with a charmed

- 418 -

life even through the valley of the shadow of death. The red hot iron repels the water that touches it, and the fingers that would trifle with it: and, if we are on fire with the Holy Ghost, Satan will keep his fingers off us, and the cold water that he pours over us will roll off and leave us unharmed: "for He that was begotten of God keepeth us, and that wicked one toucheth us not."

It is said that before going into a malarious region, it is well to fortify the system with nourishing food. So we should be fed and filled by the life of Christ in such a way that the evil does not really touch our life.

March 19.

"Launch out into the deep" (Luke v. 4).

Many difficulties and perplexities in connection with our Christian life might be best settled by a simple and bold decision of our will to go forward with the light we have and leave the speculations and theories that we cannot decide for further settlement. What we need is to act, and to act with the best light we have, and as we step out into the present duty and full obedience, many things will be made plain which it is no use waiting to decide.

Beloved, cut the Gordian knot, like Alexander, with the sword of decision. Launch out into the deep with a bold plunge, and Christ will settle for you all the questions that you are now debating, and more probably show you their insignificance, and let you see that the only way to settle them is to overleap them. They are Satan's petty snares to waste your time and keep you halting when you should be marching on.

The mercy of God is an ocean divine,
A boundless and fathomless flood;
Launch out in the deep, cut away the shore line,
And be lost in the fulness of God.

March 20.

"They which receive abundance of grace and the gift of righteousness shall reign in life" (Rom. v. 17).

Precious souls sometimes fight tremendous battles in order to attain to righteousness in trying places. Perhaps the heart has become wrong in some matter where temptation has been allowed to overcome, or at least to turn it aside from its singleness unto God; and the conflict is a terrible one as it seeks to adjust itself and be right with God, and finds itself baffled by its own spiritual foes, and its own helplessness, perplexity and perversity. How dark and dreary the struggle, and how helpless and ineffectual it often seems at such times! It is almost sure to strive in the spirit of the law, and the result always is, and must ever be, condemnation and failure. Every disobedience is met by a blow of wrath, and discouragement, and it well nigh sinks to despair. Oh, if the tempted and struggling one could only understand or remember what perhaps he has learned before, that Christ is our righteousness, and that it is not by law but by grace alone, "For sin shall not have dominion over you, for ye are not under the law, but under grace." That is the secret of the whole battle.

March 21.

"Casting all your care upon Him" (I. Peter v. 7).

Some things there are that God will

not tolerate in us. We must leave them. Nehemiah would not talk with Sanballat about his charges and fears, but simply refused to have anything to do with the matter—even to go into the temple and pray about it. How very few things we really have to do with in life. If we would only drop all the needless things and simply do the things that absolutely touch and require our attention from morning till night, we would find what a small slender thread life was; but we string upon it a thousand imaginary beads that never come, and burden ourselves with cares and flurries that if we had trusted more, would never have needed to preoccupy our attention. Wise indeed was the testimony of the dear old saint who said, in review of her past life, "I have had a great many troubles in my life, especially those that never came."

Trust and rest with heart abiding,

Like a birdling in its nest,

Underneath His feathers hiding,

Fold thy wings and trust and rest.

Trust and rest, trust and rest,

God is working for the best.

March 22.

"Hold fast the confidence and the rejoicing of the hope firm unto the end" (Heb. iii. 6).

The attitude of faith is simple trust. It is Elijah saying to Ahab, "There is a sound of abundance of rain." But then there comes usually a deeper experience in which the prayer is inwrought; it is Elijah on the mount, with his face between his knees, travailing, as it were, in birth for the promised blessing. He has believed for it—and now he must take. The first is

Joash shooting the arrow out of the windows, but the second is Joash smiting on the ground and following up his faith by perseverance and victorious testing.

It is in this latter place that many of us come short. We ask much from God, and when God proceeds to give it to us we are not found equal to His expectation. We are made partakers of Christ if we hold the beginning of our confidence steadfast to the end, and trust Him through it all.

Fainting soldier of the Lord,

Hear His sweet inspiring word,

"I have conquered all thy foes.

I have suffered all thy woes;

Struggling soldier, trust in Me,

I have overcome for thee."

March 23.

"He is a new creature" (II. Cor. v. 17).

Resurrected, not raised. There is so much in this distinction. The teaching of human philosophy is that we are to raise humanity to a higher plane. This is not the Gospel. On the contrary, the teaching of the cross is that humanity must die and sink out of sight and then be resurrected, not raised. Resurrection is not improvement. It is not elevation, but it is a new supernatural life lifting us from nothingness into God and making us partakers of the Divine nature. It is a new creation. It is an infinite elevation above the highest plane. Let us not take less than resurrection life.

I am crucified with Jesus,

And the cross has set me free;

I have ris'n again with Jesus,

And He lives and reigns in me.

This the story of the Master,

Through the cross He reached the throne,

And like Him our path to glory,

Ever leads through death alone.

Lord, teach me the death-born life.
Lord, let me live in the power of Thy resurrection!

March 24.

"And again I say, rejoice" (Phil. iv. 4).

It is a good thing to rejoice in the Lord. Perhaps you found the first dose ineffectual. Keep on with your medicine, and when you cannot feel any joy, when there is no spring, and no seeming comfort and encouragement, still rejoice, and count it all joy. Even when you fall into divers temptations, reckon it joy, and delight, and God will make your reckoning good. Do you suppose your Father will let you carry the banner of His victory and His gladness on to the front of the battle, and then coolly stand back and see you captured or beaten back by the enemy? Never! the Holy Spirit will sustain you in your bold advance, and fill your heart with gladness and praise, and you will find your heart all exhilarated and refreshed by the fulness of the heart within.

Lord, teach me to rejoice in Thee, and to rejoice evermore.

The joy of the Lord is the strength of His people.

The sunshine that scatters their sadness and gloom;

The fountain that bursts in the desert of sorrow,

And sheds o'er the wilderness, gladness and bloom.

March 25.

"The beauty of holiness" (Ps. xxix. 2).

Some one remarked once that he did not know more disagreeable people than sanctified Christians. He probably meant people that only profess sanctification. There is an angular, hard, unlovely type of Christian character that is not true holiness; at least, not the highest type of it. It is the skeleton without the flesh covering; it is the naked rock without the vines and foliage that cushion its rugged sides. Jesus was not only virtuous and pure, but He was also beautiful and full of the sweet attractiveness of love.

We read of two kinds of graces: First, "Whatsoever things are just, whatsoever things are lovely and of good report." There are a thousand little graces in Christian life that we cannot afford to ignore. In fact, the last stages in any work of art are always the finishing touches; and so let us not wonder if God shall spend a great deal of time in teaching us the little things that many might consider trifles.

God would have His Bride without a spot or even a wrinkle.

March 26.

"Jesus, the author and finisher of our faith" (Heb. xii. 2).

Add to your faith—do not add to yourself. This is where we make the mistake. We must not only enter by faith, but we must advance by faith each step of the way. At every new stage we shall find ourselves as incompetent and unequal for the pressure as before, and we must take the grace and the victory simply by faith. Is it courage? We shall find ourselves lacking in the needed courage; we must claim it by faith. Is

it love? Our own love will be inadequate; but we must take His love, and we shall find it given. Is it faith itself? We must have the faith of God, and Christ in us will be the spirit of faith, as well as the blessing that faith claims. So our whole life from beginning to end, is but Christ in us—in the exceeding riches of His grace; and our everlasting song will be: Not I; but Christ who liveth in me.

'Tis so sweet to walk with Jesus,

Step by step and day by day;

Stepping in His very footprints,

Walking with Him all the way.

March 27.

"What time I am afraid, I will trust in Thee" (Ps. lvi. 3).

We shall never forget a remark Mr. George Mueller once made in answer to a gentleman who asked him the best way to have strong faith. "The only way," replied the patriarch of faith, "to learn strong faith is to endure great trials. I have learned my faith by standing firm amid severe testings." This is very true. The time to trust is when all else fails. Dear one, if you scarcely realize the value of your present opportunity, if you are passing through great afflictions, you are in the very soul of the strongest faith, and if you will only let go, He will teach you in these hours the mightiest hold upon this throne which you can ever know. "Be not afraid, only believe"; and if you are afraid, just look up and say, "What time I am afraid, I will trust in Thee," and you will yet thank God for the school of sorrow which was to you the school of faith.

O brother, give heed to the warning,

And obey His voice to-day.

The Spirit to thee is calling,

O do not grieve Him away.

March 28.

"The fruit of the Spirit is all goodness" (Gal. v. 22).

Goodness is a fruit of the Spirit. Goodness is just "Godness." It is to be like God. And God-like goodness has special reference to the active benevolence of God. The apostle gives us the difference between goodness and righteousness in this passage in Romans, "Scarcely for a righteous man would one die, yet peradventure for a good man some would even dare to die." The righteous man is the man of stiff, inflexible uprightness; but he may be as hard as a granite mountain side. The good man is that mountain side all covered with velvet moss and flowers, and flowing with cascades and springs. Goodness respects "whatsoever things are lovely." It is kindness, affectionateness, benevolence, sympathy, rejoicing with them that do rejoice, and weeping with them that weep. Lord, fill us with Thyself, and let us be God-men and good men, and so represent Thy goodness.

There are lonely hearts to cherish,

While the days are going by;

There are weary souls who perish,

While the days are going by.

March 29.

"He will keep the feet of His saints" (I. Sam. ii. 9).

Perils as well as privileges attend the higher Christian life. The nearer we come to God, the thicker the hosts of darkness in heavenly places. The safe

place lies in obedience to God's Word, singleness of heart, and holy vigilance.

When Christians speak of standing in a place where they do not need to watch, they are in great danger. Let us walk in sweet and holy confidence, and yet with holy, humble watchfulness, and "He will keep the feet of His saints." And "now unto Him who is able to keep us from stumbling, and present us faultless before the presence of His glory, to the only wise God, our Saviour, be glory, and majesty, dominion and power, both now and forever. Amen."

What to do we often wonder,

As we seek some watchword true,

Lo, the answer God has given,

What would Jesus do?

When the shafts of fierce temptation,

With their fiery darts pursue,

This will be your heavenly armor,

What would Jesus do?

March 30.

"I wish above all things that thou mayest prosper and be in health even as thy soul prospereth" (III. John 2).

In the way of righteousness is life and in the pathway thereof is no death. That is the secret of healing. Be right with God. Keep so. Live in the consciousness of it, and nothing can hurt you. Off from the breastplate of righteousness will glance all of the fiery darts of the devil, and faith is stronger for every fierce assault. How true it is, "Who is he that shall harm you if ye be followers of that which is good?" And how true also, "Holding faith and a good conscience, which some having put away, concerning faith, have made shipwreck."

And yet again, "If thou wilt diligently hearken to the voice of the Lord thy God, and wilt keep all His statutes and commandments, I will put none of these diseases upon thee that I have brought upon the Egyptians; for I am the Lord that healeth thee."

There's a question God is asking

Every conscience in His sight,

Let it search thine inmost being,

Is it right with God, all right?

March 31.

"What things soever ye desire when ye pray, believe that ye receive them and ye shall have them" (Mark xi. 24).

Faith is not working up by will power a sort of certainty that something is coming to pass, but it is seeing as an actual fact that God has said that this thing shall come to pass, and that it is true, and then rejoicing to know that it is true, and just resting and entering into it because God has said it. Faith turns the promise into a prophecy. While it is merely a promise it is contingent upon our co-operation; it may or may not be. But when faith claims it, it becomes a prophecy and we go forth feeling that it is something that must be done because God cannot lie.

Faith is the answer from the throne saying, "It is done." Faith is the echo of God's voice. Let us catch it from on high. Let us repeat it, and go out to triumph in its glorious power.

Hear the answer from the throne,

Claim the promise, doubting one,

God hath spoken, "It is done."

Faith hath answered, "It is done";

Prayer is over, praise begun,

Hallelujah! It is done.

April 1.

"Vessels of mercy which he had afore prepared unto glory" (Rom. ix. 23).

Our Father is fitting us for eternity. A vessel fitted for the kitchen will find itself in the kitchen. A vessel for the art gallery or the reception room will generally find itself there at last.

What are you getting fitted for? To be a slop-pail to hold all the stuff that people pour into your ears, or a vase to hold sweet fragrance and flowers for the King's palace and a harp of many strings that sounds the melodies and harmonies of His love and praise? Each one of us is going to his own place. Let us get fitted now.

The days of heaven are Christly days,

The Light of Heaven is He;

So walking at His side, our days

As the days of heaven would be.

The days of heaven are endless days—

Days of eternity;

So may our lives and works endure

While the days of heaven shall be.

Walk with us, Lord, through all the days,

And let us walk with Thee;

'Til as Thy will is done in heaven,

On earth so shall it be.

April 2.

"He shall dwell on high" (Isa. xxxiii. 16).

It is easier for a consecrated Christian to live an out and out life for God than to live a mixed life. A soul redeemed and sanctified by Christ is too large for the shoals and sands of a selfish, worldly, sinful life. The great steamship, St. Paul, could sail in deep water without an effort, but she could make no progress in the shallow pool, or on the Long Branch sands; the smallest tugboat is worth a dozen of her there; but out in mid-ocean she could distance them in an hour.

Beloved, your life is too large, too glorious, too divine for the small place that you are trying to live in. Your purpose is too petty; arise and dwell on high in the resurrection life of Jesus, and the inspiring hope of His blessed coming.

Rise with thy risen Lord,

Ascend with Christ above,

And in the heavenlies walk with Him,

Whom seeing not, you love.

Walk as a heavenly race,

Princes of royal blood;

Walk as the children of the light,

The sons and heirs of God.

April 3.

"My expectation is from Him" (Ps. lxii. 5).

When we believe for a blessing, we must take the attitude of faith, and begin to act and pray as if we had our blessing. We must treat God as if He had given us our request. We must lean our weight over upon Him for the thing that we have claimed, and just take it for granted that He gives it, and is going to continue to give it. This is the attitude of trust. When the wife is married, she at once falls into a new attitude, and acts in accordance with the fact, and so when we take Christ as a Saviour, as a Sanctifier, as a Healer, or as a Deliverer, He expects us to fall into the attitude of recognizing Him in the capacity that we have claimed, and expect Him to be to us all that we have trusted Him for.

You may bring Him ev'ry care and burden,

You may tell Him ev'ry need in pray'r,

You may trust Him for the darkest moment,

He is caring, wherefore need you care?

Faith can never reach its consummation,

'Til the victor's thankful song we raise:

In the glorious city of salvation,

God has told us all the gates are praise.

April 4.

"Resist the devil and he will flee" (James iv. 7).

Resist the devil, and he will flee from you. This is a promise, and God will keep it to us. If we resist the adversary, He will compel him to flee, and will give us the victory. We can, at all times, fearlessly stand up in defiance, in resistance to the enemy, and claim the protection of our heavenly King just as a citizen would claim the protection of the government against an outrage or injustice on the part of violent men. At the same time we are not to stand on the adversary's ground anywhere by any attitude or disobedience, or we give him a terrible power over us, which, while God will restrain in great mercy and kindness, He will not fully remove until we get fully on holy ground. Therefore, we must be armed with the breastplate of righteousness, as well as the shield of faith, if we would successfully resist the prince of darkness and the principalities in heavenly places.

Your full redemption rights

With holy boldness claim,

And to the utmost fulness prove

The power of Jesus' name.

April 5.

"Many shall be purified and made white and tried" (Dan. xii. 10).

This is the promise for the Lord's coming. It is more than purity. It is to be made white, lustrous, or bright. To be purified is to have the sin burned out; to be made white is to have the glory of the Lord burned in. The one is cleansing, the other is illumination and glorification. The Lord has both for us, but in order for us to have both, we must be put into the fire to be tried, and to be led into difficult and peculiar places where Christ shall be more to us because of the very extremity of the situation. We are approaching these days. Indeed, they are already around us, and they are the precursors of the Lord's coming.

Blessed is he that keepeth his garments lest he walk naked.

There are voices in the air, filling men with hope and fear;

There are signals everywhere that the end is drawing near,

There are warnings to prepare, for the King will soon be here;

O it must be the coming of the Lord!

April 6.

"As we have many members in one body, so we being many are one body in Christ" (Rom. xii. 4, 5).

Sometimes our communion with God is cut off, or interrupted because of something wrong with a brother, or some lack of unity in the body of Christ. We try to get at the Lord, but we cannot, because we are separated from some member of the Lord's body, or because there is not the freedom of His love flowing through every organic part. It does not need a

blow upon the head to paralyze the brain; a blow upon some nerve may do it; or a wound in some artery at the extremities may be fatal to the heart. Therefore we must stand right with all His children, and meet in the body of Christ in the sweetest, fullest fellowship, if we would keep our perfect communion with Christ Himself. Sometimes we will find that an altered attitude to one Christian will bring us into the flood-tides of the Holy Ghost. It seems impossible to have faith without love, or to have Christ alone without the fulness of fellowship with all His dear saints; and if one member suffer, all suffer together, and if one rejoice, all are blessed in common.

April 7.

"In Him we live and move" (Acts xvii. 28).

The hand of Gehazi, and even the staff of Elisha could not heal the lifeless boy. It needed the living touch of the prophet's own divinely quickened flesh to infuse vitality into the cold clay. Lip to lip, hand to hand, heart to heart, he must touch the child ere life could thrill his pulseless veins.

We must come into personal contact with the risen Saviour, and have His very life quicken our mortal flesh before we can know the fulness and reality of His healing. This is the most frequent cause of failure. People are often trusting to something that has been done to them, or to something that they have done, or something that they have believed intellectually; but their spirit has not felt its way to the heart of Christ, and they have not drawn His love into their being by the hunger and thirst of love and faith, and so they are not quickened. The greatest need of our souls and bodies is to know Jesus personally, to touch Him constantly, to abide in Him continually.

May we this day lay aside all things that could hinder our near approach to Him, and walk hand in hand, heart to heart, with Jesus.

April 8.

"A merry heart doeth good like a medicine" (Prov. xvii. 22).

King Solomon left among his wise sayings a prescription for sick and sad hearts, and it is one that we can safely take. "A merry heart doeth good like a medicine." Joy is the great restorer and healer. Gladness of spirit will bring health to the bones and vitality to the nerves when all other tonics fail, and all other sedatives cease to quiet. Sick one, begin to rejoice in the Lord, and your bones will flourish like an herb, and your cheeks will glow with the bloom of health and freshness. Worry, fear, distrust, care, are all poison drops; joy is balm and healing; and if you will but rejoice, God will give power. He has commanded you to be glad and rejoice; and He never fails to sustain His children in keeping His commandments. Rejoice in the Lord always, He says; which means no matter how sad, how tempted, how sick, how suffering you are, rejoice in the Lord just where you are, and begin this moment.

The joy of the Lord is the strength of our body,

The gladness of Jesus, the balm for our pain,

His life and His fulness, our fountain of healing,

His joy, our elixir for body and brain.

April 9.

"I do always those things that please Him" (John viii. 29).

It is a good thing to keep short accounts with God. We were very much struck some years ago with an interpretation of this verse: "So every one of us shall give an account of himself to God." The thought conveyed to our mind was, that of accounting to God every day of our lives, so that our accounts were settled daily, and for us judgment was passed, as we lay down on our pillows every night.

This is surely the true way to live. It is the secret of great peace, and it will be a delightful comfort when life is closing, or the Master coming, to know that our account is settled, and our judgment over, and for us there is only waiting the glad "Well done, good and faithful servant, enter thou into the joy of thy Lord."

Step by step I'll walk with Jesus,
Just a moment at a time,
Heights I have not wings to soar to,
Step by step my feet can climb.
Jesus, keep me closer—closer,
Step by step and day by day
Stepping in Thy very foot-prints,
Walking with Thee all the way.

April 10.

"Hold fast the confidence" (Heb. iii. 6).

Seldom have we seen a sadder wreck of even the highest, noblest Christian character than when the enemy has succeeded in undermining the simple trust of a child of God, and got him into self-accusing and condemnation. It is a fearful place when the soul allows Satan to take the throne and act as God, sitting in judgment on its every thought and act; and keeping it in the darkness of ceaseless condemnation. Well indeed has the apostle told us to hold firmly the shield of faith!

This is Satan's objective point in all his attacks upon you, to destroy your trust. If he can get you to lose your simple confidence in God, he knows that he will soon have you at his feet.

It is enough to wreck both the reason and the life for the soul that has known the sweetness of His love to lose its perfect trust in God. "Beloved, hold fast your confidence and the rejoicing of your hope firm unto the end."

Fear not to take your place

With Jesus on the throne,

And bid the powers of earth and hell,

His sovereign sceptre own.

April 11.

"Commit thy way unto the Lord" (Ps. xxxvii. 5).

Seldom have we heard a better definition of faith than was given once in one of our meetings by a dear old colored woman, as she answered the question of a young man how to take the Lord for needed help.

In her characteristic way, pointing her finger toward him, she said with great emphasis: "You've just got to believe that He's done it, and it's done." The great danger with most of us is, that after we ask Him to do it, we do not believe that it's done, but we keep on helping Him, and getting others to help Him; superintending God and waiting to see how He is going to do it.

Faith adds its amen to God's yea, and then takes its hands off, and leaves God to finish His work. Its language

is, "Commit thy way unto the Lord, trust also in Him; and He worketh."

Lord, I give up the struggle,
To Thee commit my way,
I trust Thy word forever,
And settle it all to-day.

April 12.

"They were as it were, complainers" (Num. xi. 1).

There is a very remarkable phrase in the book of Numbers, in the account of the murmuring of the children of Israel in the wilderness. It reads like this: "When the people, as it were, murmured." Like most marginal readings it is better than the text, and a great world of suggestive truth lies back of that little sentence.

In the distance we may see many a vivid picture rise before our imagination of people who do not dare to sin openly and unequivocally, but manage to do it "as it were" only. They do not lie straight, but they evade or equivocate, or imply enough falsehood to escape a real conviction of conscience. They do not openly accuse God of unkindness or unfaithfulness, but they strike at Him through somebody else. They find fault with circumstances and people and things that God has permitted to come into their lives, and, "As it were," murmur. They do not perhaps go any farther. They feel like doing it if they dared to "charge God foolishly."

These things were written for our warning.

April 13.

"Rejoice evermore" (I. Thess. v. 16).

Do not lose your joy whatever else you lose. Keep the spirit of spring. "Rejoice evermore," and "Again I say, rejoice."

The loss of Canaan began in the spirit of murmurings, "When the people, as it were, murmured, it displeased the Lord." The first break in their fellowship, the first falter in their advance, came when they began to doubt, and grieve, and fret.

Oh, keep the heart from the perforations of depression, discouragement, distrust and gloom, for Satan cannot crush a rejoicing and praiseful soul.

Look out for the beginning of sin. Don't let the first touch of evil be harbored. It is the first step that loses all. Oh, to keep so encased in the Holy Ghost and in the very life of Jesus that the evil cannot reach us!

The little fly on the inside of the window-pane may be attacked by the little bird on the outside, and it may seem to him that he is lost, but the crystal pane between keeps him safely from all danger as certainly as if it were a mighty wall of iron.

April 14.

"I if I be lifted up from the earth will draw all men unto Me" (John xii. 32).

A true and pure Christian life attracts the world. There are hundreds of men and women who find no inducements whatever in the lives of ordinary Christians to interest them in practical religion, but who are won at once by a true and victorious example. We believe that more men of the world step at a bound right into a life of entire consecration than into the intermediate state which is usually presented to them at the first stage.

In an audience once there was a man

who for half a century or more had lived without Christ, and who was a very prominent citizen, a man in public life, of irreproachable character, lofty intellect, and a most winning spirit and manners, but utterly out of sympathy with the Christian life.

At the close of a service for the promotion of deeper spiritual life he rose to ask the prayers of the congregation, and before the end of the week he was himself a true and acknowledged follower of the Lord Jesus Christ. He said, as he went home that night, "If that is the religion of Jesus Christ, I want it."

April 15.

"Rooted and grounded in love" (Eph. iii. 17).

There is a very singular shrub, which grows abundantly in the west, and is to be found in all parts of Texas. It is no less than the "mosquito tree." It is a very slim, and willowy looking shrub, and would seem to be of little use for any industrial purposes; but is has extraordinary roots growing like great timbers underground, and possessing such qualities of endurance in all situations that it is used and very highly valued for good pavements. The city of San Antonio is said to be paved with these roots. It reminds one of those Christians who make little show externally, but their growth is chiefly underground—out of sight, in the depth of God. These are the men and women that God uses for the foundation of things, and for the pavements of that city of God which will stand when all earthly things have crumbled into ruin and dissolved into oblivion.

Deeper, deeper let the living waters flow;

Blessed Holy Spirit! River of Salvation!

All Thy fulness let me know.

April 16.

"Quit you like men" (I. Cor. xvi. 13).

Be brave. Cowards always get hurt. Brave men generally come out unharmed. Jeremiah was a hero. He shrank from nothing. He faced his king and countrymen with dauntless bravery, and the result was he suffered no harm, but came through the siege of Jerusalem without a hair being injured. Zedekiah, the cowardly king, was always afraid to obey God and be true, and the result was that he at last met the most cruel punishment that was ever inflicted on human heart.

The men and women that stand from the beginning true to their convictions have the fewest tests. When God gives to you a good trial, if you can stand the strain, He is not always repeating it. When Abraham offered up his son Isaac at Mount Moriah, it was a final testing for the rest of his life. Do not let Satan see that you are afraid of him, for he will pursue to the death if he thinks that he has a chance of getting you.

Be true, be true,

Whether friends be false or few,

Whatsoe'er betide, ever at His side,

Let Him always find you true.

April 17.

"He that ruleth his spirit is better than he that taketh a city" (Prov. xvi. 32).

Temperance is true self-government. It involves the grace of self-denial and the spirit of a sound mind. It is that poise of spirit that holds us quiet, self-

possessed, recollected, deliberate, and subject ever to the voice of God and the conviction of duty in every step we take. Many persons have not that poise and recollected spirit. They are drifting at the impulse of their own impressions, moods, the influence of others, or the circumstances around them. No desire should ever control us. No purpose, however right, should have such mastery over us that we are not perfectly free. The pure affection may be an inordinate affection. Our work itself may be a selfish passion. That thing that we began to do because it was God's will, we may cling to and persist in ultimately, because it is our own will. Lord, give us the spirit ever controlled by Thy Spirit and will, and the eye that looks to Thee every moment as the eyes of a servant to the hands of her mistress. So shall Thy service be our perfect freedom, and our subjection divinest liberty.

April 18.

"They shall mount up with wings" (Isa. xl. 31).

"They shall mount up with wings as eagles," is God's preliminary; for the next promise is, "They shall run and not be weary, and they shall walk and not faint." Hours of holy exultation are necessary for hours of patient plodding, waiting and working. Nature has its springs, and so has grace.

Let us rejoice in the Lord evermore, and again we say, rejoice. And let us take Him to be our continual joy, whose heart is a fountain of blessedness, and who is anointed with the oil of gladness above His fellows. We must not be disappointed if the tides are not always equally high. Even at low tide the ocean is just as

full. Human nature could not stand perpetual excitement, even of a happy kind, and God often rests in His love. Let us live as self-unconsciously as possible, filling up each moment with faithful service, and trusting Him to stir the springs at His will, and as we go on in faithful service we shall hear, again and again, His glad whisper: "Well done, good and faithful servant, enter thou into the joy of thy Lord."

April 19.

"Rest in the Lord and wait patiently for Him" (Ps. xxxvii. 7).

It is a very suggestive thought that it is in the Gospel of Mark, which is the Gospel of service, we hear the Master saying to His disciples, "Come ye apart into a desert place, and rest awhile." God wants rested workers. There is an energy that may be tireless and ceaseless, and yet still as the ocean's depth, with the peace of God, which passes all understanding. The two deepest secrets of rest are, first, to be in harmony with the will of God, and, secondly, to trust. "Great peace have they that love Thy law," expresses the first. "Thou will keep him in perfect peace whose mind is stayed on Thee, because he trusteth in Thee," describes the second. There is a good deal in learning to "stay." Sometimes we forget that it literally means to stop. It is a great blessing even to stop all thought, and this is frequently the only way to answer the devil's whirlwind of irritating questions and thoughts, to be absolutely still and refuse to even think, and meet his evil voice with a simple and everlasting "No!" If we will be still God will give us peace.

April 20.

"There they dwelt with the King for His work" (I. Chron. iv. 23).

It is easy for water to run down from the upper springs, but it requires a divine impulse to flow up from the valley in the nether springs. There is nothing that tells more of Christ than to see a Christian rejoicing and cheerful in the humdrum and routine of commonplace work, like the sailors that stand on the dock loading the vessel and singing as they swing their loads, keeping time with the spirit of praise to the footsteps and movements of labor and duty. No one has a sweeter or higher ministry for Christ than a business man or a serving woman who can carry the light of heaven in their faces all day long. Like the sea fowl that can plunge beneath the briny tide with its beautiful and spotless plumage, and come forth without one drop adhering to its burnished breast and glowing wings because of the subtle oil upon the plumage that keeps the water from sticking, so, thank God, we too may be so anointed with the Holy Ghost that sin, sorrow and defilement will not adhere to us, but we shall pass through every sea as the ship passes through the waves, in, but above the floods around us.

April 21.

"The anointing which ye have received" (I. John ii. 27).

This is the secret of the deeper life, but "That ye may be rooted and grounded in love," is the substance of it, and the sweetness of it. The fulness of the divine love in the heart will make everything easy. It is very easy to do things that we love to do, and it is very easy to trust one whom we love, and the more we realize their love the more we will trust them for it. It is the source of healing. The tide of love flowing through our bodies will strangely strengthen our very frame, and the love of our Lord will become a continual spring of youth and freshness in our physical being. The secret of love is very simple. It is to take the heart of Jesus for our love and claim its love for every need of life, whether it be toward God or toward others. It is very sweet to think of persons in this way, "I will take the heart of Jesus toward them, to let me love them as He loves them." Then we can love even the unworthy in some measure, if we shall see them in the light of His love and hope, as they shall be, and not as they now are, unworthy of our love.

April 22.

"Christ is the head" (Eph. v. 23).

Often we want people to pray for us and help us, but always defeat our object when we look too much to them and lean upon them. The true secret of union is for both to look upon God, and in the act of looking past themselves to Him they are unconsciously united. The sailor was right when he saw the little boy fall overboard and waited a minute before he plunged to his rescue. When the distracted mother asked him in agony why he had waited so long, he sensibly replied: "I knew that if I went in before he would clutch and drag me down. I waited until his struggles were over, and then I was able to help him when he did not grasp me too strongly."

When people grasp us too strongly, either with their love or with their dependence, we are intuitively

conscious that they are not looking to God, and we become paralyzed in our efforts to help them. United prayer, therefore, requires that the one for whom we pray be looking away from us to the Lord Jesus Christ, and we together look to Him alone.

April 23.

"An high priest touched with the feeling of our infirmities" (Heb. iv. 15).

Some time ago we were talking with a greatly suffering sister about healing, who was much burdened physically and desirous of being able to trust the Lord for deliverance. After a little conversation we prayed with her, committing her case to the Lord for absolute trust and deliverance as she was prepared to claim. As soon as we closed our prayer she grasped our hand, and asked us to unite with her in the burden that was most upon her heart, and then, without a word of reference to her own healing, or the burden under which she was being crushed to death, she burst into such a prayer for a poor orphan boy, of whom she had just heard that day, as we have never heard surpassed for sympathy and love, imploring God to help him and save him, and sobbing in spasmodic agony of love many times during her prayer, and then she ceased without even referring to her own need. We were deeply touched by the spectacle of love, and we thought how the Father's heart must be touched for her own need.

April 24.

"Fret not thyself in any wise" (Ps. xxxvii. 8).

A life was lost in Israel because a pair of human hands were laid unbidden upon the ark of God. They were placed upon it with the best intent to steady it when trembling and shaking as the oxen drew it along the rough way, but they touched God's work presumptuously, and they fell paralyzed and lifeless. Much of the life of faith consists in letting things alone. If we wholly trust an interest to God we can keep our hands off it, and He will guard it for us better than we can help Him. "Rest in the Lord and wait patiently for Him. Fret not thyself in any wise because of him that prospereth in the way, because of the man that bringeth wicked devices to pass." Things may seem to be going all wrong, but He knows as well as we; and He will arise in the right moment if we are really trusting Him so fully as to let Him work in His own way and time. There is nothing so masterly as inactivity in some things, and there is nothing so hurtful as restless working, for God has undertaken to work His sovereign will.

April 25.

"The very God of Peace sanctify you wholly" (I. Thess. v. 23).

A great tidal wave is bearing up the stranded ship, until she floats above the bar without a straining timber or struggling seaman, instead of the ineffectual and toilsome efforts of the struggling crew and the strain of the engines, which had tried in vain to move her an inch until that heavenly impulse lifted her by its own attraction.

It is God's great law of gravitation lifting up, by the warm sunbeams, the mighty iceberg which a million men could not raise a single inch, but melts away before the rays and the warmth

of the sunshine, and rises in clouds of evaporation to meet its embrace until that cold and heavy mass is floating in fleecy clouds of glory in the blue ocean of the sky.

How easy all this! How mighty! How simple! How divine! Beloved, have you come into the divine way of holiness! If you have, how your heart must swell with gratitude! If you have not, do you not long for it, and will you not unite in the prayer of the text that the very God of peace will sanctify you wholly?

April 26.

"Strangers and pilgrims" (Heb. xi. 13).

If you have ever tried to plough a straight furrow in the country—we are sorry for the man that does not know how to plough and more sorry for the man that is too proud to want to know—you have found it necessary to have two stakes in a line and to drive your horses by these stakes. If you have only one stake before you, you will have no steadying point for your vision, but you can wiggle about without knowing it and make your furrows as crooked as a serpent's coil; but if you have two stakes and ever keep them in line, you cannot deviate an inch from a straight line, and your furrow will be an arrow speeding to its course.

This has been a great lesson to us in our Christian life. If we would run a straight course, we find that we must have two stakes, the near and the distant. It is not enough to be living in the present, but it is a great and glorious thing to have a distant goal, a definite object, a clear purpose before us for which we are living, and unto which we are shaping our present.

April 27.

"The sweetness of the lips" (Prov. xvi. 21).

Spiritual conditions are inseparably connected with our physical life. The flow of the divine life-currents may be interrupted by a little clot of blood; the vital current may leak out through a very trifling wound.

If you want to keep the health of Christ, keep from all spiritual sores, from all heart wounds and irritations. One hour of fretting will wear out more vitality than a week of work; and one minute of malignity, or rankling jealousy or envy will hurt more than a drink of poison. Sweetness of spirit and joyousness of heart are essential to full health. Quietness of spirit, gentleness, tranquility, and the peace of God that passes all understanding, are worth all the sleeping draughts in the country.

We do not wonder that some people have poor health when we hear them talk for half an hour. They have enough dislikes, prejudices, doubts, and fears to exhaust the strongest constitution.

Beloved, if you would keep God's life and strength, keep out the things that kill it; keep it for Him, and for His work, and you will find enough and to spare.

April 28.

"For it is God which worketh in you" (Phil. ii. 13).

Sanctification is the gift of the Holy Ghost, the fruit of the Spirit, the grace of the Lord Jesus Christ, the prepared inheritance of all who enter in, the greatest obtainment of faith, not the attainment of works. It is divine holiness, not human self-

improvement, nor perfection. It is the inflow into man's being of the life and purity of the infinite, eternal and Holy One, bringing His own perfection and working out His own will. How easy, how spontaneous, how delightful this heavenly way of holiness! Surely it is a "highway" and not the low way of man's vain and fruitless mortification.

It is God's great elevated railway, sweeping over the heads of the struggling throngs who toil along the lower pavement when they might be borne along on His ascension pathway, by His own almighty impulse. It is God's great elevator carrying us up to the higher chambers of His palace, without over-laborious efforts, while others struggle up the winding stairs and faint by the way.

Let us to-day so fully take Him that He can "cause us to walk in His statutes."

April 29.

"Love never faileth" (I. Cor. xiii. 8).

In our work for God it is a great thing to find the key to men's hearts, and recognize something good as a point of contact for our spiritual influence. When Jesus met the woman at Samaria He immediately seized hold of the best things in her, and by this He reached her heart, and drew from her a willing confession of her salvation. A Scotchman once said that his salvation was all due to the fact that a good man (Lord Shaftsbury, we believe) once put his arms around him and said, "John, by the grace of God we will make a man of you yet."

The old legend tells the story of a poor, dead dog lying on the street in the midst of the crowd, every one of whom was having something to say, until Jesus came along, and

immediately began to admire its beautiful teeth. He had something kind to say even of him.

There is but One can live and love like this;

The Christ-love from the living Christ must spring.

O! Jesus! come and live Thy life in me,

And all Thy heaven of love and blessing bring.

April 30.

"Love believeth all things" (I. Cor. xiii. 7).

Beautiful is the expression in the Book of Isaiah which reflects with exceeding sweetness the love of our dear Lord. He said, "They are My people, children that will not lie; so He was their Saviour." They did lie, but He would not believe it. At least He speaks as if He would not believe it in the greatness of His love, because they were His people. He has not seen iniquity in Jacob nor perversity in Israel. There is plenty of it to see, and the devil sees it all, and a good many people are only too glad to see it; but the dear Father will not see it. He covers it with His love and the precious blood of His dear atoning Son. Such a wonderful love ought surely to make us gentler to others, and more anxious to cause our Father less need to hide His loving eyes from our imperfections and faults.

If we have the mind and heart of Christ, we shall clothe even the world with those graces which faith can claim for them, and try our best to count them as if they were real, and by love and prayer we shall at length make them real. "Love believeth all things."

May 1.

"The fruit of the Spirit is gentleness" (Gal. v. 22).

Nature's harshness has melted away and she is now beaming with the smile of spring, and everything around us whispers of the gentleness of God. This beautiful fruit is in lovely harmony with the gentle month of which it is the keynote. May the Holy Spirit lead us, beloved, these days, into His sweetness, quietness, and gentleness, subduing every coarse, rude, harsh, and unholy habit, and making us like Him, of whom it is said, "He shall not strive, nor cry, nor cause His voice to be heard in the streets."

The man who is truly filled with Jesus will always be a gentleman. The woman who is baptized of the Holy Ghost, will have the instincts of a perfect lady, although low born and little bred in the schools of earthly refinement. Beloved, let us receive and reflect the gentleness of Christ, the spirit of the holy babe, until the world will say of us, as the polished and infidel Chesterfield once said of the saintly Fenelon, "If I had remained in his house another day, I should have had to become a Christian."

Lord, help us to-day, to so yield to the gentle Dove-Spirit, that our lives shall be as His life.

May 2.

"Always causeth us to triumph" (II. Cor. ii. 14).

How these words help us. Think of them when the people rasp you, when the devil pricks you with his fiery darts, when your sensitive, self-willed spirit chafes or frets; let a gentle voice be heard above the strife, whispering, "Keep sweet, keep sweet!" And, if you will but heed it quickly, you will be saved from a thousand falls and kept in perfect peace.

True, you cannot keep yourself sweet, but God will keep you if He sees that it is your fixed, determined purpose to be kept sweet, and to refuse to fret or grudge or retaliate. The trouble is, you rather enjoy a little irritation and morbidness. You want to cherish the little grudge, and sympathize with your hurt feelings, and nurse your little grievance.

Dear friends, God will give you all the love you really want and honestly choose. You can have your grievance or you can have the peace that passeth all understanding; but you cannot have both.

There is a balm for a thousand heartaches, and a heaven of peace and power in these two little words— KEEP SWEET.

May 3.

"My peace I give unto you" (John xiv. 27).

Here lies the secret of abiding peace— God's peace. We give ourselves to God and the Holy Spirit takes possession of our breast. It is indeed "Peace, Peace." But it is just then that the devil begins to turn us away, and he does it through our thoughts, diverting or distracting them as occasion requires. This is the time to prove the sincerity of our consecration and the singleness of our heart. If we truly desire His Presence more than all else, we will turn away from every conflicting thought and look steadily up to Jesus. But if we desire the gratification of our impulse more than His Presence, we will yield to the

passionate word or the frivolous thought or the sinful diversion, and when we come back our Shepherd has gone, and we wonder why our peace has departed. Failure occurs often in some trifling thing, and the soul failure has occurred in some trifling thing, usually a thought or word, and the soul which would not have feared to climb a mountain has really stumbled over a straw.

The real secret of perfect rest is to be jealously, habitually occupied with Jesus.

May 4.

"Greater is He that is in you than he that is in the world" (I. John iv. 4).

Satan loves to trip us over little things. The reason of this is because it is generally a greater victory for him, and shows that he can upset us by a shaving and knock us down with a straw. It is the old boast of the Jebusite, when they told David they could defend Jerusalem by a garrison of the blind and lame. Most of us get on better in our great struggles than we do in our little ones. It was over a little apple that Adam fell, but all the world was wrecked. Look out, beloved, for the little stumbling blocks, and do not let Satan laugh at you, and tell his myrmidons how he tripped you over an orange peel. And, too, when the devil wants to stop some great blessing in our lives, he generally throws some ugly shadow over it and makes it look distasteful to us. How many of us have been keeping back from truths, places and persons in which God has reappeared, the greatest blessing of our lives, and the devil has succeeded in keeping us away from them by some false or foolish prejudice!

May 5.

"If ye then be risen" (Col. iii. 1).

God is waiting this morning to mark the opening hours for every ready and willing heart with a touch of life and power that will lift our lives to higher pleasures and offer to our vision grander horizons of hope and holy service.

We shall not need to seek far to discover our risen Lord. He was in advance even of the earliest seeker that Easter morning, and He will be waiting for us before the break of day with His glad "All Hail," if we have only eyes to see and hearts to welcome and obey Him.

What is His message to us this spring time? "If ye then be risen with Christ, seek those things which are above, where Christ sitteth on the right hand of God. For ye are dead, and your life is hid with Christ in God."

It is not risen with Christ, but *resurrected.* It is not rising a little higher in the old life, but it is rising from the dead. The resurrection will mean no more than the death has meant. Only so far as we are really dead shall we live with Him.

May 6.

"Reckon ye also yourselves to be alive unto God" (Rom. vi. 11).

Death is but for a moment. Life is forevermore. Live, then, ye children of the resurrection, on His glorious life, more and more abundantly, and the fulness of your life will repel the intrusion of self and sin, and overcome evil with good, and your existence will be, not the dreary repression of your own struggling, but the springing tide of Christ's spontaneous overcoming life.

Once in a religious meeting a dear brother gave us a most exhilarating talk on the risen life. Then another brother got up and talked for a long time on the necessity of self-crucifixion. A cold sweat fell over us all, and we could scarcely understand why. But after he had got through, a good sister clarified the whole situation by saying, that "Pastor S. had taken us all out of the grave by his address, and then Pastor P. has put us back again."

Don't go back into the grave again after you have got out, but live like Him, who "liveth and was dead, and lo! He is alive forevermore, and has the keys of hell and of death." Keep out of the tomb, and keep the door locked, and the keys in His risen hands.

May 7.

"I travail in birth again until Christ be formed in you" (Gal. iv. 19).

It is a blessed moment when we are born again and a new heart is created in us after the image of God. It is a more blessed moment when in this new heart Christ Himself is born and the Christmas time is reproduced in us as we, in some real sense, become incarnations of the living Christ. This is the deepest and holiest meaning of Christianity. It is expressed in Paul's prayer for the Galatians. "My little children, for whom I travail in birth again till Christ be formed in you."

There will yet be a more glorious era when we, like Him, shall be transformed and transfigured into His glory, and in the resurrection shall be, in spirit, soul and body, even as He.

Let us live, under the power of the inspiring thought, incarnations of

Christ; not living our life, but the Christ-life, and showing forth the excellencies, not of ourselves, but of Him who hath called us "out of darkness into His marvelous light"; so our life shall be to all the re-living in our position of the Christ life, as He would have lived it, had He been here.

May 8.

"Except a corn of wheat fall into the ground and die" (John xii. 24).

Death and resurrection are the central ideas of nature and Christianity. We see them in the transformation of the chrysalis, in the buried seed bursting into the bud and blossom of the spring, in the transformation of the winding sheet of winter to the many tinted robes of spring. We see it all through the Bible in the symbol of circumcision, with its significance of death and life, in the passage of the Red Sea and the Jordan leading out and leading in, and in the Cross of Calvary and the open grave of the Easter morning. We see it in every deep spiritual life. Every true life is death-born, and the deeper the dying the truer the living. We doubt not the months that have been passing have shown us all many a place where there ought to be a grave, and many a lingering shred of the natural and sinful which we would gladly lay down in a bottomless grave. God help us to pass the irrevocable sentence of death and to let the Holy Ghost, the great undertaker, make the interment eternal. Then our life shall be ever budding and blossoming and shedding fragrance over all.

May 9.

"All hail" (Matt. xxviii. 9).

It was a stirring greeting which the

Lord of Life spake to His first disciples on the morning of the resurrection. It is a bright and radiant word which in His name we would speak to His beloved children at the commencement of another day. It means a good deal more than appears on the surface. It is really a prayer for our health, but which none but those who believe in the healing of the body can fully understand. A thoughtful friend suggested once that the word "hail" really means health, and it is just the old Saxon form of the word. We all know that a hale person is a healthy person. Our Lord's message, therefore, was substantially that greeting which from time immemorial we give to one another when we meet. "How is your health?" "How are you?" or, better still, "I wish you health." Christ's wish is tantamount to a promise and command. It is very similar to the Apostle John's benediction to his dear friend Gaius, and we would re-echo it to our beloved friends according to the fulness of the Master's will.

May 10.

"I am alive forevermore" (Rev. i. 18).

Here is the message of the Christ of the cross and the still more glorious and precious Christ of the resurrection. It is beautiful and inspiring to note the touch of light and glory with which these simple words invest the cross. It is not said I am He that was dead and liveth, but "I am He that liveth and was dead, but am alive forevermore." Life is mentioned before the death. There are two ways of looking at the cross. One is from the death side and the other from the life side. One is the Ecce Homo and the other is the glorified Jesus with only the marks of the nails and the spear. It is thus we

are to look at the cross. We are not to carry about with us the mould of the sepulchre, but the glory of the resurrection. It is not the Ecce Homo, but the Living Christ. And so our crucifixion is to be so complete that it shall be lost in our resurrection and we shall even forget our sorrow and carry with us the light and glory of the eternal morning. So let us live the death-born life, ever new and full of a life that can never die, because it is "dead and alive forevermore."

May 11.

"Whosoever will save his life shall lose it" (Luke ix. 24).

First and foremost Christ teaches resurrection and life. The power of Christianity is life. It brings us not merely law, duty, example, with high and holy teaching and admonition. It brings us the power to follow the higher ideal and the life that spontaneously does the things commanded. But it is not only life, but resurrection life.

And it begins with a real crisis, a definite transaction, a point of time as clear as the morning dawn. It is not an everlasting dying and an eternal struggle to live. But it is all expressed in a tense that denotes definiteness, fixedness and finished action. We actually died at a certain point and as actually began to live the resurrection life.

Let us reckon ourselves to be dead indeed unto sin, but alive unto God through Jesus Christ.

And death is only the pathway and portal,

To the life that shall die nevermore;

And the cross leadeth up to the crown everlasting,

The Jordan to Canaan's bright shore.

May 12.

"Tell me where Thou makest Thy flock to rest at noon" (Song of Solomon i. 7).

Beloved, do you not long for God's quiet, the inner chambers, the shadow of the Almighty, the secret of His presence? Your life has been, perhaps, all driving and doing, or perhaps straining, struggling, longing and not obtaining. Oh, for rest! to lie down upon His bosom and know that you have all in Him, that every question is answered, every doubt settled, every interest safe, every prayer answered, every desire satisfied. Lift up the cry, "Tell me, O Thou whom my soul loveth, where Thou feedest, where Thou makest Thy flock to rest at noon"!

Blessed be His name! He has this for us, His exclusive love—a love which each individual somehow feels is all for himself, in which he can lie alone upon His breast and have a place which none other can dispute; and yet His heart is so great that He can hold a thousand millions just as near, and each heart seem to possess Him just as exclusively for his own, even as the thousand little pools of water upon the beach can reflect the sun, and each little pool seems to have the whole sun embosomed in its beautiful depths. And Christ can teach us this secret of His inmost love.

May 13.

"Abide in Me" (John xv. 4).

Christianity may mean nothing more than a religious system. Christian life may mean nothing more than an earnest and honest attempt to follow and imitate Christ.

Christ life is more than these, and expresses our actual union with the Lord Jesus Christ, and He is undoubtedly in us as the life and source of all our experience and work.

This conception of the highest Christian life is at once simpler and sublimer than any other. We do not teach in these pages, that the purpose of Christ's redemption is to restore us to Adamic perfection, for if we had it we should lose it to-morrow; but rather to unite us with the Second Adam, and lift us up to a higher plane than our first parents ever knew.

This is the only thing that can reconcile the warring elements of diverse schools of teaching with respect to Christian life.

The Spirit of God will lead us to have no controversy respecting mere theories, but simply hold to the person and life of Jesus Christ Himself, and the privilege of being united to Him, and living in constant dependence upon His keeping power and grace.

May 14.

"But God" (Luke xii. 20).

What else do we really need? What else is He trying to make us understand? The religion of the Bible is wholly supernatural. The one resource of faith has always been the living God, and Him alone. The children of Israel were utterly dependent upon Jehovah as they marched through the wilderness, and the one reason their foes feared them and hastened to submit themselves was that they recognized among them the shout of a King, and the presence of One compared with whom all their strength was vain.

"Wherein," asked Moses, "shall we be separated from all other peoples of the

earth, except it be in this that Thou goest before us."

A church relying on human wisdom, wealth or resources, ceases to be the body of Christ and becomes an earthly society. When we dare to depend entirely upon God and without doubt, the humblest and feeblest agencies will become "mighty through God, to the pulling down of strongholds." May the Holy Spirit give to us at all times, His own conception of these two great words, "But God."

May 15.

"I press toward the mark" (Phil. iii. 14).

We have thought much about what we have received. Let us think of the things we have not received, of some of the vessels that have not yet been filled, of some of the places in our life that the Holy Ghost has not yet possessed for God, and signalized by His glory and His presence.

Shall the coming months be marked by a diligent, heart-searching application of "the rest of the oil," to the yet unoccupied possibilities of our life and service?

Have we known His fulness of grace in our spiritual life? Have we tasted a little of His glory? Have we believed His promise for the mind, the soul, the spirit? Have we known all His possibilities for the body? Have we tested Him in His power to control the events of providence, and to move the hearts of men and nations? Has He opened to us the treasure-house of God, and met our financial needs as He might? Have we even begun to understand the ministry of prayer, as God would have us exercise it? God give us "the rest of the oil"!

May 16.

"It is not in man that walketh to direct his steps" (Jer. x. 23).

United to Jesus Christ as your Redeemer, you are accepted in the Beloved. He does not merely take my place as a man and settle my debts. He does that and more. He comes to give a perfect ideal of what a man should be. He is the model man, not for us to copy, for that would only bring discouragement and utter failure; but He will come and copy Himself in us. If Christ lives in me, I am another Christ. I am not like Him, but I have the same mind. The very Christ is in me. This is the foundation of Christian holiness and Divine healing. Christ is developing a perfect life within us. Some say man can never be perfect. "It is not in man that walketh to direct his steps." We are all a lot of failures. This is true, but we should go further. We must take God's provision for our failure and rise above it through His grace. We must take Jesus as a substitute for our miserable self. We must give up the good as well as the bad and take Him instead. It is hard for us to learn that the very good must go, but we must have Divine impulses instead of even our best attainments.

May 17.

"To him that overcometh, will I give" (Rev. ii. 17).

A precious secret of Christian life is to have Jesus dwelling within the heart and conquering things that we never could overcome. It is the only secret of power in your life and mine, beloved. Men cannot understand it, nor will the world believe it; but it is true, that God will come to dwell within us, and be the power, and the purity, and the victory, and the joy of our life. It is no

longer now, "What is the best that I can do?" but the question is, "What is the best that Christ can do?" It enables us to say, with Paul, in that beautiful passage in Philippians, "I know both how to be abased, and I know how to abound, everywhere and in all things, I am instructed both to be full and to be hungry, both to abound and to suffer need. I can do all things through Christ, which strengtheneth me."

With this knowledge I go forth to meet my testings, and the secret stands me good. It keeps me pure and sweet, as I could never keep myself. Christ has met the adversary and defeated him for me. Thanks be unto God who giveth us the victory through Jesus Christ.

May 18.

"For ye are dead" (Col. iii. 3).

Now, this definite, absolute and final putting off of ourselves in an act of death, is something we cannot do ourselves. It is not self-mortifying, but it is dying with Christ. There is nothing can do it but the Cross of Christ and the Spirit of God. The church is full of half dead people who have been trying, like poor Nero, to slay themselves for years, and have not had the courage to strike the fatal blow. Oh, if they would just put themselves at Jesus' feet, and let Him do it, there would be accomplishment and rest. On that cross He has provided for our death as well as our life, and our part is just to let His death be applied to our nature just as it has been to our old sins, and then leave it with Him, think no more about it, and count it dead, not recognizing it any longer as ourselves, but another, refusing to listen or fear it, to be identified with it, or even try to

cleanse it, but counting it utterly in His hands, and dead to us forever, and for all our new life depending on Him at every breath, as a babe just born depends upon its mother's life.

May 19.

"He purgeth it that it may bring forth more fruit" (John xv. 2).

Recently we passed a garden. The gardener had just finished his pruning, and the wounds of the knife and saw were just beginning to heal, while the warm April sun was gently nourishing the stricken plant into fresh life and energy. We thought as we looked at that plant how cruel it would be to begin next week and cut it down. Now, the gardener's business is to revive and nourish it into life. Its business is not to die, but to live. So, we thought, it is with the discipline of the soul. It, too, has its dying hour; but it must not be always dying: Rather reckon ourselves to be dead indeed unto sin, but alive unto God through Jesus Christ our Lord. Death is but a moment. Live, then, ye children of the resurrection, on His glorious life more and more abundantly, and the fulness of your life will repel the intrusion of self and sin, and overcome evil with good, and your existence will be, not the dreary repression of your own struggling, but the springing tide of Christ's spontaneous overcoming and everlasting life.

May 20.

"Ye are not your own" (I. Cor. vi. 19).

What a privilege that we may consecrate ourselves. What a mercy that God will take us worthless worms. What rest and comfort lie hidden in those words, "Not my own."

Not responsible for my salvation, not burdened by my cares, not obliged to live for my interests, but altogether His; redeemed, owned, saved, loved, kept in the strong, unchanging arms of His everlasting love. Oh, the rest from sin and self and cankering care which true consecration brings! To be able to give Him our poor weak life, with its awful possibilities and its utter helplessness, and know that He will accept it, and take a joy and pride in making out of it the utmost possibilities of blessing, power and usefulness; to give all, and find in so doing we have gained all; to be so yielded to Him in entire self surrender, that He is bound to care for us as for Himself. We are putting ourselves in the hands of a loving Father, more solicitous for our good than we can be and only wanting us to be fully submitted to Him that He may be more free to bless us.

May 21.

"We will come unto Him and make our abode with Him" (John xiv. 23).

The Bible has always held out two great promises respecting Christ. First, I will come to you; and, second, I will come into you. For four thousand years the world looked forward to the fulfilment of the first. The other is the secret which Paul says has been hid from ages and generations, but is now made manifest to His saints, which is Christ in you, the hope of glory. This is just as great a revelation of God as the incarnation of Jesus, for it makes you like Christ, as free from sin as He is. If Christ is in you, what will be the consequences? Why, He will put you aside entirely. The I in you will go. You will say, "Not I, but Christ." Christ undertakes your battles for you. Christ becomes purity and grace and

strength in you. You do not try to attain unto these things, but you know you have obtained them in Him. It is glorious rest with the Master. Jesus does not say, "Now we must bring forth fruit, we must pray much, we must do this or that." There is no constraint about it, except that we must abide in Him. That is the center of all joy and help.

May 22.

"Fight the good fight of faith" (I. Tim. vi. 12).

Oh, beloved, how must God feel about us after He has given us His heart's blood, put so many advantages in our way, expended upon us so much grace and care, if we should disappoint Him. It makes the spirit cry, "Who is sufficient for these things?" Evermore I can see before me the time when you and I shall stand on yonder shore and look back upon the years that have been, these few short years of time. Oh, may we cast ourselves at Jesus' feet and say: "Many a time have we faltered; many a hard fight has come, but Thou hast kept me and held me, thanks to God, who has given me the victory through the Lord Jesus Christ." From the battlefields of the Peninsula, a little band of veterans came forth, and they gave each a medal with the names of all their battles on one side, and on the other side this little sentence, "I was there." Oh, when that hour shall come, may it be a glad, glad thought to look back over the trials and sacrifices of these days and remember, "I was there, and by the help of God and the grace of Jesus, I am here."

May 23.

"The fulness of the blessing of the

Gospel of Christ" (Rom. xv. 29).

Many Christians fail to see these blessings as they are centered in Him. They want to get the blessing of salvation, but that is not the Christ. They want to get the blessing of His grace to help, but that is not Him. They want to get answered prayer from Him to work for Him. You might have all that and not have the blessing of Christ Himself. A great many people are attached rather to the system of doctrine. They say, "Yes, I have got the truth; I am orthodox." That is not the Christ. It may be the cold statue in the fountain with the water passing from the cold hands and lips, but no life there. A great many other people want to get the blessing of joy, but it is not the blessing of Christ personally. A great many people are more attached to their church and pastor, or to dear Christians friends, but that is not the Christ. The blessing that will alone fill your heart when all else fails is the loving heart of Jesus united to you, the fountain of all your blessings and the unfailing one when they all wither and are exhausted—Jesus Christ Himself.

May 24.

"Where is the way where light dwelleth" (Job xxxviii. 19).

Jewels, in themselves, are valueless, unless they are brought in contact with light. If they are put in certain positions they will reflect the beauty of the sun. There is no beauty in them otherwise. The diamond that is back in its dark gallery or down in the deep mine, displays no beauty whatever. What is it but a piece of charcoal, a bit of common carbon, unless it becomes a medium for reflecting light? And so it is also with the other precious gems.

Their varied tints are nothing without light. If they are many-sided, they reflect more light, and display more beauty. If you put paste beside a diamond there is no brilliancy in it. In its crude state it does not reflect light at all. So we are in a crude state and are of no use at all until God comes and shines upon us. The light that is in a diamond is not its own possession; it is the beauty of the sun. What beauty is there in the child of God? Only the beauty of Jesus. We are His peculiar people, chosen to show forth His excellencies who hath called us out of darkness into His marvelous light. Let its reflect to-day His light and love.

May 25.

"That I may know Him" (Phil. iii. 10).

Better to know Jesus Himself than to know the truth about Him for the deep things of God as they are revealed by the Holy Ghost. It was Paul's great desire, "That I may know Him," not about Him, not the mysteries of the wonderful world, of the deeper and higher teachings of God, but to enter into the Holy of Holies, where Christ is, where the Shekinah is shining and making the place glorious with the holiness of God, and then to enter into the secret of the Lord Himself. It was what Jacob strove for at Peniel, when he pleaded with God, "Tell me Thy name." He has told us His name, giving us "the light of the knowledge of the glory of God in the face of Jesus Christ." That is the secret. It is the Lord Himself, and nothing else; it is acquaintance with God; it is knowing Jesus Christ as we know no one else; it is being able to say, not only "I believe Him," but "I know Him"; not about Him, but I know Him. That is the secret above all others that God wants us to have; it is His provision for glory

and power, and it is given freely to the single-hearted seeker.

May 26.

"Be careful for nothing; but in everything by prayer and supplication with thanksgiving let your requests be made known unto God" (Phil. iv. 6).

Commit means to hand over, to trust wholly to another. So, if we give our trials to Him, He will carry them. If we walk in righteousness He will carry us through. "Humble yourselves, therefore, under the mighty hand of God that He may exalt you in due time." There are two hands there—God's hand pressing us down, humbling us, and then God's hand lifting us up. Cast all your care on Him, then His hand will lift you up, exalt you in due time. There are two cares in this verse—your care and His care. They are different in the original. One means anxious care, the other means Almighty care. Cast your anxious care on Him and take His Almighty care instead. Make no account of trouble any more, but believe He is able to sustain you through it. The government is on His shoulder. Believe that, if you trust and obey Him, and meet His will, He will look after your interests. Simply exchange burdens. Take His yoke upon you, and let Him care for you.

May 27.

"The government shall be upon His shoulder" (Isa. ix. 6).

You cannot make the heart restful by stopping its beating. Belladonna will do that, but that is not rest. Let the breath of life come—God's life and strength—and there will be sweet rest. Home ties and family affection will not bring it. Deliverance from trouble will not bring it. Many a tried heart has said: "If this great trouble was only gone, I should have rest." But as soon as one goes another comes. The poor, wounded deer on the mountain side, thinks if he could only bathe in the old mountain stream he would have rest. But the arrow is in its flesh and there is no rest for it till the wound is healed. It is as sore in the mountain lake as on the plain. We shall never have God's rest and peace in the heart till we have given everything up to Christ—even our work—and believe He has taken it all, and we have only to keep still and trust. It is necessary to walk in holy obedience and let Him have the government on His shoulder. Paul said this: "This one thing I do." There is one narrow path for us all—Christ's will and work for us.

May 28.

"He humbled Himself" (Phil. ii. 8).

One of the hardest things for a lofty and superior nature is to be under authority, to renounce his own will, and to take a place of subjection. But Christ took upon Him the form of a servant, gave up His independence, His right to please Himself, His liberty of choice, and after having from eternal ages known only to command, gave Himself up only to obey. I have seen occasionally the man who was once a wealthy employer a clerk in the same store. It was not an easy or graceful position, I assure you. But Jesus was such a perfect servant that His Father said: "Behold, My Servant in whom My soul delighteth." All His life His watchword was, "The Son of Man came to minister." "I am among you as He that doth serve." "I can do nothing of Myself." "Not My will, but Thine, be done." Have you, beloved,

learned the servant's place?

And once more, "He became obedient unto death, even the death of the cross." His life was all a dying, and at last He gave all up to death, and also shame, the death of crucifixion. This last was the consummation of His love.

May 29.

"The body is for the Lord and the Lord for the body" (I. Cor. vi. 13).

Now, just as it was Christ Himself who justified us, and Christ Himself who was made unto us sanctification, so it is only by personal union with Him that we can receive this physical life and redemption. It is, indeed, not a touch of power upon our body which restores and then leaves it to the mere resources of natural strength and life for the future; but it is the vital and actual union of our mortal body with the risen body of our Lord Jesus Christ, so that His own very life comes into our frame and He is Himself made unto us strength, health and full physical redemption.

He is alive forevermore and condescends to live in these houses of clay. They who thus receive Him may know Him as none ever can who exclude Him from the bodies which He has made for Himself. This is one of the deep and precious mysteries of the Gospel. "The body is for the Lord, and the Lord for the body." "Know ye not that your body is the temple of the Holy Ghost, which is in you, and ye are not your own, for ye are bought with a price; therefore, glorify God in your body, which is God's." (R. V.)

May 30.

"I will put My Spirit within you" (Ez. xxxvi. 27).

"I will put My Spirit within you, and I will cause you to walk in My statutes, and ye shall keep My judgments." "I will put My fear in your hearts, and ye shall not turn away from Me." Oh, friend, would not that be blessed, would not that be such a rest for you, all worn out with this strife in your own strength? Do you not want a strong man to conquer the strong man of self and sin? Do you not want a leader? Do you not want God Himself to be with you, to be your occupant? Do you not want rest? Are you not conscious of this need? Oh, this sense of being beaten back, longing, wanting, but not accomplishing. That is what He comes to do; "Ye shall receive power after that the Holy Ghost has come upon you." Better than that, "Ye shall receive the power of the Holy Ghost coming upon you." That is the true version, and really it is immensely different from the other. You shall not receive power yourself, so that people shall say: "How much power that man has. You shall not have any power whatever, but you shall receive the power of the Holy Ghost coming upon you, He having the power, that is all."

May 31.

"Whosoever therefore shall humble himself as this little child" (Matt. xviii. 4).

You will never get a humble heart until it is born from above, from the heart of Christ. For man has lost his own humanity and alas, too often has a demon heart. God wants us, as Christians, to be simple, human, approachable and childlike. The Christians that we know and love best, and that are nearest to the Lord, are the most simple. Whenever we grow stilted we are only fit for a picture

gallery, and we are only good on a pedestal; but, if we are going to live among men and love and save them, we must be approachable and human. All stiffness is but another form of self-consciousness. Ask Christ for a human heart, for a smile that will be as natural as your little child's in your presence. Oh, how much Christ did by little touches! He never would have got at the woman of Samaria if He had come to her as the prophet. He sat down, a tired man, and said: "Give me a drink of water." And so, all through His life, it was His simple humanness and love that led Him to others, and led them to Him and to His great salvation.

June 1.

"That the righteousness of the law might be fulfilled in us" (Rom. viii. 4).

Beloved friends, do you know the mistake some of you are making? Some of you say: "It is not possible for me to be good; no man ever was perfect, and it is no use for me to try." That is the mistake many of you are making. I agree with the first sentence, "No man ever was perfect"; but I don't agree with the second, "There is no use trying." There is a divine righteousness that we may have. I don't mean merely that which pardons your sins—I believe that, too—but I mean far more; I mean that which comes into your soul and unites itself with the fibers of your being; I mean Christ; your life, your purity, making you feel as Christ feels; think as Christ thinks, love as Christ loves, hate as Christ hates, and be "partakers of the divine nature." That is God's righteousness; "that the righteousness of the law might be fulfiled in us," not by us, but in us; not our hands and feet merely, but our very instincts, our very

desires, our very nature springing up in harmony with His own. Have you got Him, dear friends? He will come and fulfil all right things in you if to-day you will open your heart.

June 2.

"As ye have therefore received Christ Jesus the Lord so walk ye in Him" (Col. ii. 6).

Here is the very core of spiritual life. It is not a subjective state so much as a life in the heart. Christ for us is the ground of our salvation and the source of our justification; Christ in us of our sanctification. When this becomes real, "Ye are dead"; your own condition, states and resources are no longer counted upon any more than a dead man's, but "your life is hid with Christ in God." It is not even always manifest to you. It is hid and so wrapped up and enfolded in Him that only as you abide in Him does it appear and abide. Nay, "Christ who is your life," must Himself ever maintain it, and be made unto you of God all you need. Therefore, Christian life is not to come to Christ to save you, and then go on and work out your sanctification yourself, but "as ye have received Christ Jesus, the Lord, so to walk in Him," just as dependent and as simply trusting as for your pardon and salvation.

Ah friends, how much it would ease our tasks

For the day that's just begun,

To live our life a step at a time

And our moments one by one.

June 3.

"Ye shall receive the power of the Holy Ghost" (Acts i. 8).

There is power for us if we have the Holy Ghost. God wants us to speak to men so that they will feel it, so that they will never forget it. God means every Christian to be effective, to count in the actual records and results of Christian work. Dear friends, God sent you here to be a power yourself. There is not one of you but is an essential wheel of the machinery, and can accomplish all that God calls you to. I solemnly believe that there is not a thing that God expects of man but that God will give the man power to do. There is not a claim God makes on you or me but God will stand up to, and will give what He commands. I believe when Christ Jesus lived and died and sent down the Holy Ghost, He sent resources for all our need, and that there is no place for failure in Christian life if we will take God's resources. Jesus, the ascended One, and the Holy Ghost, the indwelling energy, life and efficiency of God, are sufficient for all possible emergencies. Do you believe this? If you believe it, let Him into your heart, without reserve and allow Him to control and work through you to-day by His power.

June 4.

"Looking unto Jesus" (Heb. xii. 2).

There must be a constant looking unto Jesus, or, as the German Bible gives it, an off-looking upon Jesus; that is, looking off from the evil, refusing to see it, not letting the mind dwell upon it for a second. We should have mental eyelashes as well as physical ones, which can be used like shields, and let no evil thing in; or, like a stockade camp in the woods, which repels the first assault of the enemy. This is the use of the fringes to our eyes, and so it should be with the soul. Many do not seem to know that they have spiritual eyes. They go through the world as if somebody had cut off their eyelashes, and they stare away on the good and evil alike. The devil comes along with his evil pictures and bids them look. We cannot look upon evil without being defiled. Sometimes, in going down the street, the sight of some of the pictures on the way will cast their filth upon the soul so that we shall feel the need of being bathed in Jesus' blood for hours for cleansing. There has been no consent unto sin, but the sight of it has defiled. There is no help for it but in the resolute, steady, inner view of Christ.

June 5.

"My heart is fixed, O God" (Ps. lvii. 7).

We do not always feel joyful, but we are always to count it joy. This word *reckon* is one of the keywords of Scripture. It is the same word used about our being dead. We are painfully conscious of something which would gladly return to life. But we are to treat ourselves as dead, and neither fear nor obey the old nature. So we are to reckon the thing that comes a blessing; we are determined to rejoice, to say, "My heart is fixed, Lord; I will sing and give praises." This rejoicing by faith will soon become a habit, and will ever bring speedily the spirit of gladness and the spontaneous overflow of praise.

Then, although the fig tree may wither and no fruit appear in the vines, the labor of the olive fail, and the field yield no increase, the herd be cut off from the stall, and the cattle from the field, yet will we rejoice in the Lord and joy in the God of our salvation.

Though the everlasting mountains

And the earth itself remove,

Naught can change His loving kindness

Or His everlasting love.

June 6.

"He emptied Himself" (Phil. ii. 8, R. V.).

The first step to the righteousness of the kingdom is "poor in spirit." Then the next is a little deeper, "they that mourn." Because now you must get plastic, you must get broken, you must get like the metal in the fire, which the Master can mould; and so, it is not enough to see your unrighteousness, but deeply to feel it, deeply to regret it, deeply to mourn over it, to own it not a little thing that sin has come into your life. And so God leads a soul unto His righteousness. He usually leads it through some testings and trials. This generally comes after conversion. I do not think it necessary for a soul to have deep and great suffering before it is saved. I think He will put it into the fire when He knows it is saved; when it realizes it is accepted; when it is not afraid of the discipline; when it is not the hand of wrath, but the hand of love. Oh, then, God, takes you down and makes you poor in spirit, and makes you mourn until you get to the third step, which is to be meek, broken, yielded, submissive, willing, surrendered, and laid low at His feet, crying: "What wilt Thou have me to do?"

June 7.

"When ye go; ye shall not go empty" (Ex. iii. 21).

When we are really emptied He would have us filled with Himself and the Holy Spirit. It is very precious to be conscious of nothing good in ourselves; but, oh, are we also conscious of His great goodness? We may be ready to admit our own disability, but are we as ready to admit His ability? There are many Christians who can say, "We are not sufficient of ourselves to think anything as of ourselves"; but the number I fear is very small who can say, "Our sufficiency is of God."

Are you sure that He is able to provide every want in you, or do you feel that you must supply it yourself? Are you believing that God does now supply every lack in your heart and your life, so that all stumbling is taken away, and you are endowed with power for His service, as Elisha took the empty vessels and filled them before they were set aside to be used? Our Saviour, at Cana, ordered the water-pots to be filled to the brim. Then the water was made into wine, but not until the vessels were full. God wants His children to have always a full heart.

June 8.

"Bread corn is bruised" (Isa. xxviii. 28).

The farmer does not gather timothy and blue grass, and break it with a heavy machine. But he takes great pains with the wheat. So God takes great pains with those who are to be of much use to Him. There is a nature in them that needs this discipline. Don't wonder if the bread corn is treated with the wise, discriminating care that will fit it for food. He knows the way He is taking, and there is infinite tenderness in the oversight He gives. He is watching the furnace you are in lest the heat should be too intense. He wants it great enough to purify, and then it is withdrawn. He knoweth our

frame. He will not let any temptation take us but such as is common to man, and He will with the temptation also make a way to escape, that we may be able to bear it. Do you believe in this disciplining love of the Husbandman, and are you trusting Him with the leading and government of your life? Oh, that you would cease to envy or be disturbed by the people around you! Some day you will be glad for the training and blessing they have brought you.

June 9.

"Ye are the light of the world" (Matt. v. 14).

We are called the lights of the world, light-bearers, reflectors, candle-sticks, lamps. We are to be kindled ourselves, and then we will burn and give light to others. We are the only light the world has. The Lord might come down Himself and give light to the world, but He has chosen differently. He wants to send it through us, and if we don't give it the world will not have it. We should be giving light all the time to our neighbors. God does not put a meteor in the sky to tell us when to shine. We are to be giving light all the time wherever we are, at home, or in the social circle, or in our place in the church. We should feel always we may never have another opportunity for it, and so we should always be burning and shining for Him. Let our lamps be trimmed and burning and full of the oil of the Spirit. Above all, let us be a steady light to the lost ones.

Let me dwell in Timnath Serah,

Where the sun forever shines,

Where the night and darkness come not,

And the day no more declines.

June 10.

"Your heavenly Father knoweth ye have need" (Matt. vi. 32).

Christ makes no less of our trust for temporal things than He does for spiritual things. He places a good deal of emphasis upon it. Why? Simply because it is harder to trust God for them. In spiritual matters we can fool ourselves, and think that we are trusting when we are not; but we cannot do so about rent and food, and the needs of our body. They must come or our faith fails. It is easy to say that we trust Him in things that are a long way off, but there can be no trifling about it in things where the faith must bring practical answers. It is easy to have faith for our needs, and to trust Him when the sun is shining. But let some things arise which irritate and rasp and fret us, and we soon find whether we have real trust or not. And so the things of everyday life are tests of our real faith in God, and He often puts us where we have to trust for tangible matters—for money and rent, and food and clothes. If you are not trusting here wholly, when you are placed in such tests you will break down. Are you trusting God for everything through the six ordinary days of the week?

June 11.

"Thou hast the dew of thy youth" (Ps. cx. 3).

Oh, that you might get such a view of Him as would make it impossible for little things ever to fret you again! The petty cares and silly trifles that have troubled you so much ought rather to fill you with wonder that you can think so much about them. Oh, if you had the dew of His youth you should go forth as the morning and fulfil the

promise of a glorious day! What a difference it has made in life since we have seen it was possible to do this! How easy it seems now when the little troubles come, to draw a little closer to Christ, to drink in a little more of that fountain of life, to get a little nearer to that loving heart, and to draw in great draughts of refreshing and strength from it. How clear it makes the brain for work! Coming to Him thus, heavy and dull and tired, how rested you become and able to spring forth ready for work. How inspiring to think that our living Head never grows weary. He is as fresh as He ever was; He is a glorious conqueror; He is ever the victorious Christ. Let Him take you to-day, and He will cause you to see in Him the invincible Leader!

June 12.

"We would see Jesus" (John xii. 21).

Glory to Him for all the things laid up for us in the days to come. Glory to Him for all the visions of service in the future; the opportunities of doing good that are far away as well as close at hand. Our Saviour was able to despise the cross for the joy that was before Him. Let us look up to Him, and rise up to Him till we get on high and are able to look out from the mount of vision over all the land of far distances. There shall not a single thing come to us in all the future in which we may not be able to see the King in His beauty. Let us be very sure that we do not see anything else. Our pupils will become impressed as they look at this vision, so that they will not be able to reflect anything else. My little child came to me once and said: "Papa, look at that golden sign across the street a good while; now look at that brick wall and tell me what you see." "Why, I see the golden sign on the brick wall." And he laughed merrily over it. So, if we look a long time upon Jesus we cannot look at anything else without seeing a reflection of Him. Everything which we behold will become a part of Him.

June 13.

"The sweetness of the lips increaseth learning" (Prov. xvi. 21).

Life is very largely made up of words. They are not so emphatic, perhaps, as deeds. Deeds are more deliberate expressions of thought. One of the most remarkable authors of the New Testament has said, "If any man offend not in word, the same is a perfect man." It is very often a test of victory in Christian life. Our triumph in this often depends on what we say, or what we do not say. It is said by James of the tongue, "It is set on fire of hell." The true Christian, therefore, is righteous in his ways and upright in his words. His deeds appeal to men; but in speech he is looking up, for God is listening. His words are sent upward and recorded for the judgment. I believe that this is an actual fact, and I can almost fancy that the skies above, which seem so transparent, the beautiful blue ether over our heads, is like a waxen tablet with a finely sensitive surface, and receives an impression of every word we speak, and that then these tablets are hardened and preserved for the eternal judgment. So we should speak, dear friends, with our eyes ever upward, never forgetting that we shall some day meet the words that we have spoken.

June 14.

"The secret of the Lord is with them that fear Him" (Ps. xxv. 14).

There are secrets of Providence which God's dear children may learn. His dealing with them often seems, to the outward eye, dark and terrible. Faith looks deeper and says, "This is God's secret. You look only on the outside; I can look deeper and see the hidden meaning." Sometimes diamonds are done up in rough packages, so that their value cannot be seen. When the tabernacle was built in the wilderness there was nothing rich in its outside appearance. The costly things were all within, and its outward covering of rough badger skin gave no hint of the valuable things which it contained. God may send you, dear friends, some costly packages. Do not worry if they are done up in rough wrappings. You may be sure there are treasures of love, and kindness and wisdom hidden within. Do not be so foolish as to throw away a nugget of gold because there is some quartz in it. If we take what He sends, and trust Him for the goodness in it, even in the dark, we shall learn the meaning of the secrets of His providence.

June 15.

"Grow up into Him in all things" (Eph. iv. 15).

Harvest is a time of ripeness. Then the fruit and grain are fully developed, both in size and weight. Time has tempered the acid of the green fruit. It has been mellowed and softened by the rains and the heat of summer. The sun has tinted it into rich colors, and at last it is ready and ripe to fall into the hand. So Christian life ought to be. There are many things in life that need to be mellowed and ripened. Many Christians have orchards full of fruit, but they are all green and sharp to the taste. There is a great deal in them that is good, but it is incomplete, and very

sharp and sour. Perhaps something goes wrong in your domestic life, and you get flurried and cross and lose your confidence in God, and then, of course, your Christian joy. These things produce regret and all kinds of misery. There are many things day after day you are sorry for. You know you are not ripe and mellow and you cannot become so by trying. You cannot bring the sweetness in. It must be wrought out from within.

June 16.

"Ye cannot serve God and Mammon" (Matt. vi. 24).

He does not say ye cannot very well serve God and mammon, but ye cannot serve two masters at all. Ye shall be sure to end by serving one. The man who thinks he is serving God a little is deceived; he is not serving God. God will not have his service. The devil will monopolize him before he gets through. A divided heart loses both worlds. Saul tried it. Balaam tried it. Judas tried it, and they all made a desperate failure. Mary had but one choice. Paul said: "This one thing I do." "For me to live is Christ." Of such a life God says: "Because he hath set his love upon Me therefore will I deliver him. I will set him on high because he hath known My name." God takes a peculiar pride in showing His love to the heart that wholly chooses Him. Heaven and earth will fade away before its trust can be disappointed. Have we chosen Him only and given Him all our heart?

Say is it all for Jesus,

As you so often sing?

Is He your Royal Master?

Is He your heart's dear King?

June 17.

"The glory of the Lord shall be thy reward" (Isa. lviii. 8).

He comes by our side as our helper; nay, more. He comes to dwell within us; to be the life in our blood, the fire in our thought, the faith within us, both in inception and consummation. Thus He becomes not only the recompense of the victor, but the resources of the victory. He is the Captain and the Overcomer in our lives. If we have caught any help that has relieved us of a troubled morning, it has been of Him. He lifts our eyes up unto Himself and delivers us from apathy, from discontent and from fears. He is always the helper in this heavenly competition, and will be the great reward in all the ages to come. If our life is hidden with Him we shall have to go through the same trials that He went through, but we shall not find them too hard. If once we take Him fully as the strength of our life, and our all in all, we shall be able to lay aside all the hindering things that press upon us day by day.

I have overcome, overcome,

Overcome for thee,

Thou shalt overcome, overcome,

Overcome thro' Me.

June 18.

"I am doing a great work, so that I cannot come down" (Neh. vi. 3).

When work is pressing there are many little things that will come and seem to need attention. Then it is a very blessed thing to be quiet and still, and work on, and trust the little things with God. He answers such trust in a wonderful way. If the soul has no time to fret and worry and harbor care, it has learned the secret of faith in God. A desperate desire to get some difficulty right takes the eye off of God and His glory. Some dear ones have been so anxious to get well, and have spent so much time in trying to claim it, that they have lost their spiritual blessing. God sometimes has to teach such souls that there must be a willingness to be sick before they are so thoroughly yielded as to receive His fullest blessing.

The enemy often keeps at this work. Sanballat came four times to Nehemiah and received always the same answer. It is best to stick to a good answer. How many fears we have stopped to fight which have proved to be nothing at last. Nehemiah recognized that fear was sin, and did not dare to yield to it.

June 19.

"Who hath first given to Him, and it shall be recompensed unto him again" (Rom. xi. 35).

The Christian women of the world have it in their power, by a very little sacrifice, to add millions to the treasury of the Lord. Beloved sisters, have you found the joy of sacrifice for Jesus? Have you given up something that you might give it to Him? Are you giving your substance to Jesus? He will take it, and He will give you a thousandfold more. I should rather be connected with a work founded on great sacrifice than on enormous endowments. The reason God loved the place where His ancient temple rose in majesty was because there Abraham offered his son and David his treasure. The reason redemption is so dear to the Father and the heavenly world is because its foundation-stone is the Cross of Calvary. And the

Christian life that is dearest to the heart of God, and will rise to the highest glory and usefulness, is the one whose foundation principle is sacrifice and self-renunciation. This is why the Master teaches us to give, because giving means loving, and love is but another name for life.

June 20.

"Let every man abide in the same calling wherein he was called" (I. Cor. vii. 20).

O ye who complain about your calling or fret about the changes and trials of life, how do you know but that these very changes are the divine methods by which God's purposes of blessing and usefulness concerning you be fulfilled? Had Aquila not been compelled to leave Rome and break up his home and business, he would probably have never met with Paul, and been called to the knowledge and service of Christ through this providential meeting. Had he not been a working man, and pursuing his ordinary avocation he would not have been brought into contact with the apostle. It was in the line of their calling, their common duties, and the providential changes of their life that God called them. And so He meets us. Do not try hard to run away from it, but, as the apostle has so finely put it, "Let every man abide in the same calling wherein he is called, let him therein abide with God." Make the most of your incidental opportunities.

June 21.

"God hath set some in the church ... helps" (I. Cor. xii. 28).

In the apostle's lists of officers in the church the "helps" are mentioned before the "governments." By the ministry of prayer, by the ministry of giving, by the ministry of encouragement, by the shining face and mute pressure of the hand, and a little word of cheer, and by the countless ways in which we can help, or at least can keep from hindering, we can all find still the footprints of Aquila and Priscilla, if we want to follow them. It is a great grace to be able to rejoice in another's work and pour our lives, like affluent rivers, into great streams. But God knows whence every drop has come, and in the greater day of recompense many of the helps shall have the chief reward. Beloved, are you helping? Are you helping your pastor, your brother, your husband, your mother, your fellow-worker, and when the harvest comes shall he that soweth and he that reapeth rejoice together?

You can help by holy prayer,

Helpful love and joyful song,

O, the burdens you may bear,

O, the sorrows you may share,

O, the crowns you yet may wear,

If you help along.

June 22.

"This is that bread which came down from heaven" (John vi. 58).

We had the sentence of death in ourselves that we should not trust in ourselves, but in God which raiseth the dead; who delivereth us from so great a death, who doth deliver; in whom we trust that He will yet deliver us. This was the supernatural secret of Paul's life; he drew continually in his body from the strength of Christ, his Risen Head. The body which rose from Joseph's tomb was to him a physical reality and the inexhaustible

fountain of his vital forces. More than any other he has imparted to us the secret of His strength; "We are members of His body, of His flesh and of His bones"; "The Lord is for the body and the body is for the Lord." Marvelous truth! Divine Elixir of Life and Fountain of Perpetual Youth! Earnest of the Resurrection! Fulfilment of the ancient psalms and songs of faith! "The Lord is the strength of my life, of whom shall I be afraid? My flesh and my heart faint and fail, but God is the strength of my heart and my portion forever." Beloved, have we learned this secret, and are we living the life of the Incarnate One in our flesh?

June 23.

"Now we are the sons of God, and it doth not yet appear what we shall be" (I. John iii. 2).

We are the sons of God. We are not merely called and even legally declared, but actually are sons of God by receiving the life and nature of God; and so we are the very brethren of our Lord; not only in His human nature, but still more in His divine relationship. "Therefore, He is not ashamed to call us brethren." He gives us that which entitles us to that right, and makes us worthy of it. He does not introduce us into a position for which we are uneducated and unfitted, but He gives us a nature worthy of our glorious standing; and as He shall look upon us in our complete and glorious exaltation reflecting His own likeness and shining in His Father's glory, He shall have no cause to be ashamed of us. Even now He is pleased to acknowledge us before the universe and call us brethren in the sight of all earth and heaven. Oh, how this dignifies the humblest saint of God!

How little we need mind the misunderstanding of the world if He "is not ashamed to call us brethren."

So let us go out to-day to represent His royal family.

June 24.

"I will clothe thee with change of raiment" (Zech. iii. 4).

For Paul every exercise of the Christian life was simply the grace of Jesus Christ imparted to him and lived out by him, so that holiness was to put on the Lord Jesus and all the robes of His perfect righteousness which he loves to describe so often in his beautiful epistles. "Put on therefore, as the elect of God, holy and beloved," he says to the Colossians, "bowels of mercies, kindness, humbleness of mind, meekness, long suffering"; and, "above all these things, put on love which is the bond of perfectness." None of these things are regarded as intrinsic qualities in us, but as imparted graces from the hand of Jesus. And even in the later years of his life, and after the mature experience of a quarter of a century we find him exclaiming, "I count all things but loss for the excellency of the knowledge of Christ Jesus, my Lord; for whom I have suffered the loss of all things, and count them but refuse, that I might win Christ and be found in Him."

Lord, enable us to-day to go out, clothed in Thy robes of perfect rightness and with our hearts in adjustment with Thy perfect love.

June 25.

"Who leadeth us in triumph" (II. Cor. ii. 14).

Every victor must first be a self-conqueror. But the method of Joshua's victory was the uplifted arm of Moses on the Mount. As he held up his hands Joshua prevailed, as he lowered them Amalek prevailed. It was to be a battle of faith and not of human strength, and the banner that was to wave over the discomfited foe, "Jehovah-nissi." This, too, is the secret of our spiritual triumph. "If we are led of the Spirit we shall not fulfil the lusts of the flesh." "Sin shall not have dominion over you, for ye are not under the law but under grace."

Have we thus begun the battle and in the strength of Christ planted our feet on our own necks, and thus victorious over the enemy in the citadel of the heart been set at liberty for the battle of the Lord and the service of others? It was the lack of this that hindered the life of Saul and it has wrecked many a promising career. One enemy in the heart is stronger than ten thousand in the field. May the Lord lead us all into Joshua's first triumph, and show us the secret of self-crucifixion through the greater Joshua, who alone can lead us on to holiness and victory!

June 26.

"When He saw the multitudes He was moved" (Matt. ix. 36).

He is able to be "touched with the feeling of our infirmities." The word "touched" expresses a great deal. It means that our troubles are His troubles, and that in all our afflictions He is afflicted. It is not a sympathy of sentiment, but a sympathy of suffering.

There is much help in this for the tired heart. It is the foundation of His Priesthood, and God meant that it should be to us a source of unceasing consolation. Let us realize, more fully, our oneness with our Great High Priest, and cast all our burdens on His great heart of love. If we know what it is to ache in every nerve with the responsive pain of our suffering child, we can form some idea of how our sorrows touch His heart, and thrill His exalted frame. As the mother feels her babe's pain, as the heart of friendship echoes every cry from another's woe, so in heaven, our exalted Saviour, even amid the raptures of that happy world, is suffering in His Spirit and even in His flesh with all His children bear. "Seeing then we have such a great high Priest, let us come boldly to the throne of grace," and let us come to our great High Priest.

June 27.

"Be filled with the Spirit" (Eph. v. 18).

Some of the effects of being filled with the Spirit are:

1. Holiness of heart and life. This is not the perfection of the human nature, but the holiness of the divine nature dwelling within.

2. Fulness of joy so that the heart is constantly radiant. This does not depend on circumstances, but fills the spirit with holy laughter in the midst of the most trying surroundings.

3. Fulness of wisdom, light and knowledge, causing us to see things as He sees them.

4. An elevation, improvement and quickening of the mind by an ability to receive the fulfilment of the promise, "We have the mind of Christ."

5. An equal quickening of the physical life. The body was made for the Holy Ghost, as well as the mind and soul.

6. An ability to pray the prayer of the

Holy Ghost. If He is in us there will be a strange accordance with God's working in the world around us. There is a divine harmony between the Spirit and Providence.

June 28.

"Leaning upon her beloved" (Songs of Solomon viii. 5).

Shall you make the claim most practical and real and lean like John your full weight on the Lord's breast? That is the way He would have us prove our love. "If you love me lean hard," said a heathen woman to her missionary, as she was timidly leaning her tired body upon her stalwart breast. She felt slighted by the timorous reserve, and asked the confidence that would lay all its weight upon the one she trusted. And He says to us, "Casting all your care upon Him for He careth for you." He would have us prove our love by a perfect trust that makes no reserve. He is able to carry all our care, to manage all our interests, to satisfy all our needs. Let us go forth leaning on His breast and feeding on His life. For John not only leaned but also fed. It was at supper that he leaned. This is the secret of feeding on Him, to rest upon His bosom. This is the need of the fevered heart of man. Let us cry to Him, "Tell me whom my soul loveth, where thou feedest, where thou makest thy flock to rest at noon."

June 29.

"He dwelleth with you and shall be in you" (John xiv. 17).

Do not fail to mark these two stages in Christian life. The one is the Spirit's work in us, the other is the Spirit's personal coming to abide within us.

All true Christians know the first, but few, it is to be feared, understand and receive the second. There is a great difference between my building a house and my going to reside in that house and make it my home. And there is a great difference between the Holy Spirit's work in regenerating a soul—the building of a house, and His coming to reside, abide and control in our innermost spirit and our whole life and being.

Have we received Him Himself not as our Guest, but as the Owner, Proprietor and Keeper of the temple He has built to be "an habitation of God through the Spirit"?

This is my wonderful story,

Christ to my heart has come,

Jesus the King of glory,

Finds in my heart a home.

I am so glad I received Him,

Jesus, my heart's dear King,

I, who so often have grieved Him,

All to His feet would bring.

June 30.

"Therefore, choose" (Deut. xxx. 19).

Men are choosing every day the spiritual or earthly. And as we choose we are taking our place unconsciously with the friends of Christ, or the world. It is not merely what ye say, it is what we prefer.

When Solomon made his great choice at Gibeon, God said to him, "Because this was in thine heart to ask wisdom, therefore will I give it unto thee, and all else besides that thou didst not choose." It was not merely that he said it because it was right to say, and would please God if he said it. But it was the thing his heart preferred, and

God saw it in his heart and gave it to him with all besides that he had not chosen. What are we choosing, beloved? It is our choice that settles our destiny. It is not how we feel, but how we purpose. Have we chosen the good part? Have we said, "Whatever else I am or have, let me be God's child, let me have His favor and blessing, let me please Him?" Or have we said, "I must have this thing, and then I will see about religion." Alas, God has seen what was in thine heart, and perhaps He has already said, "They have their reward."

July 1.

"After that ye have suffered awhile" (I. Peter v. 10).

Beloved, are we learning love in the school of suffering? Are our hearts being mellowed and deepened by the summer heat of trial until the fruit of the Spirit, "which is love, joy, peace, long-suffering, gentleness, meekness, temperance, faith, is ripening for the harvest of His coming, and our sufferings are easily borne for His sake"? Oh, this is the school of love, and makes Him unutterably more dear to our hearts and us to His. And thus only can we ever learn with Him the heavenly charity which "suffers long, and is kind."

We see the very first and the very last feature of the face of love, as delineated in St. Paul's portrait (I. Cor. xiii.), are marks of pain and patient suffering, "suffers long," "endureth all things." So let us learn thus in the school of love to suffer and be kind, to endure all things.

Surely it will not be hard to love through all when it is the heart of Jesus within us which will love and continue to love to the very end.

I want the love that suffers and is kind,

That envies not nor vaunts its pride or fame,

Is not puffed up, does no discourteous act,

Is not provoked, nor seeks its own to claim.

July 2.

"And hath raised us up together" (Eph. ii. 6).

Ascension is more than resurrection. Much is said of it in the New Testament. Christ riseth above all things. We see Him in the very act of ascending as we do not in the actual resurrection, as, with hands and lips engaged in blessing, He gently parts from their side, so simply, so unostentatiously, with so little imposing ceremony as to make heaven so near to our common life that we can just whisper through. And we, too, must ascend, even here. "If ye then be risen with Christ, seek those things that are above." We must learn to live on the heaven side and look at things from above. How it overcomes sin, defies Satan, dissolves perplexities, lifts us above trials, separates us from the world and conquers the fear of death to contemplate all things as God sees them, as Christ beholds them, as we shall one day look back upon them from His glory, and as if we were now really "Seated with Him," as indeed we are, "in the heavenly places." Let us arise with His resurrection and in fellowship with His glorious ascension learn henceforth to live above.

July 3.

"Look from the top" (Song of Solomon iv. 8).

Yes, our perplexities would become plain if we kept on a spiritual elevation. How often when the traveler quite loses his way he can soon find it again from some tree top or some hill top where all the winding paths he has gone spread behind him, and the whole homeward road opens before. So, from the heights of prayer and faith, we too can see the plain path, and know that we are going home.

There is no other way in which we can gain the victory over the world. We must get above it. We must see it from the side of our great reward. Then it looks like earthly objects after we have gazed upon the sun for a while. We are blind to them. When the Italian fruit-seller finds that he is heir to a ducal palace you cannot tempt him any more with the paltry profits of his trade or the company of his old associates. He is above it all. They who know the hope of their calling and the riches of the glory of their inheritance can well despise the world. It is the poor starving ones who go hungering for the husks of earth. We are born from above and have a longing to go home. Let us go forth to-day with our hearts on the homestretch.

July 4.

"Whosoever abideth in Him sinneth not" (I. John iii. 6).

In sanctification what becomes of the old nature? Many people are somewhat unduly concerned to know if it can be killed outright, and seem to desire a sort of certificate of its death and burial. It is enough to know that it is without and Christ is within. It may show itself again, and even knock at the door and plead for admittance, but it is forever outside while we abide in Him. Should we step out of Him and into sin we might find the old corpse in the ghastly cemetery, and its foul aroma might yet revive and embrace us once more. But he that abideth in Him sinneth not and cannot sin while he so abides.

Therefore let us abide and let us not be anxious to escape the hold of eternal vigilance and ceaseless abiding. Our paths are made and the strength to pursue them; let us walk in them. God has provided for us a full sanctification. Is it strange that He should demand it of us, and require us to be holy, even as He is holy, seeing He has given us His own holiness. So let us put on our beautiful garments and prepare to walk in white with Him.

July 5.

"A garden enclosed" (Song of Solomon iv. 12).

The figure here is a garden enclosed, not a wilderness. The garden soil is a cultivated soil, very different from the roadside or the wilderness. The idea of a garden is culture. The ground has to be prepared, to be broken up by ploughing, to be mellowed by harrowing, all the stones removed, the roots of all natural growth dug up, for the good things we are seeking are not natural growths and will not grow in our soil. We all start on the old basis and try to improve the old nature, but that is not God's way. His way is to get self out of the way entirely, and let Him create anew out of nothing, so that all shall be of Him; and we must find Jesus the Alpha and Omega.

The thing you want to learn here is to die. There can be no real life till self dies, and don't try to die yourself, but ask God to slay you, and He will make

a thorough work of it.

This the secret nature hideth,

Summer dies and lives again,

Spring from winter's grave ariseth,

Harvest grows from buried grain.

July 6.

"I am my beloved's" (Song of Solomon vii. 10).

If you want power you must compress. It is the shutting in of the steam that moves the engine. The amount of powder on a flat surface that sends a ball to its destination when shut up in a gun only makes a flash. If you want to carry the electric current you must be insulated. Stand a man on a glass platform and turn a battery on him and he will be filled with electricity. Let him step off the glass, and the moment he touches earth he loses power.

We must be inclosed by His everlasting Covenant. That holds us and keeps us from falling. He will be a wall of fire round about us. He comes Himself and envelops us round about with the old Shekinah glory, and will be the glory in the midst. He wants us inclosed—by a distinct act of consecration dedicated wholly to Him. Are you inclosed by His fences, His commandments, His promises, His covenant? Is your heart really and only for the Lord?

If not, come to Him now and let Him separate you from all the things that take your life, and let Him separate you unto Himself, the Life Giver.

July 7.

"And the glory of the Lord filled the tabernacle" (Ex. xl. 35).

In the last chapter of Exodus we read all the Lord commanded Moses to do, and that as he fulfilled these commands the glory of the Lord descended and filled the tabernacle till there was no room for Moses, and from that time the pillar of cloud overshadowed them, their guide, their protection. And so we have been building as the Lord Himself commanded, and now the temple is to be handed over to Him to be possessed and filled. He will so fill you, if you will let Him that yourself and everything else will be taken out of the way, the glory of the Lord will fill the temple, encompassing, lifting up, guiding, keeping; and from this time your moon shall not withdraw its light, nor your sun go down.

Do you want power? You have God for it. Do you want holiness? You have God for it; and so of everything. And God is bending down from His throne to-day to lift you up to your true place in Him. From this time may the cloud of His glory so surround and fill us that we shall be lost sight of forever.

July 8.

"Having begun in the Spirit, are ye now made perfect by the flesh" (Gal. iii. 3).

Grace literally means that which we do not have to earn. It has two great senses always; it comes for nothing and it comes when we are helpless; it doesn't merely help the man that helps himself—that is not the Gospel; the Gospel is that God helps the man who can't help himself. And then there is another thing; God helps the man to help himself, for everything the man does comes from God. Grace is given to the man who is so weak and helpless he cannot take the first step.

That is the meaning of grace—a little of the meaning of it; we can never know the fulness it has. Now, this river is as free as it is full, but you know some people have an idea when they get a little farther on they have got to pay an admission, and reserved seats are very high, and they shrink back from the higher blessings of the Gospel; ordinary Christians scarcely dare to claim them. If I understand the meaning of this, God has not put the higher blessings apart for a separate class who somehow are nearer to Him. God is no respecter of persons.

July 9.

"Cast thy burden on the Lord" (Ps. lv. 22).

Dear friends, sometimes we bring a burden to God, and we have such a groaning over it, and we seem to think God has a dreadful time, too, but in reality it does not burden Him at all. God says: It is a light thing for Me to do this for you. Your load, though heavy for you, is not heavy for Him. Christ carries the whole on one shoulder, not two shoulders. The government of the world is upon His shoulder. He is not struggling and groaning with it. His mighty arm is able to carry all your burdens. There is power in Christ for our sanctification. He is able to sanctify you. Yes, yes, the Lord can sanctify, the Lord can heal, the Lord can do anything. You must have faith in God. If you come to this river this morning, it will take you as your Niagara would take a little boat, and just bear you down—to a precipice? Oh, no, but to the bosom of love and blessing forever.

Oft there comes a wondrous message,
When my hopes are growing dim,

I can hear it thro' the darkness
Like some sweet and far-off hymn.
Nothing is too hard for Jesus,
No man can work like Him.

July 10.

"That we might know the things that are freely given to us of God" (I. Cor. ii. 12).

The highest blessings of the Gospel are just as free as the lowest; and when you have served Him ten years you cannot sit down and say, "I have got an experience now and I count on that." How often we do that; we say, "Now I know I am saved, I feel it." And so we are building a different foundation—we are building on something in ourselves. Always take grace as something you don't deserve, something that is freely bestowed. The long, deep, boundless river is free; it is as free at the mouth as it is at the little stream, and free all the way along, and anybody can come and drink, and anybody can come and bathe in its boundless waters. Are you going to believe it?

God has given us His Holy Spirit that we may "know the things that are freely given of us of God." It is a hard thing for the poor child to look in through the window and see a fire, and the happy family sitting around the table when it is starving. What is the good of knowing that there is warmth, and love, and light, if it is not free? God has freely given all the goodness of His grace and love.

July 11.

"For it is God which worketh in you" (Phil. ii. 13).

A day with Jesus. Let us seek its plan

and direction from Him. Let us take His highest thought and will for us in it. Let us look to Him for our desires, ideals, expectations in it. Then shall it bring to us exceeding abundantly above all that we can ask or think. Let Him be our Guide and Way. Let us not so much be thinking even of His plan and way as of Him as the Personal Guide of every moment, on whom we constantly depend to lead our every step.

Let Him also be the sufficiency and strength of all the day. Let us never forget the secret: "I can do all things through Christ who strengtheneth me." Let us have Jesus Christ Himself in us to do the works, and let us every moment fall back on Him, both to will and do in us of His good pleasure. Let our holiness be "the law of the spirit of life in Christ Jesus." Let our health be the "life of Jesus manifest in our mortal flesh." Let our faith be "the faith of the Son of God who loved us." Let our peace and joy be His peace and joy. And let our service be not our works, but the grace of Christ within us.

July 12.

"When ye pray, believe that ye receive" (Mark xi. 24).

Consecration is entered by an act of faith. You are to take the gift from God, believe you have, and confess that you have it. Step out on it firmly, and let the devil know you have it as well as the Lord. When once you say to Him boldly, "I am Thine," He answers back from the heavenly heights, "Thou art Mine," and the echoes go ringing down through all your life, "Mine! Thine!" If you dare confess Christ as your Saviour and Sanctifier He has bound Himself to

make it a reality, but you must stand behind His mighty Word. It is the essence of testimony to tell of what Jesus has promised to become to you. It is right to have glorious words of thanksgiving, but these are not exactly testimony. God would have us put our seal on the promises, and lift up our hands and acknowledge them as ours.

Then you are to ignore the old life and reckon it no longer yours if it should come up again. Every time it appears say, "This is from the under world. I am sitting in the heavenly places with Christ."

July 13.

"Even Christ pleased not Himself" (Rom. xv. 3).

Let this be a day of self-forgetting ministry for Christ and others. Let us not once think of being ministered unto, but say ever with Him: "I am among you as He that doth serve." Let us not drag our burdens through the day, but drop all our loads of care and be free to carry His yoke and His burden. Let us make the happy exchange, giving ours and taking His. Let the covenant be: "Thou shalt abide for Me, I also for thee." So shall we lose our heaviest load—ourselves— and so shall we find our highest joy, divine love, the more blessed "to give" than "to receive." Let us do good to all men as we have opportunity. Let us lose no opportunity of blessing, and let us study ingenious ways of service and usefulness. Especially let us seek to win souls.

The Days of Heaven are busy days,

They serve continually,

So spent for Thee and Thine, our days,

As the Days of Heaven would be.

The Days of Heaven are loving days,

As one they all agree,

So linked in loving unity

May our days as Heaven be.

July 14.

"Men ought always to pray" (Luke xviii. 1).

Let this be a day of prayer. Let us see that our highest ministry and power is to deal with God for men. Let us be obedient to all the Holy Spirit's voices of prayer in us. Let us count every pressure a call to prayer. Let us cherish the spirit of unceasing prayer and abiding communion. Let us learn the meaning of the ministry of prayer. Let us reach persons this day we cannot reach in person; let us expect results that we have never dared to claim before; let us count every difficulty only a greater occasion for prayer, and let us call on God, who will show us many great and mighty things which we know not.

And let it be a day of joy and praise. Let us live in the promises of God and the outlook of His deliverance and blessing. Let us never dwell on the trial but always on the victory just before. Let us not dwell in the tomb, but in the garden of Joseph and the light of the resurrection. Let us keep our faces toward the sun rising. Arise, shine. Rejoice evermore. In everything give thanks. Praise ye the Lord.

Lord, give us Thy joy in our hearts which shall lift us to lift others, and fill us so we may overflow to others.

July 15.

"I am my Beloved's and my Beloved is mine" (Song of Solomon vi. 3).

If I am the Lord's then the Lord is mine. If Christ owns me I own Him. And so faith must reach out and claim its full inheritance and begin to use its great resources. Moment by moment we may now take Him as our grace and strength, our faith and love, our victory and joy, our all in all. And as we thus claim Him we will find His grace sufficient for us, and begin to learn that giving all is just receiving all. Yes, consecration is getting Him fully instead of our own miserable life. There are, indeed, two sides of it. There are two persons in the consecration. One of them is the dear Lord Himself. "And for their sakes," He says, "I consecrate Myself that they also might be consecrated through the truth." The moment we consecrate ourselves to Him He consecrates Himself to us, and henceforth, the whole strength of His life and love and everlasting power is dedicated to keep and complete our consecration, and to make the very best and most of our consecrated life. Who would not give himself to such a Saviour? Surely we will to-day, first give ourselves and then give Him each moment as it comes, to be filled and used.

July 16.

"As the hart panteth after the waterbrooks, so panteth my soul after Thee, O God" (Ps. xlii. 1).

First in order to a consecrated life there must be a sense of need, the need of purity, of power, and of a greater nearness to the Lord. There often comes in Christian life a second conviction. It is not now a sense of guilt and God's wrath so much as of the power and evil of inward sin, and the unsatisfactoriness of the life the soul is living. It usually comes from

the deeper revelation of God's truth, from more spiritual teaching, from definite examples and testimonies of this life in others, and often from an experience of deep trial, conflict and temptation in which the soul has found its attainments and resources inadequate for the real issues and needs of life. The first result is often a deep discouragement and even despair, but the valley of Achor is the door of hope, and the seventh chapter of Romans with its bitter cry, "O wretched man that I am," is the gateway to the eighth with its shout of triumph, "The Spirit of life in Christ hath made me free from the law of sin and death."

July 17.

"By one offering He hath perfected forever them that are sanctified" (Heb. x. 14).

Are you missing what belongs to you? He has promised to sanctify you. He has promised sanctification for you by coming to you Himself and being made of God to you sanctification. Jesus is my sanctification. Having Him I have obedience, rest, patience and everything I need. He is alive forevermore. If you have Him nothing can be against you. Your temptations will not be against you; your bad temper will not be against you; your hard life, your circumstances, even the devil himself will not be against you. Every time he comes to attack you, he will only root you deeper in Christ. You will become a coward at the thought of being alone; you will be thrown on Jesus every time a trouble assails you. All things henceforth will work together for good to your own soul. Since God is for you nothing can be against you.

My heavenly Bridegroom sought me and called me one glad day,

"Arise, my love, my fair one, arise and come away,"

I listened to His pleading, I gave Him all my heart,

And we are one forever and nevermore shall part.

July 18.

"Ye are complete in Him" (Col. ii. 10).

In Him we are now complete. The perfect pattern of the life of holy service for which He has redeemed and called us, is now in Him in heaven, even as the architect's model is planned and prepared and completed in his office. But now it must be wrought into us and transferred to our earthly life, and this is the Holy Spirit's work. He takes the gifts and graces of Christ and brings them into our life, as we need and receive them day by day, just as the sections of the vessel are reproduced in the distant Continent, and thus we receive of His fulness, even grace for grace, His grace for our grace, His supply for our need, His strength for our strength, His body for our body, His Spirit for our spirit, and He just "made unto us of God wisdom, righteousness, sanctification and redemption."

But it is much more than mere abstract help and grace, much more even than the Holy Spirit bringing us strength, and peace, and purity. It is personal companionship with Jesus Himself!

Lord, help us receive from Thee to-day, that grace in all trial that shall mean our perfecting in Thee.

July 19.

"Nevertheless, David took the castle of Zion" (I. Chron. xi. 5).

Many of you have so much fighting to do because you do not have one sharp, decisive battle to begin with. It is far easier to have one great battle than to keep on skirmishing all your life. I know men who spend forty years fighting what they call their besetting sin, and on which they waste strength enough to evangelize the world.

Dear friends, does it pay to throw away your lives? Have one battle, one victory and then praise God. So they had rest from their enemies round about. There is labor to enter in. The height is steep. The way of the cross is not an easy way. It is hard to enter in, but having entered in there is perfect rest. May God help us and give us His perfect rest.

O come and leave thy sinful self forever

Beneath the fountain of the Saviour's blood;

O come, and take Him as thy Sanctifier,

Come thou with us and we will do thee good.

Come to the land where all the foes are vanquished,

And sorrow, sin, disease and death subdued;

O weary soul! by Satan bruised and baffled,

Come thou with us and we will do thee good.

July 20.

"Forget also thine own" (Ps. xlv. 10).

We, too, like the ancient Levites, must be "consecrated every one upon our son and upon our brother," and "forget our kindred and our father's house" in every sense in which they could hinder our full liberty and service for the Lord. We, too, must let our business go if it stands between us and the Lord, and in any case let it henceforth be His business and His alone, pursued for Him, controlled by Him, and its profits wholly dedicated to Him, and used as He shall direct. And, like James and John, you must be willing to give up "the hired servants" too. It will make a great difference in your way of living. It will be a change to give up your ease and luxury, your being waited upon and indulged in every wish, and have to do your own work, to give up the attentions of others, to put with privations, and inconveniences, and humiliations, but it will be easy to do it with Him. He never owned a foot of land. He never rode in a carriage. He never had a hired servant. He lay down at last in a borrowed grave. But He is rich enough now, and so will you be some day if you can only be willing to suffer and to wait.

July 21.

"Look from the place where thou art" (Gen. xiii. 14).

Let us now see the blessedness of faith. Our own littleness and nothingness sometimes becomes bondage. We are so small in our own eyes we dare not claim God's mighty promises. We say: "If I could be sure I was in God's way I could trust." This is all wrong. Self-consciousness is a great barrier to faith. Get your eyes on Him and Him alone; not on your faith, but on the Author of your faith; not a half look, but a steadfast, prolonged look, with a true heart and fixedness of

purpose, that knows no faltering, no parleying with the enemy without a shadow of fear. When you get afraid you are almost sure to fail.

Travelers who have crossed the Alps know how dangerous those mountain passes are, how narrow the foothold, how deep the rocky ravines and how necessary to safety it is that you should look up continually; one downward glance into the dizzy depths would be fatal; and so if we would surmount the heights of faith we must look up—look up. Get your eyes off yourself, off surrounding circumstances, off means, off gifts, to the Great Giver.

July 22.

"He that ministereth let us wait on our ministering" (Rom. xii. 7).

Beloved, are you ministering to Christ? Are you doing it with your hands? Are you doing it with your substance and with what you have? Is He getting the best of what is most real to you? Has He a place at your table? And when He does not come to fill the chair, is it free to His representative, His poor and humble children? Your words and wishes are cheap if they do not find expression in your actual gifts. Even Mary did not put Him off with the incense of her heart, but laid her costliest gifts at His feet.

Ye busy women, who work so hard to dress your children and furnish your houses and tables, what have your hands earned for the Master, what have you done or sacrificed for Jesus? "Can you afford it?" was asked of a noble woman, as she promised a costly offering for the Master's work. "No," was her noble reply, "but I can sacrifice it." Let us to-day look around us and see, what we do and give more to the loving Saviour, who gave up His whole life for us.

[pg 210]

July 23.

"Bring them hither to Me" (Matt. xiv. 18).

Why have ye not received all the fulness of the Holy Spirit? And how may we be anointed with "the rest of the oil?" The greatest need is to make room when God makes it. Look around you at your situation. Are you not encompassed with needs at this very moment, and almost overwhelmed with difficulties, trials and emergencies? These are all divinely provided vessels for the Holy Spirit to fill, and if you would but rightly understand their meaning, they would become opportunities for receiving new blessings and deliverances which you can get in no other way.

Bring these vessels to God. Hold them steadily before Him in faith and prayer. Keep still, and stop your own restless working until He begins to work. Do nothing that He does not Himself command you to do. Give Him a chance to work, and He will surely do so, and the very trials that threatened to overcome you with discouragement and disaster, will become God's opportunity for the revelation of His grace and glory in your life, as you have never known Him before. "Bring them (all needs) to Me."

July 24.

"The righteousness of the law might be fulfilled in us" (Rom. vii. 4).

In our earlier experiences we know the Holy Ghost only at a distance, in things that happen in a providential direction, or in the Word alone, but after awhile we receive Him as an inward Guest, and He dwells in our very midst, and He speaks to us in the innermost chambers of our being. But then the external working of His power does not cease, but it only increases, and seems the more glorious. The Power that dwells within us works without us, answering prayer, healing sickness, overruling providences, "Doing exceeding abundantly above all that we ask or think, according to the Power that worketh in us."

There is a double presence of the Lord for the consecrated believer. He is present in the heart, and is mightily present in the events of life. He is the Christ in us, the Christ of all the days, with all power in heaven and earth.

And so the Holy Ghost is our wonder-worker, our all sufficient God and Guardian, and He is waiting in these days to work as mightily in the affairs of men as in the days of Moses, of Daniel and of Paul.

July 25.

"He that in these things serveth Christ is acceptable to God" (Rom. xiv. 18).

God can only use us while we are right. Satan cared far less for Peter's denial of his Master than for the use he made of it afterwards to destroy his faith. So Jesus said to him: "I have prayed for thee that thy faith fail not." It was Peter's faith he attacked, and so it is our faith that Satan contests. "The trial of our faith is much more precious than gold that perisheth."

Whatever else we let go let us hold steadfastly to our trust. "Cast not away, therefore, your confidence," and "hold fast the rejoicing of our hope firm unto the end." And if you would hold your trust, hold your sweetness, your rightness of spirit, your obedience to Christ, your victory in every way.

Whatever comes, regard it as of less consequence, than that you should triumph and stand fast, and accepting every circumstance as God is pleased to let occur, wave the banner of your victory in the face of every foe, and go on, shouting in His name, "Thanks be unto God that always causeth us to triumph in Christ Jesus."

July 26.

"Now mine eye seeth Thee" (Job xlii. 5).

We must recognize the true character of our self-life and its real virulence and vileness. We must consent to its destruction, and we must take it ourselves, as Abraham did Isaac, and lay it at the feet of God in willing sacrifice.

This is a hard work for the natural heart, but the moment the will is yielded and the choice is made, that death is past, the agony is over, and we are astonished to find that the death is accomplished.

Usually the crisis of life in such cases hangs upon a single point. God does not need to strike us in a hundred places to inflict a death wound. There is one point that touches the heart, and that is the point God usually strikes, the dearest thing in our life, the decisive thing in our plans, the citadel of the will, the center of the heart, and when we yield there, there is little left to yield anywhere else, and when we

refuse to yield at this point, a spirit of evasion and compromise enters into all the rest of our life. Lord, we take Thee to enable us to will Thy will to be done in all things in our life without and within.

July 27.

"The building up of the body of Christ" (R. V., Eph. iv. 13).

God is preparing His heroes, and when the opportunity comes He can fit them into their place in a moment and the world will wonder where they came from. Let the Holy Ghost prepare you, dear friend, by all the discipline of life; and when the last finishing touch has been given to the marble, it will be easy for God to put it on the pedestal, and fit it into its niche.

There is a day coming, when, like Othniel, we, too, shall judge the nations, and rule and reign with Christ on the millennial earth; but ere that glorious day can be, we must let God prepare us as He did Othniel at Kirjethsepher, amid the trials of our present life, and in the little victories, the significance of which, perhaps, we little dream. At least, let us be sure of this, that if the Holy Ghost has got an Othniel ready, the Lord of heaven and earth has a throne prepared for him.

Is it for me to be used by His grace,

Helping His kingdom to bring,

Is it for me to inherit a place,

E'en on the throne of my King?

July 28.

"Not my will, but Thine" (Luke xxii. 42).

He who once suffered in Gethsemane will be our strength and our victory, too. We may fear, we may also sink, but let us not be dismayed, and we shall yet praise Him, and look back from a finished course, and say, "Not one word hath failed of all that the Lord hath spoken."

But in order to do this, we must, like Him, meet the conflict, not with a defiant, but with a submissive spirit. He had to say, "Not My will, but Thine be done"; but in saying it, He gained the very thing He surrendered. So the submission of Gethsemane is not a blind and dead submission of a heart that abandons all its hope; but it is the free submission that bows the head, in order to get double strength through the faith and prayer.

We let go, in order that we may take a firmer hold. We give up, in order that we may more fully receive. We lay our Isaac on Mount Moriah, and we ask him back, no longer our Isaac, but God's Isaac, and infinitely more secure, because given back in the resurrection life.

July 29.

"My helpers in Christ Jesus" (Rom. xvi. 3).

Christ's Church is overrun with captains. She is in great need of a few more privates. A few rivers run into the sea, but a larger number run into other rivers. We cannot all be pioneers, but we can all be helpers, and no man is fitted to go in the front until he has learned well how to go second.

A spirit of self-importance is fatal to all work for Christ. The biggest enemy of true spiritual power is spiritual self-consciousness. Joshua must die before Jericho can fall.

God often has to test His chosen

servants by putting them in a subordinate place before He can bring them to the front. Joseph must learn to serve in the kitchen and to suffer in prison before he can rise to the throne, and as soon as Joseph is ready for the throne, the throne is always waiting for Joseph. God has more places than accepted candidates. Let us not be afraid to go into the training class, and even take the lowest place, for we shall soon go up, if we really deserve to. Lord, use me so that Thou shalt be glorified and I shall be hid from myself and others.

July 30.

"If thou wilt diligently hearken unto the voice of the Lord thy God and wilt keep all His statutes" (Ex. xv. 26).

Sometimes people fail because they have not confidence in the Physician. The very first requirement of this Doctor is, that you trust Him, and trust Him implicitly, so implicitly that you go forward on His bare word, and act as if you had received His healing the moment you claimed His promise. But no one would expect to be healed by an earthly doctor as soon as they obeyed his directions.

You must do what the Great Physician tells you, if you expect Him to make you whole.

You cannot expect to be healed if you are living in sin, any more than you could expect the best physician to cure you while you lived in a malarial climate and inhaled poison with every breath. So you must get up into the pure air of trust and obedience before Christ can make you whole. And then, if you will trust Him, and attend to His directions, you will find that there is balm in Gilead, and that there is a Great Physician there.

July 31.

"We were troubled on every side" (II. Cor. vii. 5).

Why should God have to lead us thus, and allow the pressure to be so hard and constant?

Well, in the first place, it shows His all-sufficient strength and grace much better than if we were exempt from pressure and trial. "The treasure is in earthen vessels, that the excellency of the power may be of God, and not of us."

It make us more conscious of our dependence upon Him. God is constantly trying to teach us our dependence, and to hold us absolutely in His hand and hanging upon His care.

This was the place where Jesus Himself stood and where He wants us to stand, not with a self-constituted strength, but with a hand ever leaning upon His, and a trust that dare not take one step alone.

It teaches us trust. There is no way of learning faith except by trial. It is God's school of faith, and it is far better for us to learn to trust God than to enjoy life.

The lesson of faith, once learned, is an everlasting acquisition and an eternal fortune made; and without trust even riches will leave us poor.

August 1.

"For we must all appear before the judgment seat of Christ; that every one may receive the things done in his body, according to that he hath done" (II Cor. v. 10).

It will not always be the day of toil and trial. Some day, we shall hear our names announced before the universe,

and the record read of things that we had long forgotten. How our hearts will thrill, and our heads will bow, as we shall hear our own names called, and then the Master shall recount the triumph and the services which we had ourselves forgotten! And, perhaps, from the ranks of the saved He shall call forward the souls that we have won for Christ and the souls that they in turn had won, and as we see the issue of things that have, perhaps, seemed but trifling at the time, we shall fall before the throne, and say, "Not unto us, O Lord, not unto us, but unto Thy name give glory!"

Beloved, the pages are going up every day, for the record of our life. We are setting the type ourselves, by every moment's action. Hands unseen are stereotyping the plates, and soon the record will be registered, and read before the audience of the universe. and amid the issues of eternity.

August 2.

"Thy gentleness hath made me great" (Ps. xviii. 35).

The blessed Comforter is gentle, tender, and full of patience and love. How gentle are God's dealings even with sinners! How patient His forbearance! How tender His discipline, with His own erring children! How He led Jacob, Joseph, Israel, David, Elijah, and all His ancient servants, until they could truly say, "Thy gentleness hath made me great."

The heart in which the Holy Spirit dwells will always be characterized by gentleness, lowliness, quietness, meekness, and forbearance. The rude, sarcastic spirit, the brusque manner, the sharp retort, the unkind cut—all these belong to the flesh, but they have nothing in common with the gentle teaching of the Comforter.

The Holy Dove shrinks from the noisy, tumultuous, excited, and vindictive spirit, and finds His home in the lowly breast of the peaceful soul. "The fruit of the Spirit is gentleness, meekness."

Lord, make me gentle. Hush my spirit. Refine my manner. Let me have Christ in my bearing and my very tones as well as in my heart.

August 3.

"Humble yourselves therefore under the mighty hand of God" (I. Peter v. 6).

The pressure of hard places makes us value life. Every time our life is given back to us from such a trial, it is like a new beginning, and we learn better how much it is worth, and make more of it for God and man.

The pressure helps us to understand the trials of others, and fits us to help and sympathize with them.

There is a shallow, superficial nature, that gets hold of a theory or a promise lightly, and talks very glibly about the distrust of those who shrink from every trial; but the man or woman who has suffered much never does this, but is very tender and gentle, and knows what suffering really means.

This is what Paul meant when he said, "Death worketh in us, but life in you." Trials and hard places are needed to press us forward; even as the furnace fires in the hold of that mighty ship give the force that moves the piston, drives the engine, and propels that great vessel across the sea, in the face of the winds and waves.

August 4.

"Ye are not in the flesh but in the Spirit if so be that the Spirit of God dwell in you. Now if any man have not the Spirit of Christ he is none of His" (Rom. viii. 9).

A spiritual man is not so much a man possessing a strong spiritual character as a man filled with the Holy Spirit. So the apostle said: "Ye are not in the flesh, but in the Spirit, if so be that the Spirit of God dwelleth in you."

The glory of the new creation, then, is not only that it recreates the human spirit, but that it fits it for the abode of God Himself, and makes it dependent upon the sun, as the child upon the mother. The highest spirituality, therefore, is the most utter helplessness, the most entire dependence and the most complete possession of the Holy Spirit. Therefore, the beautiful act of Christ in breathing upon His disciples, and imparting to them from His own lips the very Spirit that was already in Him, expressed in the most vivid manner the crowning glory of the new creation. And when the Holy Spirit thus possesses us, He fills every part of our being.

August 5.

"If any man hear My voice and open the door I will come into him and will sup with him and he with Me" (Rev. iii. 20).

Some of us are starving, and wondering why the Holy Spirit does not fill us. We have plenty coming in, but we do not give it out. Give out the blessing you have, start larger plans for service and blessing, and you will soon find that the Holy Ghost is before you, and He will "prevent you with the blessings of goodness," and give you all that He can trust you to give away to others.

There is a beautiful fact in nature which has its spiritual parallels. There is no music so heavenly as an Aeolian harp, and the Aeolian harp is nothing but a set of musical cords arranged in harmony, and then left to be touched by the unseen fingers of the wandering winds. And as the breath of heaven floats over the chords, it is said that notes almost divine float out upon the air, as if a choir of angels wandering around and touching the strings.

And so it is possible to keep our hearts so open to the touch of the Holy Spirit that He can play upon them at will, as we quietly wait in the pathway of His service.

August 6.

"As many as are led by the Spirit of God they are the sons of God" (Rom. viii. 14).

The blessed Holy Spirit is our Guide, our Leader, and our Resting-place. There are times when He presses us forward into prayer, into service, into suffering, into new experiences, new duties, new claims of faith, and hope, and love, but there are times when He arrests us in our activity, and rests us under His overshadowing wing, and quiets us in the secret place of the Most High, teaching us some new lessons, breathing into us some deeper strength or fulness, and then leading us on again, at His bidding alone. He is the true Guide of the saint, and the true Leader of the Church, our wonderful Counsellor, our unerring Friend; and he who would deny the personal guidance of the Holy Ghost in order that he might honor the Word of God

as our only guide, must dishonor that other word of promise, that His sheep shall know His voice, and that His hearkening and obedient children shall hear a voice behind them saying, "This is the way, walk ye in it."

August 7.

"Knowing this that our old man is crucified" (Rom. vi. 6).

It is purely a matter of faith, and faith and sight always differ, so that to your senses it does not seem to be so, but your faith must still reckon it so. This is a very difficult attitude to hold, and only as we thoroughly believe God can we thus reckon upon His Word and His working, but as we do so, faith will convert it into fact, and it will be even so.

These two words, "yield" and "reckon," are passwords into the resurrection life. They are like the two edges of the "Sword of the Spirit" through which we enter into crucifixion with Christ.

This act of surrender and this reckoning of faith are recognized in the New Testament as marking a very definite crisis in the spiritual life. It does not mean that we are expected to be going through a continual dying, but that there should be one very definite act of dying, and then a constant habit of reckoning ourselves as dead, and meeting everything from this standpoint.

"Reckon yourselves dead indeed unto sin, but alive unto God, through Jesus Christ."

August 8.

"Be like the dove" (Jer. xlviii. 28).

Harmless as a dove, is Christ's

interpretation of the beautiful emblem. And so the Spirit of God is purity itself. He cannot dwell in an unclean heart. He cannot abide in the natural mind. It was said of the anointing of old, "On man's flesh it shall not be poured."

The purity which the Holy Spirit brings is like the white and spotless little plant which grows up out of the heap of manure, or the black soil, without one grain of impurity adhering to its crystalline surface, spotless as an angel's wing.

So the Holy Spirit gives a purity of heart which gives its own protection, for it is essentially unlike the evil things which grow around it. It may be surrounded on every side with evil, but it is uncontaminated and pure because its very nature is essentially holy and divine. Like the plumage of the dove, it cannot be soiled, but comes forth from the miry pool unstained and unsullied by the dark waters, because it is protected by the oily covering which sheds off every defilement and makes it proof against the touch of every stain.

August 9.

"He shall lay both his hands upon the head of the live goat, and confess over him all the iniquities of the children of Israel; transgressions and sins" (Lev. xvi. 21).

As any evil comes up, and the consciousness of any unholy thing touches our inner senses, it is our privilege at once to hand it over to the Holy Ghost and to lay it upon Jesus, as something already crucified with Him, and as of old, in the case of the sin offering, it will be carried without the camp and burned to ashes.

There may be deep suffering, there may be protracted pain, it may be intensely real; but throughout all there will be a very sweet and sacred sense of God's presence, and intense purity in our whole spirit, and our separation from the evil which is being consumed. Truly, it will be borne without the camp, and even without the smell of the flames upon our garments.

It is so blessed to have the Holy Spirit slay things. No swords but His can pass so perfectly between us and the evil, so that it consumes the sin without touching the spirit.

Lord Jesus, my Sin Offering, I lay my sin, my self, my whole nature, upon Thy Cross. Consume me by Thy holy fire, and let me die to all but Thee!

August 10.

"There is no spot in thee" (Song of Solomon iv. 7).

The blessed Holy Spirit who possesses the consecrated heart is intensely concerned for our highest life, and watches us with a sensitive, and even a jealous love. Very beautiful is the true translation of that ordinary passage in the Epistle of James, "The Spirit that dwelleth in us loveth us to jealousy."

The heart of the Holy Ghost is intensely concerned in preserving us from every stain and blemish, and bringing us into the very highest possibilities of the will of God.

The Heavenly Bridegroom would have His Church not only free from every spot, but also from "every wrinkle, or any such thing." The spot is the mark of sin, but the wrinkle is the sign of weakness, age, and decay, and He wants no such defacing touch upon the holy features of His Beloved;

and so the Holy Ghost, who is the Executor of His will, and the Divine Messenger whom He sends to call, separate, and bring home His Bride, is jealously concerned in fulfilling in us all the Master's will.

Lord, take from me every blemish and mark of weakness and decay, and make me Thy spotless Bride.

August 11.

"All the land which thou seest" (Gen. xiii. 15).

The actual provisions of His grace come from the inner vision.

He who puts the instinct in the bosom of yonder bird to cross the continent in search of summer sunshine in yonder Southern clime is too good to deceive it, and just as surely as He has put the instinct in its breast, so has He also put the balmy breezes and the vernal sunshine yonder to meet it when it arrives.

He who gave to Abraham the vision of the Land of Promise, also said in infinite truth and love: "All the land that thou seest will I give thee." He who breathes into our hearts the heavenly hope, will not deceive or fail us when we press forward to its realization. There is nothing unfaithful in Him who has said: "If it were not so, I would have told you," and we may know that He never will deceive us nor fail us, but all that He reveals by His Holy Spirit He will make our own, as we press forward and enter into its realization.

Lord, give me first the vision and then the victory. Show me all my inheritance, and then give it all to me in Christ Jesus.

August 12.

"Not ourselves, but Christ Jesus" (II. Cor. iv. 5).

Your Christian influence, your reputation as a worker for God, and your standing among your brethren, may be an idol to which you must die, before you can be free to live for Him alone.

If you have ever noticed the type on a printed page, you must have seen that the little "*i*" has always a dot over it, and it is that dot that elevates it above the other letters in the line.

Now, each us us is a little *i*, and over every one of us there is a little dot of self-importance, self-will, self-interest, self-confidence, self-complacency, or something to which we cling and for which we contend, which just as surely reveals self-life as if it were a mountain of real importance.

This *i* is a rival of Jesus Christ, and the enemy of the Holy Ghost, and of our peace and life, and therefore God has decreed its death, and the Holy Spirit, with His flaming sword is waiting to destroy it, that we may be able to enter through the gates and come to the Tree of Life. Lord, crowd me out by Thy fulness even as the glory of the Lord left no room for Moses in the Tabernacle.

August 13.

"Clouds and darkness are round about Him" (Ps. xcvii. 2).

The presence of clouds upon your sky, and trials in your path, is the very best evidence that you are following the pillar of cloud, and walking in the presence of God. They had to enter the cloud before they could behold the glory of the transfiguration, and a little later that same cloud became the chariot to receive the ascending Lord, and it is still waiting as the chariot that will bring His glorious appearing.

Still it is true that white "clouds and darkness are round about His throne, mercy and truth" are ever in their midst, and "shall go before His face."

Perhaps the most beautiful and gracious use of the cloud was to shelter them from the fiery sun. Like a great umbrella, that majestic pillar spread its canopy above the camp, and became a shielding shadow from the burning heat in the treeless desert. No one who has never felt an Oriental sun can fully appreciate how much this means—a shadow from the heat.

So the Holy Spirit comes between us and the fiery, scorching rays of sorrow and temptation.

August 14.

"Touch not Mine anointed, and do My prophets no harm" (Ps. cv. 15).

I would rather play with the forked lightning, or take in my hands living wires, with their fiery current, than speak a reckless word against any servant of Christ, or idly repeat the slanderous darts which thousands of Christians are hurling on others, to the hurt of their own souls and bodies.

You may often wonder, perhaps, why your sickness is not healed, your spirit filled with the joy of the Holy Ghost, or your life blessed and prosperous. It may be that some dart which you have flung with angry voice, or in an idle hour of thoughtless gossip, is pursuing you on its way, as it describes the circle which always bring back to the source from which it came every shaft of bitterness, and every idle and evil word.

Let us remember that when we

persecute or hurt the children of God, we are but persecuting Him, and hurting ourselves far more.

Lord, make me as sensitive to the feelings and rights of others as I have often been to my own, and let me live and love like Thee.

August 15.

"He will guide you into all truth" (John xvi. 13).

The Holy Ghost does not come to give us extraordinary manifestations, but to give its life and light, and the nearer we come to Him, the more simple will His illumination and leading be. He comes to "guide us into all truth." He comes to shed light upon our own hearts, and to show us ourselves. He comes to reveal Christ, to give, and then to illumine, the Holy Scriptures, and to make Divine realities vivid and clear to our spiritual apprehension. He comes as a Spirit of wisdom and revelation in the knowledge of Christ, to "enlighten the eyes of our understanding, that we may know what is the hope of His calling, and what the riches of the glory of His inheritance in the saints, and what is the exceeding greatness of His power to us-ward who believe, according to the working of His mighty power."

Spirit of Power! with heavenly fire,
Our souls endue, our tongues inspire;
Stretch forth Thy mighty Hand,
Thy Pentecostal gifts restore,
The wonders of Thy power once more
Display in every land.

August 16.

"I am with you alway" (Matt. xxviii. 20).

Oh, how it helps and comforts us in the plod of life to know that we have with us the Christ who spent the first thirty years of His life in the carpenter shop at Nazareth, swinging the hammer, covered with sweat and grimy dust, physically weary as we often are, and able to understand all our experiences of drudgery and labor! and One who still loves to share our common tasks and equip us for our difficult undertakings of hand and brain!

Yes, humble sister, He will help you at the washboard and the kitchen-sink as gladly as at the hour of prayer. Yes, busy mechanic, He will go with you and help you to swing the hammer, or handle the saw, or hold the plow in the toil of life, and you shall be a better mechanic, a more skilled workman, and a more successful man, because you take His wisdom for the common affairs of life. There is no place or time where He is not able and willing to walk by our side, to work through our hands and brains, and to unite Himself in loving and all-sufficient partnership with all our needs and tasks and trials, and prove our all-sufficiency for all things.

August 17.

"Speak ye unto the Rock" (Num. xx. 8).

The Holy Ghost is very sensitive, as love always is. You can conquer a wild beast by blows and chains, but you cannot conquer a woman's heart that way, or win the love of a sensitive nature; that must be wooed by the delicate touches of trust and affection. So the Holy Ghost has to be taken by a faith as delicate and sensitive as the gentle heart with whom it is coming in touch. One thought of unbelief, one expression of impatient distrust or fear, will instantly check the perfect

freedom of His operations as much as a breath of frost would wither the petals of the most sensitive rose or lily.

Speak to the Rock, do not strike it. Believe in the Holy Ghost and treat Him with the tenderest confidence and the most unwavering trust, and He will meet you with instant response and confidence.

Beloved, have you come to the rock in Kadesh? Have you opened all your being to the fulness of the Spirit, and then, with the confidence of the child to the mother, the bride to the husband, the flower to the sunshine, have you received by faith, and are you drinking of His blessed life?

August 18.

"The three hundred blew the trumpets" (Judges vii. 22).

We little dream, sometimes, what a hasty word, a thoughtless speech, an imprudent act, or a confession of unbelief and fear may do to hinder our highest usefulness, or turn it aside from some great opportunity which God has been preparing for us.

Although the Holy Ghost uses weak men, He does not want them to be weak after He chooses and calls them. Although He uses the foolish things to confound the wise, He does not want us to be foolish after He comes to give us His wisdom and grace. He uses the foolishness of preaching, but, not necessarily, the foolishness of preachers. Like the electric current, which can supply the strength of a thousand men, it is necessary that it should have a proper conductor, and a very small wire is better than a very big rope.

God wants fit instruments for His power—wills surrendered, hearts trusting, lives consistent, and lips obedient to His will; and then He can use the weakest weapons, and make them mighty through God to the pulling down of strongholds.

August 19.

"Have faith in God" (Mark xi. 22).

He requires of us a perfect faith, and He tells us that if we believe and doubt not, we shall have whatsoever we ask. The faintest touch of unbelief will neutralize our trust.

But how shall we have such perfect faith? Is it possible for human nature? Nay, but it is possible to the Divine nature, it is possible to the Christ within us. It is possible for God to give it; and God does give it. But Christ is the Author and Finisher of our faith, and He bids us have the faith of God, and as we have it through the imparting of the Spirit of Christ, we believe even as He.

We pray in His name, and in His very nature, and we live by the faith of the Son of God who loved us and gave Himself for us. The love that He requires of us is not mere human love, nor even the standard of love required in the Old Testament, but something far higher. The new commandment is, Love one another, not as yourselves, but as I have loved you.

How shall such love be made possible? Herein is our love made perfect, because as He is so are we also in this world. Our love is simply His love wrought in us, and imparted to us through the Spirit.

August 20.

"Herein is My Father glorified" (John xv. 8).

The true way to glorify God is, for God to show His glory through us, to

shine through us as empty vessels reflecting His fulness of grace and power.

The sun is glorified when he has a chance to show his light through the crystal window, or reflect it from the spotless mirror or the glassy sea.

There is nothing that glorifies God so much as for a weak and helpless man or woman to be able to triumph, through His strength, in places where the highest human qualities will fail us, and carry in Divine power through every form of toil and suffering, a spirit naturally weak, irresolute, selfish, and sinful, transformed into sweetness, purity, power and standing victorious amid circumstances from which its natural qualities must utterly unfit it. A mind not naturally wise or strong, directed by a Divine wisdom, and carried along the line of a great and mighty plan, and used to accomplish stupendous results for God and man—this is what glorifies God.

So let me glorify my Lord this day and adorn the doctrine of God in all things.

August 21.

"The battle is not yours" (II. Chron. xx. 15).

The thing is to count the battle God's. "The battle is not yours, but God's." Ye shall not need to fight in this battle. As long as we count the dangers and responsibilities ours, we shall be distracted with fear, but when we realize He is bound to take care of us, as His property and His representatives, we shall feel infinite relief and security.

If I send my servant on a long journey I am responsible for his expenses and protection, and if God sends me anywhere, He is responsible. If we belong to God, and put our life, our family, and our all in His hands, we may know He will take care of us.

If our body belongs to Him, it is His interest to keep us well, just as much as it is for the interest of the shepherd to have his sheep well fed and well cared for, and a credit to him.

"Thanks be unto God who always causeth us to triumph."

Stand up, stand up for Jesus,

Stand in His strength alone;

The arm of flesh will fail you,

Ye dare not trust your own.

August 22.

"I the Lord, the first and with the last" (Isa. xli. 4).

Thousands of people get stranded after they have embarked on the great voyage of holiness, because they have depended upon the experience rather than on the Author of it. They had supposed that they were thoroughly and permanently delivered from all sin, and in the ecstacy of their first experience they imagine that they shall never again be tried and tempted as before, and when they step out into the actual facts of Christian life and find themselves failing and falling, they are astonished and perplexed, and they conclude that they must have been mistaken in their experience, and so they make a new attempt at the same thing, and again fall, until at last, worn out, with the experiment, they conclude that the experience is a delusion, or, at least, that it was never intended for them, and so they fall back into the old way, and their last state is worse than the first.

What men and women need to-day is to know, not sanctification as a state,

but Christ as a living Person.

Lord Jesus, give me Thy heart, Thy faith, Thy life, Thyself.

August 23.

"Even as He is pure" (I. John iii. 3).

God is now aiming to reproduce in us the pattern which has already appeared in Jesus Christ, the Son of God. The Christian life is not an imitation of Christ, but a direct new creation in Christ, and the union with Christ is so complete that He imparts His own nature to us and lives His own life in us and then it is not an imitation, but simply the outgrowth of the nature implanted within.

We live Christ-like because we have the Christ-life. God is not satisfied with anything less than perfection. He required that from His Son. He requires it from us, and He does not, in the process of grace, reduce the standard, but He brings us up to it. He does not let down the righteousness of the law, but He requires of us a righteousness that far exceeds the righteousness of the Scribes and Pharisees, and then He imparts it to us. He counts us righteous in sanctification, and He says of the new creation, "He that doeth righteousness is righteous even as He is righteous."

Lord, live out thy very life in me.

August 24.

"Let your moderation be known unto all men" (Phil. iv. 5).

The very test of consecration is our willingness not only to surrender the things that are wrong, but to surrender our rights, to be willing to be subject. When God begins to subdue a soul, He often requires us to yield the things that are of little importance in themselves, and thus break our neck and subdue our spirit.

No Christian worker can ever be used of God until the proud self-will is broken, and the heart is ready to yield to God's every touch, no matter through whom it may come.

Many people want God to lead them in their way and they will brook no authority or restraint. They will give their money, but they want to dictate how it shall be spent. They will work as long as you let them please themselves, but let any pressure come and you immediately run up against, not the grace of resignation, but a letter of resignation, withdrawing from some important trust, and arousing a whole community of criticising friends, equally disposed to have their own opinions and their own will about it. It is destructive of all real power.

August 25.

"And I will put My Spirit within you, and cause you to walk in My statutes, and ye shall keep My judgments and do them" (Ezek. xxxvi. 27).

This is a great deal more than a new heart. This a heart filled with the Holy Ghost, the Divine Spirit, the power that causes us to walk in God's commandments.

This is the greatest crisis that comes to a Christian's life, when into the spirit that was renewed in conversion, God Himself comes to dwell and make it His abiding place, and hold it by His mighty power in holiness and righteousness.

Now, after this occurs, one would suppose that we would be lifted into a much more hopeful and exuberant spirit, but the prophet gives a very

different picture. He says when this comes to pass we shall loathe ourselves in our own eyes.

The revelation of God gives a profound sense of our own nothingness and worthlessness, and lays us on our face in the dust in self-abnegation.

The incoming of the Holy Ghost displaces self and disgraces self forever, and the highest holiness is to walk in self-renunciation.

August 26.

"Thine handmaid hath not anything in the house save a pot of oil" (II. Kings iv. 2).

He asked her, "What hast thou in the house?" And she said, "Nothing but a pot of oil." But that pot of oil was adequate for all her wants, if she had only known how to use it.

In truth it represented the Holy Spirit, and the great lesson of the parable is that the Holy Ghost is adequate for all our wants, if we only know how to use Him.

All that she needed was to get sufficient vessels to hold the overflow, and then to pour out until all were filled.

And so the Holy Spirit is limited only by our capacity to receive Him, and when God wants us to have a larger fulness, He has to make room for it by creating greater needs.

God sends us new vessels to be filled with His Holy Spirit in the needs that come to us, and the trials that meet us. These are God's opportunities for God to give us more of Himself, and as we meet them He comes to us in larger fulness for each new necessity.

Lord, help me to see Thee in all my trying situations and to make them vessels to hold more of Thy grace.

August 27.

"Take no thought for your life" (Matt. vi. 25).

Still the Lord is using the things that are despised. The very names of Nazarene and Christian were once epithets of contempt. No man can have God's highest thought and be popular with his immediate generation. The most abused men are often most used.

There are far greater calamities than to be unpopular and misunderstood. There are far worse things than to be found in the minority. Many of God's greatest blessings are lying behind the devil's scarecrows of prejudice and misrepresentation. The Holy Ghost is not ashamed to use unpopular people. And if He uses them, what need they care for men?

Oh, let us but have His recognition and man's notice will count for little, and He will give us all we need of human help and praise. Let us only seek His will, His glory, His approval. Let us go for Him on the hardest errands and do the most menial tasks. Honor enough that He uses us and sends us. Let us not fear in this day to follow Him outside the camp, bearing His reproach, and by-and-by He will own our worthless name before the myriads of earth and sky.

August 28.

"According to the power that worketh in us" (Eph. iii. 20).

When we reach the place of union with God, through the indwelling of the Holy Ghost, we come into the

inheritance of external blessing and enter upon the land of our possession. Then our physical health and strength come to us through the power of our interior life; then the prayer is fulfilled, that we shall be in health and prosper, as our soul prospereth. Then, with the kingdom of God and His righteousness within us, all things are added unto us.

God's external working always keeps pace with the power that worketh in us. When God is enthroned in a human soul, then the devil and the world soon find it out. We do not need to advertise our power. Jesus could not be hid, and a soul filled with Divine power and purity should become the center of attraction to hungry hearts and suffering lives.

Let us receive Him and recognize Him in His indwelling glory, and then will we appropriate all that it means for our life in all its fulness. Lord, give me the "hiding of Thy power," and let Christ be glorified in me.

August 29.

"To obey is better than sacrifice" (I. Sam. xv. 22).

Our healing is thus represented as a special recompense for obedience. If, therefore, we would please the Lord and have the reward of those who please Him, there is no service so acceptable to Him as our praise.

Let us ever meet Him with a glad and thankful heart and He will reflect it back in the health of our countenance and the buoyant life and springing health, which is but the echo of a joyful heart.

Further, thankfulness is the best preparation for faith. Trust grows spontaneously in the praiseful heart.

Thankfulness takes the sunny side of the street and looks at the bright side of God, and it is only thus that we can ever trust Him. Unbelief looks at our troubles and, of course, they seem like mountains, and faith is discouraged by the prospect. A thankful disposition will always find some cause for cheer, and gloomy one will find a cloud in the brightest sky and a fly in the sweetest ointment. Let us cultivate a spirit of cheerfulness, and we shall find so much in God and in our lives to encourage us that we shall have no room for doubt or fear.

August 30.

"Happy are ye if ye do them" (John xiii. 17).

You little know the rest that comes from the yielded will, the surrendered choice, the abandoned world, the meek and lowly heart that lets the world go by, and knows that it shall inherit the earth which it has refused! You little know the relish that it gives to the blessing to hunger and thirst after righteousness, and to be filled with a satisfaction that worldly delight cannot afford, and then to rise to the higher blessedness of the merciful, the forgiving, the hearts that have learned that it is "more blessed to give than to receive," and the lives that find that "letting go is twice possessing," and blessing others is to be doubly blessed!

Nay, there is yet one jewel brighter than all the rest in this crown of beatitudes. It is the tear-drop crystallized into the diamond, the blood-drop transfigured into the ruby of heaven's eternal crown. It is the joy of suffering with Jesus, and then forgetting all the sorrow in the overflowing joy, until with the

heavenly Pascal we know not which to say first, and so we say them both together, "Tears upon tears, joy upon joy".

August 31.

"Lead me in the way everlasting" (Ps. cxxxix. 24).

There is often apparently but little difference in two distinct lives between constant victory and frequent victory. But that one little difference constitutes a world of success or failure. The one is the Divine, the other is the human; the one is the everlasting way, the other the transient and the imperfect. God wants to lead us to the way everlasting, and to establish us and make us immovable as He. We little know the seriousness of the slightest surrender. It is but the first step in a downward progression, and God only knows where it shall end.

Let us be "not of them that draw back unto perdition, but of them that believe unto the saving our the soul."

Your victory to-day is but preparing the way for a greater victory to-morrow, and your surrender to-day is opening the door for a more terrible defeat in the days to come. Let us, therefore, whatever we have claimed from our blessed Master, commit it to His keeping, and take Him to establish us and hold us fast in the rejoicing of the hope firm unto the end.

September 1.

"Afterward that which is spiritual" (I. Cor. xv. 46).

God has often to bring us not only into the place of suffering, and the bed of sickness and pain, but also into the place where our righteousness breaks down and our character falls to pieces, in order to humble us in the dust and show us the need of entire crucifixion to all our natural life. Then, at the feet of Jesus we are ready to receive Him, to abide in Him and depend upon Him alone, and draw all our life and strength each moment from Him, our Living Head.

It was thus that Peter was saved by his very fall, and had to die to Peter that he might live more perfectly to Christ.

Have we thus died, and have we thus renounced the strength of our own self-confidence?

We begin life with the natural, next we come into the spiritual; but then, when we have truly received the kingdom of God and His righteousness, the natural is added to the spiritual, and we are able to receive the gifts of His providence and the blessings of life without becoming centered in them or allowing them to separate us from Him.

September 2.

"Who hath despised the day of small things" (Zech. iv. 10).

The oak comes out of the acorn, the eagle out of that little egg in the nest, the harvest comes out of the seed; and so the glory of the coming age is all coming out of the Christ life now, even as the majesty of His kingdom was all wrapped up that night in the babe of Bethlehem.

Oh, let us take Him for all our life. Let us be united to His person and His risen body. Let us know what it is to say, "The Lord is for the body and the body is for the Lord"! We are members of His body and His flesh and His bones.

He that gave that little infant, His own blessed babe and His only begotten Son, on that dark winter night to the arms of a cruel and ungrateful world, will not refuse to give Him in all His fulness to your heart if you will but open your heart and give Him right of way and full ownership and possession. Then shall you know in your measure His quickening life, even in this earthly life, and by-and-by your hope shall reach its full fruition when you shall sit with Him on His throne with every fiber of your immortal being even as He.

September 3.

"The God of Israel hath separated you" (Num. xvi. 9).

The little plant may grow out of a manure heap, and be surrounded by filth, and covered very often with the floating dust that is borne upon the breeze, but its white roots are separated from the unclean soil, and its leaves and flowers have no affinity with the dust that settles upon them; and after a shower of summer rain they throw off every particle of defilement, and look up, as fresh and spotless as before, for their intrinsic nature cannot have any part with these defiling things.

This is the separation which Christ requires and which He gives. There is no merit in my staying from the theater if I want to go. There is no value in my abstaining from the foolish novel or the intoxicating cup, if I am all the time wishing I could have them. My heart is there, and my soul is defiled by the desire for evil things. It is not the world that stains us, but the love of the world. The true Levite is separated from the desire for earthly things, and even if he could, he would not have the forbidden pleasures which others prize.

September 4.

"Come ye yourselves apart" (Mark vi. 31).

One of the greatest hindrances to spirituality is the lack of waiting upon God. You cannot go through twenty-four hours with two or three breaths of air, in the morning, as you sip your coffee. But you must live in the atmosphere, and you must breathe it all day long. Christians do not wait upon God enough. It needs hours and hours daily of spiritual communion with the Holy Spirit to keep your vitality healthful and full. Every moment should find you breathing out yourself into Christ, and breathing afresh His life, and love and power.

God is waiting to send us the Holy Spirit. He is longing to bless us. His one business is to quicken and sustain our spiritual life. He has nothing else to do with His infinite and great resources. Let us receive Him. Let us live in Him. Let us give to Him the joy of knowing that His infinite grace has not been bestowed in vain, but that we appreciate and improve the blessings which He oft has so freely bestowed.

Lord, help me this day to dwell in Thee as the flower in the sunshine, as the fish in the sea, living in Thy love as the atmosphere and element of my being.

September 5.

"He breathed on them" (John xx. 22).

The beautiful figure suggested by this passage is full of simple instruction. It is as easy to receive the Holy Ghost as it is to breathe. It almost seems as if

the Lord had given them the very impression of breathing, and had said, "Now, this is the way to receive the Holy Ghost."

It is not necessary for you to go to a smallpox hospital to have your lungs contaminated with impure air. It is enough for you to keep in your lungs the air you inhaled a minute ago and it will kill you. All the pure elements have been absorbed from it, and there is nothing left but carbon and other deadly gases and fluids.

Therefore, if you are to be filled with the Holy Spirit, you must first get emptied not only of your old sinful life, but of your old spiritual life. You must get a new breath every moment, or you will die. God wants you to empty out all your being into Him, and then you will take Him in, without needing to try too hard. A vacuum always gets filled, an empty pair of lungs unavoidably breathes in the pure air. If you are only in the true attitude, there will be no trouble about receiving the Holy Ghost.

September 6.

"Finally, my brethren, rejoice in the Lord" (Phil. iii. 1).

There is no spiritual value in depression. One bright and thankful look at the cross is worth a thousand morbid, self-condemning reflections. The longer you look at evil the more it mesmerizes and defiles you into its own likeness. Lay it down at the cross, accept the cleansing blood, reckon yourself dead to the thing that was wrong, and then rise up and count yourself as if you were another man and no longer the same person; and then, identifying yourself with the Lord Jesus, accept your standing in Him and look in your Father's face as blameless as Jesus. Then out of your every fault will come some lesson of watchfulness or some secret of victory which will enable you some day to thank Him, even for your painful experience.

But praise is a sacrifice, for "it is acceptable to God." It goes up to heaven sweeter than the songs of angels, "a sweet smelling savor to your Lord and King." It should be unintermittent—"the sacrifice of praise continually." One drop of poison will neutralize a whole cup of wine, and make it a cup of death, and one moment of gloom will defile a whole day of sunshine and gladness. Let us "rejoice evermore."

September 7.

"I will joy in the God of my salvation" (Hab. iii. 18).

The secret of joy is not to wait until you feel happy, but to rise, by an act of faith, out of the depression which is dragging you down, and begin to praise God as an act of choice. This is the meaning of such passages as these: "Rejoice in the Lord alway, and again I say, rejoice"; "I do rejoice; yes, and I will rejoice." "Count it all joy when ye fall into divers temptations." In all these cases there is an evident struggle with sadness and then the triumphs of faith and praise.

Now, this is what is meant—in part, at least—by the sacrifice of praise. A sacrifice is that which costs us something. And when a man or woman has some cherished grudge or wrong and is harboring it, nursing it, dwelling on it, rolling it as a sweet morsel under the tongue, and quite determined to enjoy a miserable time in selfish morbidness and grumbling, it costs us no little sacrifice to throw

off the morbid spell, to refuse the suggestions of injury, neglect and the remembrance of unkindness, to rise out of the mood of self-commiseration in wholesome and holy determination, and say, "I will rejoice in the Lord"; I will "count it all joy."

September 8.

"He that eateth Me, even He shall live by Me" (John vi. 57).

What the children of God need is not merely a lot of teaching, but the Living Bread. The best wheat is not good food. It needs to be ground and baked before it can be digested and assimilated so as to nourish the system. The purest and the highest truth cannot sanctify or satisfy a living soul.

He breathes the New Testament message from His mouth with a kiss of love and a breath of quickening power. It is as we abide in Him, lying upon His bosom and drinking in His very life that we are nourished, quickened, comforted and healed.

This is the secret of Divine healing. It is not believing a doctrine, it is not performing a ceremony, it is not wringing a petition from the heavens by the logic of faith and the force of your will; but it is the inbreathing of the life of God; it is the living touch which none can understand except those whose senses are exercised to know the realities of the world unseen. Often, therefore, a very little truth will bring us much more help and blessing than a great amount of instruction.

September 9.

"All things are lawful for Me" (I. Cor. x. 23).

I may be perfectly free myself to do many things, the doing of which might hurt my brother and wound his conscience, and love will gladly surrender the little indulgence, that she may save her brother from temptation. There are many questions which are easily settled by this principle.

So there are many forms of recreation which, in themselves might be harmless, and, under certain circumstances, unobjectionable, but they have become associated with worldliness and godlessness, and have proved snares and temptations to many a young heart and life; and, therefore, the law of love would lead you to avoid them, discountenance them, and in no way give encouragement to others to participate in them.

It is just in these things that are not required of us by absolute rules, but are the impulses of a thoughtful love, that the highest qualities of Christian character show themselves, and the most delicate shades of Christian love are manifested.

September 10.

"Wherefore, receive ye one another as Christ also received us, to the glory of God" (Rom. xv. 7).

This is a sublime principle, and it will give sublimity to life. It is stated elsewhere in similar language, "Whatsoever ye do in word or deed, do all in the name of the Lord Jesus."

This is our high calling, to represent Christ, and act in His behalf, and in His character and spirit, under all circumstances and toward all men. "What would Jesus do?" is a simple question which will settle every difficulty, and always settle it on the

side of love.

But we cannot answer this question rightly without having Jesus Himself in our hearts. We cannot *act* Christ. This is too grave a matter for acting. We must *have* Christ, and simply be natural and true to the life within us, and that life will act itself out.

Oh, how easy it is to love every one, and see nothing but loveliness when our heart is filled with Christ, and how every difficulty melts away and every one we meet seems clothed with the Spirit within us when we are filled with the Holy Ghost!

September 11.

"Lo, I am with you all the days, even unto the end of the age" (Matt. xxviii. 20).

It is "all the days," not "always." He comes to you each day with a new blessing. Every morning, day by day, He walks with us, with a love that never tires and a blessing that never grows old. And He is with us "all the days"; it is a ceaseless abiding. There is no day so dark, so commonplace, so uninteresting, but you find Him there. Often, no doubt, He is unrecognized, as He was on the way to Emmaus, until you realize how your heart has been warmed, your love stirred, your Bible so strangely vivified, and every promise seems to speak to you with heavenly reality and power. It is the Lord! God grant that His living presence may be made more real to us all henceforth, and whether we have the consciousness and evidence, as they had a few glorious times in those forty days, or whether we go forth into the coming days, as they did most of their days, to walk by simple faith and in simple duty, let us know at least that the fact is true forevermore, THAT

HE IS WITH US, a Presence all unseen, but real, and ready if we needed Him any moment to manifest Himself for our relief.

September 12.

"The furnace for gold; but the Lord trieth the hearts" (Prov. xvii. 3.)

Remember that temptation is not sin unless it be accompanied with the consent of your will. There may seem to be even the inclination, and yet the real choice of your spirit is fixed immovably against it, and God regards it simply as a solicitation and credits you with an obedience all the more pleasing to Him, because the temptation was so strong.

We little know how evil can find access to a pure nature and seem to incorporate itself with our thoughts and feelings, while at the same time we resist and overcome it, and remain as pure as the sea-fowl that emerges from the water without a single drop remaining upon its burnished wing, or as the harp string, which may be struck by a rude or clumsy hand and gives forth a discordant sound, not from any defect of the harp, but because of the hand that touches it. But let the Master hand play upon it, and it is a chord of melody and a note of exquisite delight.

"In nothing terrified by your adversaries which is to you an evident token of salvation and that of God."

September 13.

"Think it not strange concerning the fiery trial which is to try you" (I. Peter xii. 16).

Most persons after a step of faith are looking for sunny skies and unruffled

seas, and when they meet a storm and tempest they are filled with astonishment and perplexity. But this is just what we must expect to meet if we have received anything of the Lord. The best token of His presence is the adversary's defiance, and the more real our blessing, the more certainly it will be challenged. It is a good thing to go out looking for the worst, and if it comes we are not surprised; while if our path be smooth and our way be unopposed, it is all the more delightful, because it comes as a glad surprise.

But let us quite understand what we mean by temptation. You, especially, who have stepped out with the assurance that you have died to self and sin, may be greatly amazed to find yourself assailed with a tempest of thoughts and feelings that seem to come wholly from within and you will be impelled to say, "Why, I thought I was dead, but I seem to be alive." This, beloved, is the time to remember that temptation, the instigation, is not sin, but only of the evil one.

September 14.

"For the Lord God will help me, therefore shall I not be confounded; therefore, have I set my face like a flint, and I know I shall not be ashamed" (Isa. l. 7).

This is the language of trust and victory, and it was through this faith, as we are told in a passage in Hebrews, that in His last agony, "Jesus, for the joy that was set before Him, endured the cross, despising the shame." His life was a life of faith, His death was a victory of faith, His resurrection was a triumph of faith, His mediatorial reign is all one long victory of faith, "From henceforth expecting till all His enemies be made His footstool."

And so, for us He has become the pattern of faith, and in every situation of difficulty, temptation and distress has gone before us waving the banner of trust and triumph, and bidding us to follow in His victorious footsteps.

He is the great Pattern Believer. While we must claim our salvation by faith, the Great Forerunner also claimed the world's salvation by the same faith.

Let us therefore consider this glorious Leader our perfect example, and as we follow close behind Him, let us remember where He has triumphed we may triumph, too.

September 15.

"Though it tarry, wait for it, for it will surely come, and will not tarry" (Hab. ii. 3).

Some things have their cycle in an hour and some in a century; but His plans shall complete their cycle whether long or short. The tender annual which blossoms for a season and dies, and the Columbian aloe, which develops in a century, each is true to its normal principle. Many of us desire to pluck our fruit in June rather than wait until October, and so, of course, it is sour and immature; but God's purposes ripen slowly and fully, and faith waits while it tarries, knowing it will surely come and will not tarry too long.

It is perfect rest to fully learn and wholly trust this glorious promise. We may know without a question that His purposes shall be accomplished when we have fully committed our ways to Him, and are walking in watchful obedience to His every prompting. This faith will give a calm and tranquil

poise to the spirit and save us from the restless fret and trying to do too much ourselves.

Wait, and every wrong will righten,

Wait, and every cloud will brighten,

If you only wait.

September 16.

"I will never leave Thee nor forsake Thee" (Heb. xiii. 5).

It is most cheering thus to know that although we err and bring upon ourselves many troubles that might have been easily averted, yet God does not forsake even His mistaken child, but on his humble repentance and supplication is ever really both to pardon and deliver. Let us not give up our faith because we have perhaps stepped out of the path in which He would have led us. The Israelites did not follow when He called them into the Land of Promise, yet God did not desert them; but during the forty years of their wandering He walked by their side bearing their backsliding with patient compassion, and waiting to be gracious unto them when another generation should have come. "In all their afflictions He was afflicted, but the Angel of His presence saved them; He bare them and carried them all the days of old." And so yet, while our wanderings bring us many sorrows and lose us many blessings, to the heart which truly chooses His, He has graciously said: "I will never leave thee nor forsake thee."

September 17.

"Thy people shall be a freewill offering in the day of Thy power" (Ps. cx. 3).

This is what the term consecration properly means. It is the voluntary surrender or self-offering of the heart, by the constraint of love to be the Lord's. Its glad expression is, "I am my Beloved's." It must spring, of course, from faith. There must be the full confidence that we are safe in this abandonment, that we are not falling over a precipice, or surrendering ourselves to the hands of a judge, but that we are sinking into a Father's arms and stepping into an infinite inheritance. Oh, it is an infinite inheritance. Oh, it is an infinite privilege to be permitted thus to give ourselves up to One who pledges Himself to make us all that we would love to be, nay, all that His infinite wisdom, power and love will delight to accomplish in us. It is the clay yielding itself to the potter's hands that it may be shaped into a vessel of honor, and meet for the Master's use. It is the poor street waif consenting to become the child of a prince that he may be educated and provided for, that he may be prepared to inherit all the wealth of his guardian.

September 18.

"We walk by faith, not by sight" (II. Cor. v. 7).

There are heavenly notes which have power to break down walls of adamant and dissolve mountains of difficulty. The song of Paul and Silas burst the fetters of the Philippian gaol; the choir of Jehoshaphat put to flight the armies of the Ammonites, and the song of faith will disperse our adversaries and lift our sinking hearts into strength and victory. Beloved, is it the dark hour with us? the winter of barrenness and gloom? Oh, let us remember that it is God's chosen time for the education of faith and that He conceals beneath the surface, precious and untold harvests

of unthought-of fruit! It will not be always winter, it will not be always night, and when the morning comes and spring spreads its verdant mantle over the barren fields then we shall be glad that we did not disappoint our Father in the hour of testing, but that faith had already claimed and seen in the distance the glad fruition which sight now beholds, with a rapture even less than the vision of naked faith.

Lord, help me to believe when I cannot see, and learn from my trials to trust Thee more.

September 19.

"In due season we shall reap if we faint not" (Gal. vi. 9).

If the least of us could only anticipate the eternal issues that will probably spring from the humblest services of faith, we should only count our sacrifices and labors unspeakable heritages of honor and opportunity, and would cease to speak of trials and sacrifices for God.

The smallest grain of faith is a deathless and incorruptible germ, which will yet plant the heavens and cover the earth with harvests of imperishable glory. Lift up your head, beloved, the horizon is wider than the little circle that you can see. We are living, we are suffering, we are laboring, we are trusting, for the ages yet to come. "Let us not be weary in well doing for in due season we shall reap if we faint not," and with tears of transport we shall cry some day, "Oh, how great is thy goodness which Thou hast laid up for them that fear Thee, which Thou hast wrought for them that trust in Thee before the sons of men."

Help me to-day to live under the powers of the world to come, and to live as a man in heaven walking upon the earth.

September 20.

"They shall not be ashamed that wait" (Isa. xlix. 23).

Often He calls us aside from our work for a season and bids us be still and learn ere we go forth again to minister. Especially is this so when there has been some serious break, some sudden failure and some radical defect in our work. There is no time lost in such waiting hours. Fleeing from his enemies the ancient knight found that his horse needed to be reshod. Prudence seemed to urge him without delay, but higher wisdom taught him to halt a few minutes at the blacksmith's forge by the way to have the shoe replaced, and although he heard the feet of his pursuers galloping hard behind, yet he waited those minutes until his charger was refitted for his flight, and then, leaping into his saddle just as they appeared a hundred yards away, he dashed away from them with the fleetness of the wind, and knew that his halting had hastened his escape. So often God bids us tarry ere we go, and fully recover ourselves for the next great stage of the journey and work.

Lord, teach me to be still and know that Thou art God and all this day to walk with God.

September 21.

"Faint, yet pursuing" (Judges viii. 4).

It is a great thing thus to learn to depend upon God to work through our feeble resources, and yet, while so depending, to be absolutely faithful and diligent, and not allow our trust to

deteriorate into supineness and indolence. We find no sloth or negligence in Gideon, or his three hundred; though they were weak and few, they were wholly true, and everything in them ready for God to use to the very last. "Faint yet pursuing" was their watchword as they followed and finished their glorious victory, and they rested not until the last of their enemies were destroyed, and even their false friends were punished for their treachery and unfaithfulness.

So God still calls the weakest instruments, but when He chooses and enables them they are no longer weak, but "mighty through God," and faithful through His grace to every trust and opportunity; "trusting," as Dr. Chalmers used to say, "as though all depended upon God, and working as though all depended upon themselves."

Teach me, my blessed Master, to trust and obey.

September 22.

"We see not yet all things put under Him, but we see Jesus" (Heb. ii. 8, 9).

How true this is to us all! How many things there are that seem to be stronger than we are, but blessed be His name! they are all in subjection under Him, and we see Jesus crowned above them all; and Jesus is our Head, our representative, our other self, and where He is we shall surely be. Therefore when we fail to see anything that God has promised, and that we have claimed in our experience, let us look up and see it realized in Him, and claim it in Him for ourselves. Our side is only half the circle, the heaven side is already complete, and the rainbow of which

we see not the upper half, shall one day be all around the throne and take in the other hemisphere of all our now unfinished life. By faith, then, let us enter into all our inheritance. Let us lift up our eyes to the north and to the south, to the east and to the west, and hear Him say, "All the land that thou seest will I give thee." Let us remember that the circle, is complete, that the inheritance is unlimited, and that all things are put under His feet.

September 23.

"I am the Lord that healeth thee" (Ex. xv. 26).

It is very reasonable that God should expect us to trust Him for our bodies as well as our souls, for if our faith is not practical enough to bring us temporal relief, how can we be educated for real dependence upon God for anything that involves serious risk? It is all very well to talk about trusting God for the distant and future prospect of salvation after death! There is scarcely a sinner in a Christian land that does not trust to be saved some day, but there is no grasp in faith like this. It is only when we come face to face with positive issues and overwhelming forces that we can prove the reality of Divine power in a supernatural life. Hence as an education to our very spirits as well as a gracious provision for our temporal life, God has trained His people from the beginning to recognize Him as the supply of all their needs, and to look to Him as the Physician of their bodies and Father of their spirits. Beloved, have you learned the meaning of Jehovah-rophi, and has it changed your Marah of trial into an Elim of blessing and praise?

September 24.

"He calleth things that are not as though they were" (Rom. iv. 17).

The Word of God creates what it commands. When Christ says to any of us "Now are ye clean through the word which I have spoken unto you," We are clean. When He says "no condemnation" there is none, though there has been a lifetime of sin before. And when He says, "mighty through God to the pulling down of strongholds," then the weak are strong. This is the part of faith, to take God at His Word, and then expect Him to make it real. A French commander thanked a common soldier who had saved his life and called him captain, although he was but a private, but the man took the commander at his word, accepted the new name and was thereby constituted indeed a captain.

Shall we thus take God's creating word of justification, sanctification, power and deliverance and thus make real the mighty promise, "He giveth power to the faint, and to them that have no might He increaseth strength; for they that wait on the Lord shall renew their strength."

September 25.

"The faith of the Son of God" (Gal. ii. 20).

Let us learn the secret even of our faith. It is the faith of Christ, springing in our heart and trusting in our trials. So shall we always sing, "The life that I now live I live by the faith of the Son of God, who loved me and gave Himself for me." Thus looking off unto Jesus, "the Author and Finisher of our faith," we shall find that instead of struggling to reach the promises of God, we shall lie down upon them in blessed repose and be borne up by them with the faith which is no more our own than the promises upon which it rests. Each new need will find us leaning afresh on Him for the grace to trust and to overcome.

Further we see here the true spirit of prayer. It is the Spirit of Christ in us. "In the midst of the church will I sing praises unto thee." Christ still sings these praises in the trusting heart and lifts our prayers into songs of victory! This is the true spirit of prayer, like Paul and Silas in the prison at Philippi, turning prayer into praise, night into day, the night of sorrow into the morning of joy, and when He is in us, the spirit of faith, He will also become the spirit of praise.

September 26.

"I will be with Him in trouble" (Ps. xci. 15).

The question often comes, "Why didn't He help me sooner!" It is not His order. He must first adjust you to the situation and cause you to learn your lesson from it. His promise is, "I will be with him in trouble; I will deliver him and honor him." He must be with you in the trouble first until you grow quiet. Then He will take you out of it. This will not come till you have stopped being restless and fretful about it and become calm and trustful. Then He will say, "It is enough."

God uses trouble to teach His children precious lessons. They are intended to educate us. When their good work is done a glorious recompense will come to us through them. There is a sweet joy and opportunity in them. He does not regard them as difficulties but as opportunities. They have come to give God a greater interest in you, and to show how He can deliver you from

them. We cannot have a mercy worth praising God for without difficulty. God is as deep, and long, and high, as our little world of circumstances.

September 27.

"The glorious liberty of the children of God" (Rom. viii. 21).

Are you above self and self-pleasing in every way? Have you got above circumstances so that you are not influenced by them? Are you above sickness and the evil forces around that would drag down your physical life into the quicksands? These forces are all around, and if yielded to would quickly swamp us. God does not destroy sickness, or its power to hurt, but He lifts us above it. Are you above your feelings, moods, emotions and states? Can you sail immovable as the stars through all sorts of weather? A harp will give out sweet music or discordant sounds as different fingers touch the strings. If the devil's hand is on your harp strings what hideous sounds it will give. Let the fingers of the Lord sweep it, and it will breathe out celestial music. Are you lifted above people, so that you are not bound by or to any one except in the dear Lord, and are you standing free in His glorious life?

"I am risen with Christ, I am dwelling above;

I am walking with Jesus below,

I am shedding the light of His glory and love

Around me wherever I go."

September 28.

"The trial of your faith being much more precious than gold" (I. Peter i. 7).

Our trials are great opportunities. Too often we look on them as great obstacles. It would be a heaven of rest and an inspiration of unspeakable power if each of us would henceforth recognize every difficult situation as one of God's chosen ways of proving to us His love and power, and if instead of calculating upon defeat we should begin to look around for the messages of His glorious manifestations. Then indeed would every cloud become a rainbow, and every mountain a path of ascension and a scene of transfiguration. If we will look upon the past, many of us will find that the very time our heavenly Father has chosen to do the kindest things for us and give us the richest blessings has been the time when we were strained and shut in on every side. God's jewels are often sent us in rough packages and by dark liveried servants, but within we find the very treasures of the King's palace and the Bridegroom's Love.

Fire of God, thy work begin,

Burn up the dross of self and sin;

Burn off my fetters, set me free,

And through the furnace walk with me.

September 29.

"Call not thou common" (Acts x. 15).

"There is nothing common of itself" (Rom. xiv. 14).

We can bring Christ into common things as fully as into what we call religious services. Indeed, it is the highest and hardest application of Divine grace, to bring it down to the ordinary matters of life, and therefore God is far more honored in this than even in things that are more specially sacred.

Therefore, in the twelfth chapter of Romans, which is the manual of practical consecration, just after the passage that speaks of ministering in sacred things, the apostle comes at once to the common, social and secular affairs into which we are to bring our consecration principles. We read: "Be kindly affectioned one to another with brotherly love; in honor preferring one another; not slothful in business; fervent in spirit; serving the Lord."

God wants the Levites scattered all over the cities of Israel. He wants your workshop, factory, kitchen, nursery, editor's room and printing-office, as much as your pulpit and closet. He wants you to be just as holy at high noon on Monday or Wednesday, as in the sanctuary on Sabbath morning.

September 30.

"In the secret places of the stairs" (Song of Solomon ii. 14).

The dove is in the cleft of the rock—the riven side of our Lord. There is comfort and security there. It is also in the secret places of the stairs. It loves to build its nest in the high towers to which men mount the winding stairs for hundreds of feet above the ground. What a glorious vision is there obtained of the surrounding scenery. It is a picture of ascending life. To reach its highest altitudes we must find the secret places of the stairs. That is the only way to rise above the natural plane. Our life should be one of quiet mounting with occasional resting places; but we should be mounting higher step by step. Everybody does not find this way of secret ascent. It is for God's chosen ones. The world may think you are going down. You may not have as much public work to do as

formerly. "Blessed are the poor in spirit." It is a secret, hidden life. We may be hardly aware that we are growing, till some day a test comes and we find we are established. Have you got above the power of sin so that Christ is keeping you from wilful disobedience? Does it give you a shudder to know the consciousness of sin? Are you lifted above the world?

October 1.

"That in the ages to come He might show the exceeding riches of His grace" (Eph. ii. 7).

Christ's great purpose for His people is to train them up to know the hope of their calling, and the riches of the glory of their inheritance and what the exceeding greatness of His power toward us who believe.

Let us prove, in all our varied walks of life, and scenes of conflict, the fulness of His power and grace and thus shall we know "In the ages to come the exceeding riches of His grace in His kindness to us in Jesus Christ."

Beloved, are you thus following your Teacher in the school of faith, and finishing the education which is by and by to fit you for "a far more exceeding and eternal weight of glory"? This is only the School of Faith.

Little can we now dream what these lessons will mean for us some day, when sitting with Him on His throne and sharing with Him the power of God and the government of the universe. Let us be faithful scholars now and soon with Him, we too, will have "endured the cross despising the shame," and shall "sit down at the right hand of the throne of God."

October 2.

"Moses gave not any inheritance; the Lord God of Israel was their inheritance, as He said unto them" (Josh. xiii. 33).

This is very significant. God gave the land to the other tribes but He gave Himself to the Levites. There is such a thing in Christian life as an inheritance from the Lord, and there is such a thing as having the Lord Himself for our inheritance.

Some people get a sanctification from the Lord which is of much value, but which is variable, and often impermanent. Others have learned the higher lesson of taking the Lord Himself to be their keeper and their sanctity, and abiding in Him they are kept above the vicissitudes of their own states and feelings.

Some get from the Lord large measures of joy and blessing, and times of refreshing.

Others, again, learn to take the Lord Himself as their joy.

Some people are content to have peace with God, but others have taken "the peace of God that passeth all understanding."

Some have faith *in* God, while others have the faith *of* God. Some have many touches of healing from God, others, again, have learned to live in the very health of God Himself.

October 3.

"The little foxes that spoil the vines" (Song of Solomon, ii. 15).

There are some things good, without being perfect. You don't need to have a whole regiment cannonading outside your room to keep you awake. It is quite enough that your little alarm clock rings its little bell. It is not necessary to fret about everything; it is quite enough if the devil gets your mind rasped with one little worry, one little thought which destroys your perfect peace. It is like the polish on a mirror, or an exquisite toilet table, one scratch will destroy it; and the finer it is the smaller the scratch that will deface it. And so your rest can be destroyed by a very little thing. Perhaps you have trusted in God about your future salvation; but have you about your present business or earthly cares, your money and your family?

What is meant by the peace that passeth all understanding? It does not mean a peace no one can comprehend. It means a peace that no amount of reasoning will bring. You cannot get it by thinking. There may be perfect bewilderment and perplexity all round the horizon, but yet your heart can rest in perfect security because He knows, He loves, He leads.

October 4.

"Instead of the brier, the myrtle tree" (Isa. lv. 13).

God's sweetest memorial is the transformed thorn and the thistle blooming with flowers of peace and sweetness, where once grew recriminations.

Beloved, God is waiting to make just such memorials in your life, out of the things that are hurting you most to-day. Take the grievances, the separations, the strained friendships and the broken ties which have been the sorrow and heartbreak of your life, and let God heal them, and give you grace to make you right with all with whom you may be wrong, and you will wonder at the joy and blessing that will come out of the things that

have caused you nothing but regret and pain.

"Blessed are the peacemakers, for they shall be called the children of God." The everlasting employment of our blessed Redeemer is to reconcile the guilty and the estranged from God, and the highest and most Christ-like work that we can do is, to be like Him.

Shall we go forth to dry the tears of a sorrowing world, to heal the broken-hearted, to bind up the wounds of human lives, and to unite heart to heart, and earth to heaven?

October 5.

"He hath triumphed gloriously" (Ex. xv. 1).

Beloved, God calls us to victory. Have any of you given up the conflict, have you surrendered? Have you said, "This thing is too much"? Have you said, "I can give up anything else but this"? If you have, you are not in the land of promise. God means you should accept every difficult thing that comes in your life. He has started with you, knowing every difficulty. And if you dare to let Him, He will carry you through not only to be conquerors, but "more than conquerors." Are you looking for all the victory?

God gives His children strength for the battle and watches over them with a fond enthusiasm. He longs to fold you to His arms and say to you, "I have seen thy conflict, I have watched thy trials, I have rejoiced in thy victory; thou hast honored Me." You know He told Joshua at the beginning, "There shall not any man be able to stand before thee all the days of thy life; as I was with Moses, so shall I be with thee: I will not fail thee, nor forsake thee." And again, He says to us, "Fear thou not, for I am with thee."

October 6.

"Ephraim, he hath mixed himself" (Hos. vii. 8).

It is a great thing to learn to take God first, and then He can afford to give us everything else, without the fear of its hurting us.

As long as you want anything very much, especially more than you want God, it is an idol. But when you become satisfied with God, everything else so loses its charm that He can give it to you without harm, and then you can take just as much as you choose, and use it for His glory.

There is no harm whatever in having money, houses, lands, friends and dearest children, if you do not value these things for themselves.

If you have been separated from them in spirit, and become satisfied with God Himself, then they will become to you channels to be filled with God to bring Him nearer to you. Then every little lamb around your household will be a tender cord to bind you to the Shepherd's heart. Then every affection will be a little golden cup filled with the wine of His love. Then every bank, stock and investment will be but a channel through which you can pour out His benevolence and extend His gifts.

October 7.

"He opened not His mouth" (Isa. liii. 7).

How much grace it requires to bear a misunderstanding rightly, and to receive an unkind judgment in holy sweetness! Nothing tests a Christian character more than to have some evil

thing said about him. This is the file that soon proves whether we are electro-plate or solid gold. If we could only know the blessings that lie hidden in our lives, we would say, like David, when Shimei cursed him, "Let him curse; it may be the Lord will requite me good for his cursing this day."

Some people get easily turned aside from the grandeur of their life-work by pursuing their own grievances and enemies, until their life gets turned into one little petty whirl of warfare. It is like a nest of hornets. You may disperse the hornets, but you will probably get terribly stung, and get nothing for your pains, for even their honey is not worth a search.

God give us more of His Spirit, who, when reviled, reviled not again; but committed Himself to Him that judgeth righteously.

Consider Him that endured such contradiction of sinners against Himself.

October 8.

"There failed not aught of any good thing which the Lord had spoken" (Josh. xxi. 45).

Some day, even you, trembling, faltering one, shall stand upon those heights and look back upon all you have passed through, all you have narrowly escaped, all the perils through which He guided you, the stumblings through which He guarded you, and the sins from which He saved you; and you shall shout, with a meaning you cannot understand now, "Salvation unto Him who sitteth upon the throne, and unto the Lamb."

Some day He will sit down with us in that glorious home, and we shall have all the ages in which to understand the story of our lives. And He will read over again this old marked Bible with us, He will show us how He kept all these promises, He will explain to us the mysteries that we could not understand, He will recall to our memory the things we have long forgotten, He will go over again with us the book of life, He will recall all the finished story, and I am sure we will often cry: "Blessed Christ! you have been so true, you have been so good! Was there ever love like this?" And then the great chorus will be repeated once more—"There failed not aught of any good thing that He hath spoken; all came to pass."

October 9.

"Peace be unto you" (John xx. 19, 21).

This is the type of His first appearing to our hearts when He comes to bring us His peace and to teach us to trust Him and love Him.

But there is a second peace which He has to give. Jesus said unto them again, "Peace be unto you." There is a "peace," and there is an "again peace." There is a peace with God, and there is "the peace of God that passeth understanding." It is the deeper peace that we need before we can serve Him or be used for His glory.

While we are burdened with our own cares, He cannot give us His. While we are occupied with ourselves, we cannot be at leisure to serve Him. Our minds will be so filled with our own anxieties that we would not be equal to the trust which He requires of us, and so, before He can entrust us with His work, He wants to deliver us from every burden and anxiety.

"Peace, perfect peace, in this dark world of sin,

The blood of Jesus whispers peace within.

Peace, perfect peace, by thronging duties pressed,

To do the will of Jesus, this is rest."

October 10.

"If ye, through the Spirit, do mortify the deeds of the body, ye shall live" (Rom. viii. 13).

The Holy Spirit is the only one who can kill us and keep us dead. Many Christians try to do this disagreeable work themselves, and they are going through a continual crucifixion, but they can never accomplish the work permanently. This is the work of the Holy Spirit, and when you really yield yourself to the death, it is delightful to find how sweetly He can slay you.

By the touch of the electric spark they tell us life is extinguished almost without a quiver of pain. But, however this may be in natural things, we know the Holy Spirit can touch with celestial fire the surrendered thing, and slay it in a moment, after it is really yielded up to the sentence of death. That is our business, and it is God's business to execute that sentence, and to keep it constantly operative.

Don't let us live in the pain of perpetual and ineffectual suicide, but reckoning ourselves dead indeed, let us leave ourselves in the hands of the blessed Holy Spirit, and He will slay whatever rises in opposition to His will, and keep us true to our heavenly reckoning, and filled with His resurrection life.

October 11.

"And He that searcheth the hearts knoweth what is the mind of the Spirit, because He maketh intercession for the saints according to the will of God" (Rom. viii. 27).

The Holy Spirit becomes to the consecrated heart the Spirit of intercession. We have two Advocates. We have an Advocate with the Father, who prays for us at God's right hand; but the Holy Spirit is the Advocate within, who prays in us, inspiring our petitions and presenting them, through Christ, to God.

We need this Advocate. We know not what to pray for, and we know not how to pray as we ought, but He breathes in the holy heart the desires that we may not always understand, the groanings which we could not utter.

But God understands, and He, with a loving Father's heart, is always searching our hearts to find the Spirit's prayer, and to answer it. He finds many a prayer there that we have not discovered, and answers many a cry that we never understood. And when we reach our home and read the records of life, we shall better know and appreciate the infinite love of that Divine Friend, who has watched within as the Spirit of prayer, and breathed out our every need to the heart of God.

October 12.

"The law of the Spirit of life in Christ Jesus hath made me free" (Rom. viii. 2).

The life of Jesus Christ brought into our heart by the Holy Spirit, operates there as a new law of divine strength and vitality, and counteracts, overcomes and lifts us above the old law of sin and death.

Let us illustrate these two laws by a

simple comparison. Look at my hand. By the law of gravitation it naturally falls upon the desk and lies there, attracted downward by that natural law which makes heavy bodies fall to the earth.

But there is a stronger law than the law of gravitation—my own life and will. And so through the operation of this higher law—the law of vitality—I defy the law of gravitation, and lift my hand and hold it above its former resting-place, and move it at my will. The law of vitality has made me free from the law of gravitation.

Precisely so the indwelling life of Christ Jesus, operating with the power of a law, lifts me above, and counteracts the power of sin in my fallen nature.

October 13.

"The carnal mind is enmity against God" (Rom. viii. 7).

The flesh is incurably bad. "It is not subject to the law of God, neither, indeed, can be." It never can be any better. It is no use trying to improve the flesh. You may educate it all you please. You may train it by the most approved methods, you may set before it the brightest examples, you may pipe to it or mourn to it, treat it with encouragement or severity; its nature will always be incorrigibly the same.

Like the wild hawk which the little child captures in its infancy and tries to train in the habits of the dove, before you are aware it will fasten its cruel beak upon the gentle fingers that would caress it, and show the old wild spirit of fear and ferocity. It is a hawk by nature, and it can never be made a dove. "For the carnal mind is enmity against God. It is not subject to the law

of God, neither, indeed, can be."

The only remedy for human nature is to destroy it, and receive instead the divine nature. God does not improve man. He crucifies the natural life with Christ, and creates the new man in Christ Jesus.

October 14.

"Get thee, behind me, Satan" (Matt. xvi. 23).

When your old self comes back, if you listen to it, fear it, believe it, it will have the same influence upon you as if it were not dead; it will control you and destroy you. But if you will ignore it and say: "You are not I, but Satan trying to make me believe that the old self is not dead; I refuse you, I treat you as a demon power outside of me, I detach myself from you"; if you treat it as a wife would her divorced husband, saying: "You are nothing to me, you have no power over me, I have renounced you, in the name of Jesus I bid you hence,"—lo! the evil thing will disappear, the shadow will vanish, the wand of faith will lay the troubled spirit, and send it back to the abyss, and you will find that Christ is there instead, with His risen life, to back up your confidence and seal your victory.

Satan can stand anything better than neglect. If you ignore him he gets disgusted and disappears. Jesus used to turn His back upon him and say, "Get thee behind Me, Satan." So let us refuse him, and we shall find that he will be compelled to act according to our faith.

October 15.

"Faith is the evidence of things not seen" (Heb. xi. 1).

True faith drops its letter in the post-office box, and lets it go. Distrust holds on to a corner of it, and wonders that the answer never comes.

I have some letters in my desk that have been written for weeks, but there was some slight uncertainty about the address or the contents, so they are yet unmailed. They have not done either me or anybody else any good yet. They will never accomplish anything until I let them go out of my hands and trust them to the postman and the mail.

This is the case with true faith. It hands its case over to God, and then He works.

That is a fine verse in the thirty-seventh Psalm: "Commit thy way unto the Lord, trust also in Him, and He worketh." But He never worketh until we commit.

Faith is a receiving, or still better, a taking of God's proffered gifts. We may believe, and come, and commit, and rest, but we will not fully realize all our blessing until we begin to receive and come into the attitude of abiding and taking.

October 16.

"Whereas thou hast been forsaken and hated, I will make thee a joy" (Isa. lx. 15).

God loves to take the most lost of men, and make them the most magnificent memorials of His redeeming love and power. He loves to take the victims of Satan's hate, and the lives that have been the most fearful examples of his power to destroy, and to use them to illustrate and illuminate the possibilities of Divine mercy and the new creations of the Holy Spirit.

He loves to take the things in our own lives that have been the worst, the hardest and the most hostile to God, and to transform them so that we shall be the opposites of our former selves.

The sweetest spirits are made out of the most stormy and self-willed, the mightiest faith is created out of a wilderness of doubts and fears, and the Divinest love is transformed out of stony hearts of hate and selfishness.

The grace of God is equal to the most uncongenial temperaments, to the most unfavorable circumstances; and its glory is to transform a curse into blessing, and show to men and angels of ages yet to come, that "where sin abounded, there grace did much more abound."

October 17.

"Abraham believed God" (Rom. iv. 3).

Abraham's faith reposed on God Himself. He knew the God he was dealing with. It was a personal confidence in one whom he could utterly trust.

The real secret of Abraham's whole life was that he was the friend of God, and knew God to be his great, good and faithful Friend, and, taking Him at His word, he had stepped out from all that he knew and loved, and gone forth upon an unknown pathway with none but God.

Beloved, are we trusting not only in the word of God, but have we learned to lean our whole weight upon Himself, the God of infinite love and power, our covenant God and everlasting Friend?

We are told that Abraham glorified God by this life of faith. The true way to glorify God is to let the world see what He is, and what He can do. God

does not want us so much to do things, as to let people see what He can do. God is not looking for extraordinary characters as His instruments, but He is looking for humble instruments through whom He can be honored throughout the ages.

October 18.

"All things are naked and open unto the eyes of Him with whom we have to do" (Heb. iv. 13).

The literal translation of this phrase is, all things are stripped and stunned. This is the force of the Greek words. The figure is that of an athlete in the Coliseum who has fought his best in the arena, and has at length fallen at the feet of his adversary, disarmed and broken down in helplessness. There he lies, unable to strike a blow, or lift his arm. He is stripped and stunned, disarmed and disabled, and there is nothing left for him but to lie at the feet of his adversary and throw up his arms for mercy.

Now this is the position that God wants to bring us to, where we shall cease our struggles and our attempts at self-defence or self-improvement, and throw ourselves helplessly upon the mercy of God. This is the sinner's only hope, and when he thus lies at the feet of mercy, Jesus is ready to lift him up and give him that free salvation which is waiting for all.

This, too, is the greatest need of the Christian seeking a deeper and higher life, to come to a full realization of his nothingness and helplessness, and to lie down, stripped and stunned at the feet of Jesus.

October 19.

"Denying ungodliness" (Titus ii. 12).

Let us say, "No," to the flesh, the world and the love of self, and learn that holy self-denial in which consists so much of the life of obedience. Make no provision for the flesh; give no recognition to your lower life. Say "No" to everything earthly and selfish. How very much of the life of faith consists in simply denying ourselves.

We begin with one great "Yes," to God, and then we conclude with an eternal "No," to ourselves, the world, the flesh and the devil.

If you look at the ten commandments of the Decalogue, you will find that nearly every one of them is a "Thou shalt not." If you read the thirteenth chapter of First Corinthians, with its beautiful picture of love, you will find that most of the characteristics of love are in the negative, what love "does not, thinks not, says not, is not." And so you will find that the largest part of the life of consecration is really saying, "No."

I am not my own,

I belong to Him.

I am His alone,

I belong to Him.

October 20.

"Let us not be weary in well-doing" (Gal. vi. 9).

If Paul could only know the consolation and hope that he has ministered to the countless generations who have marched along the pathway from the cross to the Kingdom above, he would be willing to go through a thousand lives and a thousand deaths such as he endured for the blessing that has followed since his noble head rolled in the dust by the Ostian gate of Rome.

And if the least of us could only anticipate the eternal issues that will probably spring from the humblest services of faith, we should only count our sacrifices and labors unspeakable heritages of honor and opportunity, and would cease to speak of trials and sacrifices made for God.

The smallest grain of faith is a deathless and incorruptible germ, which will yet plant the heavens and cover the earth with harvests of imperishable glory. Lift up your head, beloved, the horizon is wider than the little circle that you can see. We are living, we are suffering, we are laboring, we are trusting, for the ages yet to come!

October 21.

"Who shall separate us from the love of Christ?" (Rom. viii. 35).

And then comes the triumphant answer, after all the possible obstacles and enemies have been mentioned one by one, "Nay, in all these things we are more than conquerors, through Him that loved us." Our trials will be turned to helps; our enemies will be taken prisoners and made to fight our battles. Like the weights on yonder clock, which keep it going, our very difficulties will prove incentives to faith and prayer, and occasions for God becoming more real to us.

We shall get out of our troubles not only deliverance but triumph, and in all these things be even more than conquerors through Him that loved us.

Our security depends not upon our unchanging love, but on the love of God in Christ Jesus toward us. It is not the clinging arms of the babe on the mother's breast that keep it from falling, but the strong arms of the mother about it which will never let it go. He has loved us with an everlasting love, and although all else may change, yet He will never leave us nor forsake us.

October 22.

"Touched with the feeling of our infirmities" (Heb. iv. 15).

Some of us know a little what it is to be thrilled with a sense of the sufferings of others, and sometimes, the sins of others, and sins that seem to saturate us as they come in contact with us, and throw over us an awful sense of sin and need.

This is, perhaps, intended to give us some faint conception of the sympathy that Jesus felt when He had taken our sins, our sicknesses and our sorrows. Let us not hesitate to lay them on Him! It is far easier for Him to bear them off us than to bear them with us. He has already borne them for us, both in His life and in His death. Let us roll the burden upon Him, and let it roll away, and then, strong in His strength, and rested in His life and love, let us go forth to minister to others the sympathy and help which He has so richly given us.

The world is full of sorrow, and they that have known its bitterness and healing are God's ministers of consolation to a weeping world.

O, the tears that flow around us,

Let us wipe them while we may;

Bring the broken hearts to Jesus,

He will wipe their tears away.

October 23.

"How long halt ye between two opinions?" (I. Kings xviii. 21).

It is strange that people will not get over the idea that a consecrated life is a difficult one. A simple illustration will answer this foolish impression. Suppose a street car driver were to say, "It is much easier to run with one wheel on the track and the other off," his line would soon be dropped by the public, and they would prefer to walk. Of course, it is ever so much easier to run with both wheels on the track, and always on the track, and it is much easier to follow Christ fully than to follow with a half heart and halting step. The prophet was right in his pungent question, "How long halt ye between two opinions?" The undecided man is a halting man. The halting man is a lame man and a miserable man, and the out-and-out Christian is the admiration of men and angels, and a continual joy to himself.

Say, is it all for Jesus,

As you so often sing;

Is He your Royal Master,

Is He your heart's true King?

October 24.

"First gave their ownselves to the Lord, and unto us by the will of God" (II. Cor. viii. 5).

It is essential, in order to be successful in Christian work, that you shall be loyal not only to God, but to the work with which you are associated. The more deeply one knows the Lord the easier it is to get along with Him.

Superficial Christians are apt to be crotchetty. Mature Christians are so near the Lord that they are not afraid of missing His guidance, and not always trying to assert their loyalty to Him and independence of others.

The Corinthians, who had given themselves first to the Lord, had no difficulty in giving themselves to His Apostle by the will of God. It is delightful to work with true hearts on whom we can utterly depend.

God give us the spirit of a sound mind and the heart to "help along."

You can help by holy prayer,

Helpful love and joyful song;

O, the burdens you may bear;

O, the sorrows you may share;

O, the crowns you may yet may wear,

If you help along.

October 25.

"Now it is high time to awake out of sleep. Let us cast off the works of darkness and let us put on the armor of light" (Rom. xiii. 11, 12).

Let us wake out of sleep; let us be alert; let us be alive to the great necessities that really concern us.

Let us put off the garments of the night and the indulgences of the night; the loose robes of pleasure and flowing garments of repose; the festal pleasures of the hours of darkness are not for the children of the day. Let us cast off the works of darkness.

Let us arm ourselves for the day. Before we put on our clothes, let us put on our weapons, for we are stepping out into a land of enemies and a world of dangers; let us put on the helmet of salvation, the breastplate of faith and love, and the shield of faith, and stand armed and vigilant as the dangers of the last days gather around us.

Let us put on the Lord Jesus Christ. This is our robe of day. Not our own works or righteousness, but the person and righteousness of the Lord Jesus

Christ, who gave us His very life, and becomes to us our All-Sufficiency.

October 26.

"Go out into the highways and compel them to come in" (Luke xiv. 23).

In the great parable in the fourteenth chapter of Luke, giving an account of the great supper an ancient lord prepared for his friends and neighbors, and to which, when they asked to be excused, he invited the halt and the lame from the city slums and the lepers from outside the gate, there is a significant picture and object lesson of the program of Christianity in this age.

In the first place, it is obvious to every thoughtful mind that the Master is beginning to excuse the Gospel-hardened people of Christian countries. It is getting constantly more difficult to interest the unsaved of our own land, especially those that have been accustomed to hear the Gospel and the things of Christ. They have asked to be excused from the Gospel feast, and the Lord is excusing them.

At the same time, two remarkable movements indicated in the parable are becoming more and more manifest in our time. One is the Gospel for the slums and the neglected classes at home; the other is the Gospel for the heathen or the neglected classes abroad.

October 27.

"Behold, I am the Lord, the God of all flesh; is there anything too hard for Me?" (Jer. xxxii. 27.)

Cyrus, the King, was compelled to fulfil the vision of Jeremiah, by making a decree, the instant the prophecy had foretold, declaring that Jehovah had bidden him rebuild Jerusalem and invite her captives to return to their native home. So Jeremiah's faith was vindicated and Jehovah's prophecy gloriously fulfilled, as faith ever will be honored. Oh, for the faith, that in the dark present and the darker future, shall dare to subscribe the evidences and seal up the documents if need be, for the time of waiting, and then begin to testify to the certainty of its hope like the prophet of Anathoth!

The word Anathoth has a beautiful meaning, "echoes." So faith is the "echo" of God and God always gives the "echo" to faith, as He answers it back in glorious fulfilment. Oh, let our faith echo also the brave claim of the ancient prophet and take our full inheritance, with his glorious shout, "Oh, Lord, Thou art the God of all flesh, is there anything too hard for the Lord?" and back like an echo will come the heavenly answer to our heart, "I am the God of all flesh, is there anything too hard for Me?"

October 28.

"Thou good servant, because thou hast been faithful in a very little, have thou authority over ten cities" (Luke xix. 17).

It is not our success in service that counts, but our fidelity. Caleb and Joshua were faithful and God remembered it when the day of visitation came. It was a very difficult and unpopular position, and all of us are called in the crisis of our lives to stand alone and in this very matter of trusting God for victory over sin and our full inheritance in Christ we have all to be tested as they.

Our brethren even in the church of God, while admitting in the abstract

the loveliness and advantages of such an ideal life, tell us as they told Israel that it is impracticable and impossible, and many of us have to stand alone for years witnessing to the power of Christ to save His people to the uttermost and like Caleb following Him wholly, if alone. But this is the real victory of faith and the proof of our uncompromising fidelity.

Let us not therefore complain when we suffer reproach for our testimony or stand alone for God, but thank Him that He so honors us, and so stand the test that He can afterwards use us when the multitudes are glad to follow.

October 29.

"Whatsoever ye shall ask the Father in my name, He will give it you" (John xvi. 23).

Two men go to the bank cashier, both holding in their hands a piece of paper. One is dressed in expensive style, and presents a gloved and jeweled hand; the other is a rough, unwashed workman. The first is rejected with a polite sentence, and the second receives a thousand dollars over the counter. What is the difference? The one presented a worthless name; the other handed in a note endorsed by the president of the bank. And so the most virtuous moralist will be turned away from the gates of mercy, and the vilest sinner welcomed in if he presents the name of Jesus.

What shall we give to infinite purity and righteousness? Jesus! No other gift is worthy for God to receive. And He has given Him to us for this very end, to give back as our substitute and satisfaction. And He has "testified" of this gift what He has of no other, namely, that in Him He is well pleased

and all who receive Him "are accepted in the Beloved." Shall we accept the testimony that God is satisfied with His Son? Shall we be satisfied with Him?

October 30.

"Dwell deep" (Jer. xlix. 8).

God's presence blends with every other thought and consciousness, flowing sweetly and evenly through our business plans, our social converse our heart's affections, our manual toil, our entire life, blending with all, consecrating all, and conscious through all, like the fragrance of a flower, or the presence of a friend consciously near, and yet not hindering in the least the most intense and constant preoccupation of the hands and brain. How beautiful the established habit of this unceasing communion and dependence, amid and above all thoughts and occupations! How lovely to see a dear old saint folding away his books at night and humbly saying, "Lord Jesus, things are still just the same between us," and the falling asleep in His keeping.

So let us be stayed upon Him. Let us grow into Him with all the root and fibers of our being. He will not get tired of our friendship. He will not want to put us off sometimes. Beautiful the words of the suffering saint: "He never says good-bye." He stays. So let us be stayed on Him.

October 31.

"My grace is sufficient for thee; for My strength is made perfect in weakness" (II. Cor. xii. 9).

God allowed the crisis to close around Jacob on the night when he bowed at

Peniel in supplication to bring him to the place where he could take hold of God as he never would have done; and from that narrow pass of peril Jacob came enlarged in his faith and knowledge of God, and in the power of a new and victorious life. He had to compel David, by a long and painful discipline of years, to learn the almighty power and faithfulness of his God, and to grow up into the established principles of faith and godliness, which were indispensable for his subsequent and glorious career as the king of Israel.

Nothing but the extremities in which Paul was constantly placed could ever have taught him, and taught the church through him, the full meaning of the great promise he so learned to claim, "My grace is sufficient for thee." And nothing but our trials and perils would ever have led some of us to know Him as we do, to trust Him as we have, and to draw from Him the measures of grace which our very extremities made indispensable.

November 1.

"We will come unto him and make our abode with him" (John xiv. 23).

This idea of trying to get a holiness of your own, and then have Christ reward you for it, is not His teaching. Oh, no; Christ is the holiness; He will bring the holiness, and come and dwell in the heart forever.

When one of our millionaires purchases a lot, with an old shanty on it, he does not fix up the old shanty, but he gets a second-hand man, if he will have it, to tear it down, and he puts a mansion in its place. It is not fixing up the house that you need, but to give Christ the vacant lot, and He will excavate below our old life and build a house where He will live forever.

Now that is what we mean when we say that Christ will be the preparation for the blessing, and make way for His own approach. It is as when a great Assyrian king used to set out on a march. He did not command the people to make a road, but he sent on his own men, and they cut down the trees and filled the broken places, and levelled the mountains. So He will, if we will let Him, be the Coming King, the Author and Finisher of our faith.

November 2.

"Bringing into captivity every thought to the obedience of Christ" (II. Cor. x. 5).

If we would abide in Christ we must have no confidence in self. Self-repression must be ever the prime necessity of divine fulness and efficiency. Now you know how quickly you spring to the front when any emergency arises. When something in which you are interested comes up, you say what you think under some sudden impulse, and then perhaps you have weeks of taking back your thought and taking the Lord's instead. It is only when we get out of the way of the Lord that He can use us. So, be out of self, always suspending your will about everything until you have looked at it and said: "Lord, what is your will? What is your thought about it?"

Those who thus abide in Christ have the habit of reserve and quiet; they are not rattling and reckless talkers, they will not always have an opinion about everything, and they will not always know what they are going to do. There will be a deferential holding back of judgment, and walking softly with

God. It is our headlong, impulsive spirit that keeps us so constantly from hearing and following the Lord.

November 3.

"This is my Beloved, and this is my Friend" (Song of Solomon v. 16).

He is our Friend. "Which of you shall have a friend at night?" This has deep significance through the experience of each one of us. Who has not had a friend, and more of a friend in some respects than even a father?

There are some intimacies not born of human blood that are the most intense and lasting bonds of earthly love. One by one let us count them over and recall each act and bond of love, and think of all that we may trust them for and all in which they stood by us, and then as we concentrate the whole weight of recollection and affection, let us put God in that place of confidence and think He is all that and infinitely more.

Our Friend! The one who is personally interested in us; who has set His heart upon us; who has come near to us in the tender and delicate intimacy of unspeakable fellowship; who gave us such invaluable pledges and promises; who has done so much for us, and who is ever ready to take any trouble or go to any expense to aid us—to Him we are coming in prayer, our Heavenly Friend.

November 4.

"Hath the Lord as great delight in burnt offerings as in obeying the voice of the Lord?" (I. Sam. xv. 22).

Many a soul prays for sanctification, but fails to enter into the blessing because he does not intelligently understand and believingly accept God's appointed means by Jesus Christ and the indwelling of the Spirit. Many a prayer for the salvation of others is hindered because the very friend takes the wrong course to bring about the answer, and resorts to means which are wholly fitted to defeat his worthy object.

We know many a wife who is pleading for her husband's soul, and hoping to win him by avoiding anything that may offend him, and yielding to all his worldly tastes in the vain hope of attracting him to Christ. Far more effective would be an attitude of fidelity to God and fearless testimony to Him, such as God could bless.

Many a congregation wonders why it is so poor and struggling. It may be found that its financial methods are wholly unscriptural and often unworthy of ordinary self-respect.

When we ask God for any blessing, we must allow Him to direct the steps which are to bring the answer.

November 5.

"I in them, and Thou in Me" (John xvii. 23).

If we would be enlarged to the full measure of God's purpose, let us endeavor to realize something of our own capacities for His filling.

We little know the size of a human soul and spirit. Never, until He renews, cleanses and enters the heart can we have any adequate conception of the possibilities of the being whom God made in His very image, and whom He now renews after the pattern of the Lord Jesus Himself.

We know, however, that God has made the human soul to be His temple and abode, and that He knows how to make the house that can hold His

infinite fulness. We know something of this as all our nature quickens into spring tide life at the coming of the Holy Spirit, and as from time to time new baptisms awaken the dormant powers and susceptibilities that we did not know we possessed.

Oh, let us give Him the right to make the best of us, and, with wonder filled, we shall some day behold the glorious temple which He has reared, and shall say, "Lord, what is man that Thou hast set Thine heart upon Him?"

November 6.

"Bless the Lord, O, my soul" (Ps. ciii. 1).

Bless the Lord, O my soul; and all that is within me be stirred up to magnify His holy name. "Bless the Lord, O my soul, and forget not all His benefits; who forgiveth all thine iniquities; who healeth all thy diseases; who redeemeth thy life from destruction; who crowneth thee with lovingkindness and tender mercies; who satisfieth thy mouth with good things, so that thy youth is renewed like the eagle's." Who so well can sing this thanksgiving song as we, rejoicing as most of us do, we trust, in this full salvation, and praising God for the glorious health of a risen Lord and a continual youth?

This psalm and its opening verses is in the very center of the Scriptures by an exact count of letters and verses. So let it stand in our lives, as we look backward and forward and upward in grateful thanksgiving as we sing in its closing strains, "Bless the Lord, O my soul, and all that is within me, bless His holy name." Lord, center my heart in Thee and in the spirit of love and praise.

November 7.

"I will strengthen thee; yea, I will help thee; yea, I will uphold thee" (Isa. xli. 10).

God has three ways of helping us: First, He says, "I will strengthen thee"; that is, I will make you a little stronger yourself. And secondly, "I will help thee"; that is, I will add My strength to your strength, but you shall lead and I will help you. But thirdly, when you are ready, "I will uphold thee with the right hand of My righteousness"; that is, I will lift you up bodily and carry you altogether, and it will neither be your strength or My help, but My complete upholding. Hence it must be quite true, that when we come to the end of our strength, we come to the beginning of His, and that in Him the weakest are the strongest, and the most helpless the most helped. "He giveth power to the faint," but to "them that have no might" at all "He gives more strength," and His word forever is, "My grace is sufficient for thee." The answer is a paradox of contradictions, and yet the most practical truths, "Most gladly, therefore, will I glory in my infirmities, that the power of Christ may rest upon me; for when I am weak, then am I strong."

November 8.

"For the law of the Spirit of life in Christ Jesus hath made me free" (Rom. viii. 2).

There is a natural law of sin and sickness, and if we just let ourselves go and sink into the trend of circumstances we shall go down and sink under the power of the tempter. But there is another law of spiritual life and of physical life in Christ Jesus to which we can rise and through

which we can counterpoise and overcome the other law that bears us down. But to do this requires real spiritual energy and fixed purpose and a settled posture and habit of faith. It is just the same when we bind the power in our factory. We must turn the belt on and keep it on. The power is there, but we must keep the connection and while we do so the law of this higher power will work and all the machinery will be in operation. There is a spiritual law of choosing, believing, abiding and holding steady in our walk with God which is essential to the working of the Holy Ghost either in our sanctification or healing.

There is a word that saves the soul,

"I will trust";

It makes the sick and suffering whole.

"I will trust."

November 9.

"Because I live ye shall live also" (John xiv. 19).

After having become adjusted to our Living Head and the source of our life, now our business is to abide, absorb and grow, leaning on His strength, drinking in His life, feeding on Him as the Living Bread, and drawing all of our resources from Him in continual dependence and communion. The Holy Spirit will be the great Teacher and Minister in this blessed process. He will take of the things of Christ and show them unto us, and He will impart them through all the channels and functions of our spiritual organism. As we yield ourselves to Him He will breathe His own prayer of communion, drawing out our hearts in longings and hungerings, which are the pledge of their own fulfilment, calling us apart in silent and wordless prayer and opening every pore, organ, sense and sensibility of our spiritual being to take in His life. As the lungs absorb the oxygen of the atmosphere, as the senses breathe in the sweet odors of the garden, so the heart instinctively receives and rejoices in the affection and fellowship of the beloved One by our side. Thus we become like a tree planted by the rivers of waters.

November 10.

"But prayer was made without ceasing, of the church unto God for him" (Acts xii. 5).

But prayer is the link that connects us with God. This is the bridge that spans every gulf and bears us over every abyss of danger or of need. How significant the picture of the apostolic church: Peter in prison, the Jews triumphant, Herod supreme, the arena of martyrdom awaiting the dawning of the morning to drink up the apostle's blood,—everything else against it. "But prayer was made unto God without ceasing." And what the sequel? The prison open,—the apostle free,—the Jews baffled,—the wicked king eaten of worms, a spectacle of hideous retribution, and the Word of God rolling on in greater victory.

Do we know the power of our supernatural weapon? Do we dare to use it with the authority of a faith that commands as well as asks? God baptize us with holy audacity and Divine confidence. He is not wanting great men, but He is wanting men that will dare to prove the greatness of their God.

But God! But prayer!

November 11.

"Reckon yourselves dead, indeed" (Rom. vi. 11).

Our life from the dead is to be followed up by the habit and attitude henceforth which is the logical outcome of all this. "Reckon yourselves *dead indeed*, unto sin, but *alive unto God* through Jesus Christ, and yield yourselves unto God," not to die over again every day, "*but, as those who are alive from the dead*, and your members as instruments of righteousness unto God."

Further His resurrection life is given to fit us for "the fellowship of His sufferings and to be made conformable unto His death."

It is intended to enable us to toil and suffer with rejoicing and victory. We "mount up with wings as eagles," that we may come back to "run and not be weary, to walk and not faint."

But let us not mistake the sufferings. They do not mean *our* sufferings, but His. They are not our struggles after holiness, our sicknesses and pains, but those higher sufferings which, with Him, we bear for others, and for a suffering church and a dying world. May God help us, henceforth, never to have another sorrow for ourselves, and put us at leisure, in the power of His resurrection, to bear His burdens and drink His cup.

November 12.

"The earnest of the Spirit in our hearts" (II. Cor. i. 22).

Life in earnest. What a rare, what a glorious spectacle! We see it in the Son of God, we see it in His apostle, we see it in every noble, consecrated and truly successful life. Without it there may be a thousand good things, but they lack the golden thread that binds them all into a chain of power and permanence. They are like a lot of costly and beautiful beads on a broken string, that fall into confusion, and are lost in the end for want of the bond that alone could bind them into a life of consistent and lasting power. O for the baptism of fire! O for "the earnest, the spirit!" O for lives that have but one thing to do or care for! O for the depth and everlasting strength of the heart of Christ within our breast, to love, to sacrifice, to realize, to persevere, to live and die like Him!

We are going forth with a trust so sacred,

And a truth so divine and deep,

With a message clear and a work so glorious,

And a charge—such a charge—to keep.

Let it be your greatest joy, my brother,

That the Lord can count on you;

And if all besides should fail and falter,

To your trust be always true.

November 13.

"Delight thyself in the Lord" (Ps. xxxvii. 4).

Daniel's heart was filled with God's love for His work and kingdom and his prayers were the mightiest forces of his time, through which God gave to him the restoration of Israel to their own land, and the acknowledgment by the rulers of the world of the God of whom he testified and for whom he lived.

There is a beautiful promise in the thirty-seventh Psalm, "Delight thyself in the Lord, and He will give thee the desires of thine heart," which it is,

perhaps, legitimate to translate, that not only does it mean the fulfilment of our desires, but even the inspiration of our desires, the inbreathing of His thoughts into us, so that our prayers shall be in accord with His will and so shall bring back to us the unfailing answer of His mighty providence.

Teach me Thy thoughts, O God!

Think Thou, Thyself, in me,

Then shall I only always think

Thine own thoughts after Thee.

Teach me Thy thoughts, O God!

Show me Thy plan divine:

Save me from all my plans and works,

And lead me into Thine.

November 14.

"The things which are seen are temporal" (II. Cor. iv. 18).

How strong is the snare of the things that are seen, and how necessary for God to keep us in the things that are unseen! If Peter is to walk on the water, he must walk; if he is going to swim, he must swim, but he cannot do both. If the bird is going to fly it must keep away from the fences and the trees, and trust to its buoyant wings. But if it tries to keep within easy reach of the ground, it will make poor work of flying.

God had to bring Abraham to the end of his own strength, and to let him see that in his own body he could do nothing. He had to consider his own body as good as dead, and then take God for the whole work, and when he looked away from himself, and trusted God alone, then He became fully persuaded that what He had promised, He was able also to perform.

This is what God is teaching us, and

He has to keep away encouraging results until we learn to trust without them, and then He loves to make His word real in fact as well as faith.

Let us look only to Him to-day to do all things as He shall choose and in the way He shall choose.

November 15.

"Oh, man of desires" (margin) (Dan. x. 11).

This was the divine character given to Daniel of old. It is translated in our version, "O man, greatly beloved." But it literally means "O man of desires!" This is a necessary element in all spiritual forces. It is one of the secrets of effectual prayer, "What things soever ye desire, when ye pray, believe that ye receive them." The element of strong desire gives momentum to our purposes and prayers. Indifference is an unwholesome condition; indolence and apathy are offensive both to God and nature.

And so in our spiritual life, God often has to wake us up by the presence of trying circumstances, and push us into new places of trust by forces that we must subdue, or sink beneath their power. There is no factor in prayer more effectual than love. If we are intensely interested in an object, or an individual, our petitions become like living forces, and not only convey their wants to God, but in some sense convey God's help back to them.

May God fill us to-day with the heart of Christ that we may glow with the Divine fire of holy desire.

November 16.

"Watch therefore, for ye know neither

the day" (Matt. xxv. 13).

Jesus illustrates the unexpectedness of His coming by the figure of a thief entering a house when the master was not there. Life, like the old Jewish night, may be divided into three watches, youth, maturity, old age. The summons to meet God may come to us in either of these watches. A writer tells us of his experience with a camping party, of which he was a member, and which, he tells us, always arranged to have watches at night. "We became especially careful after what I am about to narrate happened. During the first night, from sunset to sunrise, we had in turn carefully guarded our camp. But when the next night came, so impressed were we with the orderly character of the neighborhood, that we concluded that no guard was needed until bedtime. Within our main tent the evening was spent in story-telling, singing and general amusement. When the hour to retire arrived, it was discovered that our other tents had been robbed and everything of value stolen. The work was done before we thought a guard necessary." It is never too soon to begin watching against sin.

November 17.

"The ark of the covenant of the Lord went before them" (Num. x. 33).

God does give us impressions but not that we should act on them as impressions. If the impression be from God, He will Himself give sufficient evidence to establish it beyond the possibility of a doubt.

How beautifully we read, in the story of Jeremiah, of the impression that came to him respecting the purchase of the field of Anathoth, but Jeremiah did not act upon this impression until after the following day, when his uncle's son came to him and brought him external evidence by making a proposal for the purchase. Then Jeremiah said: "I knew this was the word of the Lord."

He waited until God seconded the impression by a providence, and then he acted in full view of the open facts, which could bring conviction unto others as well as himself.

God wants us to act according to His mind.

We are not to ignore the Shepherd's personal voice, but like Paul and his companions at Troas, we are to listen to all the voices that speak, and "gather" from all the circumstances, as they did, the full mind of the Lord.

November 18.

"And He that sat upon the throne said, It is done" (Rev. xxi. 5, 6).

Great is the difference between action and transaction. We may be constantly acting without accomplishing anything, but a transaction is action that passes beyond the point of return, and becomes a permanent committal. Salvation is a transaction between the soul and Christ in which the matter passes beyond recall. Sanctification is a great transaction in which we are utterly surrendered, irrevocably consecrated and wholly committed to the Holy Ghost, and then He comes and seals the transaction and undertakes the work. Our covenant for our Lord's healing should be just as explicit, definite and irrevocable. And so of the covenants to which God is leading His children from time to time in regard to other matters of obedience and service. God grant that during this hallowed day many a consecrated life may be able to say with new

significance and permanence, "'Tis done, the great transaction's done."

For the living Vine is Jesus,
In whose fulness we may hide;
And find our life and fruitfulness
As we in Him abide.

November 19.

"We would see Jesus" (John xii. 21).

When any great blessing is awaiting us, the devil is sure to try and make it so disagreeable to us that we shall miss it. It is a good thing to know him as a liar, and remember, when he is trying to prejudice us strongly against any cause, that very likely the greatest blessing of our life lies there. Spurgeon once said that the best evidence that God was on our side is the devil's growl, and we are generally pretty safe in following a thing according to Satan's dislike for it. Beloved, take care, lest in the very line where your prejudices are setting you off from God's people and God's truth, you are missing the treasures of your life. Take the treasures of heaven no matter how they come to you, even if it be as earthly treasures generally are, like the kernel inside the rough shell, or the gem in the bosom of the hard rock.

I have seen Jesus and my heart is dead to all beside,
I have seen Jesus, and my wants are all, in Him, supplied.
I have seen Jesus, and my heart, at last, is satisfied,
Since I've seen Jesus.

November 20.

"The disciple whom Jesus loved leaned on His breast" (John xxi. 20).

An American gentleman once visited the saintly Albert Bengel. He was very desirous to hear him pray. So one night he lingered at his door, hoping to overhear his closing devotions. The rooms were adjoining and the doors ajar. The good man finished his studies, closed his books, knelt down for a moment and simply said: "Dear Lord Jesus, things are still the same between us," and then sweetly fell asleep. So close was his communion with his Lord that labor did not interrupt it, and prayer was not necessary to renew it. It was a ceaseless, almost unconscious presence, like the fragrance of the summer garden, or the presence of some dear one by our side whose presence we somehow feel, even though the busy hours pass by and not a word is exchanged.

"O blessed fellowship, divine,
O joy, supremely sweet,
Companionship with Jesus here,
Makes life with joy replete;
O wondrous grace, O joy sublime,
I've Jesus with me all the time."

November 21.

"Consider the lilies how they grow" (Matt. vi. 28).

It is said that a little fellow was found one day by his mother, standing by a tall sunflower, with his feet stuck in the ground. When asked by her, "What in the world are you doing there?" he naively answered, "Why, I am trying to grow to be a man."

His mother laughed heartily at the idea of his getting planted in the ground in order to grow, like the sunflower, and then, patting him gently on the head, "Why, Harry, that is not the way to grow. You can never grow bigger by

trying. Just come right in, and eat lots of good food, and have plenty of play, and you will soon grow to be a man without trying so hard."

Well, Harry's mother was right. Mrs. H. W. Smith never said a sweeter thing than when she answered the question—"How do the lilies grow?" by simply adding, "They grow without trying."

Our sweetest spiritual life is the life of self-unconsciousness through which we become so united to Christ, and live continually on His life, nourished, fed and constantly filled with His Spirit and presence and all the fulness of His imparted life.

November 22.

"Cast the beam out of thine own eye" (Matt. vii. 5).

Greater than the fault you condemn and criticise is the sin of criticism and condemnation. There is no place we need such grace as in dealing with an erring one. A lady once called on us on her way to give an erring sister a piece of her mind. We advised her to wait until she could love her a little more. Only He who loved sinners well enough to die for them can deal with the erring. We never see all the heart. He does, and He can convict without condemning, and reprove without discouraging. Oh, for more of the heart of Christ! Take care, brother, how you speak of another's fault. Ere you know, you may be in the same or deeper condemnation. Very significantly does the Master say that the man that sees a mote in his brother's eye, usually has a rafter in his own eye! One of the two unpardonable sins of the Bible is unforgiving lovelessness.

"Give me a heart like Thine,

Give me a heart like Thine,
By Thy wonderful power,
By Thy grace every hour,
Give me a heart like Thine."

November 23.

"It is high time to awake out of sleep" (Rom. xiii. 11).

One of the greatest enemies to faith is indolence. It is much easier to lie and suffer than to rise and overcome; much easier to go to sleep on a snowbank and never wake again, than to rouse one's self and shake off the lethargy and overcome the stupor. Faith is an energetic art; prayer is intense labor; the effectual working prayer of the righteous man availeth much.

Satan tries to put us to sleep, as he did the disciples in the garden; but let us not sleep as do others, but let us wake and be sober, continuing in prayer and watching therein with all perseverance, stirring up ourselves to take hold of His strength, "not slothful, but followers of them, who, through patience, inherit the promise." It is the wind that carries the ship across the waves; but the wind is powerless unless the hand of the boatman is held firmly upon the rudder, and that rudder is set hard against the wind. In like manner we hold the rudder, God fills the sails. It is not the rudder that carries the ship; but it is the rudder which catches the wind that carries the ship, so God keeps us in perfect peace while we are stayed upon Him.

November 24.

"I can do all things through Christ" (Phil. iv. 13).

A dear sister said one day: "I have so

much work to do that I have not time to get strength to do it by waiting on the Lord." Surely that was making bricks without straw, and even if it was the name of the Lord and the church, it was the devil's bondage. God sends not His servants on their own charges; but "He is able to make all grace abound towards us, that we, always having all sufficiency in all things, may abound unto every good work." The old story of the chieftain, fleeing from his foes and almost overtaken, but stopping in the midst of his flight to get a shoe upon his horse that he might fly more successfully is a true type and lesson for Christian workers.

The old Latin motto *festina lente*, "make haste slowly," has a great lesson for us. The more work we have to do, the more frequently we have to drop our head upon our desk and wait a little for heavenly aid and love, and then press on with new strength. One hour baptized in the love of the Holy Ghost is worth ten battling against wind and tide without the heavenly life.

November 25.

"Judge nothing before the time, until the Lord come" (I. Cor. iv. 5).

Nothing will more effectually arrest the working of the Spirit in the heart than the spirit of criticism. At the end of a meeting a young minister came forward and told us of the great blessing he had received that afternoon, and the baptism of the Holy Spirit that had come into his heart and being, setting him free from the bondage of years. And then he added, "It all came through your answer to that question, 'Will a criticizing spirit hinder the Holy Ghost from filling the heart?' "

As the question was asked and answered, he said, "I was sitting in the church criticizing a good deal that was going on, objecting to this thing and to that thing, finding fault with the expressions, and praises and testimonies, and feeling thoroughly unhappy. The Lord brought the answer home to my heart and convicted me of my sin, and there and then I laid it down and began to see the good instead of the evil. Blessing fell upon me and my soul was filled with joy and praise, and I saw where my error lay, that for years I had been trying to see the truth with my head instead of my heart."

November 26.

"He purgeth it that it may bring forth more fruit" (John xv. 2).

One day we passed a garden. The gardener had finished his pruning, and the wounds of the knife and saw were beginning to heal, while the warm April sun was gently nourishing the stricken plant into fresh life and energy. We thought as we looked at that plant how cruel it would be to begin next week and cut it down again. It would bleed to death. Now, the gardener's business is to revive and nourish into life. Its business is not to die, but to live. So, we thought, it is with the discipline of the soul. It, too, has its dying hour; but it must not be always dying. Rather reckon ourselves to be dead indeed unto sin and alive unto God through Jesus Christ our Lord Everlasting.

Breathe Thine own breath through all my mortal frame,

Help me Thy resurrection life to claim,

Which, 'mid all changes, still abides

the same,

And lead me in the way Everlasting.

Give me the heavenly foretaste here, I pray;

Let faith foredate the everlasting day,

And walking in its glory all the way,

O, lead me in the way Everlasting!

November 27.

"And the remnant of the oil ... shall pour upon the head" (Lev. xiv. 18).

In the account of the healing of the Hebrew leper there is a beautiful picture of the touching of his ears, hands and feet, with the redeeming blood and the consecrating oil, as a sign that his powers of understanding, service, and conduct were set apart to God, and divinely endued for the Master's work and will.

But after all this, we are significantly told that "the rest of the oil" was to be poured upon his head.

The former anointing was from the oil in the hand of the priest, but the latter was to be from the log, or vessel of oil itself. It was to be literally emptied over him, until he was bathed with all its contents.

It is a figure of the large and boundless baptism of the Holy Ghost. It speaks of something more even than the ordinary experiences of the consecrated Christian. It tells of the abundant and redundant supply which God has for us out of His illimitable fulness.

Have we received "the rest oil"? Are we *filled* with the Spirit, and letting the overflow bless others?

November 28.

"Without Me ye can do nothing" (John xv. 5).

How much can I do for Christ? We are accustomed to say.—As much as I can. Have we ever thought we can do more than we can?

This thought was lately suggested by the remarks of a Christian friend, who told how God had laid it upon her heart to do something for His cause which was beyond her power, and when she dared to obey Him, He gave her the assurance of His power and resources, and so marvelously met her faith that she was enabled to do more than she could otherwise, and accomplish her heart's desire, and see a work fulfilled to which her resources were unequal.

The apostle says, "I can do all things through Christ, who is my strength," and yet He says we are not able to think anything, as of ourselves.

Oh, blessed insufficiency! Oh, blessed All-Sufficiency! Oh, blessed nothingness, which brings us all things! Oh, blessed faith, whose rich dowry is, "All things are possible to him that believeth"!

O to be found of Him in peace,

Spotless and free from blame.

November 29.

"Could ye not watch with Me one hour?" (Matt. xxvi. 40.)

A young lady whose parents had died while she was an infant, had been kindly cared for by a dear friend of the family. Before she was old enough to know him, he went to Europe. Regularly he wrote to her through all his years of absence, and never failed to send her money for all her wants. Finally word came that during a

certain week he would return and visit her. He did not fix the day or the hour. She received several invitations to take pleasant trips with her friends during that week. One of these was of so pleasant a nature that she could not resist accepting it. During her trip, he came, inquired as to her absence, and left. Returning she found this note: "My life has been a struggle for you, might you not have waited one week for me?" More she never heard, and her life of plenty became one of want. Jesus has not fixed the day or hour of His return, but He has said, "Watch," and should He come to-day, would He find us absorbed in thoughtless dissipation? May we be found each day, in the expectant attitude of those watching for a loved one.

November 30.

"In lowliness of mind let each esteem other better than themselves" (Phil. ii. 3).

When the apostle speaks of "the deep things of God," he means more than deep spiritual truth. There must be something before this. There must be a deep soil and a thorough foundation.

Very much of our spiritual teaching fails, because the people to whom we give it are so shallow. Their deeper nature has never been stirred.

The beatitudes begin at the bottom of things, the poor in spirit, the mourners, and the hungry hearts. Suffering is essential to profound spiritual life. We need not go to a monastery or a leper hospital to find it. The first real opportunity for unselfishness will bring into your life the anguish of crucifixion, unless you are born of some different race from Adam's.

It is because men and women have not faced this that they know so little of suffering and death. We must have deep convictions. Truth must be to us a necessity, and principle a part of our very being. Lord, make me poor in spirit. Lord help me to be even as Thou wert when on earth, always the lowest, and therefore "highly exalted."

December 1.

"As He is, so are we in this world" (I. John iv. 17).

Jesus will come into the surrendered heart and unite Himself with it, impart to it His own life and being and become anew from day to day, the supply of its spiritual needs and the substitute for its helplessness.

Our part is simply to yield ourselves fully recognizing our own worthlessness and then take Jesus Himself to live in us and be, moment by moment, our strength, purity and victory.

One in His death on the tree,

One as He rose from the dead;

I from the curse am as free

E'en as my glorious Head.

One in His merits I stand,

One as I Pray in His name,

All that His worth can demand

I may with confidence claim.

One on the Throne by His side,

One in His Sonship divine,

One as the Bridegroom and Bride,

One as the Branch and the Vine.

All that He has shall be mine,

All that He is I shall be;

Robed in His glory divine,

I shall be even as He.

December 2.

"Looking diligently lest any man fail" (Heb. xii. 15).

It is not losing all, but coming short we are to fear. We may not lose our souls, but we may lose something more precious than life—His full approval, His highest choice, and our incorruptible and star-gemmed crown. It is the one degree more that counts, and makes all the difference between hot water—powerless in the boiler—and steam—all alive with power, and bearing its precious freight across the continent.

I want, in this short life of mine,

As much as can be pressed

Of service true for God and man,

Help me to be my best.

I want to stand when Christ appears

And hear my name confessed

Numbered among the hidden ones,

His holiest and best.

I want, among the victor throng,

To have my name confessed;

And hear my Master say at last,

Well done, you did your best.

Give me, O Lord, Thy highest choice;

Let others take the rest:

Their good things have no charm for me,

For I have got Thy best.

December 3.

Thy thoughts are very deep (Ps. xcii. 5).

When a Roman soldier was told by his guide that if he insisted on taking a certain journey it would probably be fatal he answered, "It is necessary for me to go, it is not necessary for me to live." That was depth. When we are convicted like that we shall come to something.

The shallow nature lives in its impulses, its impressions, its intuitions, its instincts, and very largely in its surroundings. The profound character looks beyond all these and moves steadily on, sailing past all the storms and clouds into the clear sunshine which is always on the other side, and waiting for the afterwards which always brings the reversion of sorrow and seeming defeat and failure.

When God has deepened us, then He can give us His deeper truths, His profoundest secrets, and His mightier trusts.

Lord, lead me into the depths of Thy life and save me from a shallow experience.

On to broader fields of holy vision;

On to loftier heights of faith and love;

Onward, upward, apprehending wholly,

All for which He calls thee from above.

December 4.

"From me is thy fruit found" (Hos. xiv. 8).

Nothing keeps us from advancement more than ruts and drifts, and wheel-tracks into which our chariots roll and then move on in the narrow line with unchanging monotony, currents in life's stream on which we are borne in the old direction until the law of habit almost makes advance impossible. The true remedy for this is to commence at nothing; taking Christ afresh to be the Alpha and Omega for a deeper, higher, Divine experience,

waiting even for His conception of thought, desire, prayer, and afraid lest our highest thought should be below His great plan of wisdom and love.

O Comforter gentle and tender,
O holy and heavenly Dove,
We're yielding our heart in surrender,
We're waiting Thy fulness to prove.
O come as the heart-searching fire,
O come as the sin-cleansing flood;
Consume us with holy desire,
And fill with the fulness of God.
Anoint us with gladness and healing;
Baptize us with power from on high;
O come with filling and sealing
While low at the Thy footstool we lie.

December 5.

"With a perfect heart to make David King" (I. Chron. xii. 38).

"What is the supreme purpose of our life? They were all of one heart to make David king." Is this our purpose, to prepare the Bride, to prepare the world, to prepare His way? Does it dwarf and dim all other ambitions, all other cares? Does it fill and satisfy every capacity, every power, every desire? Does it absorb every moment, every energy, every resource? Does it give direction and tone to every plan and work of life? Does it decide for us the education of our children, the investment of our means, the friendships and associations of life, the whole activity, interest and outlook of our being? Are we in it, spirit, soul and body, all we are, all we do, all we hope for—of one heart to make Jesus King?

We're going forth united
With loyal heart and hand,
To bear His royal banner

Aboard o'er every land.
From every tribe and nation
We'll haste His Bride to bring.
And Oh, with what glad welcome
We'll make our Jesus King.

December 6.

"Humble yourselves therefore under the mighty hand of God, that He may exalt you" (I. Peter v. 6).

Opposition is essential to a true equilibrium of forces. The centripetal and centrifugal forces acting in opposition to each other keep our planet in her orbit. The one propelling, and the other repelling, so act and react, that instead of sweeping off into space in a pathway of desolation and destruction, she pursues her even orbit around her solar center.

So God guides our lives. It is not enough to have an impelling force— we need just as much a repelling force, and so He holds us back by the testing ordeals of life, by the pressure of temptation and trial, by the things that seem to be against us, but really are furthering our way and stablishing our goings. Let us thank Him for both, let us take the weights as well as the wings, and thus divinely impelled, let us press on with faith and patience in our high and heavenly calling.

Lord, help me to learn from all that comes to me this day Thy highest will.

Lord, help me to-day to sink under Thy blessed hand, that Thou mayest have Thy way and will with me.

December 7.

"Abide with us; for it is toward evening" (Luke xxiv. 29).

In His last messages to the disciples in

the 14th and 15th chapters of John, the Lord Jesus clearly teaches us that the very essence of the highest holiness is, "Abide in Me, and I in you, for without Me ye can do nothing."

The very purpose of the Holy Ghost whom He promised was to reveal Him, that at "that day, ye shall know that I am in the Father, and ye in Me, and I in you," and the closing echo of His intercessory prayer was embraced in these three small but infinite words, "I in them."

Is it for me to be cleansed by His power

From the pollution of sin?

Is it for me to be kept every hour

By His abiding within?

Is it for me to be perfectly whole

Thro' His anointing divine;

Claiming in body, and spirit, and soul,

All of His fulness as mine?

Wonderful promise so full and so free,

Wonderful Saviour, Oh, how can it be,

Cleansing and pardon and mercy for me?

Yes, it's for me, for me.

December 8.

"Is there no balm in Gilead; is there no physician there?" (Jer. viii. 22).

Divine healing is just divine life. It is the headship of Christ over the body. It is the life of Christ in the frame. It is the union of our members with the very body of Christ and the inflowing life of Christ in our living members. It is as real as His risen and glorified body. It is as reasonable as the fact that He was raised from the dead and is a living man with a true body and a rational soul to-day, at God's right hand. That living Christ belongs to us in all His attributes and powers. We are members of His body, His flesh and His bones, and if we can only believe and receive it, we may live upon the very life of the Son of God.

Lord, help me to know the "Lord for the body and the body for the Lord."

There is healing in the promise,

There is healing in the blood,

There is strength for all our weakness

In the risen Son of God.

And the feeblest of His children,

All His glorious life may share;

He has healing balm in Gilead,

He's the Great Physician there.

December 9.

"Launch out into the deep" (Luke v. 4).

One of the special marks of the Holy Ghost in the Apostolic Church was the spirit Of boldness. One of the most essential qualities of the faith that is to attempt great things for God and expect great things from God, is holy audacity. Where we are dealing with a supernatural Being, and taking from Him things that are humanly impossible, it is easier to take much than little; it is easier to stand in a place of audacious trust than in a place of cautious, timid clinging to the shore. Like wise seamen in the life of faith, let us launch out into the deep, and find that all things are possible with God, and all things are possible unto him that believeth.

Let us to-day attempt great things for God, take His faith and believe for them and His strength to accomplish them.

The mercy of God is an ocean divine,

A boundless and fathomless flood;

Launch out in the deep, cut away the shore-line,

And be lost in the fulness of God.

Oh, let us launch out in this ocean so broad,

Where the floods of salvation o'erflow,

Oh, let us be lost in the mercy of God,

Till the depth of His fulness we know.

December 10.

"According to the measure of the rule which God hath distributed" (II. Cor. x. 13).

According to thy faith be it unto thee was Christ's great law of healing and blessing in His earthly ministry. This was what He meant when He said, "With what measure ye mete it shall be measured to you again." These mighty measures are limited by the the measures that we bring. God deals out His heavenly treasures to us in these glorious vessels, but each of us must bring our drinking cup, and according to its measure we shall be filled.

But even the measure of our faith may be a Divine one. Thank God, the little cup has become enlarged through the grace of Jesus, until from its bottom there flows a pipe into the great ocean, and if that connection is kept open we shall find that our cup is as large as the ocean and never can be drained to the bottom. For He has said to us, "Have the faith of God," and surely this is an illimitable measure.

Let us claim the mighty promise,

Let us light the torches dim;

Let us join the glorious chorus,

Nothing is too hard for Him.

December 11.

"I pray not for the world, but for them" (John xvii. 9).

How often we say we would like to get some strong spirit to pray for us, and feel so helped when we think they are carrying us in their faith. But there is One whose prayers never fail to be fulfilled and who is more willing to give them to us than any human friend. His one business at God's right hand is to make intercession for His people, and we are simply coming in the line of His own appointment and His own definite promise and provision, when we lay our burdens upon Him and claim His advocacy without doubt or fear. "Seeing then that we have a great High Priest that is passed into the heavens, Jesus, the Son of God, let us come boldly to the throne of grace that we may find help in time of need."

Like a golden censer glowing,

Filled with burning odors rare,

All my heart is upward flowing,

In a cloud of ceaseless prayer.

O'er the heavenly altar bending,

Jesus interceding stands,

All our prayers to heaven ascending,

Reach the Father through His hands.

December 12.

"To abide in the flesh is more needful for you, and having this confidence, I know that I shall abide" (Phil. i. 24, 25).

One of the most blessed things about divine healing is that the strength it brings is holy strength, and finds its natural and congenial outflow in holy acts and exercises.

Mere natural strength seeks its gratification in natural pleasures and activities, but the strength of Christ leads us to do as Christ would do, and to seek our congenial employment in His holy service.

The life of Christ in a human body saves it from a thousand temptations to self-indulgence and sin, and not only gives us strength for higher service, but also a desire for it, and puts into it a zest and spring which gives it double power.

Lord, help us to-day to claim Thy life and then give it for the help of others.

Have you found the branch of healing?

Pass it on.

Have you felt the Spirit's sealing,

Pass it on.

'Twas for this His mercy sought you,

And to all His fulness brought you,

By the precious blood that bought you,

Pass it on.

December 13.

"He that abideth in Me and I in him the same bringeth forth much fruit for apart from Me ye can do nothing" (John xv. 5).

So familiar are the vine and the branches, it is not necessary to explain; only the branches and the vine are one. The vine does not say, I am the central trunk running up and you are the little branches; but I am the whole thing, and you are the whole thing. He counts us partakers of His nature. "Apart from Me ye can do nothing." The husband and the wife, and many more figures contribute to this marvelous Christ teaching, which has no parallel, no precedent in any other teaching under the sun; that

Christ is the life of His people, and that we are absolutely linked with and dependent upon Him. All other systems teach how much man is and may become. Christianity shows how a man must lose all he is if he would come into full unity with Christ in His life.

Lord, help me this day to abide in Thee.

Oh! what a wonderful place

Jesus has given to me!

Saved by His glorious grace,

I may be even as He.

December 14.

"Instead of the thorn shall come up the fir tree" (Isa. lv. 13).

Difficulties and obstacles are God's challenges to faith. When hindrances confront us in the path of duty we are to recognize them as vessels for faith to fill with the fulness and all-sufficiency of Jesus, and as we go forward, simply and fully trusting Him, we may be tested, we may have to wait and let patience have her perfect work, but we shall surely find at last the stone rolled away, and the Lord waiting to render unto us double for our time of testing, and fulfil the promise, "Instead of the thorn shall come up the fir tree, instead of the brier the myrtle tree, and it shall be to the Lord for an everlasting sign that shall not be cut off."

Oft there comes a wondrous message
When my hopes are growing dim;
I can hear it through the darkness,
Like some sweet and far-off hymn.
Nothing is too hard for Jesus,
No man can work like Him.
When my way is closed in darkness

And my foes are fierce and grim,
Still it sings above the conflict
Like some glad, victorious hymn:
Nothing is too hard for Jesus,
No man can work like Him.

December 15.

"When my heart is overwhelmed lead me to the Rock that is higher than I" (Ps. lxi. 2).

The end of self is the beginning of God. "When the tale of bricks is doubled then comes Moses." That is the old Hebrew way of putting it. "Man's extremity is God's opportunity." That is the proverbial expression of it. "When my heart is overwhelmed, lead me to the rock that is higher than I." That is David's way of expressing it. "We have no might against this company, neither know we what to do." No might, no light—"but our eyes are upon Thee," that was Jehoshaphat's experience of it. "Mine eyes fail with looking upward. I am oppressed, Lord, undertake for me."

"When I had great trouble I always went to God and was wondrously carried through; but in my little trials I used to try to manage them myself, and often most signally failed." So Miss Havergal has expressed the experience of many a Christian. God wants us "at our wit's end," and then He will show His wisdom, love and power. How often we ask God to help, and then begin to count up the human probabilities! God's very blessings become a hindrance to us if we look from Him to them.

December 16.

"I will restore to you the years that the locust hath eaten, the canker worm and the caterpillar and the palmer worm, my great army, which I sent among you" (Joel ii. 25).

A friend said to me once: "I have got to reap what I sowed, for God has said: 'Whatsoever a man soweth, that shall he also reap.' Then why don't you apply this in the spiritual world, and compel the sinner to pay the penalty of his sins?"

Christ has borne this penalty, and the same Christ has borne the natural penalties, too, and delivered us out of condemnation in every sense. Physical sufferings come to us, but not under the law of retribution, but only as a Divine discipline. Every penalty has been fulfilled by Christ and every law satisfied, and so far as we can have risen with Him into the plane of spiritual and eternal life, we are lifted above the mere realm of law, and we enter into the full effects of His complete satisfaction of every claim against us. So it is true that even the wreck that sin has brought upon our physical and temporal life is removed by His great atonement, and the promise is made real to us, "I will restore to you the years that the locust hath eaten."

December 17.

"Be careful for nothing" (Phil. iv. 6).

What is the way to lay your burden down? "Take My yoke upon you, and learn of Me; for I am meek and and lowly of heart, and ye shall find rest unto your souls."

"For My yoke is easy and My burden is light." That is the way to take His burden up. You will find that His burden is always light. Yours is a very heavy one. Happy day if you have exchanged burdens and laid down your loads at His blessed feet to take

up His own instead. God wants to rest His workers, and He is too kind to put His burden on hearts that are already bowed down with their own weight of cares.

Are you fearing, fretting or repining?

You can never know God's perfect peace.

On His bosom all your weight reclining.

All your anxious doubts and cares must cease.

Would you know the peace that God has given?

Would you find the very joy of heaven?

Be careful for nothing,

Be prayerful for everything,

Be thankful for anything,

And the peace of God that passeth understanding

Shall keep your mind and heart.

December 18.

"The faith of the Son of God" (Gal. ii. 20).

Faith is hindered most of all by what we call "our faith," and fruitless struggles to work out a faith which is but a make-believe and a desperate trying to trust God, which must ever come short of His vast and glorious promises. The truth is that the only faith that is equal to the stupendous promises of God and the measureless needs of our life, is "the faith of God" Himself, the very trust which He will breathe into the heart which intelligently expects Him as its power to believe, as well as its power to love, obey, or perform any other exercise of the new life.

Blessed be His name! He has not given us a chain which reaches within a single link of our poor helpless heart, but that one last link is fatal to all the chain. Nay, the last link, the one that fastens on the human side is as Divine as the link that binds the chain of promise in the heavens. "Have the faith of God," is His great command. "I live by the faith of the Son of God" is the victorious testimony of one who had proved it true.

Lord, teach me to have the faith of the Son of God.

December 19.

"God giveth grace unto the humble" (James iv. 6).

One of the marks of highest worth is deep lowliness. The shallow nature, conscious of its weakness and insufficiency, is always trying to advertise itself and make sure of its being appreciated. The strong nature, conscious of its strength, is willing to wait and let its work be made manifest in due time. Indeed, the truest natures are so free from all self-consciousness and self-consideration that their object is not to be appreciated, understood or recompensed, but to accomplish their true mission and fulfil the real work of life.

One of the most suggestive expressions used respecting the Lord Jesus is given by the evangelist John in the thirteenth chapter of His Gospel, where we read, "Jesus, knowing that He came from God, and went to God, riseth from supper and began to wash the disciples' feet." It was because He knew His high dignity and His high destiny that He could stoop to the lowest place and that place could not degrade Him.

God give to us the Divine insignia of heavenly rank, a bowed head, a meek and lowly spirit.

December 20.

"That I should be the minister of Jesus Christ to the Gentiles, ministering the Gospel of God" (Rom. xv. 16).

This is a very beautiful and practical conception of missionary work. There is a great difference in being consecrated to our God. We may be consecrated to our work and consecrated to our God. We may be consecrated and fitted to do missionary work, and utterly fail, if He should call us to do something different. But when we are consecrated to Him, we shall be ready for anything He may require of us, and be as well qualified to serve Him by the sick bed of a brother, or even in the secular duties of home, as in standing in the pulpit or leading a soul to Christ.

Paul's conception is holy work, or a special sacrifice, and directly unto Christ, and Christ alone; and he stood as one should stand at the altar of incense, lifting up with holy hands the Gentile nations unto God, and laying all his work like fragrant incense before the throne, pleased only with what would please his Master, and stand the test of His inspection, and the seal of His approval in that glorious day.

This is the spirit of true service.

December 21.

"Give us day by day our daily bread" (Luke xi. 3).

It is very hard to live a lifetime at once, or even a year, but it is delightfully easy to live a day at a time. Day by day the manna fell, so day by day we may live upon the heavenly bread, and live out our life for Him. Let us, breath by breath, moment by moment, step by step, abide in Him, and, just as we take care of the days, He will take care of the years.

God has given two precious promises for the days. "As thy days so shall thy strength be," is His ancient covenant, and the literal translation of our Master's parting words to His disciples is, "Lo, I am with you all the days, even unto the end of the age."

Like the little water spider that goes down beneath the waters of the pool enclosed in a bubble of air, and there builds its nest and rears its young, and lives its little life in that bright sphere down beneath the slimy pool, so let us in this dark world shut ourselves in with Christ in the little circle of each returning day, and so abide in Him, breathing the air of heaven and living in His love.

December 22.

"My tongue also shall talk of Thy righteousness all the day long" (Ps. lxxi. 24).

It is a simple law of nature, that air always comes in to fill a vacuum. You can produce a draught at any time, by heating the air until it ascends, and then the cold air rushes in to supply its place. And so we can always be filled with the Holy Spirit by providing a vacuum. This breath is dependent upon exhausting the previous breath before you can inhale a fresh one. And so we must empty our hearts of the last breath of the Holy Spirit that we have received, for it becomes exhausted the moment we have

received it, and we need a new supply, to prevent spiritual asphyxia.

We must learn the secret of breathing out, as well as breathing in. Now, the breathing in will continue if the other part is rightly done. One of the best ways to make room for the Holy Spirit is to recognize the needs that come into the life as vacuums for Him to fill, and we shall find plenty of needs all around us to be filled, and as we pour out our lives in holy service, He will pour His in—in full measure.

Jesus, empty me and fill me
With Thy fulness to the brim.

December 23.

"Out of the spoils won in battles, did they dedicate to maintain the house of the Lord" (I. Chron. xxvi. 27).

Physical force is stored in the bowels of the earth, in the coal mines, which came from the fiery heat that burned up great forests in ancient ages. And so spiritual force is stored in the depths of our being, through the very sufferings which we cannot understand. Some day we shall find that the deliverance we have won from these trials were preparing us to become true "Great Hearts" in life's Pilgrim's Progress, and to lead our fellow pilgrims triumphantly through trial to the city of the King.

But let us never forget that the source of helping other people must be victorious suffering. The whining, murmuring pang never does anybody any good. Paul did not carry a cemetery with him, but a chorus choir of victorious praise, and the harder the trial, the more he trusted and rejoiced, shouting from the very altar of sacrifice, "Yea, and if I be offered upon the service and sacrifice of your faith, I joy and rejoice with you all."

Lord, help me this day to draw strength from all that comes to me.

December 24.

"And seekest thou great things for thyself? Seek them not; for behold I will bring evil upon all flesh, saith the Lord; but thy life will I give unto thee for a prey in all places whither thou goest" (Jer. xlv. 5).

A promise given for hard places, and a promise of safety and life in the midst of tremendous pressure, a life for a prey.

It may well adjust itself to our own times, which are growing harder as we near the end of the age, and the tribulation times.

What is the meaning of "a life for a prey"? It means a life snatched out of the jaws of the destroyer, as David snatched the lamb from the lion. It means not a place of security, or of removal from the noise of the battle, and the presence of our foes, but it means a table in the midst of our enemies, a shelter from the storm, a fortress amid the foe, a life preserved in the face of continual pressure, Paul's healing when pressed out of measure so that he despaired even of life, Paul's Divine help when the thorn remained, but the power of Christ rested upon him and the grace of Christ was sufficient.

Lord, give me my life for a prey, and in the hardest places help me to-day to be victorious.

December 25.

"I bring you glad tidings" (Luke ii. 10).

A Christmas spirit should be a spirit of

humanity. Beside that beautiful object lesson on the Manger, the Cradle, and the lowly little child, what Christian heart can ever wish to be proud? It is a spirit of joy. It is right that these should be glad tidings, for, "Behold, I bring you glad tidings of great joy which shall be to all people."

It is a spirit of love. It should be the joy that comes from giving joy to others. The central fact of Christmas is the Christ who loved us, and came to live among us and die for us, and he or she has no right to share its joys who is living for himself or herself alone.

Love is always sacrificial, and so the Christmas spirit will call us to a glad and full surrender, first to God, and then the joyful sacrifice of what we call our own for His glory and the good of others.

The Christmas spirit is a spirit of worship. It finds the Magi at His feet with their gold and frankincense and myrrh. Let it find us there, too.

The Christmas spirit is a spirit of missions. Its glad tidings are for all people.

December 26.

"The Spirit that dwelleth in us lusteth to envy" (James iv. 5).

This beautiful passage has been unhappily translated in our Revised Version: "The Spirit that dwelleth in us lusteth to envy." It ought to be, "The Spirit that dwelleth in us loveth us to jealousy." It is the figure of a love that suffers because of its intense regard for the loved object.

The Holy Ghost is so anxious to accomplish in us and for us the highest will of God, and to receive from us the truest love for Christ, our Divine Husband, that He becomes jealous when in any way we disappoint Him,

or divide His love with others.

Therefore, it is said in the preceding passage, "Ye adulterers and adulteresses, know ye not that the friendship of the world is enmity with God?"

Oh, shall we grieve so kind a Friend? Shall we disappoint so loving a Husband? Shall we not meet the blessed Holy Spirit with the love He brings us, and give in return our undivided and unbounded affection?

Was there ever a Bridegroom so loving seeking our heart to gain?

December 27.

"He sent forth the dove which returned not again unto him" (Gen. viii. 12).

First, we have the dove going forth from the ark, and finding no rest upon the wild and drifting waste of sin and judgment. This represents the Old Testament period, perhaps, when the Holy Ghost visited this sinful world, but could find no resting-place, and went back to the bosom of God.

Next, we have the dove going forth and returning with the olive leaf in her mouth, the symbol and the pledge of peace and reconciliation, the sign that judgment was passed and peace was returning. Surely this may beautifully represent the next stage of the Holy Spirit's manifestation, as going forth in the ministry and death of Jesus Christ, to proclaim reconciliation to a sinful world.

There is a third stage, when, at length, the dove goes forth from the ark and returns no more; but it makes the world its home, and builds its nest amid the habitations of men. This is the third and present stage of the Holy Spirit's blessed work. Let us welcome the Dove to a nest in our hearts.

December 28.

"The Holy Ghost, whom God hath given to them that obey Him" (Acts v. 32).

We can only know and prove the fulness of the Spirit as we step out into the larger purposes and plans of Christ for the world.

Perhaps the chief reason why the Holy Spirit has been so limited in His work in the hearts of Christians, is the shameful neglect of the unsaved and unevangelized world by the great majority of the professed followers of Christ. There are millions of professing Christians—and, perhaps, real Christians—in the world, who have never given one real, earnest thought to the evangelization of the heathen world.

God will not give the Holy Spirit in His fulness for the selfish enjoyment of any Christian. His power is a great trust, which we must use for the benefit of others and for the evangelization of the lost and sinful world. Not until the people of God awake to understand His real purpose for the salvation of men, will the Church ever know the fulness of her Pentecost. God's promised power must lie along the line of duty, and as we obey the command, we shall receive His promise in his fulness.

Lord, help me to understand Thy plan.

December 29.

"I have not shunned to declare unto you all the counsel of God" (Acts xx. 27).

It is probable that God lets every human being, that crosses our path, meet us, in order that we may have the opportunity of leaving some blessing in his path, and dropping into his heart and life some influence that will draw him nearer to God. It would be blessed, indeed, if we could meet every immortal soul, at last, that we have ever touched in the path of life, and truly say, "I am pure from the blood of all men."

Beloved, is it so? The servant that works in your household; the man that sat beside you in the train; the laborer that wrought for you, and, above all, the members of your household and family, your fellow-laborer in the shop or factory, have you done your best to lead them to Christ?

The early Christians regarded every situation as an opportunity to witness for Christ. Even when brought before kings and governors, it never occurred to them that they were to try to get free, but the Master's message to them was, "It shall turn to you for a testimony." It was simply an occasion to preach to kings and rulers, whom otherwise they could not reach.

December 30.

"That God would fulfil in you all the good pleasure of His goodness, and the work of faith with power" (II. Thess. i. 11).

Our God is looking to-day for pattern men, and when He gets a true sample, it is very easy to reproduce it in a thousand editions, and multiply it in other lives without limitation.

All the experiences of life come to us as tests, and as we meet them, our loving Father is watching with intense and jealous love, to see us overcome, and if we fail He is deeply disappointed, and our adversary is filled with joy.

We are a gazing-stock continually for angels and principalities, and every

step we take is critical and decisive for something in our eternal future.

When Abraham went forth that morning to Mount Moriah, it was an hour of solemn probation, and when he came back he was one of God's tested men, with the stamp of His eternal approbation. God could say, "I know him, that he will do judgment and justice, that the Lord may bring upon Abraham all that He hath spoken."

God is looking for such men to-day. Lord, help me to be such an one.

December 31.

"I pray not that Thou shouldst take them out of the world, but that Thou shouldst keep them from the evil" (John xvii. 15).

He wants us here for some higher purpose than mere existence. That purpose is nothing else than to represent Him to the world, to be the messengers of His Gospel and His will to men, and by our lives to exhibit to them the true life, and teach them how to live it themselves.

He is representing us yonder, and our one business is to represent Him here. We are just as truly sent into this world to represent Him as if we had gone to China as the ambassador of the American Government.

While engaged in the secular affairs of life, it is simply that we may represent Him there, carry on His business, and have means to use for His affairs. He came here from another realm, and with a special message, and when His work was done He was called to go home to His Father's dwelling-place and His own.

Lord, help me to worthily represent Thee.

And carry music in our heart

Through busy street and wrangling mart;

Plying our daily task with busier feet,

Because our souls a heavenly strain repeat.